THE THEFT ACTS

AUSTRALIA
The Law Book Company
Brisbane · Sydney · Melbourne · Perth

CANADA
Carswell
Ottawa · Toronto · Calgary · Montreal · Vancouver

AGENTS
Steimatzky's Agency Ltd., Tel Aviv;
N.M. Tripathi (Private) Ltd., Bombay;
Eastern Law House (Private) Ltd., Calcutta;
M.P.P. House, Bangalore;
Universal Book Traders, Delhi;
Aditya Books, Delhi;
MacMillan Shuppan KK, Tokyo;
Pakistan Law House, Karachi, Lahore

THE THEFT ACTS

By

EDWARD GRIEW, MA., LL.B.

of Gray's Inn, Barrister
Emeritus Professor of Law,
University of Nottingham

SEVENTH EDITION

LONDON
SWEET & MAXWELL
1995

First Edition	1968
Second Edition	1974
Third Edition	1978
Fourth Edition	1982
Fifth Edition	1986
Sixth Edition	1990
Seventh Edition	1995

Published in 1995 by Sweet & Maxwell Limited of
South Quay Plaza, 183 Marsh Wall, London E14 9FT
Phototypeset by MFK Information Services Ltd., Hitchin, Herts
Printed in Great Britain by The Bath Press, Bath, Avon

*No natural forests were destroyed to make this product; only farmed timber
was used and replanted.*

A CIP catalogue record for this book is available from the British Library

ISBN 0421 522704

PREFACE TO THE SEVENTH EDITION

In the Preface to the sixth edition I complained that the topic of appropriation in theft was "quite beyond my capacity to expound both simply and accurately". Since then the problem has changed. The decision of the majority of the House of Lords in *Gomez* [1993] A.C. 442 has enabled the same topic to be expressed in the present edition in quite a simple, but an extraordinarily wide, proposition (stated in §2–88). The decision was conveyed in a speech that eschewed resort to evidence of the intention of those who framed the modern law of theft and quite failed to engage with the elaborate reasoned and scholarly dissenting speech of Lord Lowry. In consequence, when read together with authorities (on the word "dishonestly") to which it does not refer, it achieves a substantial distortion of the offence; and it gives rise to inevitable speculation about the way in which the courts will deal with some of its surely unintended implications. Much of Chapter 2 has had to be rewritten in the light of this decision. I have decided that the time has come to provide a brief overview of the offence of theft near the beginning of this chapter (§2–03), to give newcomers to the subject a glimpse of the wood before it becomes obscured by the trees.

Gomez is only one of the reasons justifying the Law Commission's recent decision to undertake a review of the whole law of criminal dishonesty. Another is the strange scheme of the deception offences. But one unnecessary difficulty in this area, caused by the surprising decision in *Halai* [1983] Crim.L.R. 624 that obtaining a loan is not an "obtaining of services", could and should be eliminated by the enactment of the Commission's own recommended provision appended to its report on *Conspiracy to Defraud*, Law Com. No. 228 (1994).

Parliament has enacted, in Part I of the Criminal Justice Act 1993, valuable provisions for enlarging the jurisdiction of courts in England and Wales. These provisions, surprisingly, have not yet been brought into force; but, full of hope, I have created Chapter 17 for their consideration.

Dr A.T.H. Smith's massive work *Property Offences* was published just before the copy for this edition was due. It is wonderfully stocked with learning and ingenious argument, of which, thankful for the time lag between copy day and galley proofs, I have done my best to take reasonable account in the footnotes.

This edition attempts to state the law as at March 15, 1995.

Edward Griew

CONTENTS

Contents

Contents

TABLE OF CASES

Table of Cases

Table of Cases

TABLE OF STATUTES

In the case of the Theft Acts 1968 and 1978 the principal references only are noted

Abbreviations

The following abbreviations are used in this book:

The Act	The Theft Act 1968 (unless the context otherwise implies)
The Bill	The Theft Bill subsequently enacted as Theft Act 1968 (unless the context otherwise implies)
Arlidge and Parry	Anthony Arlidge Q.C. and Jacques Parry, *Fraud* (1985)
C.L.R.C.	Criminal Law Revision Committee
Draft Bill	Draft Theft Bill appended to *Eighth Report*
Eighth Report	C.L.R.C.'s *Eighth Report: Theft and Related Offences* (1966, Cmnd. 2977)
Smith (A. T. H.)	A. T. H. Smith, *Property Offences* (1994)
Smith (J. C.)	J. C. Smith, *The Law of Theft* (7th ed. 1993)
Thirteenth Report	C.L.R.C.'s *Thirteenth Report: Section 16 of the Theft Act 1968* (1977, Cmnd. 6733)
Williams, *C.L.G.P.*	Glanville Williams, *Criminal Law—The General Part* (2nd ed. 1961)
Williams, *Textbook*	Glanville Williams, *Textbook of Criminal Law* (2nd ed. 1983)

Chapter 1

PRELIMINARY AND MISCELLANEOUS

1. THE BACKGROUND TO THE ACTS

The Theft Act 1968

Before the passing of the Act, the law of theft and related offences was **1–01** largely contained in the Larceny Act 1916. That statute enshrined most of the indictable offences of dishonesty. It stated, but did not reform, the complex law of larceny and other common law offences; and it consolidated, but did not rationalise, numerous accretions to the statute book in the form of special offences of larceny and other crimes.

In March 1959 Mr. R. A. Butler, the Home Secretary, asked the newly created Criminal Law Revision Committee

> "to consider, with a view to providing a simpler and more effective system of law, what alterations in the criminal law are desirable with reference to larceny and kindred offences and to such other acts involving fraud or dishonesty as, in the opinion of the committee, could conveniently be dealt with in giving effect to the committee's recommendations on the law of larceny."

There was then no talk of a general codification of a revised criminal law. But this reference of "larceny and kindred offences" to the Committee was well justified; the law in this area was generally acknowledged to be in an unsatisfactory state. It is not necessary now to conduct a post–mortem on the old law, but an indication of some of its outstanding deficiencies will be given as necessary in the introductory passages to later chapters of this book.

The subject occupied the C.L.R.C. for seven years. Their *Eighth Report: Theft and Related Offences*, with a Draft Theft Bill annexed, was presented to Parliament in May 1966. The draft Bill, slightly amended, was the basis of the Theft Bill introduced in the House of Lords in December 1967. After further amendments during its passage, that Bill received the Royal Assent in July 1968. The Act came into force on January 1, 1969.

The Theft Act 1978

It was, before long, a matter of general agreement that section 16(2)(*a*) of **1–02** the 1968 Act required replacing. The highly unsatisfactory nature of that provision justified special amending legislation in advance of a general review of fraud offences that had been promised by the Law Commission.[1] Proposals for such legislation were made by the C.L.R.C. on a reference from the Home

---

[1] See Law Com. No. 76, *Report on Conspiracy and Criminal Law Reform* (1976), para. 1.15; *Thirteenth Report*, para. 3.

1

Secretary. The outcome was the Theft Act 1978, which came into force on October 20, 1978.[2]

2. MODE OF TRIAL. THE TRIBUNAL OF FACT

Mode of trial

1–03   Most offences under the two Theft Acts are triable either way.[3] The exceptions are referred to in the relevant chapters.

The tribunal of fact

1–04   It follows that it would seem appropriate, throughout most of this book, to refer equally to juries and to magistrates, either by mentioning both in terms or by gathering up both in a single phrase—the "tribunal (or trier) of fact." Either course, however, would be tedious. Moreover, a great deal of the case law is expressed in terms of the way in which a trial judge should deal with the jury; and the issues which are for determination by magistrates as judges of fact are precisely those which are conventionally described as "jury issues." So the general method of this book, when discussing the function of the tribunal of fact or the way in which it ought to be directed or advised, will be to refer to the jury, and to the judge directing the jury, alone. It is hoped that this will not be misunderstood, even by magistrates and their clerks who are well aware that they are dealing with the great majority of the Theft Act cases coming before the courts. Clerks to justices will no doubt understand that they are to advise their benches in much the way that the Crown Court judge is to direct the jury; stipendiary magistrates will direct themselves in the same way. For "jury" read also "magistrate(s)" whenever the context permits.

3. VERDICTS

Criminal Law Act 1967, s.6(3) and (4)

1–05   The Criminal Law Act 1967, s.6, contains provisions, of general application to trial on indictment (but not to summary trial), which it is convenient to mention here rather than repeatedly throughout the book.

Provision for alternative verdicts

Section 6(3) of the Criminal Law Act 1967 confers important powers on a jury who find an accused person not guilty of an offence with which he is specifically charged. If "the allegations in the indictment amount to or include (expressly or by implication) an allegation of another offence" within the trial court's jurisdiction, the jury may find him guilty of that other offence;

---

[2] The background to the 1978 Act is more fully treated below, at §§7–04 to 7–08 and §§13–02 to 13–05.

[3] Magistrates' Courts Act 1980, Sched. 1, para. 28.

or they may find him guilty of an offence of which he could be found guilty if he were specifically indicted for that other offence. For the purposes of section 6(3) an allegation of an offence always includes an allegation of an attempt to commit it (section 6(4)).

The offence of which the jury may convict by virtue of section 6(3) is commonly called the 'lesser offence' (as opposed to the 'major offence' charged). This language has been judicially frowned upon as not being justified by the terms of the subsection. But it is convenient shorthand; and the provision may be expected to achieve in practice convictions of offences less serious than those charged.[4]

'Included' allegations

An allegation of a lesser offence may be found to be expressly included in   **1–06**
the allegations in an indictment by applying "the red pencil test", that is, by "striking out all the averments which have not been proved"[5] and seeing whether what is left amounts to an allegation of the lesser offence.

It was at one time understood that an allegation of a lesser offence was included by implication in the allegation of a major offence only where the lesser offence was "an essential ingredient of the major offence"—as theft, for example, is an essential ingredient of robbery.[6] This was a clear, soundly-based rule. But it was overthrown by the controversial decision of the House of Lords in *Wilson*.[7] This held that an allegation of one offence may be included by implication in the allegation of another, even though the former is not a necessary element of the latter. Specifically, an allegation of inflicting grievous bodily harm includes an allegation of assault occasioning actual bodily harm even though "inflicting" does not require an assault. The explanation seems to be that an allegation of grievous bodily harm *includes* (in one sense of that term) an allegation of actual bodily harm, as the greater includes the less; and that an assault is one way, no doubt the commonest way, of inflicting bodily harm and is therefore *included* (in another sense of that term) in "inflicting" as being an example of it; " 'inflicting' can … include "inflicting by assault."[8] This shift from one sense of "includes" to another is not explicitly noticed in the opinion of Lord Roskill, with which the other lords agreed; it must be regarded as a serious flaw in the reasoning.

The application of section 6(3) to indictments for Theft Act offences is not   **1–07**
always clear in the light of the *Wilson* decision, as the following discussion shows. The headings refer to the offences charged.

Theft (s.1). An allegation of theft does not by implication include an alle-

---

[4] The trial judge is not invariably obliged to tell the jury of the possibility of conviction of a less serious offence: see *Maxwell* [1990] 1 W.L.R. 401; [1990] 1 All E.R. 801, and cases there cited.
[5] *Lillis* [1972] 2 Q.B. 236 at 241–242.
[6] *Springfield* (1969) 53 Cr.App.R. 608; *Lillis* [1972] 2 Q.B. 236 at 241.
[7] [1984] A.C. 242. Although the decision and its reasoning caused astonishment (see J. C. Smith [1984] Crim.L.R. 37; Emmins, *ibid.* at 152; Glanville Williams [1984] C.L.J. 290 and (1991) 55 J.C.L. 234), they were re-affirmed by the House in *Savage* [1992] 1 A.C. 699.
[8] [1984] A.C. 242 at 261.

gation of handling (s.22) by receiving[9] or by any other means. This surely remains true since *Wilson*, even though handling by receiving stolen goods is a way of stealing those goods.[10] Precisely because the handling will almost inevitably be a theft, there must be a strong argument that a conviction of handling on a theft charge would be inconsistent with acquittal of the theft itself.

1–08   *Robbery (s. 8(1)); assault with intent to rob (s. 8(2))*. Robbery involves theft as an essential ingredient. On a charge of robbery, therefore, the jury may find the accused not guilty of robbery but guilty of theft.[11] The other ingredient of robbery is the use of force on any person or the putting, or seeking to put, any person in fear of being then and there subjected to force. One charged with robbery could not formerly be convicted of assault with intent to rob, for robbery may be committed without an assault (by a mere seeking to put in fear).[12] But as an assault will occur in most robberies, the alternative verdict may now be possible by analogy with *Wilson*. There cannot be conviction of a mere assault, however, on a charge of robbery or of assault with intent to rob, as "common assault and battery" are now summary offences and not within the jurisdiction of the Crown Court, as section 6(3) requires.[13]

1–09   *Burglary (s.9)*. One way of committing burglary is to enter a building as a trespasser and to steal (or attempt to steal) therein or to inflict (or attempt to inflict) on any person therein any grievous bodily harm (s.9(1)(*b*)). An allegation of entering a building as a trespasser and stealing therein includes an allegation of theft. If the trespass is not proved, the allegation of it may be struck out, as may the word "therein" and even the date alleged, to reveal an express allegation of theft committed wheresoever and whensoever.[14]

An allegation of entry followed by theft has been held, applying *Wilson*, to include by implication an allegation of entry with intent to steal[15]; and an allegation of entry followed by inflicting grievous bodily harm includes by implication an allegation of assault occasioning actual bodily harm.[16]

It seems, notwithstanding *Wilson*, that on an indictment (under section

---

[9] Compare *Woods* [1969] 1 Q.B. 447.

[10] See below, §15–50.

[11] *Shendley* [1970] Crim.L.R. 49. Similarly, a conviction of conspiracy to steal should be available on a charge of conspiracy to rob (where all that is not proved is the agreement to use force); but see to the contrary, unconvincingly, *Barnard* (1979) 70 Cr.App.R. 28 at 33.

[12] *Tennant* [1976] Crim.L.R. 133 (as to assault); compare *Springfield* (1969) 53 Cr.App.R. 608. (Otherwise, if force or an actual putting in fear is expressly alleged?)

[13] Criminal Justice Act 1988, s.39; *Mearns* [1991] 1 Q.B. 82; *Savage* (1990) 91 Cr.App.R. 317. (This is so although a count for common assault might have been added under s.40.)

[14] *Lillis* [1972] 2 Q.B. 236. But before leaving to the jury the possibility of a conviction of theft, the judge should ensure that the defendant "has had the opportunity of fully meeting that alternative": see *per* Lord Roskill in *Wilson* [1984] A.C. 242 at 261. *Lillis* is criticised by J.C. Smith [1972] Crim.L.R. 459.

[15] *Whiting* (1987) 85 Cr.App.R. 78, (regarding *Hollis* [1971] Crim.L.R. 525, to the contrary, as no longer good law); for compelling criticism, see Smith (A.T.H.), para. 28–08.

[16] *Jenkins* (decided with *Wilson*) [1984] A.C. 242.

9(1)(*a*)) charging burglary by entering a building as a trespasser with intent to commit an offence mentioned in section 9(2) (say, theft or rape), it is not possible to acquit of the burglary and convict of an attempt to commit the intended offence (still less of the intended offence itself); an allegation of entry with intent to steal, for instance, does not imply an allegation of conduct that has got as far as an attempted theft.[17]

Aggravated burglary (s.10). A person charged with aggravated burglary **1–10** may be convicted of burglary as described in the indictment or of any offence of which he could be found guilty on an indictment charging burglary so described.

Handling (s.22). Many (maybe most) persons guilty of handling stolen **1–11** goods are also guilty of theft. But a handling charge does not imply an allegation that the accused intended to deprive the victim permanently of the goods, which is essential for theft; nor is theft a way of committing handling, so as to be implied by an allegation of handling in the sense apparently intended in *Wilson*. So a verdict of theft is not possible on a handling indictment.

Attempt or preliminary act charged; complete offence proved

Section 6(4) of the Criminal Law Act 1967 goes on to provide for the situ- **1–12** ation in which an indictment charges a mere attempt or an assault or other act preliminary to an offence, but in which it is proved that the accused was in fact guilty of the completed offence. In such a case the accused can be convicted of the attempt[18] or other preliminary offence charged, or the court can discharge the jury so that an indictment for the completed offence can be preferred. An example under the present Act might arise from a charge of assault with intent to rob under section 8(2) where the jury find that the accused in fact committed the full offence of robbery.

Summary trial

There is no power on summary trial to acquit of the only offence charged **1–13** but to convict of an attempt to commit it or of some other offence. So a failure to anticipate a difficulty of proof and to charge an alternative offence, or an attempt, can lead to an unmerited acquittal or to duplication of proceedings. This was illustrated in *Bogdal v. Hall*[19]: charges of obtaining unemployment benefit girocheques by deception failed for want of proof that the particular

---

[17] Compare *Lyttle* [1969] Crim.L.R. 213 (charge, in effect, of entry with intent to rape).
[18] Similarly on summary trial, for the attempt does not merge in the completed offence: *Webley v. Buxton* [1977] Q.B. 481.
[19] [1987] Crim.L.R. 500.

girocheques were received; attempts in the form of the making of fraudulent claims were proved but not separately charged.

Provision in the Theft Acts

1–14 Only in two cases do the Theft Acts themselves provide for conviction of one offence on the charge of another: a person charged on indictment with theft (but not one tried summarily) may be found guilty of taking a conveyance if that offence rather than theft is proved[20]; and a person charged with aggravated vehicle–taking and found not guilty of that offence (whether on trial on indictment or summary trial) may likewise be convicted of taking a conveyance if that offence is proved.[21]

Nowhere do the Acts provide for conviction of the offence charged where some other offence, but not the offence charged, is found to have been committed. Yet the Court of Appeal has on one occasion allowed a conviction of theft to stand on the ground that, if that offence was not committed, the appellant was guilty of obtaining a pecuniary advantage by deception, so that (as the court asserted) no miscarriage of justice had occurred.[22] To convict a person of an offence not proved to have been committed because he has committed an offence with which he has not been charged surely requires statutory warrant. The decision should be regarded as an aberration.[23]

4. HUSBAND AND WIFE

The spouse as offender

1–15 The Theft Acts apply in relation to the parties to a marriage as if they were not married (s.30(1)), so that a husband can commit any offence under the Acts against his wife or in connection with her property, and vice versa. Any argument to the effect that, if the parties were not married, the victim would have no interest in the property which is the subject–matter of the alleged offence is defeated by the same subsection, which requires any interest derived from the marriage to be treated as if it subsisted independently of the marriage.

The subsection does not, of course, affect general doctrines of the criminal law relating to husband and wife. The defence of marital coercion will be as available to a wife on a prosecution under the Acts as on other prosecutions[24]; and husband and wife will no more be able to conspire together to commit an offence under the Acts than they are able to conspire to commit other offences.[25]

---

[20] s. 12(4).
[21] s. 12A(5).
[22] *McHugh* (1976) 64 Cr.App.R. 92.
[23] But compare *Ayres* [1984] A.C. 447: conviction of conspiracy to defraud upheld although indictment defective because such charge not at that time possible where agreement was to commit another offence, as was the case; no miscarriage of justice because conspiracy (not charged) to commit the other offence plainly found on the facts.
[24] Criminal Justice Act 1925, s.47; Williams, *C.L.G.P.*, pp. 764–768.
[25] Criminal Law Act 1977, s.2(2)(*a*).

The spouse as prosecutor

Section 30(2) assimilates the position of the married to that of the unmar-   **1–16**
ried in another respect and is not limited to offences under the Acts. It provides that:

"a person shall have the same right to bring proceedings against that person's wife
or husband for any offence (whether under this Act or otherwise) as if they were
not married."

The prosecution of spouses

Section 30(2) is subject to a restriction on some prosecutions imposed, in   **1–17**
respect of prosecutors generally, by section 30(4).[26] This provides that certain
proceedings are to be instituted only by or with the consent of the Director of
Public Prosecutions save in special cases. The proceedings in respect of
which the limitation is imposed are proceedings against a person "for any
offence of stealing or doing unlawful damage to property which at the time of
the offence belongs to that person's husband or wife, or for any attempt,
incitement or conspiracy to commit such an offence." The phrase "belongs
to" in this passage is to be interpreted in accordance with section 5(1),[27] which
is discussed in the chapter on theft.[28]

The restriction on prosecution does not apply   **1–18**
   (i) if the accused spouse is charged with committing the offence jointly
       with the other spouse (an example would be a case in which a wife is
       alleged to have stolen with her husband partnership property belong-
       ing to him and his partner); or
  (ii) "if by virtue of any judicial decree or order (wherever made)" the
       spouses "are at the time of the offence under no obligation to co-
       habit"[29] (s.30(4), proviso (*a*)).

The restriction would, on the other hand, appear to apply (unless the case
falls within either of these exceptions) even where the marriage is at an end
before the institution of proceedings, for the subsection is expressed in terms
of marriage "at the time of the offence."
Subsection (4) does not in general prevent the arrest without warrant, or
the issue or execution of a warrant for the arrest, of a person for any offence,
or the remand in custody or on bail of a person charged with any offence.[30]
But the spouse–victim cannot himself or herself arrest without warrant for an

---

[26] The subsection operated to render the proceedings a nullity in *Withers* [1975] Crim.L.R. 647.
[27] s.34(1).
[28] See below, §§2–28 *et seq.*
[29] See *Woodley v. Woodley* [1978] Crim.L.R. 629 (proviso applied to divorce judge's committal
order suspended on terms that husband did not molest wife or approach within 200 yards of her
home).
[30] Prosecution of Offences Act 1985, s.25(2)(*a*).

offence within the subsection, and a warrant of arrest cannot be issued on an information laid by him or her without the Director's consent (subs. (5)[31]).

5. INTERPRETATION[32]

1–19　　The Theft Act 1968, as has been judicially observed in several cases, "is an Act designed to simplify the law."[33] It greatly reduced the number of offences employed to cover the range of conduct penalised; it employs, on the whole, simpler, more modern and less technical language than was formerly used; and it removed a good many "technicalities and subtleties"[34] that had marred the old law.

The Act's aim of simplifying the law should not be frustrated by gratuitous subtlety in its interpretation. The courts for their part may be expected to reject a subtle reading in favour of a simple reading where both are truly available, and they will be right to do so. Still, it is a practitioner's proper function to take a subtle point on behalf of his client when the need arises; and a commentator will occasionally feel bound to suggest an analysis of the Act that appears to be available, even if he regards it as unattractive on the ground of undue subtlety or of policy.

Questions of civil law

1–20　　Closely associated with the view of the Act as one designed to simplify the law is the proposition (which does not follow from it) that it ought to be capable of being understood by a lay person. From this proposition proceeds the notion (which also does not follow) that the Act should receive a plain person's interpretation; there seems sometimes to be a feeling that, the plain person being no lawyer, there is something disreputable about construing it in a lawyerly way.[35] This, it is thought, has contributed to some errors and inconsistencies in the case law on the Act and to an insupportable doctrine concerning the relation between the criminal law in this Act and other principles of law. In the case of *Baxter*,[36] Sachs L.J. elaborated the statement that the Act is one "designed to simplify the law" by saying that

> "it uses words in their natural meaning and is to be construed thus to produce sensible results; when [the] Act is under examination this court deprecates attempts to bring into too close consideration the finer distinctions in civil law as to the precise moment when contractual communications take effect or when property passes."

---

[31] Added by the Criminal Jurisdiction Act 1975, s.14(4) and Sched. 5, and amended by the Prosecution of Offences Act 1979, s.11(1) and Sched. 1.
[32] Rodney Brazier [1974] Crim.L.R. 701.
[33] *Baxter* [1972] 1 Q.B. 1 at 13, *per* Sachs L.J.
[34] *Bonner* (1970) 54 Cr.App.R. 257 at 264–265, *per* Edmund Davies L.J.
[35] Close kin to this is a tendency to resort to the ordinary person's supposed conception of theft as a factor in interpreting the elaborate provisions on that offence: see especially, below, §2–39.
[36] See n. 33, above; compare *Nordeng* (1975) 62 Cr.App.R. 123 at 128 (and commentary by J. C. Smith [1976] Crim.L.R. at 195).

To the same effect was the suggestion of Lord Roskill in *Morris*[37] that:

"it is on any view wrong to introduce into this branch of the criminal law questions whether particular contracts are void or voidable on the ground of mistake or fraud or whether any mistake is sufficiently fundamental to vitiate a contract. These difficult questions should so far as possible be confined to those fields of law to which they are immediately relevant and I do not regard them as relevant questions under the 1968 Act."

The major difficulty with this benignly-intentioned approach is that the **1–21** Act inevitably defines offences against property in terms of the categories of the civil law (see, for instance, ss.4, 5, 9 and 15). Words by means of which reference to those categories is made (such as "things in action", "ownership", "possession", "proprietary right or interest", "trespasser") do not have "natural' meanings but technical ones. This is helpful, not harmful; it makes for certainty in the criminal law. The Act should of course be read sensibly; but that does not mean that there is a painless plain person's route to its meaning. There are, in particular, bound to be cases in which the practitioner cannot do his full duty without an adequate grasp of relevant principles of the civil law. And the courts should be prepared to make careful application of those principles, for two reasons: as an indispensable means of fixing the boundaries of criminal liability with adequate certainty; and to avoid incongruous and even unjust conflict between the respective demands on citizens of the civil and criminal law.[38]

A valuable corrective to the judicial statements quoted above is the case of *Walker*,[39] decided by the Court of Appeal a few days after the decision in *Morris*. P had bought a video recorder from D. He found it to be defective and returned it to D for repair. He later issued a summons to recover the price and this was served on D. D resold the recorder and was charged with theft of it. D's resale could be theft only if P had still a "proprietary right or interest"in the recorder at the time of the resale.[40] This depended on civil law principles relating to the rejection of goods by buyers which the trial judge had failed to apply or to explain to the jury. D's conviction was inevitably quashed. The law of contract and of property applies in all courts and in all contexts. There is in truth, as the Court of Appeal insisted, "no distinction between the civil law and the criminal law."[41]

---

[37] [1984] A.C 320 at 334.
[38] See J. C. Smith [1972 B] C.L.J. 197, *passim* and especially at 197–198; Glanville Williams [1977] Crim.L.R. 127 at 128 *et seq.*
[39] (1983) 80 L.S. Gaz. 3238; [1984] Crim.L.R. 112.
[40] See ss.1(1) and 5(1).
[41] See also, *e.g. Shadrokh–Cigari* [1988] Crim.L.R. 465, referring to a doctrine of equity; *Dobson v. General Accident Fire and Life Assurance Corp. plc* [1990] Q.B. 274 at 289, *per* Bingham L.J., as to the need to resort to the civil law on, in effect, questions of ownership; *Wheeler* (1990) 92 Cr.App.R. 279, applying principles in the Sale of Goods Act 1979.

"Ordinary words"

1–22   There has, in fact, been a judicial tendency to leave the interpretation of particular statutory words to the lay tribunal. The relevant doctrine is that an "ordinary word" does not need judicial explanation; its "natural" or "ordinary" meaning is known to the jury.[42] This view has been pervasive, though it is not always given effect.[43] Its application has sometimes been very puzzling, as when for a time the identification of an "obligation" was said to be a matter for the jury although the word means "legal obligation." [44] And generally—and especially in relation to the central word "dishonestly" [45]—the doctrine has proved controversial.[46] It may be contended that there is much to be said for the criminal law's ability to reflect community values, as represented by justices and juries, and to respond to changes in those values; and that there is a real difficulty about tying down the meaning of words by judicial pronouncement. The present book, however, will be found to reflect the belief that a person's liability to conviction should not depend upon the accidental composition of the bench or jury that tries him when it might depend upon a proposition of law[47]; that the prevailing view makes unjustified assumptions about the existence of clear community norms in a morally and socially plural society, and also about the existence of generally apprehended "natural meanings" of words[48]; and that it is the business of the judiciary, gradually by a course of decisions, to help the lay tribunal to as consistent an application of the criminal law as can reasonably be achieved.

---

[42] The *locus classicus* is a dictum of Lord Reid in *Brutus v. Cozens* [1973] A.C. 854, on the later fortunes of which see D.W. Elliott [1989] Crim.L.R. 323.

[43] As to the impact of the doctrine in early Theft Act cases, see D. W. Elliott [1976] Crim.L.R. 707.

[44] See below, §2–44.

[45] See below, §§2–132 *et seq*.

[46] See Glanville Williams [1976] Crim.L.R. 472 and 532; and, as to the issue of dishonesty, see the references in §2–136, nn. 41, 42.

[47] Compare, in other contexts, C.L.R.C., *Fourteenth Report: Offences against the Person* (1980: Cmnd. 7844), para. 7; *Pearlman v. Harrow School* [1979] Q.B. 56 at 66–67, *per* Lord Denning M.R.

[48] There are several references in Theft Act cases to the "natural meaning" of words: *e.g. Baxter*, n. 33, above; *Treacy* [1971] A.C. 537 at 543, *per* John Stephenson J.; *D.P.P. v. Turner* [1974] A.C. 357 at 364, *per* Lord Reid. Nevertheless, it is thought that scepticism about this notion is permissible. In one case the jury asked for and were granted the use of a dictionary, probably to look up the word "dishonestly". The conviction was quashed; the jury should have been told to apply the "ordinary meaning" of the word, which was said to be "quite clear": *Swift* (C.A. No. 1396/B/79), unreported. It is not unknown for courts to consult dictionaries in search of "ordinary meanings"; see *e.g. Peters* (1886) 16 Q.B.D. 636, cited by Cross, *Statutory Interpretation* (2nd ed.), 54.

Chapter 2

THEFT

1. DEFINITION AND INTRODUCTION

Basic definition

Section 1(1) provides a "basic definition of theft":   **2–01**

"A person is guilty of theft if he dishonestly appropriates property belonging to another with the intention of permanently depriving the other of it."

The offence is punishable with a maximum of seven years' imprisonment on conviction on indictment.[1]

Introduction

Background

This offence replaced a number of pre-existing offences which in modern   **2–02**
times were contained in the Larceny Act 1916. A brief reference to those offences may be useful.

Historically, *larceny* was an offence against another's possession of goods; and it involved a violation of that possession by "taking and carrying away" his goods without his consent, with the intention of permanently depriving him of them. Such a "taking" could not occur where there was a consensual delivery; nor could it occur where the offender was himself already in possession, for instance as a bailee. But one who induced a delivery by fraud was regarded as "taking" without consent because the fraud was treated as negativing the victim's apparent consent; and a bailee became capable of larceny (by conversion of the goods bailed) by a statutory extension of the offence. The element of "carrying away" (or "asportation") required some physical removal of the goods, however slight. Another important limitation on the scope of larceny was the requirement that the intention to deprive the victim permanently should exist at the moment of the taking, though this rule was somewhat mitigated by intellectual ingenuity on the part of the judges.

Embezzlement was an offence of statutory origin designed to deal with the dishonest misappropriation by a servant of any chattel, money or valuable security delivered to the servant on account of his employer; for such misappropriation could not be larceny if it occurred before the property was reduced into the employer's possession.

---

[1] s.7, as amended by Criminal Justice Act 1991, s.26(1). The maximum was originally 10 years. A person convicted of stealing or attempting to steal a motor vehicle may be disqualified for holding or obtaining a driving licence: Road Traffic Offenders Act, 1988, Sched. 2, Pt. II.

Fraudulent conversion was another statutory creation. Its main *raison d'être* was the fact that, whereas a bailee could by statute be guilty of larceny by misappropriating the property bailed, one who had ownership of property could not, even though he had been entrusted with it otherwise than for his own beneficial enjoyment. The offence covered absconding trustees, club treasurers and the like. Unlike larceny and embezzlement it extended to any kind of property.

In the notion of a fraudulent conversion of any property the model was found for a single new offence of theft to replace the three crimes mentioned above. Or rather, to replace a great many crimes; for under the old law there was a large number of different forms of larceny with different maximum penalties. There is now one offence of theft—though robbery, which is no mere aggravated theft but rather theft-plus-force, is preserved as a distinct crime and is separately treated in Chapter 3.

An overview

2–03   It is as well to offer readers who are new to the subject a brief overview of the offence of theft before embarking on a detailed examination of it. This is the more desirable because the law on the subject is in a remarkable condition as a result of some decisions of high authority. It is hoped that what follows may assist in an understanding of the subject as it unfolds.

2–04   *Breadth of the offence.* Theft is in some ways a very broadly defined offence. First, "property" of any description—whether tangible or intangible, real or personal—can in principle be stolen (though the circumstances in which land can be stolen are specifically limited by the Act). Secondly, the Act treats property as "belonging to" virtually everyone having any possessory or proprietary connection with it; so that the range of available victims of theft is unexpectedly wide. Thirdly, decisions of the House of Lords have given extraordinary width to the crucial concept of an "appropriation" of property: if those decisions are taken at face value, almost any act done in relation to property belonging to another, the doing or authorising of which is one of "the rights of an owner" of such property, may be an appropriation of the property, even if the other person in fact consented to or authorised that act.

2–05   *Some limiting factors.* The breadth of the offence is restricted, however, by the following factors. First, it is important to emphasise at the outset that theft requires the appropriation of some particular property. The fact that, as a result of dishonest conduct on D's part, the totality of a person's assets has been reduced, or he has suffered some general economic loss or been disappointed in some expectation of economic gain or of being rendered what is due to him, does not mean that D has committed theft. D must be shown to have stolen *something.*[2] Secondly, theft is not committed by a dishonest act

---

[2] See below, §2–26.

that merely reduces the value of property[3]; nor by one that for a time deprives a person of his property or of the opportunity to use it or to profit by it. Although judicial decisions make it surprisingly easy to identify an appropriation of property, that appropriation is no theft unless committed with the "intention of permanently depriving" the victim of the property.[4]

Thirdly, no act is theft unless done "dishonestly." It is plain that the greater **2–06** the range of the conduct capable of being theft, the greater the significance of the requirement of dishonesty as a limiting factor. So an effect of the decisions on appropriation referred to above is to place on the word "dishonestly" a quite unforeseen weight. It is therefore desirable to offer an early sketch of the law on this aspect of theft. "Dishonestly" is not given a meaning either by the Act or by judicial decisions. But section 2(1) specifies three cases in which the belief with which D acts will render his appropriation of property not dishonest as a matter of law: cases in which he believes (a) that he is entitled in law to deprive P of the property, or (b) that P would consent if he knew what D was doing, or (c) that P cannot be discovered by taking reasonable steps. For the rest, the decision whether D's appropriation of property was dishonest is, according to the ruling Court of Appeal authorities, a matter for the tribunal of fact. The jury or magistrates are to say whether D's appropriation of property was dishonest (in the meaning of that word as an ordinary word of the English language, without judicial explanation) according to the ordinary standards of reasonable and honest people; and if they say that it was, they are to convict if, but only if, they are satisfied that D himself must have realised that his conduct was dishonest by those standards.

The analysis of theft; sections 2–6

The "basic definition" of theft is to some extent elaborated in sections 2-6. **2–07** Those sections have varying functions. Section 4 insists that everything properly called *"property"* can be stolen but introduces limits to that proposition for some types of property, notably land. Section 5 alone constitutes a genuine definition: it contains an exhaustive explanation of the phrase *"belonging to another."* Section 3 provides a broad explanation of the term *"appropriates"* without strictly speaking defining it. Section 6, by contrast, does no more than marginally extend the meaning of *"with the intention of permanently depriving the other of it"* beyond what might otherwise be regarded as its ordinary meaning. And section 2, as said above, declares that certain cases of appropriation of property are not to be regarded as dishonest; it makes no contribution to a definition of *"dishonestly,"* if such a thing were possible.

Detailed treatment of the offence must inevitably proceed, however artificially, by way of a separate consideration of each of its elements; and the following five parts of this chapter consider those elements in the order just

---

[3] A case in which D's act diminishes a "thing in action" (*e.g.* a bank credit) is an apparent exception to this. See below, §§2–145, *et seq.*
[4] But not necessarily, it seems, by the appropriation itself. See below, §2–72.

indicated. Subsequent parts gather together important principles relating to the theft of intangible property, which presents peculiar difficulties; summarise the principles governing the charging of theft in informations and indictments; and deal with the specialised offence of abstracting electricity.

2. "PROPERTY"

2–08   "'Property' includes money and all other property, real or personal, including things in action and other intangible property" (s.4(1)); and wild creatures, tamed or untamed, are to be regarded as property (s.4(4)). Section 4 provides specially for land and wild creatures by limiting the circumstances in which they can be stolen. These special cases will be dealt with below.

Reduced to its shortest form, without any change in its meaning, section 4(1) reads: "'Property' includes ... all ... property." Such a statement might be thought unworthy of the draftsman of the Act. It had a point, however, as a plain indication to those accustomed to the former law that the new theft was, in respect of its subject-matter, much wider than the old larceny. Only things capable of being "taken and carried away"—in effect, money and other tangible personalty—could formerly be stolen. The draftsman made his point emphatically by mentioning land and intangible forms of property as capable now of being stolen.

Land; and things growing wild thereon

2–09   Land can be stolen, but only by certain persons in certain particular ways. A person who appropriates "land, or things forming part of land and severed from it by him or by his directions", is not guilty of theft unless he falls within one of the exceptional cases mentioned below, or unless what he appropriates is an incorporeal hereditament (s.4(2)).[5]

Land is not defined in the Act. Any difficulty that exists concerns the meaning of the phrase "things forming part of land". Problems can arise in connection with (i) things annexed to the land and (ii) materials deposited on the land.

(i) As to *things annexed to the land*, "the general maxim of the law is, that what is annexed to the land becomes part of the land; but it is very difficult, if not impossible, to say with precision what constitutes an annexation sufficient for this purpose."[6] There is no difficulty with houses and similar permanent structures or with things that are clearly integral parts of such structures.[7] In the case of anything resting on or attached to land or to a building thereon, the tests to be applied are those applied in the law relating to fixtures: whether such a thing forms part of the land depends in part upon the

---

[5] The most important incorporeal hereditaments are easements, *profits à prendre* and rent charges. See Megarry and Wade, *The Law of Real Property* (5th ed.), Chap. 13.
[6] *Holland v. Hodgson* (1872) L.R. 7 C.P. 328 at 334, *per* Blackburn J.
[7] See *per* Lord Goddard C.J. in *Billing v. Pill* [1954] 1 Q.B. 70 at 75.

degree of annexation and in part upon the object of annexation.[8] In *Billing v. Pill*[9] the floor of an army hut built in seven sections was secured to concrete foundations by bolts let into the concrete. It was held that, although the foundations formed part of the realty, the hut, in the light of the evidence as to the temporary object of its attachment to the land, did not. On the other hand "blocks of stone placed one on top of another without any mortar or cement for the purpose of forming a dry stone wall would become part of the land,"[10] at least if the wall was not purely temporary.

(ii) *Materials deposited on land*, such as sand and cinders, will not form part of the land if they lie in heaps on the ground; but if they are spread on the land they are likely to be found to have become part of the soil.[11]

When land can be stolen

Section 4(2) provides that land can exceptionally be stolen in the following situations. **2–10**

(a) A trustee or personal representative or one authorised[12] to sell or dispose of land belonging to another[13] can steal the land or anything forming part of it by dealing with it in breach of the confidence[14] reposed in him (s.4(2)(a)).

(b) A person not in possession of land[15] can in general steal something **2–11** forming part of the land: he can appropriate it by severing it or causing it to be severed, or after it has been severed[16] (s.4(2)(b)). To come onto a person's land and take the tiles from his roof (severing) is obviously as much theft as to take the books from his shelves; and one may steal another's pasture by grazing cattle on his land[17] (causing to be severed).

The general rule that a person not in possession of land can steal by sever-

---

[8] See, as to the meaning of fixtures, Megarry and Wade, *op. cit.*, p. 731; Halsbury, *Laws of England* (4th ed.), Vol. 27, p. 111.
[9] [1954] 1 Q.B. 70.
[10] *Holland v. Hodgson* (1872) L.R. 7 C.P. 328 at 335, *per* Blackburn J. Compare *Skujins* [1956] Crim.L.R. 266 (a decision of quarter sessions); farm gate held to form part of the realty.
[11] As in *Morgan v. Russell & Sons* [1909] 1 K.B. 357.
[12] "by power of attorney, or as liquidator of a company, or otherwise. . . ."
[13] See s.5(1)(2). Land held on trust, for instance, will belong to the beneficiaries.
[14] The word "confidence" is purposely used in preference to "trust", which might have been understood in a technical sense. An agent, for example, authorised to sell land, will commit theft if he dishonestly sells to his own nominee at an undervalue for the purpose of making a profit by then selling it to a sub-purchaser on his own account.
[15] No doubt including a member of the household of one in possession.
[16] When it will surely not form part of the land.
[17] *McGill v. Shepherd* (1976: Victoria), unreported, cited by Williams and Weinberg, *Property Offences* (2nd ed.), p. 94.

ance is subject to a large exception, provided by section 4(3), in relation to things growing wild. Save in one class of case, no one steals if he picks mushrooms[18] growing wild or if he picks flowers, fruit or foliage from a plant[19] growing wild. The excepted case is that in which the picking is done "for reward or for sale or other commercial purpose."

This piling of exception upon exception is confusing. We may approach these provisions in another way by observing that the Act makes a series of distinctions:

(i) One who is in possession of land and one who is not. The former cannot steal by severing (unless he is a tenant and he severs a fixture: see exception (c), below). The latter can, but in respect of him a distinction is drawn between—

(ii) Mushrooms and plants growing wild, and anything else "forming part of the land" (including cultivated plants). The latter can always be stolen by one not in possession of the land. As to "plants growing wild" the Act makes a third distinction:

(iii) Severing and picking.[20] Uprooting a plant, even one growing wild, will be "severing"; if the plant belongs to anyone and the severing is dishonest, it will be theft. But taking individual blooms from a wild shrub or a basketful of wild berries or a quantity of wild holly will be mere "picking" and cannot be theft, subject to one final distinction:

(iv) Commercial and non-commercial purpose. Even the picking of another's wild mushrooms or flowers, fruit or foliage from another's wild plants will be theft if dishonestly done "for reward or for sale or other commercial purpose." So whether you steal when you pick wild flowers may depend on your motive: if you desire to decorate your house[21] or your friend, it is not theft; if you are picking for pay or to sell in the market, it is. This distinction is contrary to the general principle that theft does not depend upon motive, or even upon a view to gain (s.1(2)). It may also present disproportionate problems of proof. The burden is on the prosecution to prove the commercial purpose; and this will no doubt usually be very hard to do—save, for instance, where a known market trader is caught in the act of amassing a large quantity of flowers, fruit or foliage.

2–12   (c) The third exceptional case in which an appropriation of land or things forming part thereof may be theft is that in which a tenant[22] in possession appropriates a fixture or structure let to be used with the land (s.4(2)(c)).

---

[18] Includes any fungus.

[19] Includes any shrub or tree.

[20] The uprooting of any wild plant, or the picking, uprooting or destroying of a protected plant, may be a summary offence under s.13 of the Wildlife and Countryside Act 1981.

[21] If you desire to decorate your shop-window for the sake of the aesthetic effect, this could be construed as a "commercial purpose". The phrase is very vague.

[22] For the meaning of "tenancy" in this provision, see the text of s.4(2) in Appendix 1.

Some cases that are not theft

The following, in conclusion, are examples of cases in which appropriation **2–13** of land or things forming part of land will not be theft:

(i) D is a lessee of land. He removes and sells ore or plants from the land. If he is "in possession of the land" (which he may not be; he may have sub-let it), he is not guilty of theft, for he is not within exception (b) above, and the thing taken is not a "fixture or structure" within exception (c).

(ii) D is in possession of land under a mere licence. He severs and appropriates a fixture. He is not within either exception (b) or exception (c) and so does not steal. It is odd perhaps that the licensee should have this advantage over the tenant.

(iii) D squats on P's land, or extends his fences so as to take in part of P's land, or forcibly turns P off his land. He does not steal, because exception (b) concerns only the severance of things forming part of the land.

Wild creatures

From the terms of section 4(4) it is clear that "a wild creature" means "a **2–14** creature wild by nature." This was the language of the Larceny Act[23] and cases decided under the old law therefore remain relevant for the classification of some creatures as wild or otherwise. The last of those cases amusingly illustrated the ambiguity of the word "wild". The case concerned mussels on the sea shore. The prosecution's concession that they were wild creatures was both inevitable and mildly incongruous.[24]

Wild creatures that have been tamed or are ordinarily kept in captivity can be stolen as readily as any other property. As to creatures at liberty, the problem was whether by means of the law of theft to protect the owner of, or the person having sporting rights over, the land on which they may be taken or killed. More tersely: should poaching be theft? The C.L.R.C. recommended[25] that it should be theft when done "for reward or for sale or other commercial purpose", and the Bill so provided. This would have been a substantial departure from the pre-existing law and would have rendered the offender liable to very much greater penalties than those provided under other statutes controlling poaching. In the end the relevant provision was excluded from the Bill during its passage.

The result is that if a wild creature is "not tamed nor ordinarily kept in **2–15** captivity," it cannot normally be stolen. The rationale of this is that, although P may own the land on which the creature is and Q may have sporting rights over the land, no one owns the creature until it is killed or taken.[26] But when it

---

[23] Larceny Act 1916, s.1(3) proviso (b).
[24] *Howlett* [1968] Crim.L.R. 222.
[25] *Eighth Report*, para. 52.
[26] See *Blades v. Higgs* (1865) 11 H.L.C. 621.

has been reduced into someone's possession (and so long as it has not subsequently been lost or abandoned), or when someone is in course of reducing it into possession, it can be treated as the proper subject of theft. Section 4(4) provides accordingly, treating a wild creature and the carcass of a wild creature in identical terms. So it is not theft to kill and take game on P's land, unless, for instance, the creature is taken from P's snares (even from another poacher's snares) or from a hut in which P has put the product of his own day's shooting.

2–16   *Fish and deer*. Schedule 1 to the Act preserves in a modified form certain provisions of the Larceny Act 1861 concerning the unlawful taking or destroying of fish in water which is private property or in which there is any private right of fishery. Other provisions, originally preserved by Schedule 1, relating to the taking or killing of deer, are now contained in the Deer Act 1991, s.1. This creates summary offences of (1) entering any land, without the consent of the owner or occupier or other lawful authority, in search or pursuit of any deer with the intention of taking, killing or injuring it; (2) on any land, (a) intentionally taking, killing or injuring any deer (or attempting to do so), or (b) searching for or pursuing any deer with the intention of taking, killing or injuring it, or (c) removing the carcass of any deer, without the consent of the owner or occupier of the land or other lawful authority.

"Money"

2–17   A question about the legal meaning of "money" is invariably a question as to the classes of assets referred to by the word in a particular context.[27] The Theft Act concerns the appropriation (or the obtaining by deception: s.15) of particular items of property,[28] some of which are singled out for mention as "money." All that the word seems to include in this context is current coins and bank notes (including, of course, foreign coins and notes).[29] So, if a person deals dishonestly with a cheque for £x, he can be convicted on a charge of stealing "£x in money" only if he cashes the cheque and appropriates the cash as property belonging to another.[30] It is tempting to give the word "money" a wider meaning than this. After all, it is rightly observed in a different connection that according to "the ordinary language and usage of mankind, when a man says, 'I have so much money at my bankers,' he considers and treats it as his money"[31]; so that, even when a testator's reference to his "money" is to be construed in a strict sense, it is allowed to include what he has on current and deposit account.[32] It is one thing, however, to permit a testamentary gift of

---

[27] See F. A. Mann, *The Legal Aspect of Money* (5th ed.), Chap. I.
[28] See below, §2–26.
[29] That is, coins and notes issued by the authority of the law and currently capable of serving as universal means of exchange in their country of origin: adapting language of Mann, *op. cit.*, p.8.
[30] *Davis* (1988) 88 Cr.App.R. 347 (below, §2–49); *Brady v. Inland Revenue Commissioners* [1989] S.T.C. 178 (obtaining payment by cheque is not obtaining "money" for Theft Act purposes).
[31] *Manning v. Purcell* (1855) 7 De G.M. & G. 55, *per* Turner L.J. at 67.
[32] *Re Collings* [1933] Ch. 920.

"money" to pass the benefit of a bank account. It is quite another thing to suppose that a person's bank account is "money" for Theft Act purposes. The "property" in which a bank's customer can have a "proprietary right or interest" (s.5(1)) is a thing in action—namely, the debt owed to him by the bank when the account is in credit.[33] If, say, £74.74 is credited to the account, the property available to be stolen is not, strictly, "the sum of £74.74" but a "chose (or thing) in action."[34]

"Things in action and other intangible property"[35]

"Things in action" are "all personal rights of property which can only be **2–18** claimed or enforced by action and not by taking physical possession."[36] They include intangible things such as a debt,[37] a right under a trust and, it seems, any obligation owed in law by one person to another and capable of being enforced by that other[38]: the creditor, the beneficiary and the obligee have "property" that can be stolen.

It was for a long time believed that the category, "things in action," embraced all kinds of personal property other than things in possession (moveable chattels, including money as defined above).[39] But it is now clear that there are some kinds of intangible property that are not things in action. Patents and applications for patents are declared by statute not to be things in action.[40] Another kind was revealed in *Attorney-General of Hong Kong v. Nai-keung*,[41] where a company had export quotas issued by a government department. The quotas conferred an expectation of a licence to export textiles to the amount of the quotas but no enforceable right to such a licence. There was a flourishing market in such quotas. The quotas (although not things in action) were held to be "intangible property" and therefore capable of being stolen by a dishonest director of the company who sold them at an undervalue for his own benefit.[42]

Nothing, in truth, turns for theft purposes on whether a species of intangible property is a "thing in action." There is no doubt that, for example,

---

[33] *Foley v. Hill* (1848) 2 H.L.C. 28; *Space Investments Ltd. v. Canadian Imperial Bank of Commerce Trust Co. (Bahamas) Ltd.* [1986] 1 W.L.R. 1072; [1986] 3 All E.R. 75 (as to trust funds deposited with bank). (Lord Goddard C.J. made the same point for Larceny Act purposes in *Davenport* (1954) 38 Cr.App.R. 37 at 41.)

[34] *Attorney-General's Reference (No. 1 of 1983)* [1985] Q.B. 182 at pp. 187–188. See also *Kohn* (1979) 69 Cr.App.R. 395; *Golechha* (1989) 90 Cr.App.R. 241 at 246.

[35] See below, §2–143, as to theft of such property generally; §2–145, as to theft of bank credits.

[36] *Torkington v. Magee* [1902] 2 K.B. 427, *per* Channell J. at 430; adopted in *Kohn* (1979) 69 Cr.App.R. 395.

[37] But not the mere appearance of a debt, created by a fraudulent entry in an account: *Thompson* (1984) 79 Cr.App.R. 191.

[38] See, *e.g.*, below, §2–146.

[39] *Colonial Bank v. Whinney* (1885) 30 Ch.D. 261, *per* Fry L. J. at 285; Crossley Vaines, *Personal Property* (5th ed.), pp. 11–13.

[40] Patents Act 1977, s.30(1).

[41] (1987) 86 Cr.App.R. 174.

[42] For a more doubtful application of the phrase, "other intangible property", see below, §8–08.

intangibles such as shares and copyrights are property; there is no need to classify them further.

2–19   The tempting possibility of convicting a dishonest person of theft of intangible property can lead to too energetic an attempt to identify available property. The potential difficulties of analysis and, it is submitted, the dangers, are illustrated by *Baruday*.[43] D, an insurance broker, acted as the agent of P, a large employer, in relation to workers' compensation policies with I, insurers. Premiums were paid in advance on the basis of estimates of P's wages bill; on subsequent adjustment P might be entitled to some return of premiums from I. D had a monthly running account with I on which he was constantly in debit. I credited to this account the amount of certain "return premiums."[44] D failed to pass on these credits to P by payment or by credit in account. The Supreme Court of Victoria upheld D's convictions of theft of things in action. The Crown had contended that the things in question were the debts due from I to P; but any such debts were discharged by the accounting with P's agent, D. Still, the court held that I's "creation of the credit [in favour of D] involved the creation of a 'thing in action'" which was "property belonging to [P]," and that D's "retention" of that property was an appropriation of it. This, with respect, makes the notion of a "thing in action" work altogether too hard. On I's discharge of its indebtedness the only relevant thing in action seems to have been P's claim against D himself. The credit allowed by I in its accounting with D was not itself "property" of any kind; it was not, and it did not create, any right of action against I (which was, in any case, D's creditor, not his debtor). There was no "property" for D to "retain". D became P's debtor. But the Theft Act does not make a thief of a debtor who dishonestly decides not to discharge his indebtedness and therefore conceals it.

Cheques and other instruments

2–20   If D dishonestly draws a cheque on P's cheque form in his own favour, or draws such a cheque in E's favour and delivers it to E, the gravamen of D's conduct is best conveyed by a charge of stealing P's bank credit, if such a charge is available. The theft of bank credits is a topic to be considered in detail below,[45] where it will appear that no such theft can occur if P's bank account is not in credit and P has no overdraft facility to drawn upon at the relevant time. This difficulty can be avoided, it seems, by charging theft of the cheque form. For the purpose of such theft it is immaterial whether the cheque is met or whether it is drawn within the limits of P's credit or overdraft

---

[43] [1984] V.R. 685. (Victoria's Crimes Act 1958 contains provisions in relevant respects identical to those of the Theft Act 1968.)
[44] The headnote refers to "cheques" received by D from I; but all indications in the judgment are of credits in account rather than cheques. If cheques had been received, theft convictions might have been based on the equivalent of s.5(3) of the English Act (see §2–40, below); no reference to things in action need have been made.
[45] §§2–145 *et seq.*

facility.[46] The temptation has not always been resisted to describe the property stolen (the cheque) as itself a thing in action, on the ground that a cheque is an instrument embodying a right in the person entitled to it to receive payment of the amount for which it is drawn.[47] But the property stolen must be property belonging to P and the thing in action created in the payee's favour by the transaction of drawing and delivering a cheque is not a thing that has ever belonged to the drawer. It is therefore more accurate, to say that D has stolen P's cheque form—that is, a piece of paper.[48]

Excluded or doubtful things

Nothing that is not "property" can be stolen. There are some categories of   **2–21** things that are not, or are possibly not, "property."

Electricity

The fact that section 13 of the Act creates a separate offence of abstracting electricity suggests that electricity is not intended to be property for the purpose of theft. This was confirmed by the Divisional Court in *Low v. Blease*.[49]

The human body and its parts[50]

Dead bodies. There could be no larceny of a corpse at common law; for, it   **2–22** was consistently asserted, there could be no property in a dead body. Whatever the credentials of this principle,[51] it no doubt survives to limit the modern law of theft, at least to the extent that there can be no theft of a buried corpse. Nor, it is thought, does the theft sanction protect the possession of anyone having the right to possess the body for a limited purpose—such as the executor who has the right to possession of it until burial,[52] or a licensed anatomist who is authorised to have possession of it for a "statutory period" for teaching or research purposes.[53] "Property" within the Act is probably

---

[46] *Kohn* (1979) 69 Cr.App.R. 395 at 410. As to the necessary intention of permanently depriving P of the cheque form, which will in due course revert to his bank and be available to him, see below, §8–71. There may be theft of the cheque although in part it represents payment of a debt owed by P to E: see *Sobel* [1986] Crim.L.R. 261. In *Kohn*, above, there were convictions of stealing both cheque and bank credit in respect of the same transaction; but in *Wille* (1988) 86 Cr.App.R. 296, counts in respect of cheques were, surely more properly, withdrawn from the jury as superfluous.

[47] *ibid.*, at 409–410.

[48] Compare *Davis (Gary)* (1988) 88 Cr.App.R. 347 at 350–351 (see below, §2–49); *Shadrokh-Cigari* [1988] Crim.L.R. 465, below, §2–35 (banker's drafts).

[49] [1975] Crim.L.R. 513.

[50] P. Matthews [1983] C.L.P. 193; A. T. H. Smith [1976] Crim.L.R. 622; Roger S. Magnusson "Proprietary Rights in Human Tissue" in N. Palmer and E. McKendrick (eds.), *Interests in Goods*.

[51] See P. Matthews, *op. cit.*, p. 197.

[52] *Williams v. Williams* (1882) 20 Ch.D. 659.

[53] Anatomy Act 1984, ss.2–4.

limited to that which is capable of being owned or of indefinite lawful possession. If this is right, the law is unsatisfactory; the cadaver store of a university anatomy department should be within the protection of the Act.

2–23   A body may perhaps become capable of ownership by "the lawful exercise of work or skill" which gives it "some attributes differentiating it from a mere corpse awaiting burial." Such an operation, it has been suggested, would give "a right to permanent possession" and render the body "the subject of property."[54] This principle cannot apply to a dissected corpse, which, after dissection, can be retained "for the purpose only of its decent disposal."[55] But it would apply to a mummified corpse preserved as a museum piece and (*a fortiori*) to a part of a body, such as a skeleton, lawfully preserved after dissection. Sections 5 and 6 of the Anatomy Act 1984 provide that, under licence granted in the interests of education and research, and in accordance with the deceased's permission, a person may be authorised to possess parts of bodies after dissection is concluded. No time limit is imposed upon such possession. There seems here to be a source of "property".

Parts of bodies removed after death for therapeutic purposes under section 1 of the Human Tissue Act 1961 ought certainly to be recognised as property, and so as capable of being stolen, before transplantation occurs.

2–24   *Parts and products of living bodies.* It seems that specimens of urine and blood provided to the police can be stolen.[56] Blood and sperm banks must surely be protected by the law of theft. Nor need the status of "property" be denied to parts of living donors removed for transplantation or of ova removed for *in vitro* fertilisation. The case of an ovum fertilised *in vitro* is, to say the least, more doubtful.

Trade secrets and other confidential information

2–25   It is probably a good guess that few of the people responsible for the Act contemplated trade secrets (secret industrial processes, for example) as "property" within the meaning of section 4(1) or as capable of being stolen. During the debates on the Bill, however, Lord Wilberforce took a wide view of the word "property" as including "things like business secrets."[57] He did not pursue in detail the analysis required to demonstrate that the law of theft has become an effective weapon against modern forms of industrial espionage. It seems that it has not. One can in popular parlance describe a person who "bugs" a private conversation or photocopies a confidential document as "stealing" a secret. But to achieve that result in law would involve reading the Act in a very robust way for the purpose of producing a dramatic new

---

[54] *Doodeward v. Spence* (1908) 6 C.L.R. 406, *per* Griffith C.J. at 414. (The case was an action of detinue relating to the long-preserved corpse of a still-born two-headed child. Barton J., while agreeing with the Chief Justice's judgment holding that the action would lie, did not regard this curiosity as a "corpse" within the meaning of the general rule.)
[55] Anatomy Act 1984, s.5.
[56] *Welsh* [1974] R.T.R. 478; *Rothery* [1976] R.T.R. 550 (pleas of guilty).
[57] H.L. Deb., Vol. 259, col. 1309.

offence not hinted at by the C.L.R.C. The Act is not in fact the appropriate instrument to deal with this specialised kind of mischief.[58] The short way of disposing of an argument to the contrary is to deny that trade secrets are "property" within the Act. They should be treated in the same way as the confidential information contained in the proof copy of an examination paper; such information has been held to be incapable of being stolen because it is not "property."[59] But even if a secret were property, it would be peculiarly difficult to steal, for a reason to be noticed later in this chapter.[60]

"Property" means a particular asset

The word "property" in the definition of theft refers to particular assets. **2–26** For that alone can be stolen which can be the subject of "possession or control" or of a "proprietary right or interest" (section 5(1)) and which can be "appropriated" with the intention of "depriving" another of it. So a dishonest act cannot be theft simply because (as its doer knows) it involves or must lead to the diminution of another's net wealth.

These observations are stimulated by *Navvabi*,[61] in which theft convictions were sought on a novel basis. D issued cheques which his bank account would be unable to meet. But they were backed by a banker's card, so that his bank was bound to honour them. The Court of Appeal quashed D's convictions of theft. There was held to be no appropriation of "that part of the bank's funds to which the sum specified in the cheque corresponded". The decision was expressed as turning on the meaning of "appropriation".[62] But the reason for denying theft in this kind of case is more fundamental. When the guaranteed cheque is delivered to the payee, there is no "part" of the bank's "funds" corresponding to the sum specified. The bank's obligation to pay does not attach to particular property. When the cheque is collected by the payee's bank (the common procedure), no "funds" are "transferred by the [paying] bank to the [payee]".[63] Rather, the transaction features in a general accounting between the banks. No particular asset of the paying bank is diminished. The element of "property" is not satisfied; there is no need to discuss appropriation. Only if the payee obtains cash for an open cheque is particular property of the paying bank affected. *Navvabi* was not such a case; but it is submitted, and the decision suggests, that the drawer of the guaranteed cheque does not appropriate the cash later paid to the payee.

---

[58] Compare the Supreme Court of Canada in *Stewart v. R.* (1988) 50 D.L.R. (4th) 1 at 12–13, reversing *Stewart* (1983) 149 D.L.R. (3rd) 583; R. G. Hammond (1984) 100 L.Q.R. 252. In *Stewart v. R.*, at 12, Lamer J. pointed out the difficulty of defining a category of "confidential information".

[59] *Oxford v. Moss* (1978) 68 Cr.App.R. 183.

[60] Below, §2–144. If a secret is written on a piece of paper and the paper is taken, a charge of theft naturally presents no difficulty.

[61] (1986) 83 Cr.App.R. 271.

[62] *ibid.*, at 276.

[63] *Pace* the language, *ibid.*

3. "BELONGING TO ANOTHER"

Generally

2–27   In order that property may be stolen it must "belong to another".

When D picks P's pocket and extracts money, or when he removes valuables from P's house, it is obvious that the *actus reus* of a theft has occurred; but even in such simple cases the property does not necessarily belong to P in the loosest sense of the word "belong": P may be carrying Q's money for him or have Q's valuables on loan or for safe keeping. Yet clearly D steals from P, and whether P owns the property or not it is necessary to regard the property, for the purpose of the law of theft, as belonging to P as well as to Q.

Moreover, experience with the law of larceny showed that to exclude from the ambit of the offence all cases in which D himself was already the owner of the property or became the owner by the transaction alleged to involve a dishonest appropriation—to say that an owner could not steal, or that one could not both become owner and steal as a result of the same transaction—was unsatisfactory in a number of ways.[64]

Section 5 therefore gives the phrase "belonging to another" a much wider meaning than it bears in common speech.[65] For purposes of the law of theft, property may "belong" at the same time to a number of different people, including its legal owner, almost anyone with an equitable interest in it and its present possessor or controller (subss. (1) and (2)). And some special cases are provided for, in which property (or its proceeds) is artificially regarded, as against D, as belonging to another because of some legal obligation owed by D to that other as a result of the circumstances in which he came by the property (subss. (3) and (4)).

Possession or control; proprietary right or interest

2–28   Section 5(1) provides that property "shall be regarded as belonging to any person having possession or control of it, or having in it any proprietary right or interest (not being an equitable interest arising from an agreement to transfer or grant an interest)."

(i) *Possession or control*

The word "possession" in English law is a veritable chameleon, changing its meaning with every change in the context in which it occurs. If it had been used alone in section 5(1) there might have been much room for argument as to its meaning in this context; whereas the addition of the words "or control"

---

[64] It led among other things to multiplicity of offences (special provisions being made for some appropriations by owners); to artificial reasoning and impure doctrine (some owners being speciously treated as non-owners in order to secure convictions of larceny); and to the acquittal of a number of persons whom a law of theft should arguably catch.

[65] The issue of whether property belonged to another may involve a question of law, including a question on the construction of documents, on which it is up to the judge to direct the jury: see, *e.g.* §§2–33, 2–44, below.

ensures that some cases doubtfully of possession are in fact to be treated as equivalent to cases of possession. For instance, if D seizes goods from the hands of P, a customer handling them in a shop, there is clearly a theft from P, who has control if not possession, and there is no need to discover whether P has yet acquired a proprietary right by purchase.

Things on P's land. It is submitted that P can always be treated as having　**2–29** "control" of property lying on land that he occupies, even if he does not know of it. In *Woodman*,[66] a company had sold all the scrap metal on the site of its disused factory but retained control of the site. The company did not know that the purchasers had left some of the metal on the site. One who entered the site and removed the metal was properly convicted on an indictment describing the metal as belonging to the company. The language of the judgment was perhaps unduly cautious; a person in control of a site was described as "prima facie" having control of articles on it in "ordinary and straightforward cases".[67]

The point is not of significance except in the case of property abandoned by its former owner. If property on P's land has not been abandoned it can be described (by amendment if necessary) as belonging to its named owner,[68] if known, or to "a person unknown." Abandoned property, on the other hand, may belong to P or to no one. The leading case on the relative claims of D and P to property found by D on P's land holds that D's claim prevails unless P had, expressly or impliedly, manifested an intention to exercise control over such property on the land.[69] An exception was asserted where D is a trespasser; and the exception was said to be reflected in a case of larceny where D scavenged for lost golf balls and was convicted of stealing from the golf club.[70] Such a scavenger no doubt steals under the present law. But the club's "control" of the balls within the meaning of section 5(1) can hardly depend on the fact of trespass. So the better view appears to be that P, as occupier, has "control" (which he is taken to intend to exercise at least against a trespasser) of anything on his land. But if he has manifested no "intention to exercise control" over particular property, or a particular class of property, the taking of such property by D (not being a trespasser), ought not to be theft, his claim being superior to that of P.[71]

Theft by owner. One result of the protection of possession is that an owner　**2–30** can steal his own property. D may, for instance, have pledged his goods with P; or he may have entrusted goods to P for repair so that P has acquired an

---

[66] [1974] Q.B. 754.

[67] *ibid.*, at 758.

[68] If to the Crown as owner of treasure trove, the fact that the property is treasure trove must be proved beyond reasonable doubt in the criminal proceedings: *Hancock* (1989) 90 Cr.App.R. 422.

[69] *Parker v. British Airways Board* [1982] Q.B. 1004.

[70] *Hibbert v. McKiernan* [1948] 2 K.B. 142.

[71] For the case where D claims to have been unaware of P's interest in the property, see below, §2–101. For an extended discussion of the application of the law of theft to finders of property, see Smith (A. T. H.), paras. 4–13 *et seq.*

artificer's lien entitling him to retain possession until the repair bill is paid. If in either of these cases, in order to defeat P's possessory rights, D dishonestly takes the goods from P's possession, he may be convicted of theft.

The Court of Appeal has in fact gone further than this in *Turner (No. 2)*,[72] where P, having repaired D's car, left it in the road near his (P's) garage. D came and took the car away. The possible existence of a lien was disregarded. D was nevertheless held rightly convicted of theft if he acted dishonestly, for P had "possession or control" (presumably as a bailee at will). The decision goes very far and its correctness is not clear. Once P's possible lien is ignored, D did nothing in relation to the car that he was not perfectly entitled to do. This should on principle have ruled out liability for theft.[73]

(ii) *Proprietary right or interest*

2–31   Something of the scope of theft is indicated by the inclusion among the possible victims of the offence of "any person ... having ... any proprietary right or interest" in the property appropriated. The phrase clearly includes the owner of an estate in land or of any interest therein; a beneficiary under an express trust; the owner of a thing in action (the creditor in respect of a debt, for instance); a partner in respect of partnership property; and so on.[74] If D's act of appropriation is done with the intention of defeating P's right or interest in the property, it will properly be described as an appropriation of property "belonging to" P—even though other people may have other, and larger, rights in the same property. D himself may have a proprietary right or interest and still be guilty of theft: a part-owner or a partner, for example, may dishonestly appropriate property, as by selling it or by absconding with it, so as to defeat his co-owner or his partners[75]; and a dishonest sale by a trustee of trust property for his own purposes will be a theft of property belonging to the beneficiaries.

2–32   *Equitable interests*. Two express provisions make it perfectly clear that, in general, equitable interests in property are "proprietary interests" within the meaning of section 5(1). First, section 5(1) itself includes a parenthesis excepting, from those to whom property is to be regarded as belonging, a person who has in it "an equitable interest arising only from an agreement to transfer or grant an interest". Since land cannot be stolen save in cases not material to this point, the exception will mainly affect dealings in shares and similar property. D contracts to transfer shares to P and receives money from P; he then transfers them to Q; he does not steal the shares, for P has only an

---

[72] (1971) 55 Cr.App.R. 336.
[73] See below, §2–93. *Turner (No. 2)* was perhaps overlooked in *Meredith* [1973] Crim.L.R. 253 (Judge da Cunha), where D, without reference to the police, had removed his car from a police pound and a charge of theft was said to be improper. This view has generally been preferred.
[74] But the interest must be a proprietary one. A copyright owner was held not to have a proprietary interest in material infringing the copyright, notwithstanding the Copyright Act 1956, s.18: *Storrow and Poole* [1983] Crim.L.R. 332 (Judge Lowry Q.C.); see now the Copyright, Designs and Patents Act 1988, ss.99, 100, 114.
[75] *Bonner* (1970) 54 Cr.App.R. 257.

equitable interest arising from the agreement to transfer.[76] It seems that, this exception apart, anyone else with an equitable interest is intended to be included.

Secondly, section 5(2) provides that the persons to whom property subject to a trust is to be regarded as belonging include "any person having a right to enforce the trust". The purpose of this subsection is to ensure that a misappropriation of property held on trust for a charitable object shall not fail to be theft merely because no particular person has a beneficial interest in the property. Charitable trusts are enforced under the Charities Act 1960, s.28, by (among others) the Attorney-General.

Clowes (No. 2)[77] provides two examples of equitable interests protected by the law of theft. The Barlow Clowes group of companies (BC) advertised investment schemes based on investment in gilts; and members of the public subscribed to the schemes. (i) C used monies so invested for his own purposes. The Court of Appeal held that the trial judge had properly directed the jury as a matter of law that the monies had belonged to the investors. The investments (on the true construction of BC's brochures as contractual documents) had created a relationship of trustee and beneficiary between BC and the investors. (ii) N, a senior manager in BC, stole property belonging to investors when he withdrew large sums from a bank account consisting in part of money contributed by investors and in part of funds belonging to BC. The argument that N must be presumed to have withdrawn non-trust funds rather than to have acted in breach of trust[78] was rejected. Equity applies that principle to assist a beneficiary against a trustee; but the whole mixed account was property in which the investors had an equitable interest—a "proprietary interest" within the meaning of s. 5(1).   **2–33**

Constructive trusts[79]

The apparent implication, then, of section 5(1) is that any trust beneficiary not excluded by the parenthesis has in the trust property a "proprietary interest" protected by the law of theft. The application of this principle in the case of a possible constructive trust, however, raises two kinds of difficulty: the problem of identifying the existence of such a trust; and the reluctance of   **2–34**

---

[76] There is difficulty also, on the same ground, in finding a theft from P in a third party's dishonest dealings with shares that P has contracted to buy from O: see *per* Lord Keith of Kinkel in *Tarling v. Government of the Republic of Singapore* (1978) 70 Cr.App.R. 77 at 137. But it has been suggested that there may be "property belonging to" P in his enforceable right against O—a legal thing in action (see above, §2–18): J.C. Smith [1979] Crim.L.R. at 225.
[77] [1994] 2 All E.R. 316; Jonathan S. Fisher (1994) 5 J.I.B.L. 212. Compare *Hallam and Blackburn*, [1995] Crim.L.R. 323: clients gave cheques to investment advisers for the purpose of investment in policies and bonds. These cheques (or their proceeds), and cheques (or the proceeds of cheques) from financial institutions, representing the proceeds of investments, were held on trust for the clients; and there was theft whenever there was a dishonest appropriation of such trust property. As to charging such a theft occurring at an unknown time, see below, §2–159.
[78] *Re Hallett's Estates* (1880) 13 Ch.D. 696.
[79] A. T. H. Smith [1977] Crim.L.R. 395; Arlidge and Parry, paras. 4.03–4.05.

some courts to treat the appropriation of an interest under such a trust as theft.

2–35   *Property transferred under mistake of fact.* In *Shadrokh-Cigari*,[80] about a quarter of a million U.S. dollars had been transferred in error to the account of a boy, R, with P bank. R's guardian, D, prevailed upon R to authorise the bank to issue banker's drafts drawn in favour of D for the bulk of this sum. The Court of Appeal applied to the drafts the recently-stated principle that one who transfers money to another under a mistake of fact retains an interest in that money under a constructive trust.[81] P bank had retained an equitable interest in the drafts, having issued them on the mistaken assumption that the funds in the account could be properly dealt with as authorised by R. D therefore stole the drafts[82] from the bank when he applied them to his own purposes.[83]

Such a response to a development in the law of trusts offers the prospect of a relatively active role for the criminal courts by way of response to dishonest behaviour. Consider, for example, the application to the law of theft of a more general principle that has been accepted in at least one English civil case: "the receiving of money which consistently with conscience cannot be retained is, in equity, sufficient to raise a trust in favour of the party from whom or in whose account it was received."[84] If the circumstances in which D receives money make it inconsistent with conscience for him to retain it, a conscientious jury ought to be able to find that he acts dishonestly according to the standards of ordinary decent people[85] when, aware of the circumstances, he prefers to apply the money to his own purposes rather than restore it.

2–36   *Secret profits and bribes.* (i) *Secret profits.* A strong case for the recognition of a trust would seem to have existed in *Attorney-General's Reference (No. 1 of 1985)*.[86] D was the manager of a tied public house. He was obliged, by the terms of his contract of employment with P (the brewers), to obtain from P all liquor to be sold in the public house and to pay all the takings of the house into P's bank account. D bought beer from other sources, sold it in the public house and kept the proceeds for himself. D was clearly liable to account to P for at least the profit he had made; but he could be guilty of theft only if P were beneficially entitled to the proceeds of D's sales or the profit element in them. The Court of Appeal rejected the contention that D became a constructive trustee on these facts. Its reasons were (a) that the making of a

---

[80] [1988] Crim.L.R. 465.
[81] *Chase Manhattan Bank N.A. v. Israel-British Bank (London) Ltd.* [1981] Ch. 105.
[82] That is, the pieces of paper: see above, §2–20.
[83] An alternative basis of D's conviction was section 5(4): see below, §2–48.
[84] Story, *Commentaries on Equity Jurisprudence* (2nd ed., 1839), para. 1255; applied in *Neste Oy v. Lloyds Bank plc* [1983] 2 Lloyd's Rep. 658 (cited by Goff and Jones, *The Law of Restitution* (4th ed.), p. 94).
[85] See below, §2–132.
[86] [1986] Q.B. 491. The decision was accepted without criticism by the House of Lords in *Cooke* [1986] A.C. 909 (see especially *per* Lord Mackay at 934). See also *Keatley* [1980] Crim.L.R. 505 (Judge Mendl).

secret profit by the use of a "fiduciary position" does not give rise to a trust; and (b) that in any case no separate profit element was identifiable as property to which a trust could attach.

It is convenient to comment first on proposition (b), briefly observing that it seems to confuse the existence of a trust (surely attaching, if it exists, to the proceeds of sale as a whole) and the extent of P's interest under it.

Proposition (a) was surprising in its width[87] and questionable in its application to the facts of the case. D had sold beer on P's premises to customers whom P were entitled to regard as their own. The purpose of buying and selling his own beer will have been to conceal, on a stock-taking, his purloining of the takings. Those takings, it is submitted, were P's property, just like the proceeds of any other sales (of P's goods) that D may have made to the same customers.[88] The main precedent relied on by the court[89] concerned bribes received by an employee in breach of his fiduciary duty. It is surprising that the court could see "no distinction in principle" between such a case, where the employee has not abused his employer's property, and a case like the instant case, where the employee makes a profit from the use of his employer's property, time and clientèle. The case for treating D's conduct as theft was much stronger than that for holding that the corrupt employee steals his bribe. The authority of the court's precedent, as we shall see immediately, has now been seriously undermined; so the law stated in *Attorney-General's Reference (No. 1 of 1985)*, and more generally the subject of the theft of secret profits, would seem to merit reconsideration.   **2–37**

(ii) *Bribes*. In the much-debated case of *Lister & Co. v. Stubbs*[90] in 1890 the Court of Appeal held that an employee stands in relation to his employer, in respect of bribes that he has received in breach of his fiduciary duty, in the capacity of a debtor only (having a duty to account for the bribes) and not that of a trustee. If this is so, it follows that an employer who pockets his bribe does not steal it; and it was so held in *Powell v. McRae*,[91] where C bribed D, a turnstile operator at Wembley Stadium, to let him into the stadium to see an all-ticket match.   **2–38**

The Privy Council, however, in *Attorney-General for Hong Kong v. Reid*,[92] has recently disapproved *Lister v. Stubbs*, which it found to be inconsistent

---

[87] Contrast the assertion of Goff and Jones, *The Law of Restitution* (4th ed.), pp. 646–647 (made before the decision in *Attorney-General for Hong Kong v. Reid* (below, §2–38), that the fiduciary who receives a bribe is the only exception to the general rule suggested by the English authorities, "that a fiduciary will hold any benefit made from the abuse of his fiduciary position or from the use of his beneficiary's property as a constructive trustee."
[88] The argument is, in effect, that money received for the beer should have gone straight into the till rather than into D's pocket. If that is right, there may strictly be no need to rely on the existence of a trust.
[89] *Lister & Co. v. Stubbs* (1890) 45 Ch.D. 1.
[90] (1890) 45 Ch.D. 1.
[91] [1977] Crim.L.R. 571.
[92] [1994] 1 A.C. 324; see J.C. Smith (1994) 110 L.Q.R. 180 on the Theft Act implications.

with pre-existing authorities. The principle now stated is that "a fiduciary acting dishonestly and criminally[93] who accepts a bribe and thereby causes loss or damage to his principal must ... be a constructive trustee...."[94] On that basis the principal would be beneficially entitled to the bribe or to any-thing that the corrupt agent might acquire with it; and either might be the subject of theft, the law underlying *Powell v. McRae* having changed. That conclusion assumes that the law is now as stated by the Privy Council, which (given the Judicial Committee's composition) English courts may be expected to accept. It depends also on the willingness of the criminal courts to apply the general law faithfully in the application of section 5(1) and its reference to "any proprietary ... interest". The history provides some reason for doubt on this point.

2–39   *Invocation of the general conception of theft.* It was the view of the court in *Attorney-General's Reference (No. 1 of 1985)* that D's keeping all the pro-ceeds of his improper sales was "so far from the understanding of ordinary people as to what constitutes stealing" that it "should not amount to steal-ing".[95] It might not, indeed, be stealing because D might believe that he was entitled, as against P, to keep those proceeds.[96] But objection must be taken to the apparent implication of the court's remark: that even if D were a con-structive trustee of the takings, his conduct should still be held not to be theft. It is submitted that the interpretation of "proprietary interest" in section 5(1) as not including an interest under one variety of trust would amount to a rewriting of the Act which the court ought not to undertake. The court wants the Act to produce acceptable results. That motive justifies a call for parlia-mentary, rather than an act of judicial, legislation.

Property received subject to an obligation

2–40   D may receive property in circumstances which render him bound, as between himself and another person, to deal with it in a particular way. A dishonest application of such property ought to be theft; and section 5(3) accordingly provides:

> "Where a person receives property from or on account of another, and is under an obligation to the other to retain and deal with that property or its proceeds in a

---

[93] This does not beg a question about theft but apparently refers to the offence of corruption likely to be committed by the bribe-taker; see in English law the Public Bodies Corrupt Practices Act 1889, s.1, and the Prevention of Corruption Act 1906, s.1.
[94] [1994] 1 A.C. 324, *per* Lord Templeman at 338.
[95] [1986] Q.B. 491 at 507. In *Tarling v. Government of the Republic of Singapore* (1978) 70 Cr.App.R. 77 at 110, Lord Wilberforce apparently could not conceive that the making of a secret profit could be theft.
[96] See §2–125, below. Or (depressing thought) a jury might refuse to say that D's keeping the proceeds was not dishonest "according to the ordinary standards of reasonable and honest people": see §2–132, below.

particular way, the property or its proceeds shall be regarded (as against him) as belonging to the other."

D may receive possession of goods as a bailee. Or he may become the legal owner of property (as of money that is paid to him) but receive it as a trustee. In such cases the bailor or any person entitled to enforce the trust is a person to whom the property is to be regarded as belonging, by virtue of section 5(1) or (2); so that no further provision is necessary to render the property capable of being stolen by D. It is, however, to the much more complicated provision in section 5(3) that reference is, for some reason, commonly made when an obligation such as it mentions exists, even if section 5(1) or (2) would do perfectly well.[97]

To what kind of obligation does section 5(3) refer?

It must be stressed that it is not enough that D, when he receives money or   **2–41**
other property, falls under some contractual obligation, or that a relationship of debtor and creditor is thereby created. D must be under an obligation[98] which prescribes the application of that particular property or its proceeds. In *Hall*,[99] for example, D was a travel agent who had received deposits and payments from clients in respect of air trips to be arranged by him. He paid the sums into his firm's general trading account but arranged no trips and could not repay any of the money. His conviction of theft was quashed. There had not been proved such a special arrangement between him and any of the clients as would give rise to an obligation within section 5(3).

If D is under a duty to P to collect money and to account to P for the money   **2–42**
less D's commission or other reward, the circumstances may be such as to oblige D to maintain a distinct fund representing his receipts. If so, D, dishonestly pocketing more than he is entitled to, will be guilty of theft of the excess.[1] Or the receipt of money by D as P's agent may create in D the obligation of a debtor only so that a failure to account to P for what he receives cannot be theft.[2]

Similarly, if D sells P's goods on his behalf, he may owe P a fiduciary duty in relation to the proceeds of sale; or, once again, his resulting obligation to P may merely be that of debtor to creditor. In the former case only can there be

---

[97] The C.L.R.C. itself gave as its illustration of s.5(3) the case of the treasurer of a holiday fund who misapplies the fund or part of it. His "duty to retain and deal with the property as agreed" (*Eighth Report*, p. 127) is surely that of a trustee. An executor's misappropriation of property from the deceased's estate is given by Smith (A. T. H.), para. 4–54, as a possible example of a case depending entirely on s.5(3).
[98] That is, an obligation of which he personally knows: *Wills* (1990) 92 Cr.App.R. 297. This should in principle mean that he personally knows the facts giving rise to the obligation. The existence, on those facts, of an obligation within the meaning of s.5(3) is a conclusion of law: see below, §2–44. D's ignorance of the legal consequence may be relevant to the issue of dishonesty.
[99] [1973] Q.B. 126; distinguished in *Hallam and Blackburn*, [1995] Crim.L.R. 323 (payments to investment advisers for investment).
[1] Compare *Lord* (1905) 60 J.P. 467 (debt collector); *Messer* [1913] 2 K.B. 421 (taxi-driver).
[2] *e.g. Stanley Robertson* [1977] Crim.L.R. 629 (Judge Rubin Q.C.).

any question of theft if he dissipates all his assets without paying P what he should.

The circumstances of the individual transaction, including most obviously the terms of any agreement between D and P, may plainly reveal the nature of D's obligation. If they do not, the obligation may be difficult to classify. "The cases ... do not show that there is any general principle to determine whether the agent holds property or money in trust"[3]—which is what, in truth, the prosecution must show. One reason for this is that in the civil cases referred to, the nature of the principal's remedy against the agent (whether personal, as against a debtor, or proprietary) "is not normally of consequence."[4]

2–43   The following generalisation, however, may be helpful. It seems that section 5(3) will be satisfied where, having received money or other property from P, or on account of P, D has an obligation to P to preserve a fund or corpus consisting of, or representing,[5] that money or other property, which fund or corpus is to be maintained except so far as it may or must be dealt with "in a particular way"—that is, in the manner required by the transaction with P, or by transfer to P or at his direction, or as justified by an accounting with P.

A legal obligation is required; the function of the judge

2–44   The "obligation" referred to in section 5(2) is, of course, a legal obligation.[6] The decision whether on the facts of a particular case such an obligation arose is one that must be made by the judge, applying the general law. The judge, however, does not know the facts of a contested case until the jury return their verdict. His direction to the jury must therefore be hypothetical in form. He will tell them that if they find certain facts, then the case is one in which a legal obligation arose to which section 5(3) applies. This was laid down by the Court of Appeal in *Mainwaring and Madders*.[7]

It is submitted that the guidance given in *Mainwaring* is unhappy in one respect. It contemplates that the judge will refer to section 5(3) in his direc-

---

[3] Bowstead on *Agency* (13th ed.), p. 128.

[4] *ibid.*, p. 129. See now 15th ed., pp. 160–162, 192 (not repeating the statement quoted in the text).

[5] As its "proceeds"—which must be generously interpreted to include the case where D is at liberty to set aside money which is the equivalent in value of the money received; this commonplace situation cannot be intended to be excluded. Liberal interpretation may also be needed where D mixes in a cash box or a bank account sums received from various persons for a common purpose and is entitled to do so. If proprietary interests in mixed funds are ignored (that is, if, as is common, only s.5(3) is alluded to, and not s.5(1) and (2)), it may be necessary to regard the whole of the fund as the "proceeds" of each contribution. For otherwise (proprietary interests being ignored), who is the victim if D misappropriates a part only of the fund?

[6] *D.P.P.* v. *Huskinson* [1988] Crim.L.R. 620 (no basis in relevant legislation for legal obligation to apply housing benefit to payment of rent).

[7] (1981) 74 Cr.App.R. 99; confirmed in *Dubar* [1994] 1 W.L.R. 1484, disapproving *Hall* [1973] Q.B. 126 and *Hayes* (1976) 64 Cr.App.R. 82 in this respect.

tion. But if on given facts the application of the subsection is a matter of law, why should the jury be troubled with any mention of the subsection? Its application means that the property appropriated by D (whether it is what he originally received or its proceeds) is to be regarded, for purposes of his theft liability, as "belonging to" P. Section 5(3), that is to say, provides, for a special kind of situation, an artificial interpretation of one of the terms in the basic definition of theft. It is surely enough to tell the jury that a finding of certain facts will mean that the property D dealt with (dishonestly appropriated, as the prosecution allege) was property belonging to P. The judge ought to shield the jury from legal complexities whenever he possibly can.[8]

Further examples of the application of section 5(3)

The following are some further cases within section 5(3): **2–45**

(a) P employs D to carry out repairs to P's house and advances £50 to D, not simply on account of the total cost of the job but specifically for the purpose of buying necessary materials. D may have an obligation to use the money in that way.[9] If so, a dishonest use of the £50, or any part of it, will be theft.[10]

(b) P1, P2 and D share a flat. The gas account is in the name of P1. P1 and P2 give D cheques so that, adding her own share, D may pay the gas bill. D, having no bank account, cashes the cheques with her employer. She spends the proceeds on Christmas presents and pays only a third of the gas bill. The proceeds of the cheques are to be regarded as belonging to P1 and P2. D may be convicted of theft.[11]

(c) D ran discos and other events in aid of a body established for the distribution of funds among charities. He held the monies he raised, and their proceeds (a bank account into which he paid them), subject to an obligation described in section 5(3). In fact, he held them on trust.[12]

(d) P sends D a cheque which goes astray in the post. D applies to P for a substitute payment, which is made on the understanding that if the cheque turns up it will be returned to P. D steals the cheque, if, when it arrives, he dishonestly cashes it or pays it into his bank for collection.[13]

(e) D dishonestly sells P's goods without authority and misappropriates the proceeds. The proceeds constitute a fund over which P has a proprietary

---

[8] See *A Criminal Code for England and Wales* (Law Com. No. 177), Vol. 1, para. 3.43; *Shadrokh-Cigari* [1988] Crim.L.R. 465.

[9] Or at least to preserve, and use in that way, an equivalent fund.

[10] Compare *Hughes* [1956] Crim.L.R. 835; but, by contrast, *Jones* (1948) 33 Cr.App.R. 11 and *Bryce* (1955) 40 Cr.App.R. 62 show the need for great caution.

[11] *Davidge v. Bunnett* [1984] Crim.L.R. 297.

[12] *Wain*, October 12, 1993, C.A. no. 92/0667/73; [1994] 1 Archbold News 5. *Lewis v. Lethbridge* [1987] Crim.L.R. 59 (in which a person who failed to pay to a charity the money that he had collected from sponsors of a runner in the London Marathon was held to have been, for all the evidence showed, merely a dishonest debtor) was overruled as inconsistent with *Davidge v. Bunnett*, above, and (more to the point, surely) as overlooking the existence of a trust.

[13] *Wakeman v. Farrar* [1974] Crim.L.R. 136.

claim and which therefore "belongs to" him by virtue of section 5(1). D also receives the proceeds "on account of" P with a clear obligation to retain them for him.[14]

Secret profits and bribes—not received "on account of" P

2-46 D, a servant or agent, who takes a bribe or who makes a secret profit by an abuse of his position or by an unauthorised use of the property of P, his employer or principal, will be bound to account to P for the amount of the bribe or the profit. But the existence of this duty to account for what is received does not mean that it is received "on account of" P within the meaning of section 5(3).[15] It remains unclear just what the reference to property received "on account of another" in section 5(3) adds to the scope of the phrase "belonging to another" as the latter is elaborated in section 5(1).[16]

Doubts about two cases

2-47 In *Brewster*[17] contracts between insurance companies and D, a broker, provided that premiums collected by D would vest in the companies. In practice, though, the companies permitted brokers to use money they collected for their own business purposes and to stand indebted to the companies for the amounts in question. The Court of Appeal held that this did not affect the nature of D's obligation, he having acted dishonestly. The case appears to be a rather special one of an obligation to maintain a specific fund reviving in the event of D's becoming dishonest. Until he becomes dishonest there is surely no such obligation (for the purposes of a civil action). So is not D convicted effectively as a dishonest debtor? (It is not suggested that a similar objection would apply if D could be proved dishonest from the outset.)

Finally, the curious and much discussed case of *Meech*[18] should be mentioned. D agreed with P to cash a cheque that P had obtained from Q. He paid the cheque into his bank, intending to draw cash to pay P. He then learnt that P had obtained the cheque by fraud. He drew the appropriate sum from his account and, with help from E and F, contrived the appearance of a robbery so as to have an excuse for not being able to pay the money to P. The Court of Appeal held that D was guilty of stealing the proceeds of property that he had received from P under an obligation within section 5(3). The argument that P could never have enforced the so-called "obligation" was met by holding that the question was to be looked at from D's point of view. He had "assumed an

---

[14] So also with money obtained by the fraudulent cashing of a cheque intended for P or drawn without authority on P's account: compare *Gale* (1876) 2 Q.B.D. 141; *Davenport* (1954) 38 Cr.App.R. 37.

[15] *Attorney General's Reference (No. 1 of 1985)* [1986] Q.B. 491 (*sed quaere*, on the facts of the case; see the view taken above, §2–37); compare *Cullum* (1873) L.R. 2 C.C.R. 28.

[16] As to secret profits and bribes, see above, §§2–36 to 2–38. In *Williams and Lamb* [1995] Crim.L.R. 77 a mortgagor's solicitor, who had told his client's bank that he had instructions, on receipt of the mortgage advance, to remit part of it to the bank for the reduction of the client's overdraft, was held to have received the advance in part "on account of" the bank.

[17] (1979) 69 Cr.App.R. 375.

[18] [1974] Q.B. 549.

'obligation'" which he thought was a legally binding one, and was therefore "under an obligation" within the meaning of section 5(3).[19] This is hardly acceptable. One cannot be guilty of an offence (as opposed to an attempt to commit it) just because one mistakenly believes an essential element of the offence to exist. D argued further that, because at the time of the appropriation he knew the truth, he was not then under an "obligation." This argument was rejected. The court had in any case already stated that the crucial time is "the time of the creation or the acceptance of the obligation".[20] But it has been correctly objected that, reading section 1(1) and 5(3) together, the obligation must plainly exist at the time of the appropriation.[21]

Property "got" by another's mistake[22]

Section 5(4) provides:

2–48

"Where a person gets property by another's mistake, and is under an obligation to make restoration (in whole or in part) of the property or its proceeds or of the value thereof,[23] then to the extent of that obligation the property or proceeds shall be regarded (as against him) as belonging to the person entitled to restoration, and an intention not to make restoration shall be regarded accordingly as an intention to deprive that person of the property or proceeds."

The subsection was intended to cover a case like *Moynes v. Coopper*.[24] A wages clerk, not having been told that D had received an advance on his wages, gave D a wage packet containing his full wages without deduction. D was held not guilty of larceny when, opening the packet, he realised the error but kept the excess. Section 5(4) was passed primarily to reverse this result. D has "got" his full wages by his employer's mistake; he has an obligation to make restitution ("restoration") of the value of part of the payment; to that extent the money received is now to be regarded as belonging to the employer; dishonestly spending or banking the money, having formed the intention not to repay the excess, will be theft. D's mere retention of the money, indeed, with the dishonest intention not to repay his employer, may be enough to constitute theft. D has "come by [the money] . . . without stealing it" and he seems now to be guilty of an "assumption of a right to it by keeping . . . it as owner", which section 3(1) declares to be an appropriation. The point is no doubt academic in the case of money, with which D will probably "deal . . . as owner", for example by banking it, as soon as he decides to "keep" it; moreover, the exact time of the theft is unlikely to be material.[25]

---

[19] *ibid.*, at 555.

[20] *ibid.*

[21] Smith (J. C.), para. 2–67; Glanville Williams [1977] Crim.L.R. at 337.

[22] Glanville Williams [1977] C.L..L. 62, for detailed discussion. For further discussion, see Parry, *Offences against Property*, paras. 1.34–1.36.

[23] That is, the value of the property or of its proceeds: *Stalham* [1993] Crim.L.R. 310 (though not reported on this point).

[24] [1956] 1 Q.B. 439.

[25] But as to payment into a bank account, see below, §2–50.

The subsection applied

2–49   Section 5(4) was applied on interesting facts in the case of *Davis*.[26] Because
of an administrative error, D had received from the local authority housing
benefit cheques to which he was not entitled. At one time he was entitled to
benefit but received a double payment in the form of two cheques. When he
ceased to be entitled to benefit he continued to receive (single) benefit
cheques. His appeal concerned, in part, alleged thefts of "money" which he
had obtained by cashing some of the cheques with a shopkeeper.

The later (single) cheques—the pieces of paper, rather than the things in
action they created in D's favour—were plainly property that he got by mistake; so charges of theft of these cheques would have presented no difficulty.
But D was charged with stealing "money", not cheques. The Court of Appeal
was clear that the cash into which D converted the cheques was their "proceeds" within the meaning of section 5(4). D was "under an obligation to
make restoration" of these proceeds, which he could therefore be convicted
of stealing.

In the double payment case, the two cheques (whenever each may have
arrived in relation to the other) were to be treated as "got" by mistake, just as
though the whole excessive payment had been made by a single cheque. D
was under an obligation to restore their proceeds "in part". The proceeds
were a single pool of cash which "to the extent of that obligation" was to be
regarded as belonging to the local authority. D could be convicted of stealing
cash to that amount without its being necessary to attribute the amount
stolen to either cheque.[27]

Mistaken payments and bank accounts

2–50   Situations involving bank accounts require separate analysis. Two cases
may be imagined: (i) D receives a payment in error (or an overpayment) by

---

[26] (1988) 88 Cr.App.R. 347. The close analysis to which Mustill L.J. submitted s.5(4) in this case
deserves careful study. But one passage (at 351–352) is questionable. The Lord Justice takes the
draftsman to have contemplated three possible "conditions" in which property, "got" by mistake, may be "by the time the defendant comes to commit his dishonest appropriation": it may
still exist; it may have been exchanged for money or goods ("proceeds") which are still traceable;
it may have "ceased to exist ... or ... gone out of reach of recovery." He supposes the subsection
to refer to an obligation to restore "property", "proceeds" or "value" in these situations respectively. This, with respect, seems to be a misreading. The analysis cannot work for the case of
"value", where, as the passage seems to mean, the property has been disposed of and there are
no traceable proceeds. There would be nothing to steal. It is submitted that the obligation to
restore "the property or its proceeds or ... the value ... thereof" must be an obligation existing,
because of the mistake, when the property is first "got". In some cases D will be obliged to
restore the property itself (or its proceeds if he should happen to convert them). In other cases,
typically of mistaken payment or overpayment, his only obligation from the outset is to repay a
sum equivalent to (the value of) what has been wrongly received. In all these cases, what was
originally got by mistake, or any property into which it is converted, can be stolen by an appropriation dishonestly made with knowledge of the mistake.
[27] Such an approach "may not be effective, if the proceeds ... take more than one form, and if the
prosecution is forced to identify which form is the one to have been stolen" (88 Cr.App.R. at
353).

the crediting of his bank account through the banks' direct debit system. (ii) D has in error been paid cash (or too much cash) or been given a cheque (or a cheque for too large a sum), and he banks the cash or cheque before he discovers the error. To the extent of the overpayment the thing in action represented by the bank account[28] will, in case (i), be property "got" by mistake[29]; in case (ii) it will be "the proceeds" of such property. In either case the thing in action will be regarded (as against D) as property belonging to the person making the mistake—assuming, of course, that the mistake gives rise to an obligation to restore the "value" of the overpayment. This, at any rate, describes the situation where the account is in credit on completion of the banking transaction[30] (or, perhaps, later as a result of further transactions); for only if it is in credit does D have property, in the form of a thing in action (a creditor's right against the bank), to which section 5(4) can apply. Similarly, for theft to be possible, there must still be credit available to be stolen when, D having learned of the error and formed "an intention not to make restoration", an alleged appropriation occurs. Whether D appropriates by simply forming that intention is uncertain.[31] The idea that theft may be committed by a mere decision not to pay a debt is one to be avoided if possible. A way of avoiding it may be to argue that the phrase in section 3(1), "keeping as owner," refers only to property that D ought to "restore" to P; that there is no question of restoring the bank credit itself, but only the "value" of the amount paid in error—an equivalent sum; and that an appropriation must be sought in some use of the account—perhaps a use that reduces the credit in the account (or any outstanding overdraft facility) to below the amount that ought to be paid to P.

A legal obligation is required; the overpaid punter

The "obligation" referred to in section 5(4) is a legal obligation.[32] Where D **2–51** decides to disregard a merely moral obligation to restore property got by P's mistake, the court has to resort to some other ground for holding that the property belonged to P if D is to be convicted. This was done in *Gilks.*[33] D, a punter, had won £10.62 by bets in P's betting shop. But P's manager paid D £117.25, wrongly thinking that D had backed one more winning horse than he had. D took the money knowing that he had been overpaid. His conviction of theft was upheld. He had no legal obligation to restore the overpayment of £106.63, as it had been made under a wagering contract.[34] So section 5(4)

---

[28] See below, §2–146.
[29] *Attorney-General's Reference (No. 1 of 1983)* [1985] Q.B. 182; re-affirmed in *Stalham* [1993] Crim.L.R. 310.
[30] Note that, although the amount of a cheque delivered to a bank for collection may be credited to the account at once, the credit is not usually effective, so as to give the customer any right against the bank, before the cheque is cleared.
[31] The point was left open in the *Attorney-General's Reference*, above, n. 29.
[32] *Gilks* (1972) 56 Cr.App.R. 734.
[33] (1972) 56 Cr.App.R. 734.
[34] *Morgan v. Ashcroft* [1938] 1 K.B. 49.

could not apply. But the Court of Appeal affirmed the trial judge's ruling that "the property in the £106.63 never passed to [D]". On this basis D appropriated property belonging at all times to P without recourse to section 5(4). This is not satisfactory. The court eschewed elaborate argument to defend its proposition that the mistake made by P's manager was of a kind to prevent property in the money from passing; they referred only to a long-doubted Larceny Act case that was readily distinguishable.[35] The better view, it is submitted, is that D did obtain ownership of all the money paid.[36] That is surely what would have been held if a quasi-contractual right to recover the overpayment had existed and section 5(4) could have applied.[37]

Some difficulties[38]

2–52   We have seen that the Court of Appeal in *Shadrokh-Cigari*[39] has applied in the context of theft a principle recognising P, the payer of money under a mistake, as retaining a beneficial interest in the money. If the money is converted into other property or paid into a larger fund, P's interest in the money will become an interest in that property or fund, subject only to the limits of a beneficiary's tracing remedy. Nor is there any reason why these principles should apply only to money (and to instruments giving rise to money claims, as in *Shadrokh-Cigari* itself), and not to property generally. It seems to follow that in almost any case within section 5(4) the property or proceeds referred to in that subsection will "belong to" the transferor of the property anyway by virtue of section 5(1). It might be thought an argument against the reasoning of *Shadrokh-Cigari* that it renders subsection (4) substantially redundant. But that reasoning is not the first to suggest that the reference in section 5(1) to "any proprietary...interest" added more to the scope of theft than was generally realised when the Act was drafted and passed.[40] In any event there is no question of subsection (4)'s ceasing to be invoked, its references to mistake and to an obligation to make restoration being so helpfully specific compared to the language of section 5(1).

2–53   A case of property "got" by mistake, under whichever provision it is analysed, is capable of presenting difficult problems in the law of trusts, restitution or quasi-contract. Whether a person is obliged "to make restoration" of property may, for instance, turn on difficult distinctions between mistakes

---

[35] *Middleton* (1873) L.R. 2 C.C.R. 38: 10s. due to D from post office; clerk, consulting document referring to E, handed D £8 odd; held, property did not pass (*sed quaere*).
[36] See also Glanville Williams, *loc. cit.* n. 121, above; Smith (J. C.), para. 2–78; Parry, *Offences against Property*, para. 1.54; Russell Heaton [1973] Crim.L.R. 736 at 739. In favour of the decision, see Williams and Weinberg, *Property Offences* (2nd ed.), p. 90.
[37] The point may have become academic; even if ownership did pass, it may be one of the strange results of the decision in *Gomez* [1993] A.C. 442 (below, §§2–80, 2–84) that D would be regarded as appropriating money belonging to the betting shop by the act of receiving payment of it.
[38] For an early critical discussion, see R. Stuart (1967) 30 M.L.R. 609, especially at 622–623.
[39] [1988] Crim.L.R. 465; above, §2–35.
[40] Compare the comments on s.5(3), above, §2–40.

of fact and mistakes of law. It is not clear that such distinctions should be relevant to criminal liability. Again, difficult problems attending claims in equity in respect of money paid under a mistake may infect the law of theft either via section 5(1) (if indeed "proprietary interest" includes any proprietary claim available against a constructive trustee) or via section 5(4) (for the subsection is not expressed to be limited to common law obligations). Problems in the law of tracing[41] cannot necessarily be kept out of the criminal courts.

Section 5(4) is available as a plain basis of theft liability where D "gets" **2–54** property from P by deception (inducing a "mistake") in circumstances giving P a right to recover money paid under a mistake of fact, as where D falsely states facts which (if true) would have the effect that money was due under an existing contract (say, an insurance policy) and P pays that money.[42] But, according to a decision of the House of Lords to be discussed below,[43] any obtaining of property (other than land) by deception is now regarded as an appropriation of that property, apparently as property "belonging to" the deceived party immediately before the obtaining. This principle has made resort to section 5(4) unnecessary where theft is charged in deception cases.[44]

Corporations sole

Property belonging to a corporation sole is to be regarded as belonging to **2–55** the corporation notwithstanding a vacancy in the corporation (s.5(5)).

The property must belong to P at the material time

Property never belonging to P

The fact that D dishonestly tries to get his hands on property does not **2–56** necessarily mean that he is guilty of an offence. There can, for instance, as one singularly optimistic prosecution has shown, be no theft or attempted theft of the property of a testatrix by inducing her to revoke one will and make another, or by steps taken under the latter will on her death. The executors named by the revoked will were suggested as the intended victims of theft; but they never had a proprietary interest in the property.[45]

---

[41] See Goff and Jones, *The Law of Restitution* (4th ed.), Chap. 2.
[42] D should, of course, be charged with obtaining property by deception (s.15). In *Williams* [1980] Crim.L.R. 589, s.5(4) was referred to in upholding a conviction of theft, where money had been paid under a contract doubtfully regarded by the court as *void* for fundamental mistake induced by D's fraud.
[43] *Gomez* [1993] A.C. 442; see below, §2–80.
[44] And it has rendered academic any debate (briefly indulged in in former editions of this book) as to the relevance of s.5(4) where P pays money or delivers property to D under a contract which is *voidable* for D's fraud.
[45] *Tillings and Tillings* [1985] Crim.L.R. 393 (Mann J.).

Property no longer belonging to P

2–57   A point more likely to cause difficulty is that property that has undoubtedly belonged to P must still belong to him (in some sense within section 5) at
the time of the alleged theft. The point may require the application of principles of the law of contract, sale and agency.[46] It may be illustrated by reference to retail transactions.

Ownership ("the property") in goods passes to a buyer at the time the
parties intend it to pass.[47] In the case of a supermarket or cash-and-carry store
the courts attribute to the parties the intention that ownership shall pass only
on payment. This applies no less to goods (such as meat and vegetables)
wrapped and priced by an assistant within the store, but to be paid for at the
check-out, than to goods with which the customer serves himself from the
shelves. Accordingly, where a customer leaves the store without paying for
goods so wrapped and priced, he removes goods that still belong to the
store.[48] But once the property in the goods has passed under a valid contract
and the buyer has taken delivery, there is no question of theft by any further
act of the buyer. A motorist who fills his tank with petrol at a garage and then
decides not to pay does not steal the petrol when he drives away[49]; property in
the petrol has passed to him under the sale transaction and the garage retains
neither possession nor a proprietary interest.[50] A plainer case is that of the
diner who decides at the end of his meal not to pay for it; he cannot steal the
food in his stomach, as the Divisional Court had once solemnly to hold.[51]
Another stage in the history of goods sold may be a revesting of the
ownership in the seller on the buyer's rejection of them. Then the seller does
not by re-selling the goods, even dishonestly, appropriate property that any
longer belongs to the first buyer. A jury dealing with a case of this kind plainly
needs guidance on the legal effect of the buyer's acts.[52]

Appropriation by act causing property to cease to belong to P

2–58   It is enough that the property belonged to P up to the time of the act of
appropriation although it ceased to belong to him by virtue of that very act.
An argument to the contrary failed in the early House of Lords case of *Lawrence v. Metropolitan Police Commissioner.*[53] D, a taxi-driver, was charged
with theft of an excessive sum taken in advance, by way of fare, from his passenger's proffered wallet. Even if property in the money so taken passed to

---

[46] See above, §1–21.
[47] Sale of Goods Act 1979, s.17; prima facie "rules" for the establishing of the parties' intention
are provided by s.18.
[48] *Davies v. Leighton* (1978) 68 Cr.App.R. 4.
[49] He can be convicted of making off without payment: Theft Act 1978, s.3 (see Chap. 13).
[50] *Edwards v. Ddin* (1976) 63 Cr.App.R. 218; Sale of Goods Act 1979, s.18, r. 5(1). To the like
effect, *Stewart, The Times*, December 14, 1982.
[51] *Corcoran v. Whent* [1977] Crim.L.R. 52.
[52] *Walker* [1984] Crim.L.R. 112; (1983) 80 L.S.Gaz. 3238; above, §1–21.
[53] [1972] A.C. 626.

D, the act of taking it could nevertheless be theft. Similarly, where D takes delivery of goods from P under a voidable contract of sale induced by D's fraud, he appropriates property belonging to P even if property passes under the contract by virtue of the delivery.[54]

Whether identity of victim material

The identity of the victim of an alleged theft is not normally material. The **2–59** essential matter requiring proof is that D intended to deprive permanently of the property some person (whether nameable or not and whether or not correctly identified in the indictment) falling within the generous catchment of section 5. Specification of the victim ought in general to be treated as an immaterial allegation. But it is not always so. It may exceptionally be crucial to the nature of the prosecution case; and if so, the judge cannot, without an amendment of the indictment, invite the jury to convict on the basis of an appropriation of property belonging to someone other than the person named. An example occurred in *Boakye*,[55] in which B was charged with conspiracy with M to steal money and debts belonging to an agency that was an alter ego of M himself. The evidence showed that M had drawn for his own purposes on the agency's bank account into which monies from the Manpower Services Commission, to be used only for purposes connected with a programme financed by the Commission, had been paid. It was not open to the judge, on the indictment as framed, to tell the jury that they could find a conspiracy to steal property belonging (by an application of section 5(3)) to the Commission.

4. "APPROPRIATES"

Introductory; section 3(1)

Appropriation and "conversion"

In place of larceny, embezzlement and fraudulent conversion, the **2–60** C.L.R.C., as we have seen,[56] recommended a generalised version of the last of these offences, capable of being committed in respect of any type of property, including intangibles.[57] The language of the old law of larceny, which depended on a "taking and carrying away" of movable property "without the consent of the owner"—some trespassory interference with, and movement of, "goods"—would not do for the new broad offence. You cannot "take", still less "take and carry away", a bank balance; and even in relation to tangible property, theft was no longer going to depend upon the commission of a

---

[54] *Dobson v. General Accident Fire and Life Assurance Corporation plc* [1990] Q.B. 274, *per* Bingham L.J. at 290.

[55] March 12, 1992, C.A. no. 89/5650/W4.

[56] Above, §2–02.

[57] The theft of intangibles, and especially of bank credits, has proved to be an important and complex subject. It is dealt with in a separate part of the chapter, where the main consideration of the appropriation of such property will be found: see below, §§2–143 to 2–155.

trespass. The C.L.R.C. might, indeed, have suggested that the language of "fraudulent conversion" be carried over into the new law to express the prohibited conduct. But they preferred the word "dishonestly" to "fraudulently"[58]; and the word "appropriates" to "converts", as less of a "lawyers' word". "Dishonestly appropriates", it was said, meant the same as "fraudulently converts to his own use or benefit, or the use or benefit of any other person" in the Larceny Act 1916, s.20(1)(iv).[59]

2–61   The C.L.R.C. referred to appropriation as "the familiar concept of conversion".[60] The *word* "conversion", however, though long used both in criminal law[61] and in the law of tort, does not represent a single *concept* of settled meaning. As to the criminal context, the offences of larceny as a bailee and fraudulent conversion were concerned with misappropriations by those lawfully in possession of property with the consent of the owner or entrusted with ownership or possession of property for particular purposes. But these offences covered only part of the ground now covered by theft; and the meaning of conversion in relation to them was never fully worked out.[62] On the other hand, appropriation in criminal law seems not to be a replica of its tort counterpart. In *Rogers v. Arnott*,[63] decided under the Larceny Act, the act of a bailee in attempting to sell a borrowed tape recorder was held to be a criminal conversion although it would not itself have founded liability in tort; and in *Bonner*[64] the Court of Appeal had no doubt that a partner must be held to "appropriate" partnership property with which he absconds even if in the circumstances he would not be liable to his co-partner in tort.[65] It is submitted that this refusal to equate conversion in crime and in tort is right and inevitable.

Treating "tuum" as "meum"

2–62   A person "appropriates" another's property, in the non-technical sense of the word, when he takes it to (or for) himself or makes it his own; appropriation is "the treating of 'tuum' as 'meum.'[66]"[67] Lord Lowry, dissenting in the leading case of *Gomez*,[68] referred to the "primary dictionary meaning" of

---

[58] *Eighth Report*, para. 39.
[59] *ibid*. para. 35.
[60] *ibid*. para. 34.
[61] Larceny Act 1916, ss.1(1) proviso, 20(1)(i) and (iv), 21 ("converts or appropriates").
[62] See Smith and Hogan, *Criminal Law* (1st ed.), pp. 358–360; *Russell on Crime* (12th ed.), pp. 966–969.
[63] [1960] 2 Q.B. 244; compare now, *Pitham and Hehl* (1976) 65 Cr.App.R. 45 (below, §2–75).
[64] (1970) 54 Cr.App.R. 257.
[65] Co-ownership is a defence to an action founded on conversion except as specified in the Torts (Interference with Goods) Act 1977, s.10(1). S.10(1)(a) restated the only existing exceptions as understood at the time of *Bonner*. Para. (b) added a further significant exception. The same Act made other modifications of the scope of conversion as a tort. There was no question of its thereby also casually modifying the scope of theft.
[66] Of yours as mine.
[67] *Eighth Report*, para. 33.
[68] [1993] A.C. 442 at 469.

"appropriate" as "take possession of, take to oneself, especially without authority"; and he thought that, within the meaning of section 1(1), "[t]he act of appropriating property is a one-sided act, done without the consent or authority of the owner." This is certainly close to the conception of the C.L.R.C.; for the Committee intended that a person who deceived another into consenting to transfer the *ownership* of property to him would not steal the property when he received it, but would be guilty only of obtaining it by deception contrary to section 15(1).[69] On the other hand, the Committee assumed that a person would steal—as well as commit the offence under section 15—if he induced the owner of property by deception to make a bailment of it (a mere delivery of *possession*), intending when taking delivery to make the property his own.[70] This would involve, in Lord Lowry's parlance, a "two-sided act"; but it would be one done by the rogue with a unilateral acquisitive intention going beyond the intention of the owner.

Appropriation as understood by the House of Lords

As will appear, the meaning attributed to the word "appropriates" by **2–63** decisions of the House of Lords is much wider than Lord Lowry's "primary dictionary meaning" and goes well beyond anything apparently contemplated by the C.L.R.C. If those decisions are taken at face value, almost any act done in relation to property belonging to another, the doing or authorising of which is one of "the rights of an owner", may be an appropriation of the property, even if the other person in fact consented to, or authorised, that act.[71]

Section 3(1)

The C.L.R.C. expressed the hope and belief "that the concept of 'dis- **2–64** honest appropriation' [would] easily be understood even without the aid of further definition".[72] They nevertheless offered such aid in a provision enacted as section 3(1):

> "Any assumption by a person of the rights of an owner amounts to an appropriation, and this includes, where he has come by the property (innocently or not) without stealing it, any later assumption of a right to it by keeping or dealing with it as owner."

The subsection does not read like a definition and was indeed described by the Committee as a "partial definition".[73] But it is not clear what it was intended to leave unsaid. The House of Lords has held that an assumption of any of the rights of an owner may be an appropriation[74]; but the decision to

---

[69] *Eighth Report*, para. 38.
[70] *ibid.* para. 90.
[71] See in particular, §§2–69 and §§2–77 *et seq.*, below.
[72] *Eighth Report*, para. 34.
[73] *ibid.* See also Lord Lane C.J. in *Morris* [1983] Q.B. 587 at 596.
[74] *Morris* [1984] A.C. 320; below, §2–69.

this effect was expressed as an interpretation of section 3(1) and not as giving content to an assertion that the subsection was "not exhaustive".[75]

Theft by one already in possession

2–65   Section 3(1) is at pains to provide that where a person "has come by ... property (innocently or not) without stealing it,[76] any later assumption of a right to it by keeping or dealing with it as owner" is an appropriation. It might seem that this hardly needed to be said; but the passage is explicable as a message to pre-Theft Act practitioners, to whom it made clear that certain gaps that existed under the old law had been filled. The following are examples of its operation. It will be noticed that in several of them the appropriation constituted by the "later assumption" is not D's first appropriation of the property in question; but it is that by which, if he acts dishonestly, he steals.

(i) D finds property and takes possession of it, but is not then guilty of theft (a) because he intends to restore it to its owner, or (b) because he does not believe that the owner can be found.[77] He subsequently appropriates the property if he decides (in case (a)) not to restore the property to its owner, or (in case (b)) to hold on to it although the owner turns out to be known or traceable.

(ii) D receives stolen goods, intending to take them to the victim or the police. He appropriates the goods when he subsequently changes his mind.

(iii) D takes property when he is too drunk to steal; he does not then form the intention of permanently depriving the owner. He appropriates the property when, on sobering up, he decides to deal with it as his own.

(iv) D "comes by" property as the result of an error. He discovers some time later the fact that he has the property, or that it was not intended for him, or that it is not what he was intended to have; and he decides nevertheless to keep it. This is an appropriation.

2–66   (v) *Agents, bailees and custodians.* The agent in possession of his principal's goods for sale who sells them below the authorised price, intending to keep the proceeds[78]; the coal-merchant's employee who takes a sack of coal from the coal lorry for his own use; the hirer of a camera who sells it as his own; the borrower of a library book who gives it as a birthday gift to his friend; the cashier at the supermarket check-out who deliberately rings up too low a price for goods and sells them to the customer for the reduced

---

[75] *ibid.* at 331. The rest of the relevant passage, it has been observed, "treats it as if it were exhaustive": *Philippou* (1989) 89 Cr.App.R. 290 at 299.

[76] For the significance of the words "without stealing it" see below, §2–94.

[77] See s.2(1)(c).

[78] Compare cases of dishonest dealings with intangible property: *e.g. Kohn* (1979) 69 Cr.App.R. 395 (principal's bank credit; see below, §2–149); *Attorney-General of Hong Kong v. Nai-keung* (1987) 86 Cr.App.R. 174 (transferable export quotas; see above, §2–18).

price[79]: each of these people, having lawful possession or custody of the property of another, appropriates it by assuming in it the rights of an owner.

"Keeping... as owner." Section 3(1) refers to "a later assumption of a right **2–67** to [property] by keeping or dealing with it as owner". A "dealing" will involve a positive act. A "keeping", on the other hand, may be constituted (as in several of the examples given above) by a mental act—a decision not to give up property—and an omission to do what ought to be done with it. Although, in practice, theft of this kind is most likely to be revealed when D deals with the property in some active way or expressly refuses to give it up, it seems to be technically complete on the occurrence of the dishonest non-restoration (assuming that D has an opportunity to restore). But there can be no "keeping... as owner" during a period of indecision about what to do with the property.[80] Apart from any other consideration, while D remains un-decided he does not have the intention of permanently depriving P.

Exemption for the bona fide purchaser

One person clearly within section 3(1) is nevertheless expressly saved from **2–68** liability for theft by section 3(2). This is the bona fide transferee for value of property who discovers after the transfer that his transferor's title was defective and who nevertheless keeps or deals with the property. C steals property from P and sells it to D, who buys it in good faith, believing that he is acquiring a good title to it.[81] He later learns the truth. But he does not restore the property to P. Indeed, he deals with it as his own. This is not theft.

An assumption of any of the rights of an owner

The controversial case of *Morris*[82] concerned the criminal liability of a person who takes goods from the shelf of a self-service store and substitutes for **2–69** the price label on them a label showing a lower price, intending to buy the goods for that lower price at the till. Does he steal the goods? If so, when? The effect of the decision of the House of Lords, as glossed by the later decision of the House in *Gomez*,[83] is that an appropriation occurs, and that a theft is complete, at the latest when he switches the price labels and possibly earlier. Notwithstanding the opening words of section 3(1) ("Any assumption by a person of the rights of an owner amounts to an appropriation..."), it was declared that the requirement of an appropriation was satisfied by "an

---

[79] In *Bhachu* (1976) 65 Cr.App.R. 261, however, the only appropriation identified by the Court of Appeal was that of the shopper (to which the cashier was a party) in taking the goods from the shop.
[80] *Broom v. Crowther* (1984) 148 J.P. Rep. 592.
[81] The subject of the subsection is any "later assumption of rights which he believed himself to be acquiring." The last words refer, of course, to a belief at the time of the purchase, not at the time of the "later assumption": *Adams*, April 3, 1992, C.A. no. 90/1514/W3.
[82] [1984] A.C. 320.
[83] [1993] A.C. 442.

assumption ... of *any* of the rights of the owner ...".[84] It did not matter that the dishonest shopper had not yet assumed *all* the rights of an owner.

2–70   In another passage in his opinion in *Morris* Lord Roskill asserted that a combination of acts might together amount to, or evidence, an appropriation—as, in the instant case, the removal of the goods from the shelf, the switching of the labels and perhaps the putting of the re-labelled goods into a trolley or basket.[85] But any such requirement of a combination of acts was rejected in *Gomez*. The switching of price labels was itself the assumption of one of the rights of the owner. There was "much to be said", indeed, for the view that "the mere taking of the article from the shelf and putting it in a trolley or other receptacle amounted to the assumption of one of the rights of the owner, and hence an appropriation"[86]; and later in his speech,[87] Lord Keith, effectively delivering the opinion of the majority, expressly agreed with observations of Parker L.J. in *Dobson v. General Accident Fire and Life Assurance Corp. plc*,[88] to the effect that a shoplifter would appropriate goods he intends to steal (and would therefore steal them) merely by taking them from a shelf or moving them from one place on a shelf to another.[89]

2–71   The view of appropriation as satisfied by the assumption of any of an owner's rights was already implicit in a number of cases before *Morris*.[90] And it has been expressly applied, on the authority of *Morris*, to determine the time at which a theft of credit in a bank account, by a dishonest dealing with the account, is complete: an appropriation, and therefore theft, occurs, when a cheque drawn on the account is issued or presented for payment or an instruction to debit the account is transmitted to the bank.[91] Any of these acts is the exercise of one of the rights of the owner of the account.[92]

Intention to deprive thereby or thereafter

2–72   In a case like *Morris* the appropriation of the property will precede the

---

[84] [1984] A.C. 320, at 331–332 (surprisingly claiming support in the language of the latter part of s.3(1), and in ss.2(1)(a) and 3(2)); re-affirmed in *Gomez* [1993] A.C. 442 at 459. This seems to be the only aspect of *Morris* that survives the criticism of the House in *Gomez*.

[85] [1984] A.C. 320 at 332–333.

[86] [1993] A.C. 442, *per* Lord Keith at 460.

[87] At p. 463.

[88] [1990] 1 Q.B. 274 at 283–284.

[89] See *McPherson* [1973] Crim.L.R. 191 (approved in *Anderton v. Wish* (1980) 72 Cr.App.R. 23n), as explained by Lord Lane C.J. in *Morris* [1983] Q.B. 587 at 597, and by Parker L.J.

[90] See *Pitham and Hehl* (1976) 65 Cr.App.R. 45 (offering to sell P's goods as complete theft; see below, §2–75); *Pilgram v. Rice-Smith* (1977) 65 Cr.App.R. 142 (theft at supermarket food counter when the assistant, in league with the customer, wraps goods and understates their price on the wrapper); see also *Easom* [1971] 2 Q.B. 315 (examining property to see whether it contains something worth stealing treated as an appropriation). The doctrine also supports the assertion that most cases of handling stolen goods are also cases of theft: see below, §15–50.

[91] See below, §2–151.

[92] For another application of the principle, see *Atakpu* [1994] Q.B. 69, below, §2–94.

deprivation of P which D intends. That deprivation depends upon further action by D; the store will be "deprived" of the goods whose price label has been changed only when D buys them at the till for the price he has put on them. (Although this transaction is consensual, it must involve a "deprivation" within the meaning of the Act; for by it D will commit an offence of obtaining property by deception, which itself requires an intention of permanently depriving the victim.[93]) The necessary intention in theft was probably understood until recently to be an intention of depriving P of the property by the act of appropriation itself. This understanding may have been a legacy of larceny, which, except when committed by a bailee, required a taking of possession of movable property. Under *Morris*, by contrast, there may be an appropriation now with the intention of depriving P in the future. This reading—which is not explicitly referred to in *Morris* (or in *Gomez*)—is bold, but not impossible in the more flexible context of the modern offence. It is worth pausing, however, to consider its relation to the law of attempt.

Inchoate transactions

Changing the price label upon goods is merely a step towards the intended offence of obtaining the goods by deception. It will probably not suffice to constitute an attempt to commit that offence; for an attempt requires "an act more than merely preparatory" to the offence intended.[94] So the identification of a complete theft at the point when the label is changed (or when the goods are lifted off the shelf) operates to supplement the law of inchoate offences. The suspect shopper may, strictly, be apprehended at that point. But a conviction of theft on the strength of what he has so far done will in effect deprive him of the defence which the law of attempt is carefully designed to give him—namely, that he might still have changed his mind and abandoned his dishonest purpose.[95] It is therefore suggested that (in justice, in addition to practical considerations) he should be allowed to reach the till and be dealt with for the obtaining, or the attempt to obtain, which he there commits.

2–73

Attempting to take property

There is, of course, no question of confining theft to cases where the criminal activity is in a real sense successful. A thief caught in possession of property a few seconds after seizing it has stolen and not merely attempted to steal. And there is no reason why the same should not be true of one who has gripped property so as to achieve effective control of it, but has not removed it. It seems that the courts will go as far as possible along this path. In *Corcoran v. Anderton*[96] a youth was held guilty of robbery (which involves

2–74

---

[93] s.15(1).
[94] Criminal Attempts Act 1981, s.1(1).
[95] An intending label-swopper, once equipped away from home with his substitute label, would have no answer to a charge of going equipped for theft or "cheat" under s.25.
[96] (1980) 71 Cr.App.R. 104.

theft) when he was party to an attack on a lady in which her handbag was wrested from her grasp—even though the bag fell to the ground and was never in his or his companion's control. The decisive circumstance may have been that the lady was made to lose control, if only momentarily. This, it is suggested, rendered the case a borderline one and possibly justified the court in finding a complete appropriation.[97] On the other hand, merely grasping property in an unsuccessful attempt to loosen it from P's control, or to part it from something to which it is attached, should perhaps be regarded as a mere attempt.[98]

Offering P's goods for sale

2–75   A theft of P's goods is held to be complete when D dishonestly offers to sell them to E, having no authority to do so.[99] It has been objected that the offer alone, not being a conversion of the goods, ought not to be theft.[1] It is submitted that this objection in itself ties theft too closely to the technicalities of conversion. Yet it does seem odd to describe as a complete theft an offer which E may in the event refuse; if E refuses, D will have achieved nothing at all. And it is thought that there can certainly be no theft where D does not intend to deliver the goods to E even if E accepts his offer and pays the price agreed. D's mere reference to the goods as a device to support his fraud on E can hardly be an appropriation; and in any case D has no intention of depriving P of the goods.[2]

Act preparatory to theft from till

2–76   A striking case of a preparatory act treated as theft is *Monaghan*.[3] A shop-assistant received £3.99 from a customer and put it in her till (as she was supposed to do). But she did not ring the sum up, because she had a proved intention to remove an equivalent sum later. She was arrested before proceeding further and charged with theft of "the sum of £3.99". Her conviction was upheld on appeal. It is submitted that this goes too far. It cannot be known whether in the end the defendant would have removed any money. She had not yet got as far as attempting to do so within the meaning of a general law of attempt that provides ample opportunity for a late change of

---

[97] Too often one senses the prosecution being rescued from a poor choice of charge. An apter charge here was surely assault with intent to rob (s.8(2)). For another example, see *Monaghan* below, §2–76.

[98] But Eveleigh L.J., in a supporting judgment in *Corcoran v. Anderton*, regarded D's "*seeking* to overcome [P's] efforts to retain [the bag]" as an appropriation: (1980) 71 Cr.App.R. 104 at 108 (italics supplied).

[99] *Pitham and Hehl* (1976) 65 Cr.App.R. 45; compare *Rogers v. Arnott* [1960] 2 Q.B. 244 (larceny as a bailee).

[1] Glanville Williams [1977] Crim.L.R. 127 at 131–132; for further argument, see Williams, *Textbook*, pp. 763–765.

[2] Even with the assistance of s.6(1); it is thought that D does not intend to "treat the thing as his own *to dispose of*".

[3] [1979] Crim.L.R. 673.

mind. Moreover, it is difficult to see what property she appropriated, if (as may be assumed) she mixed the sum she received with the employer's other money in the till. Her wrong was one of omission—namely, "omitting a material particular from an account", which is an offence of false accounting under section 17 of the Act.

Acts done with the consent or authority of P

Can there be an appropriation of property by an act which P has author-   **2–77**
ised or to which he has consented? A narrower question concerns the relevance of a consent of P induced by deception: can D steal property at the
same time as he obtains it by deception contrary to section 15(1)? These
questions, which have been the subject of a bewildering case law, are now
answered affirmatively by the House of Lords.

Lawrence v. Metropolitan Police Commissioner (1971).[4] P was an Italian   **2–78**
newly arrived in England. He hired D, a taxi-driver, to drive him from Victoria to Ladbroke Grove. The lawful fare for the journey was 10s. 6d. (53p). P
gave D a £1 note, but D said that this was not enough and himself took £6
more from P's still open wallet. P offered no resistance to this act. D was
charged with theft of about £6 and convicted. It was regarded as clear by the
House of Lords, and in fact conceded on D's behalf, that there had been an
appropriation of the £6. But it was argued that P had consented to that appropriation, which could not therefore be theft because the words "without the
consent of the owner" should be implied in section 1(1). The House of Lords
responded by firmly declaring that to obtain a conviction of theft it need not
be proved "that the taking was without the consent of the owner": the omission of words equivalent to the phrase "without the consent of the owner" in
the repealed definition of larceny was deliberate.[5] And it is clear that the
House's reason was not (as it might have been) that the words were unnecessary because an absence of consent is inherent in the concept of appropriation
itself; for it was also said that "[an appropriation] may occur even though the
owner has permitted or consented to the property being taken".

The Court of Appeal had regarded the additional £6 taken from P's wallet
as having been both obtained by deception and appropriated. That court
went so far as to say "that in any case where the facts would establish a charge
under section 15(1)[6] they would also establish a charge under section 1(1)".[7]
Viscount Dilhorne, for the House of Lords, confirmed that in some cases the
facts might justify conviction of both offences.[8]

---

[4] [1972] A.C. 626.
[5] *ibid.* at 630–631. Larceny required a taking and carrying away of goods "without the consent of the owner".
[6] [1971] 1 Q.B. 373 at 378. A person is guilty of an offence under s.15(1) if by deception he dishonestly obtains ownership, possession or control (see s.15(2)) of property belonging to another with the intention of permanently depriving the other of it.
[7] An exception should have been acknowledged in the case of an obtaining of land: see below, §2–82.
[8] [1972] A.C. 626 at 633.

2–79   *Morris* (1983).[9] The law of theft was for some years thrown into confusion by an apparent inconsistency between what the House of Lords had said in *Lawrence* and a dictum of Lord Roskill, speaking for the House, in *Morris*, the supermarket price-label swapping case. Disagreeing with the view, expressed by Lord Lane C.J. in the Court of Appeal, that a customer appropriates goods on sale in a supermarket when he takes them from the shelf,[10] Lord Roskill said that "[i]n the context of section 3(1), the concept of appropriation involves not an act expressly or impliedly authorised by the owner but an act by way of adverse interference with or usurpation of [the owner's] rights".[11] There was broad agreement that this was impossible to reconcile with the statement in *Lawrence* that the owner's permission or consent to property's being taken does not exclude an appropriation. In the period following *Morris*, Lord Roskill's dictum, although not necessary for the decision of the case, tended to be followed in other cases as the current orthodoxy.

2–80   *Gomez.*[12] But the authority of *Lawrence* was re-asserted in this case in December 1992. D, the assistant manager of an electrical goods shop, induced his manager to authorise a sale of goods by falsely representing that a building society cheque being tendered in payment by a rogue was "as good as cash," whereas D knew that the cheque was in fact stolen and worthless. The goods were in due course delivered to the rogue. It was held by the majority of the House, on the authority of *Lawrence*, (i) that notwithstanding the manager's consent to or authorisation of the "taking"[13] of the goods by the rogue, the taking amounted to an appropriation; and (ii) that it was irrelevant that the transaction also constituted an offence of obtaining property by deception.[14] The principle asserted in *Morris* was expressly rejected (though the correctness of the actual decision in that case was confirmed).[15]

---

[9] [1984] A.C. 320; see above, §2–69.
[10] [1983] Q.B. 587 at 596.
[11] [1984] A.C. 320 at 332.
[12] [1993] A.C. 442.
[13] The "taking" referred to is presumably the taking of delivery, which will have effected the passing of the property in the goods under this contract for the sale of unascertained goods. It is possible that an appropriation might occur at the time of the contract in the case of a sale of specific goods under which property passed, albeit voidably, at that time (Sale of Goods Act 1979, ss.17(1) and 18, r. 1): see *Dobson v. General Accident Fire and Life Assurance Corp. plc* [1990] 1 Q.B. 274, *per* Parker L.J. at 280–281; Glanville Williams [1977] Crim.L.R. 127 at 136; [1981] Crim.L.R. 666 at 667). The courts tend in fact to find an intention that the property in specific goods shall pass to the buyer on payment rather than on the mere making of a contract of sale (see *Lacis v. Cashmarts* [1969] 2 Q.B. 400, and other supermarket and cash-and-carry cases; *Dobson's case*, above); and if payment precedes delivery under a fraudulently induced sale, the buyer perhaps steals the goods when he pays for them.
[14] [1993] A.C. 442 at 464, *per* Lord Keith, with whom three Lords agreed. Lord Lowry dissented in an elaborate and scholarly opinion. He relied heavily on the "normal dictionary meaning" of "appropriates" and on the intention of the C.L.R.C. as revealed in the *Eighth Report* (see above, §2–62). Lord Keith made no attempt to engage with Lord Lowry's argument beyond indicating the view (at p. 464) that it was purposeless to seek to construe the Act by reference to the *Eighth Report* in view of the decision of the House in *Lawrence*.
[15] [1993] A.C. 442 at 464.

Two cases were declared[16] to have been wrongly decided, because they **2–81** were inconsistent with *Lawrence*. The first was *Skipp*.[17] D, a bogus haulage contractor, collected parcels of groceries from three places in London, with instructions to deliver them to Leicester. It was wrongly held that D committed one theft only, when he did an unauthorised act with respect to all the goods, by deviating from the route to Leicester. Theft of each parcel of goods in fact occurred at the same time as D obtained it by deception—namely, when he took delivery of it with the intention of permanently depriving the consignor of it.[18]

The other case expressly overruled was *Fritschy*.[19] D collected krugerrands from P with instructions to take them to Switzerland to sell. He intended from the outset to keep them for himself. It was wrongly held that, everything D did in England having been authorised, there had been no appropriation within the jurisdiction. It should be noted that there was no finding of deception in this case; a count alleging deception was withdrawn from the jury.[20]

Theft and obtaining property by deception

The effect of *Lawrence* and *Gomez* is to declare almost any case of obtain- **2–82** ing property by deception under section 15 to be a case of theft also.[21] An obtaining of land by deception (which cannot also be theft) is the only substantial exception.[22] This is certainly not what the C.L.R.C. intended[23]; it would be a mistake, they thought, to include in theft "conduct which ordinary people would find difficult to regard as theft".[24] The Committee did, however, anticipate that one who by deception obtained possession (as opposed to ownership) of property, intending to deprive the victim permanently of it—formerly larceny by a trick—would commit both offences.[25] Since deception is merely one among several improper ways of getting hold of another's

---

[16] *ibid.*
[17] [1975] Crim.L.R. 114.
[18] See also *Atakpu* [1994] Q.B. 69 (below, §2–94), confirming the overruling by *Gomez* of *Hircock* (1978) 67 Cr.App.R. 278.
[19] [1985] Crim.L.R. 745.
[20] Other cases, not involving deception, that are inconsistent with *Gomez* are: *Meech* [1974] Q.B. 549 (see above, §2–47), on the question when an appropriation occurred; *Eddy v. Niman* (1981) 73 Cr.App.R. 237 (transferring goods from supermarket shelf into trolley provided, intending to steal them, held not theft); *Kaur v. Chief Constable of Hampshire* (1981) 72 Cr.App.R 359 (shoes, one marked with wrong low price, dishonestly tendered to cashier, who reads and charges that price; completion of purchase and taking delivery held to involve no theft); and *Shuck* [1992] Crim.L.R. 209.
[21] One significant implication, revealed by *Dobson v. General Accident Fire and Life Assurance Corp. plc* [1990] Q.B. 274 is that an insurance policy providing cover against "theft" extends to the loss of property as a result of a section 15 offence, unless "theft" is specially defined by the policy.
[22] See s.4(2) for the limited circumstances in which land can be stolen. An obtaining by deception of wild creatures not tamed or ordinarily kept in captivity (s.4(4)) is an unlikely exception.
[23] See above, §2–62.
[24] *Eighth Report*, para. 38.
[25] *ibid.*, para. 90.

property, it is not in itself very shocking or disastrous that the majority in *Gomez*, scorning any assistance that the Eighth Report might afford them, should have gone further than the Committee intended and included as theft a case in which P intends, because of D's fraud, to transfer to D his entire proprietary interest in property. The eradication for all criminal law purposes of the troublesome old distinction between larceny by a trick and obtaining by false pretences is an attractive outcome.[26]

2–83   This by no means implies that the section 15 offence should be treated as virtually redundant. It will surely remain proper practice to charge an obtaining by deception when that is the nature of the criminal transaction disclosed by the evidence available to the prosecution. The charge of theft in *Gomez*, although in the end successful, was inept, not only as being of doubtful validity on the then authorities, but because it did not adequately describe the defendants' conduct. There is now the additional consideration that Parliament has recently distinguished between the two offences by reducing the maximum penalty for theft to seven years' imprisonment while retaining the original common maximum of ten years for obtaining property by deception.

Act done with consent or authority not obtained by deception

2–84   It would have been perfectly possible for the majority in *Gomez* to regard *Lawrence* as a case of deception in which any general statement about the relevance of the victim's consent was unnecessary to the decision; and to limit the holding in *Gomez* itself to a pronouncement about the relevance of a consent or authority obtained by deception.[27] But it is not easy to read the decision in this way. Lord Keith's observation, that "*Lawrence* makes it clear that consent to or authorisation by the owner of the taking by the rogue is irrelevant",[28] was, it is true, made when discussing the facts of fraud cases like *Gomez* itself, as the use of the word "rogue" reflects. But there are reasons for understanding him to mean that consent or authorisation[29] are always irrelevant to the existence of an appropriation. One reason is the express overruling, as inconsistent with *Lawrence*, of *Fritschy*[30] which was not a case of deception. A second is Lord Keith's approval of observations by Parker L.J. in *Dobson v. General Accident Fire and Life Assurance Corp plc*,[31] which he cites extensively. Discussing the removal by customers of goods from

---

[26] Compare P. R. Glazebrook [1991] C.L.J. 389; but S. Shute and J. Horder (1993) 56 M.L.R. 548 at 553 (supported in this by C. M. V. Clarkson, *ibid.* 554), regret that a distinction of "moral significance" between theft and obtaining by deception has been "largely obliterated" by *Gomez*.
[27] Mitchell C. Davies (1993) 13 L.S. 308, at 317, criticises the majority in *Gomez* for "failing to distinguish between apparent and actual consent", the former occurring, he suggests, where consent is "vitiated" by fraud.
[28] [1993] A.C. 442 at 464.
[29] No "sensible distinction can be made" between the two: [1993] A.C. 442 at 460.
[30] Above, §2–81.
[31] [1990] 1 Q.B. 274 at 283–284.

shelves in shops and supermarkets, Parker L.J. denied that any distinction is to be made between cases according to whether the owner does or does not consent to such removal; there would be an appropriation in either case, because "it was held in *Lawrence*'s case that consent is not relevant to appropriation". Lord Keith, and the other Lords who concurred in his opinion, must be taken to have adopted this understanding of the effect of *Lawrence*. Thirdly, Lord Keith agreed[32] with the opinion of Lord Browne-Wilkinson that one who dishonestly abstracts company property is guilty of theft even if those who control the company are to be regarded as consenting to the abstraction; for "your Lordships' decision ... renders the whole question of consent by the company irrelevant".[33] This passage was not concerned with consent obtained by deception.

If that is right, *Gomez* surely goes much too far, producing an interpret-   **2–85** ation of "appropriates" at variance with the notion ordinarily conveyed by that word or by "an assumption of rights". It is submitted that it remains open to the House of Lords in a future case, without using its power to overrule its own decisions, to renounce as erroneous, and as unnecessary for the decision of either *Lawrence* or *Gomez*, the larger doctrine of the irrelevance of consent. Meanwhile it is possible that inferior courts will themselves contrive to treat *Lawrence* and *Gomez* as holding only that an act may be an appropriation although, as a result of D's fraud, P consented to it or even participated in it.[34]

Theft of company assets by company controller[35]

There can be no doubt that the director of a company having authority to   **2–86** deal with property of the company for the company's purposes can commit theft by dealing with it "dishonestly and in fraud of the company".[36] But theft of company assets by a person who wholly owns and controls the company requires further discussion.[37] If he transfers company assets to himself or applies such assets to his own purposes, he undoubtedly deals with "property belonging to another", namely, the company. But it may seem somewhat unreal to describe him as stealing from the company. The true losers must always be other parties, normally loan or trade creditors or the revenue. If a

---

[32] [1993] A.C. 442 at 464.
[33] *ibid.* at 496.
[34] *Gomez* was not so understood in *McColgan*, March 26, 1993, C.A. no. 92/6992/X3; but consideration of the point was cursory and not apparently essential to the decision.
[35] G. R. Sullivan [1983] Crim.L.R. 512; [1984] Crim.L.R. 405 (replying to J. Dine [1984] Crim.L.R. 397); Arlidge and Parry, paras. 4.26 *et seq.*; G. Virgo [1991] C.L.J. 464; D. W. Elliott, *op. cit.*, n. 38, below.
[36] *Attorney-General of Hong Kong v. Nai-keung* (1987) 86 Cr.App.R. 174 (above, §2–18). For consideration of opinions apparently to the contrary in *Tarling v. Government of the Republic of Singapore* (1978) 70 Cr.App.R. 77, see J. C. Smith [1979] Crim.L.R. at 224.
[37] References to a sole controller of a company do duty also for cases where all the controllers of a company act in concert or where acts are done to which all the controllers are party or consent.

sole trader transfers the assets of his unincorporated business beyond the reach of his creditors with intent to defraud them, he commits no theft. Indeed, he may commit no offence at all save in the event of a bankruptcy order, when the transfer becomes retrospectively an offence under the Insolvency Act 1986, s. 357. It is odd that the sole trader who has turned himself into a "one-man company" should be in a different position; but it seems that he is. His liability to be convicted of theft, it has been cogently argued,[38] depends on a false description of his appropriation of the company's property as being done "dishonestly", which is to misunderstand that word in the context of theft; this argument will be referred to later in this chapter.[39] His liability also depends, of course, on a recognition of his conduct as an appropriation of the property.

2–87   The argument against regarding a company controller as appropriating company assets was expressed in a speculative proposition advanced by Mustill L.J. for the Court of Appeal in *McHugh and Tringham*[40]:

"Where the actor is beneficially entitled to the entire issued share capital (or at least the entire voting share capital) of the company it may be that his act is not an appropriation because—(a) his act is equivalent to an act of the company, and his intent is the intent of the company, so that there can be no circumstance in which any of his acts is unauthorised; and/or (b) since he has the irresistible power to determine what policies the company shall pursue, there is nothing which he himself may do in the company's name which could in practice be unauthorised."

But the doctrine (invoked in reason (a)) of identification between a company and its controllers—which applies to render a company guilty of an offence by virtue of the acts and states of mind of its "directing mind and will"—has been rejected in its suggested application to acts done in fraud of the company.[41] Lord Roskill's dictum in *Morris*[42] to the effect that an authorised act could not be an appropriation—by which Mustill L.J.'s proposition was influenced—has been deprived of its authority by *Gomez*. As has been seen,[43] the statement that the owner's consent or authority is irrelevant to an appropriation was expressly applied (*obiter*, of course) to an abstraction of a company's property with the consent of its controllers. Cases in which it had been

---

[38] D. W. Elliott [1991] Crim.L.R. 732.

[39] Below, §2–120, n. 5.

[40] (1988) 88 Cr.App.R. 385 at 393. The court did not need, on the facts, to assert the correctness of this proposition.

[41] *Attorney-General's Reference (No. 2 of 1982)* [1984] Q.B. 624 (citing *Belmont Finance Corp. Ltd. v. Williams Furniture Ltd.* [1979] Ch. 250); *Gomez* [1993] A.C. 442 at 491 (Lord Lowry) and 496 (Lord Browne-Wilkinson).

[42] Above, §2–79. The dictum was followed by the majority of the Supreme Court of Victoria in *Roffel* [1985] V.R. 511 (effective controller of company milking company's bank account; held, no appropriation).

[43] Above, §2–84.

conceded[44] or held[45] that such an abstraction by a company controller himself was an appropriation of the property were declared to have been correctly decided.

Theft after Gomez

If *Gomez* has been rightly understood, the three House of Lords cases establish the following principles: **2–88**

   (i) the assumption of any of the rights of an owner amounts to an appropriation (*Morris*, interpreting section 3(1); reinforced by observations in *Gomez*);
   (ii) P's consent to or authorisation of D's act is irrelevant to the status of that act as an appropriation (*Lawrence* and *Gomez*);
   (iii) D may be guilty of theft although he does not intend by the act of appropriation itself to deprive P permanently of the property (effect of *Morris*).

These principles in combination produce the following extraordinary proposition:

Any act done by D with respect to P's property, which it is the privilege of P alone as owner of the property to do or to authorise, is an appropriation of that property, even if the act is in fact authorised or consented to by P; and the act is theft if it is done dishonestly and with the intention, by that act or by an act yet to be done (even one to which D will consent), to deprive P permanently of the property.

The result is to "[reduce] the *actus reus* of theft almost to vanishing point"[46] and, in doing so, to put a weight upon the word "dishonestly" that it is unfit to bear—as will be argued hereafter.[47]

Gallasso. The above statement of the law is offered subject to any qualification of it that has to be derived from the strange judgment of the Court of Appeal in *Gallasso*.[48] Mrs Gallasso had charge of the patients' finances in a residential home for the severely mentally handicapped. She received three   **2–89**

---

[44] *Attorney-General's Reference (No. 2 of 1982)*, above. Two men arranged large loans and overdrafts for companies they had established and then drew massively on the bank accounts for private purposes. It was held that liability should have turned on whether the defendants may have believed that they were entitled in law to act as they did: see s.2(1)(a).
[45] *Philippou* (1989) 89 Cr.App.R. 290. But the reasoning in this case remains suspect. The Court of Appeal found an appropriation in D's abstraction of funds from the company's bank account *plus* their use of the funds for their own purposes (which showed the transaction to be dishonest). According to *Gomez*, the former act is an appropriation in itself; see above, §2–70.
[46] Sir John Smith in the course of an elaborate critique of *Gomez* at [1993] Crim.L.R. 305.
[47] Below, §§2–121 to 2–123.
[48] [1993] Crim.L.R. 459. The brief report does not adequately reflect the judgment, details of which are taken from the transcript: no. 92/5023/Z4. Argument was heard on the very day that judgment in *Gomez* was handed down; judgment was given a fortnight later.

cheques on behalf of P, a patient, made payable to "P, c/o G." With the first cheque she properly opened a trust account with a building society; but she quite unnecessarily paid the other cheques into two further accounts. P was named as the beneficiary of all three accounts. The question that fell to be decided was whether she had stolen the third cheque.[49] It was held that she had not. The court found convincing the argument that, although "*Gomez* makes clear that a taking with consent may amount to an appropriation", yet "there must still be a taking" and the defendant's paying in of the second and third cheques into trust accounts, with P as named beneficiary, "was not a taking at all"; by so doing she was not assuming the rights of the owner but affirming them.

2–90   Ignoring for the moment the strange language used here and some of the other reasoning of the court, it is possible to support the decision in a way that avoids violence to the rest of the case law and in particular to *Gomez*. It would have been acceptable to say that an appropriation of property must be an act by which the actor intends to deprive P of that very property (or an act which he at least intends as a step towards such deprivation); the basic definition of theft requires an appropriation of property "with the intention of permanently depriving [the victim] *of it*". Mrs Gallasso may have intended to deprive her patient of the *proceeds* of the second and third cheques; the jury indeed convicted her of theft from the second account. But she did not intend to deprive him of *the cheques* themselves.

It is just possible that the court understood counsel to mean something like this by his suggested requirement of "a taking". As intangible property can be stolen and as some thefts can be committed by merely "keeping ... as owner" property that D has "come by ... without stealing [it]", the court can hardly have intended to demand for theft some movement (or "asportation") of property, still less anything in the nature of a trespassory "taking". It is difficult to understand the use of this very inappropriate word. But giving it some such meaning as that suggested here would be consistent with the court's assertion that the replacing of an article knocked from a shelf or handing to a lady her dropped purse would not be an appropriation. What may be meant is that such acts are not deprivatory in intent.

2–91   But such an attempt to explain *Gallasso* runs into trouble in other parts of the judgment. In particular, it was said[50] that "the word 'appropriation', in isolation, is an objective description of the act done, irrespective of the mental state of either the owner or the accused"; so that "a dishonest motive [does not] turn an action which is not an appropriation into an appropriation." A hotel porter who, in breach of regulations, keeps a customer's suitcase under his desk was said not thereby to appropriate it even if his act indicates a dishonest design. It is not possible to reconcile this either with the

---

[49] The defendant had been acquitted of theft of the second cheque; she had been properly convicted of theft in respect of a transfer to her own bank account of funds in the second trust account; and there had been no verdicts on counts alleging thefts from the third account.
[50] Quoting Lord Browne-Wilkinson in *Gomez* [1993] A.C. 442 at 495.

explanation of the case offered above or with the general body of the case law on appropriation, including the overruling of *Fritschy* (which the court had well in mind). The fact is that *Gallasso* may after all defy rationalisation.

Argument for consistency between civil and criminal law

Many years ago Professor Glanville Williams argued that theft cannot be **2–92** committed (a) "by a person who has or obtains an indefeasible title to the property when he commits the act charged as an appropriation" or (b) "by an act that is not wrongful (under the general law) against the person to whom the property belongs".[51] This principle ought to be acknowledged as a qualification of the "extraordinary proposition" stated above.[52] Its recognition would go some way to limiting the power of the tribunal of fact, apparently given by the present condition of the law of theft, to declare almost any act to be theft because done "dishonestly".[53]

Professor Williams pointed to certain decisions, already encountered in **2–93** this chapter, as being apparently against his thesis. Two of these were *Turner (No. 2)*[54] and *Gilks*.[55] The conviction in the former depended, not on D's infringement of any lien enjoyed by the garage that had repaired his car, but solely on a finding that he did not, as he claimed, believe that he was entitled to repossess the car from outside the garage. If he was so entitled, however, his repossession should have been held no theft; he was at most a dishonest debtor.[56] As it is difficult to maintain now that D did not appropriate the car,[57] Williams' general principle is needed. When Gilks took up from the betting shop counter the excessive sum he was paid as winnings, he took what, according to civil law, could not be recovered from him. It certainly seems odd that his taking of it was theft. The conclusion was made possible by the even odder view that although Gilks could keep the money he did not become owner of it. The case has been much criticised.[58] It is not thought that

---

[51] [1977] Crim.L.R. 127 and 205; *ibid.* at 327; Williams, *Textbook*, Chap. 35. Compare Arlidge and Parry, paras. 1–10—1–15.

[52] §2–88.

[53] The problem of the transaction that, though unimpeachable according to the civil law, might (since *Gomez*) arguably involve theft by one of the parties of property acquired under it (*e.g.* by "dishonestly" taking advantage of an expensive mistake made by the other party), is discussed by Smith (A. T. H.), para. 5–18, and Smith (J. C.), para. 2–19. Parry, *Offences against Property*, paras. 1.154–1.159, argues that conduct that is lawful as a matter of civil law is not theft because not "dishonest".

[54] Above, §2–30.

[55] Above, §2–51.

[56] See on this case Smith (J. C.), para. 2–54, and [1972 B] C.L.J. 197 at 215–217; Williams, *Textbook*, pp. 749–751; Parry, *Offences against Property*, paras. 1.156 1.157.

[57] But see *Meredith* [1973] Crim.L.R. 253 (Judge da Cunha), where D, without reference to the police, removed his car from a police pound; a charge of theft was said to be improper (possibly overlooking *Turner*, but to satisfactory effect).

[58] See Glanville Williams [1977] Crim.L.R. at 205–207, and [1977] C.L.J. 62 at 72–73; Smith (J. C.), para. 2–78, and [1972] Crim.L.R. 586–590.

these two cases imply a general and final rejection of Professor Williams' thesis.

Successive appropriations—one theft only; duration of theft

2–94   *Successive appropriations.* It is clear that a person may appropriate the same property more than once. He may, for instance, find goods and keep them, thinking the owner untraceable (this is an appropriation but not dishonest, according to section 2(1)), and, when he learns who the owner is, steal by a "later assumption of a right to it", as section 3(1) confirms. But this does not mean that one can steal the same property more than once as a principal offender by successive appropriations. Only one who has originally "come by" property *without stealing it*" can steal it by such a "later assumption". So in *Atakpu*,[59] an agreement between "a pair of thoroughly dishonest rascals" to hire cars in Germany and to bring them to England; in order to "ring the changes" and sell them was a conspiracy to commit a theft abroad[60] (by obtaining the cars by deception); that theft would be over by the time the cars arrived in England; and nothing done in England could constitute a further theft. They were guilty of no conspiracy triable in England.[61]

2–95   It has been said that there may be different appropriations of the same goods by different persons during the same incident—as in a burglary in which several people take part.[62] But this seems to introduce an unnecessary complication. If D1 enters a building and takes possession of goods pursuant to an agreement with D2, D2 is all along guilty as a secondary party. But if D2 has nothing to do with the burglary until he himself enters later (by coincidence), finds D1 already at work and joins in removal of the same goods, he then becomes a party to an existing and continuing appropriation. There seems to be no need to refer to separate theft offences.

2–96   *Duration of theft.* Is theft over as soon as anything has been done that qualifies as an appropriation? Or does (or may) the activity of stealing continue, and if so for how long, beyond the first moment of appropriation? These questions did not arise for decision in *Atakpu*, in which it was enough to conclude as a matter of common sense that, even if an appropriation may continue for some time, the theft of a car stolen abroad by deception is over by the time the car has reached England. But the questions are important in robbery and in handling. In robbery it may be necessary to decide whether force was used "at the time of" stealing; and in this context it has been held that an appropriation is not a merely momentary event—how long it lasts is a jury question.[63] This answer gives the law of theft a useful flexibility for a

---

[59] [1994] Q.B. 69.
[60] But see G. R. Sullivan and C. Warbrick [1994] Crim.L.R. 650 (below, §17–01, n. 2).
[61] As to jurisdiction in such a case when Part I of the Criminal Justice Act 1993 is in force, see below, §17–09.
[62] *Gregory* (1981) 77 Cr.App.R. 41.
[63] *Hale* (1978) 68 Cr.App.R. 415; below, §3–08.

number of purposes.[64] Handling stolen goods, on the other hand, cannot be committed in "the course of the stealing". There is a temptation, therefore, to limit the duration of the theft so as to extend the scope of the handling offence; and the theft of property by offering to sell it to an alleged handler has been regarded as committed by an "instantaneous appropriation".[65] The cases on robbery and handling are in consequence not easy to reconcile.

5. "WITH THE INTENTION OF PERMANENTLY DEPRIVING THE OTHER OF IT"

The basic rule

The C.L.R.C. recommended that an intention to deprive P permanently of   **2–97** the property should be a necessary element in theft, as it was in larceny. They recognised that temporary deprivation can sometimes occasion great loss or hardship and that an intention to cause such deprivation "may involve dishonesty comparable with that involved in theft." But they considered that where there is an intention to return the property, the conduct is "essentially diferent from stealing" and that either the inclusion in theft of all dishonest borrowing or the creation of a general offence of temporary deprivation would be "a considerable extension of the criminal law [not] called for by any existing serious social evil".[66] Despite much controversy while the Bill was before Parliament, this view finally prevailed.[67]

So the general rule is that dishonest borrowing is not theft. If D takes P's property he is not normally guilty of stealing it if he intends in due course to return it or at least that P shall recover it. It is necessary to describe this as "the general rule" because section 6 is at pains to provide that one who intends a borrowing that is "equivalent to an outright taking" is to be regarded as intending to deprive permanently. Subject to this obscure provision, which is dealt with below, it is immaterial for how long D can be shown to have intended to enjoy possession of the property or for how long P is actually deprived of it. Immaterial, that is, as a matter of law. As a matter of common sense, of course, the longer the period is, the less plausible will be D's claim that he intended P to have the property back. But if that claim appeals to the tribunal of fact as a reasonable possibility, he will be entitled to an acquittal.

---

[64] *e.g.* powers of arrest: see V. Tunkel [1978] Crim.L.R. 331. For the suggestion that an appropriation of a bank credit may last from the relevant act of the thief to the debiting of the account, see below, §2–153. For the pleading notion of one "continuous" theft by successive appropriations of different things, see below, §2–158.
[65] *Pitham and Hehl* (1976) 65 Cr.App.R. 45 (as explained in *Gregory* (1981) 77 Cr.App.R. 41 at 46, and in *Atakpu* [1994] Q.B. 69 at 77); see below, §15–47.
[66] *Eighth Report*, para. 56.
[67] For full argument of the contrary view, see Glanville Williams, [1981] Crim.L.R. 129. In recent years the "borrowing" of films and cassettes to make pirate copies has afforded an example of a relevant "serious social evil"; see below, §2–109.

Some points of detail

2–98   *"With the intention. . . ."* The intention of depriving P permanently must
coincide with a dishonest appropriation. But this need not be D's first appropriation. He may take P's property intending at first merely to borrow it; he
has "come by the property . . . without stealing it". If he later decides to keep
it for good or to sell it, this is a "later assumption of a right to it by keeping or
dealing with it as owner" and a fresh appropriation (s.3(1)). Theft occurs at
this point.
        Certain varieties of "conditional intention" are considered below, §2–114.

2–99   *". . . of permanently depriving the other. . . ."* The word "permanently" must
be understood in the light of P's particular interest in the property. If P
merely has temporary "possession or control" of the property, it nevertheless belongs to him for the purpose of his being a victim of theft (s.5(1)), and
D can intend that he be "permanently" deprived of it although he might have
had to relinquish it very shortly in any event.
        It has already been noticed that (as a result of House of Lords authority on
the element of appropriation in theft) D may steal property by an act done—
the assumption of one of the owner's rights in it—as a preliminary to a later
intended acquisition of it; he need not intend that P be deprived, permanently or at all, by that particular act.[68]

2–100   *". . . of it."* It has long been understood, both in the law of larceny and under
the present Act, that even if D means to return to P the indistinguishable
equivalent of what he takes—the precise amount of cash[69] or an identical can
of baked beans—he nevertheless has the necessary intention of permanently
depriving P of the particular property appropriated. Whether he is guilty of
theft depends on whether he appropriates that property dishonestly, a matter to which his intention to replace what he takes may be relevant.[70]

Belief in abandonment as excluding intention

2–101   Suppose that D sees in the street property which he wrongly believes
(whether or not on reasonable grounds) to have been abandoned by its
owner. He believes that the property does not "belong to" anyone. This
belief by definition negatives any intention on D's part to deprive anyone of
the property when he takes possession of it. There will therefore be no need,
on a charge of theft from the owner, to consider the issue of dishonesty[71]; the
absence of the required intention excludes the theft charged. Alternatively,
D may find and take, on land occupied by P, property which he believes to

---

[68] See above, §2–72.
[69] *Velumyl* [1989] Crim.L.R. 299; *cf.* §8–65, below (obtaining property by deception).
[70] See below, §2–134.
[71] Very heavy weather was made of that issue in *Small* (1987) 86 Cr.App.R. 170, it would seem
quite unnecessarily.

have been abandoned there by its owner, O. Once again D, having that belief, does not intend to deprive O. His taking may, however, be adverse to an interest of P. If D nevertheless believes that P has no interest in the property, he might also claim, charged with theft from P, that he did not intend to deprive P of it. But it is probable that P, as occupier, had "control" within the meaning of section 5(1) and was a person to whom the property "belonged" for theft purposes.[72] D intentionally deprived P of that control. If that is right, it may strictly be more accurate in this case to understand D as denying dishonesty; he believed that he had in law the right to deprive P, or that P would have consented to the taking if he had known.[73]

A preface to section 6

Section 6 provides a partial definition of the phrase "with the intention of   **2–102** permanently depriving the other of it." That it is only a partial definition appears from the first words of the section, which show that it is concerned only with a case where a person appropriates property "without meaning the other permanently to lose the thing itself." The section identifies circumstances in which the appropriator is nevertheless to be regarded as having the intention of permanently depriving the other of the property.

The section was an unsatisfactory late amendment to the Bill.[74] It is badly drafted and employs language new to this branch of the law. For instance, a curious distinction is taken between "property" and "the thing itself"; yet, as between subsections (1) and (2), the two phrases are used indifferently in precisely the same context: subsection (1) talks of D's treating "the thing" and subsection (2) of his treating "the property" as "his own to dispose of regardless of [P's] rights". In subsection (1) the phrases "having the intention" and "meaning" are both used, with no clear difference in meaning or intention. Subsection (1) ends with the obscure expression "equivalent to an outright taking or disposal". Rarely can a provision inserted for clarification have contributed more obscurity.

Limited function of the section

The draft Bill had no clause corresponding to section 6. The C.L.R.C.   **2–103** described "cases where the offender intends to do something with the property which for practical purposes is equivalent to permanent deprivation" and thought that these cases would be treated as theft without need for special provision.[75] It was made clear in the House of Commons that the section was drafted largely with the same cases in mind. The Court of Appeal, in the leading case of *Lloyd*,[76] has declared a disposition to interpret the section "in

---

[72] See above, §2–29
[73] s.2(1)(a) and (b).
[74] For the illuminating, and remarkable, Parliamentary history of the section, see J. R. Spencer [1977] Crim.L.R. 653.
[75] *Eighth Report*, para. 58.
[76] [1985] Q.B. 829 at 836.

such a way as to ensure that nothing is construed as an intention permanently to deprive which would not prior to the 1968 Act have been so construed".[77] In other cases the same court and the Judicial Committee of the Privy Council seem to have taken a somewhat less restrictive view of the section's potential.[78] But it is certainly the case, as the court in *Lloyd* confirmed, that *the section should be referred to in exceptional cases only*. It is important to emphasise this cautionary statement because of the impression of some people to the contrary and because of the strange uses to which the section has been put at first instance in some cases.[79]

Section 6(1)

2–104   "A person appropriating property belonging to another without meaning the other permanently to lose the thing itself is nevertheless to be regarded as having the intention of permanently depriving the other of it if his intention is to treat the thing as his own to dispose of regardless of the other's rights; and a borrowing or lending of it may amount to so treating it if, but only if, the borrowing or lending is for a period and in circumstances making it equivalent to an outright taking or disposal."

The first part of the subsection

2–105   The following situations are undoubtedly within the first part of the subsection:

(i)   D takes P's chattel. His intention is to pretend that it is his own and to induce P to "buy" it. Thus P will not permanently "lose the thing itself". But D will be treating the chattel as his own to dispose of regardless of P's rights.

(ii)   D takes an exhibit from an exhibition and holds it to ransom; he will return it only if the exhibitor fulfils some condition named by D. This is identical with situation (i) save that there is no deception.

(iii)   D takes P's gold watch, intending to pawn it and to send the pawn ticket to P. He intends, that is to say, to treat the watch as his own to dispose of, although he hopes that P will recover the watch by redeeming it. (Even if D does not get as far as pawning the watch, his intention to do so is, of course, enough.)

2–106   Situations such as those in (i) and (ii) above (intended sale to owner and intended ransom) were identified by the Court of Appeal in *Lloyd*[80] as aimed at by the first part of section 6(1). There seems no reason to doubt that the

---

[77] The offence of larceny required an intention to deprive the victim permanently, but there was no statutory gloss on this requirement.
[78] See *Coffey* [1987] Crim.L.R. 498; *Bagshaw* [1988] Crim.L.R. 321; *Chan Man-sin v. R.* (1987) 86 Cr.App.R. 303.
[79] See *Warner* (1970) 55 Cr.App.R. 93; *Halstead v. Patel* (1972) 56 Cr.App.R. 334; *Cocks* (1976) 63 Cr.App.R. 79; *Harkindel Atwal* [1989] Crim.L.R. 293; *Cahill* [1993] Crim.L.R. 141.
[80] [1985] Q.B. 829 at 836.

court would regard situation (iii) as an analogous case. And it might be thought that an intention to keep P's property unless P will behave as D wishes might always be regarded in the same way as an intention to hold property to ransom; in effect, P must buy his property back. But the cases certainly do not go this far. In *Barnett and Reid*[81] the Court of Appeal thought that there might be rare circumstances in which taking property to hold as security for a supposed debt would not amount to treating it as one's own to dispose of regardless of the other's rights. And in *Coffey*[82] the court declined to treat as simply analogous to ransom the withholding of property until P should comply with D's wishes in another matter. The jury, it seemed to be said, might take the view that D's perception of the likelihood of P's complying was such that D's conduct was not "equivalent to an outright taking." But the requirement of equivalence to "an outright taking" is prescribed by section 6(1) only for a case of "borrowing"; and it is submitted that a taking of P's property to put pressure on him to do something is not a "borrowing".[83]

Although speaking restrictively of the first part of section 6(1), the court in **2–107** *Lloyd* did not directly cast doubt on the application of the subsection to some other situations illustrated by decisions of its own to which it referred:

(iv) P has written a cheque in favour of D but will deliver it only on performance of some act by D, *e.g.* the delivery of goods. D comes and takes the cheque without performing the act; he intends to pay the cheque into his bank for collection. The cheque will in due course return to P (by returning to his bank); but D's taking of it is with the intention of treating it as his own to dispose of regardless of P's rights.[84]

(v) D, an approved building contractor, is lawfully in possession of Inland Revenue vouchers to be used to claim exemption from deduction of tax upon payment of remuneration by the main contractors. D "sells" the vouchers to E so that E may claim such exemption. The vouchers, fraudulently completed by E, will in due course return to the Inland Revenue. D's appropriation by "selling" the vouchers is within section 6(1).[85]

D's intention to treat the thing as his own "to dispose of." An intention to **2–108** treat the relevant property as D's own "to dispose of" is easily identified in situations (i)–(v). It is less obvious in a situation in which the Privy Council made an important application of section 6(1):

(vi) D issues a forged cheque on P Ltd.'s bank account. The credit in the

---

[81] July 21, 1987, C.A. no. 5818/C3/86.
[82] [1987] Crim.L.R. 498.
[83] See below, §2–109.
[84] For cases and discussion, see below, §8–71, on the corresponding point in obtaining property by deception.
[85] *Downes* (1983) 77 Cr.App.R. 260; compare *Mulligan* [1990] S.T.C. 220.

account will be unaffected by the forged instrument. But D, it is held, steals the credit because he is "purporting to deal with [P Ltd.'s] property without regard to [its] rights".[86]

"Purporting to deal with" property is thus regarded as a case of "disposing of" it. This authority seems to have been relied on in one case as suggesting that any dealing with property is a disposal of it.[87] Such a reading of section 6(1) would be very remarkable; it would go far towards rendering the words "to dispose of" redundant, which the Court of Appeal has insisted they are not.[88] It is therefore desirable to mention again that the court was inclined in *Lloyd* to give the subsection a narrow application.

Borrowing

2–109   The second part of section 6(1) refers to cases of "borrowing" and "lending". None of the situations (i) to (vi) above appears to be one of "borrowing"; it is thought that the word refers to a case where D assumes possession of property without deciding never to return it to P but, equally, without having in mind a use or dealing (such as sale, ransom, pledge) that would be inconsistent with a borrowing legitimately so called. Such a taking is theft "if, and only if, [it] is for a period and in circumstances making it equivalent to an outright taking".

The view of the Court of Appeal in *Lloyd* was that this part of the subsection

> "is intended to make clear that a mere borrowing is never enough to constitute the necessary guilty mind unless the intention is to return the 'thing' in such a changed state that it can truly be said that all its goodness or virtue has gone."[89]

In *Lloyd* itself, films were removed from a cinema, each for a few hours only, to be copied on to master videotapes, so that many pirate copies of the film could be put on the market. This was not theft.[90] The films themselves,

---

[86] *Chan Man-sing v. Attorney-General of Hong Kong* (1987) 86 Cr.App.R. 303 at 306; see below, §2–155.
[87] *D.P.P. v. Lavender* [1994] Crim.L.R. 297 (D takes doors from council property under repair and uses them to replace damaged doors in another property of the same council; s.6(1) applied).
[88] *Cahill* [1993] Crim.L.R. 141 (omission of the words in direction to jury "materially altered the sense" of the subsection).
[89] [1985] Q.B. 829 at 836. This adopts a long-standing suggestion of Sir John Smith; see now Smith (J. C.), para. 2–126. The court's language is not entirely happy; its own example of the used ticket (see text below) shows that there need not always be a changed physical state. The notion of exhausted "virtue" can be overworked: see Professor Smith's comment on *Bagshaw* [1988] Crim.L.R. 321 at 322.
[90] See also *Warner* (1970) 55 Cr.App.R. 93, for a case of a mere indefinite borrowing which was not theft.

the physical property appropriated, did not lose their "virtue", however great the loss to the copyright owners and others.

The following case of "borrowing" is within the subsection: **2–110**

(vii) D takes from P's ticket office a train ticket or a ticket giving access to a place. He cannot say this was not theft merely because he meant to surrender the ticket at the end of the journey or on entering the place and because thereby the ticket would return to P.

The following seems also to qualify:

(viii) D takes P's railway season ticket, intending to use it for as long as he may wish to do so, possibly for as long as it is valid. (But if he intends to keep the ticket for a limited time substantially shorter than the period for which the ticket is valid, the case would seem to be outside the section. The section's obscurities may be illustrated by asking what the effect will be of D's intending to return the ticket, say a quarterly season ticket, a very short time before its expiry. At what point does a borrowing become "equivalent to an outright taking"?)

Borrowing and abandonment

D may take P's chattel, use it for a time and then abandon it. It will be   **2–111**
inadvisable for a court to treat such a case simply as one of "borrowing". If it does it will become enmeshed in the obscurities of section 6. The correct course, it is submitted, is to concentrate on the abandonment. If D leaves the chattel in such a place that he can virtually be regarded as returning it to P (*e.g.* he leaves a book with P's name in it in the office where P works), he will not be regarded as treating it as his own to dispose of. If, on the other hand, the facts of the abandonment show D to be indifferent whether P recovers the chattel or not, he can be regarded as, by abandoning it, "dealing with it as owner" (s.3(1)), having at that time the intention "to treat the thing as his own to dispose of". Even though D may have been content that P should recover the chattel, the case will be particularly strong if the circumstances of the abandonment show that he undoubtedly realised that P was extremely unlikely to do so.

Lending

Section 6(1) appears, finally, to contemplate the following kind of case: **2–112**

(ix) D is a bailee of P's chattel. He lends the chattel to E, telling E that he may keep and use it for as long as he likes. The circumstances, to D's knowledge, are such that the chattel may never be returned (*e.g.* E is going abroad) or that by the time it is returned its "virtue" may have gone (*e.g.* it is a ticket for a series of concerts and E may keep the ticket until the end of the series). In either situation there appears to be a "lending . . . for a period and in circumstances making it equivalent to an outright ... disposal." D is not protected by his claim that he did not mean P permanently to lose "the thing itself."

Section 6(2)

2–113   One kind of case is specifically mentioned by section 6(2) as being within section 6(1). Where D,

> "having possession or control (lawfully or not) of [P's property], parts with the property under a condition as to its return which he may not be able to perform, this ... amounts to treating the property as his own to dispose of regardless of [P's] rights"

if it is done for D's purposes and without P's authority.

An obvious case is that where D, a bailee of P's property, pledges the property with E as security for a loan by E to himself, intending to redeem it and to return it to P. There are two possible views of this situation. One is that D is guilty of theft only if he realises that he may be unable to redeem; the other is that the case must be within the subsection, as it can be asserted of every pledgor, life being full of uncertainties, that he may not be able to redeem his security. The former view is doctrinally the purer; the latter is more readily suggested by the terms of the poorly-drafted section.

"Conditional intention"

2–114   This phrase is a convenient heading under which to consider a number of states of mind in the description of which a conditional clause features as an important and possibly crucial element: "I shall steal from that pocket (or handbag or house) if, as I hope, there is anything attractive (or such as I seek) to be had in it"; "I shall keep this thing if, but only if, on examination it proves to suit my purpose"; "if this belongs to anyone, I shall deprive him of it". It will be seen that these intentions, and the conditions that qualify them, are of very different kinds. The fact is that the expression "conditional intention", which for a time had something of a vogue in this area of the criminal law, is a dangerous one—useful perhaps as a heading, but not to be used in analysis unless its meaning in the context is made very plain.

Looking for something to steal

2–115   In *Easom*[91] D took up P's handbag where it lay near P in a cinema and looked into it to see whether there was anything worth stealing. There was not; so he replaced the bag, with its contents intact, where he had found it. It was held that his "conditional appropriation" of the bag and its contents did not suffice to establish theft of those things. He had formed no intention to deprive P permanently of the property named in the indictment.[92]

---

[91] [1971] 2 Q.B. 315.
[92] "... and this was so notwithstanding the provisions of s.6(1) ... ": at 319.

Easom came in due course to be seen as the source of a doctrine that a "conditional intention to steal"—an intention, for example, to steal if there should prove to be anything worth stealing—was no intention to steal for the purpose of an offence requiring that ingredient. English law did indeed briefly flirt with such a doctrine, which for a time troubled the law of burglary and attempted theft before being renounced.[93] As to theft itself, what section 1(1) requires in terms is not an "intention to steal" but a more specific "intention of permanently depriving [P] of [the property appropriated]". It is productive of error to argue (as has been done) that what was conditional was not *Easom*'s appropriation but his intention. He had no intention to deprive P permanently either of the handbag or of the particular things he found in it. The attribution to *Easom* of a so-called "doctrine of conditional intention" is misconceived.

It was hinted in *Easom* itself that the appellant, who was plainly looking for   **2–116** something to steal, could have been convicted of attempted theft on a charge suitably framed.[94] Within a few years of *Easom* such a conviction became problematical for another reason—namely, a short-lived aberration of the law relating to "impossible attempts".[95] But impossibility of success has ceased to be a bar to conviction of attempt in such a case.[96]

Keeping property for examination and for retention or return

If D is looking for money in P's handbag and finds only cosmetic paraphernalia, or if he sorts through a pile of mail looking for registered letters and finds only unregistered ones,[97] he has no intention of permanently depriving P, or the Post Office, of the particular things he examines. But if he finds something that may on examination prove to conform to his requirements, it is strongly arguable that he does steal it, or that on the particular facts he may do so, when he keeps it for examination, even though he will return it to its owner if it proves disappointing.[98]

The Supreme Court of Victoria has held such a case to be theft by virtue of the first part of a provision identical to section 6(1): D intends "to treat the thing as his own to dispose of regardless of [P's] rights".[99] An alternative view

---

[93] As to burglary, see below, §4–31; as to attempted theft, *Scudder v. Barrett* [1980] Q.B. 195n; *Bayley and Easterbrook* [1980] Crim.L.R. 503.

[94] [1971] 2 Q.B. at 321; and see cases cited in preceding note.

[95] *Haughton v. Smith* [1975] A.C. 476; *Partington v. Williams* (1975) 62 Cr.App.R. 220. (The difficulty was overlooked or ignored in *Bayley and Easterbrook*, above.)

[96] Criminal Attempts Act 1981, s.1(2); *Smith and Smith* [1986] Crim.L.R. 166 (and see *ibid.* at 167, comment on form of charge).

[97] See *Easom* [1971] 2 Q.B. 315 at 319

[98] D's claim that he would have returned the thing in certain circumstances may stretch credulity. But if that is his defence, as it was in *Sharp v. McCormick* (next note), the jury or magistrates must be correctly advised as to its legal effect if they think it possibly true.

[99] *Sharp v. McCormick* [1986] V.R. 869. The court left open the question whether it would be theft in the absence of the provision.

would be that, for the time being, D's retention of the thing is only a "borrowing" and that it is therefore necessary to ask whether, on the facts, including D's own expectation as to the outcome of his trial of the thing, the borrowing is "equivalent to an outright taking"—a question requiring a jury judgment.[1] There is a problem, however, with either application of section 6(1). The subsection is expressed to apply only where D appropriates property "without meaning [P] permanently to lose the thing itself", by which the draftsman surely meant to indicate a case where D intends, or supposes, or at least is content, that the thing will return to P. If that is right, the typical case under consideration is outside the ambit of section 6(1): when D takes the thing he has, for the time being, no such state of mind.

2–118   Is the case, then, one of theft without resort to section 6(1)? The answer may be that it depends on the particular facts. D may best be understood as having intended to keep the thing unless (unexpectedly) it should prove unsuitable; and in this case he may properly be found to have formed a (so to speak) defeasible intention to deprive P permanently of it. But if the facts better suggest D's assumption that he will return the thing, with the reservation that he will keep it if (against the odds) it should prove suitable to his purpose, it would be acceptable (save in one kind of case) to say that theft was not (yet) committed. The excepted case is that in which it is known that the thing did in fact answer D's requirements: it is proved that he intended to keep the thing if it had certain qualities and that it had those qualities. This perhaps establishes theft.

Realising that the property probably belongs to another

2–119   It has been argued that (assuming a finding of dishonesty) D should be liable to conviction of theft if he acquires from E property belonging to P realising that E very likely has no title to it.[2] The question is whether the required intention of depriving the victim is satisfied by recklessness with respect to such deprivation or by nothing less than knowledge. What is in effect, though not in terms, suggested is that recklessness establishes a particular form of conditional intention: "If this is a deprivation of another, then it is one that I intend to commit."

This suggestion must probably be rejected.[3] It is, understandably, only for the case of strong suspicion, or realisation of a probability, that the conclusion of theft is suggested. Yet there is really no way of distinguishing between mild and strong suspicion that E has no title; in either case the conditional "intention" can be written in the same form. It seems, therefore, that D must know that he is depriving someone.

---

[1] Compare *Coffey* [1987] Crim.L.R. 498; above, §2–106.
[2] J. R. Spencer [1985] Crim.L.R. 92.
[3] As it is by Glanville Williams [1985] Crim.L.R. 432 at 438.

6. "DISHONESTLY"

Did D appropriate the property dishonestly?—introductory

Preliminary points

It may be assumed, for the purpose of what now follows that D has appro-   **2–120**
priated property belonging to P. Did he do so "dishonestly"? Some preliminary points may be made about this question.

(i) The question relates to the time of the appropriation. The Court of
Appeal has several times had occasion to emphasise this point, notably in
relation to the prosecution's difficult task of establishing theft of property to
which section 5(3) applies.[4]

(ii) The question should be understood to relate to D's conduct considered
as an appropriation—that is, as a dealing with property belonging to P—and
not from some other point of view.[5] In particular, the fact that D has a dishonest intention to default as P's debtor should not normally be relevant to a
theft issue.[6]

(iii) Both appropriation and the intention of depriving P are preliminary
issues in relation to that of dishonesty. The judge (on the strength of his
understanding of the legal position relating to the property concerned) may
rightly direct the jury as a matter of law that D's proved conduct amounted to
an appropriation of property belonging to another, while leaving it to them to
say whether D acted dishonestly. The Court of Appeal made this distinction
in *Clowes (No. 2)*.[7] The court did not advert to the third issue—namely,
whether D intended to deprive P of the property. If D's mistaken understanding of the factual or the legal position may have been such that, were he
correct, the property would not have "belonged to another" within the
meaning of section 1(1), he is not proved to have had the intention of depriving anyone of it. In that case the issue of dishonesty would not arise.

(iv) D will commonly need to ensure that the question of the honesty or
otherwise of his conduct is a live issue, by giving evidence that he acted with
one of the beliefs mentioned in section 2(1) or with some other state of mind
that may cause the tribunal of fact to withhold a finding of dishonesty.[8] But,
though D may have this evidential burden, the burden of proof on the issue
remains always with the prosecution.[9]

---

[4] *Hall* [1973] Q.B. 126; *Hayes* (1976) 64 Cr.App.R. 82; as to s.5(3), see above, §2–40.
[5] D. W. Elliott [1991] Crim.L.R. 732 at 735, persuasively argues that "dishonesty must be with
regard to the owner" (or, in the terms of the Act, the person to whom the property "belongs")
and not to some other person who may be affected by D's act. Theft is an offence against a person
in respect of his proprietary interest in the property concerned. See also Smith (A. T. H.), para.
7–68.
[6] S. 5(4) qualifies this general rule by creating theft liability out of a decision not to pay one kind
of debt; and *Turner (No. 2)* [1971] 1 W.L.R. 901 (see above, §2–30) seems to offend against it.
[7] [1994] 2 All E.R. 316; above, §2–33.
[8] See below, §2–133.
[9] *Falconer-Atlee* (1973) 58 Cr.App.R. 348, which illustrates the importance of a direction to the
jury on a part of s.2(1) rendered relevant by the evidence.

Importance and nature of the question

2–121   The point has already been made that the astonishingly wide meaning given by decisions of the House of Lords to the word "appropriates" in section 1(1) gives a correspondingly great significance to the question whether the appropriation was made dishonestly. Those decisions have been interpreted as meaning that almost any act done with respect to another's property (even with the other's consent), with the intention of thereby or thereafter acquiring it (even by a consensual transaction), is an appropriation of it[10]; and, if so, any such act will be theft unless not done dishonestly. It is submitted that the word "dishonestly" in the definition of theft is thus given a weight that it is unfit to bear. Dishonesty becomes the factor that turns otherwise legitimate behaviour into an indictable crime.

2–122   The prevailing view of appropriation, then, forces upon dishonesty the function of a positive ingredient of the offence. That is, indeed, how it was expressly presented in *Lawrence*, in which theft was said (simply following the language of section 1(1)) to have "four elements: (i) a dishonest (ii) appropriation (iii) of property belonging to another (iv) with the intention of permanently depriving the other of it"[11]—as though all were ingredients in the same positive sense. This passage is constantly quoted; and the common coinage of professional discourse, it must be admitted, suggests that its conception of the role of dishonesty is very generally shared.

It is thought, however, that this is a long-standing error. The word "dishonestly" should properly be understood, not as adding a vital ingredient to offences in whose definitions it appears, but rather as having a negative function—as meaning "otherwise than honestly". So understood, it would be similar to the word "unlawfully" or the phrase "without lawful excuse" in other offences; it would signify that conduct conforming to the other requirements of the offence (an appropriation of property committed with deprivatory intent) is prima facie criminal unless "honestly" done. That is the approach of the Theft Act itself, so far as it deals with the dishonesty issue; section 2(1) sets out three situations in which an appropriation is *not* to be regarded as dishonest. It is hardly an approach that the courts can expressly follow for the time being, given the state of the case law on appropriation; yet it is possible to detect a hint of it in recent decisions of the Court of Appeal denying the need for a direction to the jury on dishonesty in the absence of evidence raising an issue in relation to it.[12]

2–123   The word "dishonestly" is treated as standing for a concept too vague and variable for the decisive job it is being asked to do. And this is compounded by the method used by the courts (as explained below) to identify dishonesty in a particular case. The law does not declare in advance what conduct is

---

[10] See above, §2–88.
[11] [1972] A.C. 626 at 632, *per* Viscount Dilhorne, approving Megaw L.J. in the Court of Appeal, [1971] 1 Q.B. 373 at 376.
[12] See below, §2–133.

dishonest. Conduct that is prima facie innocent may be theft, it seems, only because a particular jury or bench of magistrates, representing "reasonable and honest people", say after the event that it was "dishonest"—whatever they may suppose that word to mean in the context of such conduct—and believe that the defendant would have expected them to say so. A good example of what is thought to be an unsatisfactory state of the law has been provided by a supporter of the decision in *Gomez* on the irrelevance of consent to appropriation[13]: Simon Gardner refers to "cases where the victim consents to the taking, but does so in a state of low-level, non-specific confusion"—as when "rogues" exploit elderly people (without deception[14] or any pressure amounting to blackmail or any "true mistake" on the victims' part[15]) by "dishonestly overcharging them for work or underpaying them for their treasures."[16] This, he says, is rightly theft. It would be theft if, and only because, the judges of fact (as Gardner hints) "sense" that it ought to be a crime. As a matter of form their verdict of guilty would involve the application of the epithet "dishonestly" to the transaction; but they would be using that cloudy word for all the world as though it meant "wickedly". And they would not be obliged to explain how the transaction differs from countless others that involve the ruthless exploitation of vulnerable "victims" but would never be thought of as theft. The ability to characterise conduct as theft in this way, after the event and by means of an oracular verdict, is objectionable in principle.

Section 2(1): acts declared to be not dishonest

Section 2(1) provides three grounds on which D may claim that as a matter **2–124** of law his appropriation of property belonging to another was not dishonest. Each involves his assertion that he acted with a certain belief. If it is possible that he acted with that belief he is entitled to an acquittal. A defendant asserting such a belief is therefore entitled to have the jury directed in terms of the relevant paragraph of section 2(1); the more general (*Ghosh*) dishonesty direction to be discussed below cannot strictly be adequate in such a case.[17]

Belief in a right to deprive

The appropriator who believes "that he has in law the right[18] to deprive" of **2–125** the property the person to whom it belongs, is not guilty of theft, for his appropriation is not to be regarded as dishonest (s.2(1)(a)). Such a belief will

---

[13] See above, §2–84.
[14] For deception and overcharging, see below, §8–28.
[15] So that s.5(4) does not apply.
[16] (1993) 109 L.Q.R. 194 at 195.
[17] *Pace* a mystifying dictum in *Kell* [1985] Crim.L.R. 239. In *Wootton and Peake* [1990] Crim.L.R. 201 the point was not firmly enough asserted; the court was influenced by *Woolven* (1983) 77 Cr.App.R. 231 (below, §8–75), which, however, concerned an offence to which s.2 does not apply.
[18] Whether on behalf of himself or of another: s.2(1)(a).

protect him even if it is an unreasonable one or is the result of self-induced intoxication,[19] and even if the claim he makes is of a kind completely unknown to the law.[20]

2–126   Unless D knows that the property in question is property belonging to another (within the wide meaning given to that phrase by s.5), he cannot strictly be said to intend to deprive the other of the property. So where, for example, D takes P's umbrella from a stand, mistaking it for his own, or where D has got property by another's mistake and is under an obligation to restore it or its value to P but is unaware of the mistake and believes the property was intended for him, his taking in the former case and his retention of the property in the latter case[21] do not need to be defended by resort to section 2(1)(a); D does not intend to deprive P, let alone believe that he has a right to do so.[22]

2–127   *Mistake of law.* Occasionally section 2(1)(a) may be the ground of D's immunity when he takes or retains property to which, because of a legal error, he makes a specific claim. For example, D, wrongly believing that ownership in certain goods has passed to him by virtue of a transaction, takes them from P's possession. The goods "belong to" P not only in the loose sense of the term, but as possessor under section 5(1). But D believes he has the right to deprive P.[23] D may have a similar belief where he has himself sold and delivered goods to P and repossesses them because of P's failure to pay the full price. Or D may find money whose owner he knows to be traceable, but appropriate the money because he believes "findings is keepings." In each of these cases section 2(1)(a) will protect D from liability for theft.

2–128   *Claim to equivalent sum.* Reliance on section 2(1)(a) will more often be required where D knew that the particular property (usually money) was P's, but alleges that he believed P owed him or a third person a sum equivalent in value to what he took. If with such a belief D removed the sum in question from the pocket of P's coat as it hung on a peg in their office, he will clearly not be guilty of theft. But it is important to notice that that belief would also suffice to acquit him if he chose some less acceptable and even, in other respects, seriously criminal method of debt-collecting. In *Robinson*,[24] D

---

[19] *Holden* [1991] Crim.L.R. 478; as to intoxication, compare *Jaggard v. Dickinson* [1981] Q.B. 527 (Criminal Damage Act 1971, s.5(2)).
[20] See Williams, *C.L.G.P.*, pp. 321–325; *Russell on Crime* (12th ed.), pp. 1023–1025.
[21] See s.5(4).
[22] See further, §2–101, above (belief in abandonment).
[23] The summary jurisdiction of justices is not ousted by such an assertion of belief in title to personal property: *Eagling v. Wheatley* [1977] Crim.L.R. 165 (and see commentary at 166, pointing out that even if the case concerned real property, the justices would not be called upon to decide a question of title, but only a question as to D's state of mind, and their jurisdiction should be unaffected).
[24] [1977] Crim.L.R. 173; compare *Skivington* [1968] 1 Q.B. 166 (acquitted of robbery, of which larceny was, and theft now is, an essential ingredient, but convicted of offences against the person; might now also be convicted of blackmail).

brandished a knife and used force to get from P money that he said P owed him. His conviction of theft was quashed because the jury had been directed that D could rely on section 2(1)(a) only if he believed that he was entitled to get his money in the way he did. This was a misdirection. Similarly, if D believes that she is legally entitled to £20 promised to her by P as a reward for sexual favours, she is not guilty of theft, whether she takes that sum by stealth or by force or extorts it by threatening to reveal P's indiscretions if he does not pay.[25]

Belief that the victim would consent

Section 2(1)(b) protects one who appropriates property in the belief that, **2–129** if the person to whom it belongs "knew of the appropriation and the circumstances of it", that person would consent.[26] "'The circumstances' are, of course, all the relevant circumstances"[27]; the hypothetical consent referred to would be "a true consent, honestly obtained".[28]

A typical case is that of the housewife who "borrows" a bag of sugar from a neighbour to whom she mistakenly attributes a spirit of local co-operation. She intends to deprive her neighbour permanently of the sugar she takes, though she may intend to offer later an equivalent quantity in return. So also with the man who borrows money from his colleague's wallet or his employer's till. He, like the housewife, if charged with theft, must succeed on the issue of dishonesty if he is to escape a conviction. Either of two familiar pleas may yield that success. The first is the section 2(1)(b) plea: "I thought P wouldn't mind." If this may be true it succeeds as a matter of law. The second is: "I intended to repay", which raises questions for the jury that are considered below.[29]

Belief that the owner cannot be discovered

If one appropriates property "in the belief that the person to whom [it] **2–130** belongs cannot be discovered by taking reasonable steps", the appropriation is not to be regarded as dishonest—save in the case of the appropriator to whom the property came as a trustee or personal representative (s.2(1)(c)).

The obvious example is the finder of lost property. Factors such as the place where the thing is found, its apparent value and the existence of any distinguishing marks or features will determine whether it seems worth while

---

[25] But in the latter case she might now be convicted of blackmail; see discussion of *Bernhard* [1938] 2 K.B. 264, below, §14–32.
[26] "*A fortiori*, a person is not to be regarded as acting dishonestly if he appropriates another's property believing that with full knowledge of the circumstances that other person has in fact agreed to the appropriation." *Per* Viscount Dilhorne in *Lawrence v. Metropolitan Police Commissioner* [1972] A.C. 626 at 632.
[27] *Lawrence* [1971] 1 Q.B. 373, *per* Megaw L.J. at 377.
[28] *Attorney-General's Reference (No. 2 of 1982)* [1984] 2 Q.B. 624, *per* Kerr L.J. at 641.
[29] §2–132.

handing the thing to the police, advertising for the owner or taking other steps. For the purpose of the law of theft the finder may make his own assess ment (i) of the likely outcome of the steps he might take, and (ii) (it is sug-gested[30]) of the reasonableness in the circumstances of his being required to take them. As to (i), the law seems strict in requiring a belief that the owner cannot be discovered rather than that he is unlikely to be. As to (ii), the law (if the suggestion here is correct) is both generous, in that liability for theft depends to this extent on the accused's own moral standard, and paradoxical, in that the less natural it is to him to put himself out for his neighbour, the less likely is his appropriation of his neighbour's goods to be dishonest.

Other cases besides those of finders fall within section 2(1)(c)—for instance, that of the person who gets property by another's mistake but does not know how, by reasonable steps, to identify or trace the person to whom he should make restoration.

A willingness to pay for the property

2–131   If D knows that P is unwilling to sell property to him, D cannot claim that his appropriation of the property was necessarily honest just because he was prepared to pay for it or, indeed, because he actually paid P's asking price or a reasonable price for the property. A provision designed to exclude an argu-ment to the contrary is contained in section 2(2).

Situations not within section 2(1): two questions for the jury

2–132   In any case not turning on an alleged belief within section 2(1), the quest-ion whether D appropriated the property in question "dishonestly" (if it is a live issue) is, as the authorities stand, for decision by the tribunal of fact; what is "dishonest" is not a question of law. The leading case of *Ghosh*[31] requires that for a finding of dishonesty there should be affirmative answers to two questions:

(1) Was what was done dishonest according to the ordinary standards of reasonable and honest people?
(2) Must D have realised that what he was doing was dishonest according to those standards?

When is dishonesty a live issue?

2–133   A direction in terms of the *Ghosh* questions need not, and indeed should not, always be given. The cases make clear, in particular, that the second question need not be explicitly posed if there is no evidence to suggest that D

---

[30] *Contra*, Williams, *Textbook* (1st ed.), p. 664.
[31] [1982] Q.B. 1053. Trial judges have been advised to use the precise words of Lord Lane C.J. in this case when directing juries: *Ravenshad* [1990] Crim.L.R. 398; and see *Green* [1992] Crim.L.R. 292.

believed that what he did was honest by ordinary people's standards.[32] But the Court of Appeal has tended to say that, if there is no such evidence, there is normally no need for "a *Ghosh* direction" at all—not just a lack of need to ask the second question. The reason is clear. A jury need hardly be asked as a matter of routine whether shoplifting, street mugging, a bank hold-up or obtaining property by deception is dishonest by prevailing social standards. If it is proved that D appropriated P's property with the intention of permanently depriving him of it, there would seem to be, at least in most cases, a clear prima facie case of theft. To render dishonesty a live issue there is need of further evidence—either evidence of a belief falling within section 2(1); or evidence capable of inducing a reasonable jury to deny condemnation of the appropriation as dishonest[33]; or evidence capable of raising a doubt as to whether D knew that others would regard his conduct as dishonest.

Background to the Ghosh questions

The first question. The first of the *Ghosh* questions derives from the earlier **2–134** Court of Appeal decision in *Feely*,[34] in which it was held that, the word "dishonestly" being "an ordinary word of the English language" which is "in common use", the jury do not need the help of the judge in its application.[35] They should simply decide whether an appropriation was dishonest by applying "the current standards of ordinary decent people".[36] For this purpose, of course, the jury may be taken to represent ordinary decent standards; they are in effect being invited, and may be expressly invited,[37] to apply their own standards.

In *Feely* itself D, the manager of a betting shop, took about £30 from his employers' safe. He left no IOU or other record of the transaction and did not tell his employers. His defence, when charged with theft, was that he would have repaid the money. The trial judge directed the jury that this commonplace defence was no defence in law. If D did not believe that his

---

[32] *Roberts* (1987) 84 Cr.App.R. 117 (handling); *Price* (1989) 90 Cr.App.R. 409 (deception offences); *Squire* [1990] Crim.L.R. 341 (conspiracy to defraud); and see *Hagan* [1985] Crim.L.R. 598 (intent to defraud). What the Court of Appeal has tended to say is that "a *Ghosh* direction"—not simply its second, "subjective" limb—need not be given unless there is evidence that D did not realise that others would regard his conduct as dishonest; and in *Brennen* [1990] Crim.L.R. 118 it was held to be a misdirection (so serious as to exclude application of the proviso) to say that D was guilty if the first *Ghosh* question was answered in the affirmative—even though there was no evidence on which the second question could be answered negatively. *Sed quaere?* If there is no such evidence, is not the second question a pointless ritual?
[33] For suggestions as to the limited scope of the jury issue, see below, §2–140.
[34] [1973] Q.B. 530.
[35] *ibid.* at 537–538; citing in support Lord Reid in *Brutus v. Cozens* [1973] A.C. 854 at 861: "The meaning of an ordinary word of the English language is not a question of law"—but for the "decline and fall" of this largely "ineffectual" dictum, see D. W. Elliott [1989] Crim.L.R. 323.
[36] In *Ghosh* "ordinary decent people" became "reasonable and honest people". Arlidge and Parry, para. 1.24, are tempted by, but seem in the end to reject, the possibility that "honest" people are a narrower category than "ordinary" people. Surely the reference in *Ghosh* to "honest" people is hopelessly circular and must be a slip.
[37] See, for example, the direction in *Green and Greenstein* (1975) 61 Cr.App.R. 296 at 301, approved by the Court of Appeal; *McIvor* (1981) 74 Cr.App.R. 74 at 78.

employers would have consented to his taking the money (and they had in fact prohibited the practice of borrowing from the till), he was guilty of theft even if he intended to repay, however soon, and had the means to do so. This was held to be a misdirection. Whether D had acted dishonestly was for the jury to say. D's conviction was quashed.

2–135   *The second question.* It is one thing to refer to the tribunal of fact the question whether the defendant's conduct was dishonest and therefore theft, rather than resolving the matter as a question of law. It would be quite another thing to refer the question to the defendant himself! Yet, for a time, it appeared that the courts were flirting even with this approach. There were statements in some judgments to the effect that if, at the time of his act, D may have believed that he was acting honestly, he would be entitled to an acquittal.[38] On this basis, a jury would seem to be required to prefer D's code of conduct to their own where the two appear to differ.

Perhaps these statements were merely badly expressed. On their face, however, they threatened rather serious consequences for the law of theft and other offences of dishonesty. A subsequent attempt by the Court of Appeal to clarify the law having proved unsuccessful,[39] the same court in *Ghosh* reasserted the authority of the principle in *Feely*, but (for a reason to be mentioned below[40]) added for the jury's consideration the second question, referring not to D's view of the honesty of his conduct but to his knowledge of the view that would be taken by "ordinary people."

Objections to the two questions[41]

2–136   The decisions in *Feely* and *Ghosh* have been regretted by most commentators. The objections to them include the following:

(i) *Feely*.[42] The *Feely* principle depends upon two related assumptions. One is that "dishonestly", because it is an "ordinary word", has an agreed range of meaning that the jury will identify without judicial help. But it is not true that all speakers of a language will necessarily share the same sense of the application or non-application of an "ordinary word" in a particular context. Even judges, a relatively homogeneous group of uniformly high linguistic competence, have been known to differ on the application of the epithet

---

[38] See *Boggeln v. Williams* (1978) 67 Cr.App.R. 50 at 54; *Landy* (1981) 72 Cr.App.R. 237 at 247; and compare, before *Feely*, a dictum in *Gilks* (1972) 56 Cr.App.R. 734 at 738.
[39] *McIvor* (1981) 74 Cr.App.R. 74. (An additional problem deriving from *Landy*, above, and *McIvor* was an unsupportable discrepancy between conspiracy to defraud and theft in respect of the test for dishonesty. This discrepancy was eliminated by *Ghosh* [1982] Q.B. 1053.)
[40] §2–138.
[41] See, more fully, [1985] Crim.L.R. 341.
[42] The most elaborate critiques of *Feely* are those of the Supreme Court of Victoria in *Salvo* [1980] V.R. 401, *Bonollo* [1981] V.R. 633, and *Brow*, *ibid.* 783. See also Williams, *Textbook*, p. 725; Smith (A. T. H.), paras. 7–48 *et seq.*; D. W. Elliott [1976] Crim.L.R. 707; Griew, *Dishonesty and the Jury* (Leicester U.P., 1974). The critics are themselves criticised, and the allocation of the dishonesty issue to the jury is vigorously defended, by Richard Tur in A. Phillips Griffiths (ed.), *Philosophy and Practice* (C.U.P., 1985), pp. 75–96.

"dishonest" in a marginal case.[43] The other assumption is that there are shared community standards (the "standards of ordinary decent people"— that is, the jury[44]) for application in borderline, as well as in clear, cases. If this is not just another way of expressing the notion that people will agree upon the use of ordinary words, it can be nothing less than the assumption that "ordinary decent people", set to work by the word "dishonestly", will agree on the range of conduct that ought to be condemned as offences. To this there is the obvious objection that it ignores the great diversity of our very mixed society in terms of age, class, moral outlook and cultural background. The *Feely* question must tend, rather, to promote disagreement within individual juries and inconsistency of decision between different juries.

The above difficulties derive from a refusal to acknowledge that the dishonesty issue is one of law. The jury must, of course, find the facts: what did the defendant do? and with what possible intention, belief or other state of mind that is relevant within the law of the offence charged? It is the function of the law, it is submitted, to say whether so behaving, with such a state of mind, is dishonest and therefore an offence. This appears to have been the previous law.[45] In proposing the new form of the law, the C.L.R.C. did casually refer to dishonesty as "something which laymen can easily recognise when they see it"[46]; but it is difficult to find warrant, either in the *Eighth Report* read as a whole or in a comparison of the form of the legislation with what it replaced, for the supposition that a revolution such as *Feely* effected was intended by the substitution of the word "dishonestly" for the word "fraudulently" which had occurred in the definition of larceny.[47] **2–137**

(ii) *Ghosh*.[48] The question added by *Ghosh* (must D have realised that what he was doing was dishonest according to the ordinary standards being applied by the jury?[49]) is an even more dramatic innovation than the *Feely* question. It derives from a misapplication of the notion of a "state of mind". The Court of Appeal asserted that proof of dishonesty requires reference to D's state of mind. So, on any view, it undoubtedly does, whenever there is any evidence suggesting that D's appropriation of P's property may not have been dishonest. For there must then be a finding as to whether he may have **2–138**

---

[43] *Sinclair v. Neighbour* [1967] 2 Q.B. 279.
[44] There is a substantial literature on the dishonesty of "ordinary decent people"; see, *e.g.* J. Ditton, *Part-Time Crime*; S. Henry, *The Hidden Economy*. Are all jurors truly to apply their own standards?
[45] The relevant modern cases on larceny were *Williams* [1953] Q.B. 660; *Cockburn* (1967) 52 Cr.App.R. 134. For a valuable article just before the decision in *Feely*, see D. W. Elliott [1972] Crim.L.R. 625.
[46] *Eighth Report*, para. 39.
[47] See further [1985] Crim.L.R. 341 at 349. But see Glanville Williams (1985) 5 L.S. 183 at 188–89, seeming to reveal that the C.L.R.C. did indeed expect that the jury might be left without guidance.
[48] See Smith (J. C.), para. 2–114; Williams, *Textbook*, p. 728.
[49] Note: (a) the circularity of this question as part of a test for dishonesty; (b) the oddity of the question as satirised by J. R. Spencer [1982] C.L.J. 224: "What the jury thinks the defendant thought the jury would have thought."

acted with a belief or intention that might tend to negative dishonesty. May he (as he claims) have believed that he had a right to take the property or intended to repay the money taken? D's relevant state of mind once being found, however, the only question that should remain to be answered is whether section 2(1) applies or (if not) whether the jury's sense of ordinary standards makes D's conduct with that state of mind dishonest. This is a question, not as to what state of mind D had, but as to how his state of mind is to be characterised. Dishonesty is not itself a "state of mind" in the same sense that belief as to a fact or intention as to future action is a "state of mind".

The Court of Appeal thought that the need to refer to D's "state of mind" entailed the asking of the second jury question as to D's understanding of what others would think dishonest. There is, with respect, a serious error in the court's reasoning at this point.[50] The error is clear to see when the court discusses the supposed case of a visitor from a country where public transport is free. He travels on a bus without paying. Does he do so dishonestly? The court says that "his conduct, judged objectively by what he has done, is dishonest." But this cannot be right. What the jury should judge by "ordinary standards" must be D's conduct as a whole—that is, his act in the context of the state of mind with which he did it.[51] In the case put, therefore, the jury will first have found that D believed (or may have believed) public transport to be free. Having so found, they can hardly declare his conduct dishonest. His state of mind has thus been taken into account in the only way necessary. The court, however, having mistakenly declared him dishonest when "judged objectively," has to introduce a further "subjective" element to rescue him. Hence the second question.

2–139   (iii) *Practical objection.* The Court of Appeal decisions on the dishonesty issue must have an important practical bearing on the administration of the criminal law. A different approach to the issue might make clear that given conduct was dishonest as a matter of law, and such clarity would tend to determine cases without need for a trial. *Feely* and *Ghosh*, however, provide two bases upon which it may be worth a defendant's while to take his chance with a jury.[52] He may advance a "state of mind" which would before *Feely* have offered no defence at all. Or he may claim not to have realised that others would condemn his actions. Such claims must multiply and lengthen trials; and it must be in the interests of some defendants to introduce as much evidence as possible on the dishonesty issue in order to obfuscate it. The

---

[50] [1982] Q.B. 1053 at 1063. The error is elaborately demonstrated by Kenneth Campbell [1984] C.L.J. 349.

[51] Physical acts are not in themselves honest or dishonest. The point is implicit in *Feely* itself; see, *e.g.* [1973] Q.B. 530 at 541.

[52] He is entitled to have the matter determined by the jury, however unreasonable an answer favourable to him would be: *D.P.P. v. Stonehouse* [1978] A.C. 55, for the general principle; and see *Clemo (Note)* [1973] R.T.R. 176; *Painter* [1983] Crim.L.R. 189. But an appeal based on an omission to leave the issue to the jury may fail on the ground that the jury could not but have found dishonesty: *e.g. Melwani* [1989] Crim.L.R. 565. An unreasonable acquittal by magistrates might be upset by the Divisional Court: *Bracegirdle v. Oxley* [1947] K.B. 349.

consequences in terms of expense and of increased difficulty for the jury, not to speak of the danger of unsatisfactory outcomes, are surely enough in themselves to raise serious doubts about the present state of the law.[53]

Dishonesty, laudable motive and necessity

It is submitted that matters of justification and excuse have nothing to do with the issue of dishonesty. A person charged with theft may claim that he acted with a laudable motive—perhaps in the interests of a moral or political crusade or, more prosaically, to save a commercial enterprise. This should not be recognised as a claim to have acted "honestly". Good motive being in principle irrelevant, it ought not to be allowed in by permitting the limiting adverb "dishonestly" an unlimited function. It cannot, for instance, be open to a jury to say (under the first *Ghosh* question) that a latterday Robin Hood, who takes from the rich to give to the poor, is not guilty of theft.[54] Nor can Robin claim (under the second *Ghosh* question) that he did not realise that others would say he had acted "dishonestly"; for that would simply be to admit to a misuse of the word. This may be the meaning of the decision of the Court of Appeal in *Buzalek and Schiffer*.[55] The basis of a prosecution for fraudulent trading was D's admitted lies to banks, causing losses of some £8 million. His defence was that he thought his lies justifiable in order to keep certain companies afloat. It was held that a *Ghosh* direction was not called for; D had admitted dishonesty. **2–140**

Even a claim to have acted from necessity (to save human life, perhaps) is not, it is thought, properly to be classified as a claim to have acted "honestly". If there is evidence that D was forced by "duress of circumstances" to appropriate P's property, he should be entitled to an acquittal of theft if he satisfies—but only if, and only because,[56] he satisfies—the conditions of the general defence now recognised under that name.[57]

The dishonesty issue as one of law

Section 2(1) declares some appropriations to be not dishonest as a matter of law. Moreover, the judgment in *Feely*[58] itself suggests that there are limits **2–141**

---

[53] Especially in fraud cases, to which equally the Court of Appeal decisions apply: *Ghosh* [1982] Q.B. 1053 at 1059 (deception offences; conspiracy to defraud); *Lockwood* [1986] Crim.L.R. 244 (fraudulent trading). See Fraud Trials Committee Report (H.M.S.O., 1986), paras. 3.4–3.8, 3.18 (calling for law reform consideration), and 8.16.

[54] Smith (J. C.), para. 2–114.

[55] [1991] Crim.L.R. 130.

[56] This, of course, is without prejudice to D's possible, but distinct, claim that he believed that P would consent if he knew of the situation of necessity: see s.2(1)(b), above, §2–129.

[57] See *Conway* [1989] Q.B. 290; *Martin* (1988) 88 Cr.App.R. 343. Contrast the view of the Law Commission in *Report on Defences of General Application* (Law Com. No. 83), para. 4.5, that "proof of dishonesty in theft may perhaps be negatived if, although the defendant knows an appropriation is without the owner's consent, he takes the property to avoid a greater evil, for example, to save life"; and, less tentatively, at para. 4.17: "Discussion of the defence [*sc.* of necessity] in the context of theft has now been settled by the terms of the Theft Act 1968."

[58] Above, §2–134.

to the principle that in other cases it is a question for the tribunal of fact whether the conduct charged was dishonest. The case is put of a person acting in a way "to which no one would, or could reasonably, attach moral obloquy".[59] To hold the case to be theft, it is said, "would tend to bring the law into contempt". The point is generalised: "a taking to which no moral obloquy can reasonably attach is not within the concept of stealing ... under the Theft Act 1968".[60] It appears to be proper, therefore, to instruct a jury that the meaning of the word "dishonestly" is limited at least to this extent as a matter of law. And a direction to acquit is surely contemplated in the case put.

2–142   The limiting function of the word "dishonestly" in offences under the Theft Acts is not at present a matter of law except to the extent stated in the preceding paragraph. What is submitted here, however, is that the law should play a much more active role in identifying the scope of dishonesty offences. In the light of the case law, it is hardly open to the Court of Appeal to bring this about; but the House of Lords could do so. It might, for example, hold that the word "dishonestly" in the definition of an offence operates to exclude from the scope of the offence only cases of claim of right (as well as any, or any other, cases expressly excluded by statute)[61]; or only such cases and those involving no "moral obloquy". Another suggestion has been that in the case of theft "dishonestly" might be interpreted to mean "knowing that the appropriation will or may be detrimental to the interests of the owner in a significant practical way"[62]—a suggestion that could be modified to suit the needs of other offences. Alternatively (and preferably) this suggestion might be taken up by Parliament as a basis of remedial legislation.[63]

7. THEFT OF THINGS IN ACTION AND OTHER INTANGIBLE PROPERTY

2–143   Any kind of property can be the subject of theft. But the ways in which different kinds of intangible property can be stolen are variously limited by the lack of available modes of appropriation and, more seriously, by the difficulty of depriving of the property the person to whom it belongs. Nevertheless, anyone—such as a trustee, co-owner or agent for sale—who has the power to dispose of property can steal that property by a disposition intended to defeat the interests of others to whom the property belongs.[64]

---

[59] The case is "that of a manager of a shop who, having been told that under no circumstances was he to take money from the till for his own purposes, took 40p from it, having no small change himself, to pay for a taxi hired by his wife who had arrived at the shop saying that she only had a £5 note which the cabby could not change."

[60] [1973] Q.B. 530 at 539.

[61] This is the tendency of the Victorian decisions referred to at n. 42, above.

[62] *Per* McGarvie J. in *Bonollo* [1981] V.R. 633 at 656; Smith (J. C.), para. 2–116.

[63] D. W. Elliott [1982] Crim.L.R. 395, suggesting that dishonesty is "a dispensable concept". For competing draft provisions, see *ibid.*, at 409–410; Glanville Williams (1985) 5 L.S. 183 at 189; P. R. Glazebrook [1993] C.L.J. 191 at 193.

[64] See above, §2–31; *Attorney-General of Hong Kong v. Nai-keung* (1987) 86 Cr.App.R. 174.

Moreover, both the *Morris* interpretation of the definition of appropriation as including an assumption of any of the rights of an owner,[65] and a statutory softening of the requirement of an intention of permanently depriving the victim of the property,[66] do something to facilitate the theft of intangibles. These points are illustrated in a separate discussion, below, of the theft of bank credits.[67]

Theft of certain kinds of property may be impossible in the absence of a   **2–144** power to dispose of the property or to control its disposition. The point may be illustrated by reference to trade marks, copyright and trade secrets (assuming, for the sake of discussion, the last to be a species of "property"[68]):

(i) *Trade marks*. The obvious case to be considered is the dishonest infringement of a trade mark, as by using the mark upon goods of the same description as that to which it applies. This may be an appropriation—an assumption of the rights of the owner in the trade mark. Yet there can hardly be said to be an intention to deprive the owner of the trade mark itself.[69] The infringement is therefore no theft.

(ii) *Copyright*. If D publishes copies of P's literary work without P's licence to do so, he may popularly be said to "steal" the benefit of P's skill and labour. He may also be said to appropriate P's copyright in the work by assuming one of P's exclusive rights, as copyright owner, in it.[70] Even so, he does not do so with the effect, or the intention, of depriving P of the copyright and so does not steal.[71]

(iii) *Trade secrets*. Even if trade secrets were "property", they would be difficult to steal. No doubt we may in a loose sense say that D "appropriates" P's secret if he dishonestly acquires the knowledge that P has a right to preserve to himself or makes use of the knowledge that P alone has the right to use. But D does not thereby deprive P of his knowledge: he deprives him only of an advantage attaching to it—its exclusiveness. On that analysis the thing appropriated is not the same as that of which P is deprived; but the basic definition of theft requires that it shall be ("appropriates property . . . with the intention of depriving [P] of it"). The conclusion must be that trade secrets cannot in general be stolen. But exceptional situations might be envisaged. For instance, D seduces from P's employment a chemist, Q, who alone knows a formula developed by Q for P; and D elicits from Q both the formula and the promise to keep it secret from P. This would satisfy the definition of theft, if secrets were property.[72]

---

[65] See above, §2–69.
[66] s.6: see above, §2–104.
[67] §§2–151, 2–155.
[68] Which they almost certainly are not: see above, §2–25.
[69] D can hardly be said to intend "to treat the thing as his own *to dispose of*"; so s.6(1) should not affect this case; but *cf.* below, §2–155.
[70] Copyright, Designs and Patents Act 1988, ss.1(1), 2(1).
[71] He may be guilty of an offence under the Copyright, Designs and Patents Act 1988, s.107.
[72] The oddity of acknowledging only such unlikely cases as theft is noted in *Stewart v. The Queen* (1988) 50 D.L.R. (4th) 1 at 14, as an argument against recognising confidential information as capable of being stolen.

Theft of bank credits[73]

2-145   A theft charge cannot be made out by proving that a company is so many
millions of pounds worse off as the result of the depredations of, say, a dishonest director or accountant. It must be shown that, with the required intention, he appropriated particular property belonging to the company.[74]
English law possesses no widely-defined general offence of fraud.[75] So, since
large frauds within organisations almost inevitably involve the abuse of
intangible assets such as bank accounts, the concept of the appropriation of
such assets must be capable of flexible exploitation if the law of theft is to
make an adequate contribution to the control of serious fraud. The topic now
to be examined is plainly of the first importance.

Bank credits as "property belonging to another"

2-146   *"Property".* When a bank account is in credit, the account holder has
"property" in the form of a thing in action—a claim available against the
bank as his debtor.[76] If he has an enforceable overdraft arrangement with the
bank, this too, it has been held, gives him "property" within the meaning of
that word in the Theft Act so long as the overdraft facility has not been
exhausted by drawings on the account.[77] At any time, however, when the
account is in debit and no right to draw on it exists, the account holder has no
relevant property capable of being stolen by abuse of the account.[78] It is plain
that, when possible theft of a bank credit or overdraft facility is under consideration, careful examination of the banking relationship and of the history
of the account in the relevant period may be necessary to establish whether
there was property available to steal at the time of a suggested
appropriation.[79]

2-147   *D's account as property "belonging to another".* Credit in an account may
be capable of being stolen by an account holder himself if it is to be regarded
as also "belonging to" another person by virtue of section 5. This will be the
case if D and P have a joint account upon which D may draw only for the
common purposes of himself and P[80]; if the account is one which D holds or
controls as a trustee[81]; if the account, wholly or in part, represents property
received by D which he is obliged to retain as a distinct fund and to apply only
for the purposes of the persons from, or on account of, whom he received it[82];
or if the credit derives from an erroneous transfer of funds by P to D's

---

[73] See further, [1986] Crim.L.R. 356.
[74] See above, §2-26.
[75] See below, §7-22.
[76] See above, §2-17.
[77] *Kohn* (1979) 69 Cr.App.R. 395.
[78] *ibid.* at 408. Nor can there be theft of a merely contingent liability: *Doole* [1985] Crim.L.R. 450.
[79] See [1986] Crim.L.R. at 359–360.
[80] Credit in the account "belongs to" P: s.5(1).
[81] Credit in the account "belongs to" the beneficiaries or to anyone having a right to enforce the
trust: s.5(1)(2).
[82] Credit in the account "belongs to" those persons: s.5(3).

account, or from a payment by D into his account of funds mistakenly paid to him by P.[83]

Appropriation of bank credits

Some elementary background principles. A legitimate dealing with a bank   **2–148**
credit takes place when the bank pays cash or transfers funds on the instructions (or "mandate") of the account holder, or one acting with his authority, and debits the account accordingly. If an instruction given to the bank does not constitute a mandate upon which the bank is entitled to act by making a payment against the account, a debiting of the account on the strength of that instruction is nugatory: the bank will be obliged to restore the debit or (to put it another way) the bank continues to be its customer's debtor to the same extent as before.
   A cheque issued by a bank's customer (the drawer) in favour of a third party (the payee) is an instruction by the drawer to the bank to pay to the payee (or subsequent holder) the amount for which the cheque is drawn. Payment of a crossed cheque must be to a bank; only if the cheque is uncrossed may payment be in cash. The drawing of a cheque in favour of a payee has no legal consequences until the cheque is delivered to the payee. When it is so delivered, the drawer becomes bound to honour the cheque if the bank fails to do so. But the issue of the cheque gives the payee no right against the drawer's bank; nothing in the transaction operates as an assignment to the payee of the debt represented by the credit in the drawer's account.[84]

Appropriation by authorised signatory. In the seminal case of *Kohn*,[85] D   **2–149**
was a company director who had authority to issue cheques for company purposes. He improperly issued cheques upon the company's account for his own purposes. The Court of Appeal upheld convictions of theft in respect, in the case of each cheque,[86] of the credit (or the overdraft facility) available to the company and appropriated by D. The court accepted the analysis of this kind of transaction offered in earlier editions of this book—namely, that D appropriates the debt owed by the bank, or part of it, by causing the company's credit balance to be diminished, or at least taking the risk of such diminution. The case was said to be analogous to the theft of a chattel by destruction. This analysis, however, now appears not to be adequate, for two reasons. First, it does not commit itself to a view as to when the appropriation takes place—whether on the debiting of the account ("diminution") or on the issue of the cheque ("taking the risk of . . . diminution"). This question is discussed below.[87] Secondly, the analysis is inadequate for the case of an act giving the bank no right to debit the account.

---

[83] For the application of s.5(4) to the case of credit got by mistake, see above, §2–50.
[84] Bills of Exchange Act 1882, s.53(1).
[85] (1979) 69 Cr.App.R. 395.
[86] Except in one case, where the account was overdrawn beyond the agreed limit, so that there was no property to appropriate: see above, text at n. 78.
[87] §2–151.

2–150   *Appropriation by act giving the bank no mandate.* In *Chan Man-sin v. R.*[88] the accountant of two companies, by using forged cheques, withdrew some millions of Hong Kong dollars from the bank accounts of the companies. His appeal to the Judicial Committee of the Privy Council against theft convictions[89] was based upon the undoubted fact that, as between the companies and their banks, the transactions were nullities; the banks could not sustain debits to the companies' accounts that were based on forgeries; there could be no "diminution" of the things in action said to have been stolen. The Judicial Committee nevertheless held that the appellant had appropriated the things in action: "[a]ny assumption of the rights of an owner amounts to an appropriation" (section 3(1)); this provision does not require the assumption of all the rights of an owner[90]; it was enough that the appellant had assumed the right of the companies as owners of the accounts to draw upon them. This reasoning[91] must be taken to have replaced that adopted in *Kohn*.

2–151   *When and where does the theft occur?* In *Chan Man-sin* the Judicial Committee left open the question whether theft is complete on the doing of the acts which will result in the debiting of the bank account, or only when the account is actually debited.[92] Once it is decided, however, that the appropriation consists of D's assumption of the owner's right to deal with the account, the conclusion seems inevitable that theft is complete when he does the act that constitutes that assumption. The Divisional Court subsequently so held in *Governor of Pentonville Prison, ex p. Osman.*[93] It was alleged in that case that D, in Hong Kong, had transmitted a telex message conveying an instruction to a bank in the United States relating to an account held at that bank. The question (arising under the Fugitive Offenders Act 1967[94]) was whether the act of sending this message could constitute a theft, committed in Hong Kong, of the credit in that account. It was held that it could.

A similar point had arisen earlier in *Tomsett*.[95] In that case the Court of Appeal had rejected an argument that an agreement to send a telex instruction from England to New York in relation to funds temporarily on deposit there might found a conspiracy to steal in England[96] because the funds in question were those of an English company. The court applied the principle that an appropriation, and therefore theft, of property prima facie occurs where the property is situated, and a debt is situated where the debtor is—in that case New York. But the court in *Osman* (consisting of two of the three

---

[88] (1987) 86 Cr.App.R. 303.
[89] Under the Theft Ordinance (Hong Kong), identical in relevant respects to the 1968 Act.
[90] Applying the equivalent of s.3(1), as interpreted in *Morris* [1984] A.C. 320 (above, §2–69).
[91] Applied by the Court of Appeal shortly before in *Wille* (1988) 86 Cr.App.R. 296.
[92] (1987) 86 Cr.App.R. 303 at 306. See also *Kohn* (1979) 69 Cr.App.R. 395 at 407 (*obiter*); *Doole* [1985] Crim.L.R. 450; *Navvabi* (1986) 83 Cr.App.R. 271 at 276.
[93] (1988) 90 Cr.App.R. 281 at 296–297.
[94] Repealed and replaced by the Extradition Act 1989.
[95] [1985] Crim.L.R. 369.
[96] So as to give an English court jurisdiction in relation to the conspiracy. For the effect of Part I of the Criminal Justice Act 1993, when in force, on jurisdiction in relation to conspiracy to commit theft abroad, see below, §17–09.

judges who had decided *Tomsett*) did not regard *Tomsett* as binding on it on the question whether the typing of the telex message was itself an appropriation, for it had not been argued in the earlier case that it was.

Where D, for his own purposes, draws a cheque on P's account in favour of   **2–152**
E (whether by forging P's signature or by abuse of his own status as authorised signatory), his theft of credit in the account appears to be complete when he delivers the cheque to E. If he draws a cheque in his own favour, language used in *Chan Man-sin*[97] seems to imply an understandable assumption that theft will occur at the earliest when he presents the cheque for payment or negotiates it to a third party.

An act continuing until account debited? The conclusion that theft of P's   **2–153**
bank credit is complete when D assumes any right of an owner in it, as by delivering to a payee a cheque drawn upon it or sending to the bank an instruction relating to it, may exceptionally give rise to a serious practical problem. It could require an investigation of the state of the account at the moment when D delivered the cheque or sent the instruction. For if the account were then overdrawn (beyond any agreed limit), there will have been no relevant property belonging to P for D to steal. Yet it may be difficult or impossible to show at what time D's relevant act (*e.g.* the issue of a post-dated cheque) took place. This problem would not arise if the time of the theft were the time of the debiting of the account; for there need be no doubt about the state of the account at that time.[98] A possible solution, not excluded by the cases, is to treat D's act as continuing (as an appropriation or potential appropriation) until the account is debited. Whenever the account is first in credit up to that time, the act would take effect as an appropriation of the property then existing. On that view it would be sufficient, in order to prove that a theft has occurred, to show that the account was in credit at the time of the debiting, if not before.[99]

The intention of permanently depriving P of the bank credit

D's act a mandate on which bank can act. Where D's dishonest act in deal-   **2–154**
ing with P's bank account is an effective mandate entitling the bank to debit the account, so that it will result, in the ordinary course of events, in a real diminution of the credit in the account (or of P's right to draw on the account), there is no difficulty about asserting that D intends, to that extent, to deprive P permanently of that credit (or right).[1]

D's act not a valid mandate. Where, however, D's act is not a mandate upon   **2–155**

---

[97] (1987) 86 Cr.App.R. at 306.
[98] See *Navvabi* (1986) 83 Cr.App.R. 271 at 276.
[99] If theft of a bank credit can continue from the doing of the appropriative act in one country to the debiting of the account in another, the theft may be located in both countries, with important consequences in relation to extradition.
[1] Even if he intends to repay P an equivalent amount or to restore the debited sum to the account: see above, §2–100.

which the bank is entitled to act, P's property—his right against the bank—will in law be unaffected by the transaction. If D knows this, it may safely be said that he does not intend P to lose his legal right; in the language of section 6(1)), he does not "[mean P] to lose the thing itself". Even so, he would, according to that provision, be regarded as intending to deprive P permanently of his property if his intention were "to treat the thing as his own to dispose of regardless of [P's] rights". Section 6(1) was invoked by the Judicial Committee in *Chan Man-sin v. Attorney-General of Hong Kong*,[2] a case of forged cheques, as the basis for summarily dismissing the argument that the necessary intention cannot have been present. But the Board justified reliance on the section by observing only that "the appellant was purporting *to deal with* the companies' property without regard to their rights".[3] This is no doubt so; but it is not clear how the appellant can be said to have intended to treat the thing in action as his own "to dispose of". The argument employed in *Chan Man-sin* seems inadequate. Still, it is submitted that it would be "[going] too far" to say that "unless the debit to the account can be sustained against the customer there can ... be no theft".[4] When goods are stolen (otherwise than by an act that destroys them) the owner is not deprived of his absolute interest in them but only of their enjoyment. A bank credit, similarly, may be affected by an act that is not a mandate to the bank. For so long as D's fraud remains undiscovered, the debit to the account that results from it will not be corrected and P will in a practical sense be deprived of his asset. D may reasonably be presumed to intend that his fraud should remain undetected, and therefore that the account will be permanently debited. The doubtful case, turning on the correctness of the application of section 6(1), must be that in which it appears that D intended to reveal his fraud in due course or knew that it was bound to be discovered.[5]

8. INFORMATIONS AND INDICTMENTS

One offence per count or information

2–156   Rule 1(2) of the Indictment Rules 1971 provides:

"Where more than one offence is charged in an indictment, the statement and particulars of each offence shall be set out in a separate paragraph called a count."

Rule 12 of the Magistrates' Courts Rules 1981 provides that "a magistrates'

---

[2] (1987) 86 Cr.App.R. 303 at 306.
[3] Emphasis supplied.
[4] The language of the Court of Appeal in *Doole* [1985] Crim.L.R. 450. See Arlidge and Parry, para. 3–05.
[5] When the fraud is discovered, the loser turns out to be the bank. But there is no theft from the bank: *Navvabi* (1986) 83 Cr.App.R. 271; above, §2–26. Other offences will commonly be available: *e.g.* theft of cheque; forgery; false accounting; conspiracy to defraud (if two or more are involved). The law of theft nevertheless needs amending to cater more clearly for this kind of case.

court shall not proceed to the trial of an information that charges more than one offence".[6]

Problems can arise in applying these rules where a person is alleged to have stolen a number of things on different occasions, or at different times and places on the same occasion; or where he is alleged to have stolen an amount of money or a number of items during a certain period, but the time or times at which he stole this or that amount or item cannot be demonstrated. Too narrow or technical a conception of an "offence" for the purpose of the rules quoted above could have serious consequences for the efficient prosecution of such cases. The courts have in fact avoided a restrictive view. They have tended rather to facilitate prosecution and conviction by the use of a number of concepts and devices.

One charge for a single "activity"

In *Wilson*,[7] an indictment for shoplifting contained two counts, among   **2–157** others, each of which related to D's conduct in a different store. In one count he was alleged to have stolen records and after-shave lotion from Boots; in the other, clothes of various kinds, electrical switches and a cassette tape from Debenhams. The evidence showed that in each of these stores the articles came from different "departments". The Court of Appeal applied a principle recently stated in the Divisional Court in relation to informations,[8] subsequently applied to indictments by the Court of Appeal,[9] and approved in the House of Lords in these terms: "it will often be legitimate to bring a single charge in respect of ... one activity even though that activity may involve more than one act".[10] The question whether the charge relates to one offence or to more than one is to be determined "by applying common sense and by deciding what is fair in the circumstances"[11]; it is "a question of fact and degree."[12] D's convictions on the two counts were upheld. Neither count, in the Court of Appeal's view, charged more than one offence, either on its face or in the light of the evidence.[13] In another case the court would even

---

[6] This rule is of reduced importance since the House of Lords decided that a magistrates' court may, if it is fair to do so, try two or more informations together without the consent of the defendant: *Chief Constable of Norfolk v. Clayton* [1983] 2 A.C. 473.

[7] (1979) 69 Cr.App.R. 83.

[8] *Jemmison v. Priddle* [1972] 1 Q.B. 489, *per* Lord Widgery C.J. at 495; compare *Cullen v. Jardine* [1985] Crim.L.R. 668.

[9] *Jones* (1974) 59 Cr.App.R. 120.

[10] *D.P.P. v. Merriman* [1973] A.C. 584, *per* Lord Morris of Borth-y-Gest at 593 (and see *per* Lord Diplock at 607).

[11] *ibid.*

[12] (1979) 69 Cr.App.R. at 88. See also *Heaton v. Costello* [1984] Crim.L.R. 485 (switching price labels on one article and smuggling another through the check-out may be a single activity).

[13] The court found "not clear at all" the facts of *Ballysingh* (1953) 37 Cr.App.R. 28, where a count charging theft from (as the evidence showed) several "departments" of a store was regarded as defective. They appeared to contemplate that thefts from different departments of a large store like Harrods might not necessarily constitute a single activity (69 Cr.App.R. at 88). But see *D.P.P. v. McCabe* [1992] Crim.L.R. 885 (below, §2–158).

have been prepared, if necessary, to apply the "activity" test to sanction a single theft charge where a bogus haulage contractor loaded greengrocery in three different parts of London, for carriage on the instructions of the same principal.[14]

One charge for a "continuous" offence

2–158   A number of cases decided before the Indictments Act 1915 concerned, respectively, mining operations conducted continuously over four years, involving the taking of coal belonging to many persons[15]; the cutting of eight trees with intent to steal them during a tree-felling operation carried out in a particular season[16]; the abstraction of gas from a main, by-passing the meter, day after day for several years[17]; and pilfering identified articles from an employer, the articles being found in the accused's possession on the day named in the indictment as that of the offence.[18] In each of these cases the course of conduct was held to constitute a "continuous taking". A case that seems to be of the same type is *D.P.P. v. McCabe*,[19] in which D was found to have 76 library books which could have come from as many as 32 different branches of a public library over a period of a year or more. A single charge of stealing them between specified dates was held to be appropriate.[20]

One charge for a "general deficiency"

2–159   If a trustee, agent or employee is unable to account for property held or received by him as such, it may be provable that he has at some time within a certain period appropriated part or the whole of the property but impossible to show just when such an appropriation occurred or, indeed, whether there was only one appropriation or more than one. In such a case a conviction may be had upon an indictment charging theft of the whole deficiency on a date between specified dates (or even on a particular date if, as is usually the case, the date of the theft is immaterial).[21]

---

[14] *Skipp* [1975] Crim.L.R. 114.
[15] *Bleasdale* (1848) 2 Car. & K. 765.
[16] *Shepherd* (1868) L.R. 1 C.C.R. 118.
[17] *Firth* (1869) L.R. 1 C.C.R. 173.
[18] *Henwood* (1870) 11 Cox 526.
[19] [1992] Crim.L.R. 885. But the decision was said to be justified by the principle operating in the "general deficiency" cases, next mentioned in the text.
[20] A single charge should not be used, however, where it is clear that different defences may be advanced in relation to different items: *Jackson, The Guardian*, November 20, 1991, C.A. no. 91/5435/X3.
[21] *Hallam and Blackburn*, [1995] Crim.L.R. 323, applying *Tomlin* [1954] 2 Q.B. 274 (embezzlement). See also, under the pre-existing law, *Balls* (1871) L.R. 1 C.C.R. 328; *Lawson* (1952) 36 Cr.App.R. 30; *Wilson v. Read* [1956] Crim.L.R. 418. Compare *Cain* [1983] Crim.L.R. 802 (handling). In *Tomlin* the court insisted (at p. 282) that "in the ordinary case, where it is possible to trace the individual items and to prove a conversion of individual property or money, it is undesirable to include them all in a count charging a general deficiency."

Moreover, the time of any appropriation being unknown, it may also not be known in what form the property was held at that time. D, an investment adviser, receives a cheque from P, a client, for the purchase of policies or bonds. At various times thereafter D may hold the cheque, or a resulting credit in his bank account, or payments from third parties by cheque or otherwise representing the proceeds of P's policies or bonds, or the proceeds in one form or another of such payments. If it cannot be shown at what time or times in the history of the transaction D dishonestly appropriated property (whether cheque, cash or thing in action) which belonged to P by virtue of section 5(1), (2) or (3), D can be convicted of theft of "the sum of £x"—the value of P's original cheque or of any proceeds shown to have been received by D.[22]

Conviction based on defective indictment

A summary conviction obtained upon an information that is bad for duplicity must be quashed if challenged; the magistrates' court had no jurisdiction to try the information.[23] But on appeal against conviction on indictment it may be held that, although strictly the indictment was defective, no miscarriage of justice has occurred—the defendant not having been prejudiced in his defence by the form of the indictment[24] or his counsel having refrained from objection at the trial.[25] The proviso to section 2(1) of the Criminal Appeal Act 1968 may be applied and the appeal dismissed.   **2–160**

Theft of part or whole of a collection or quantity

On a charge of stealing several specific items there may be a conviction of stealing some of them if theft of them all is not proved.[26] The same principle should apply if what is charged is theft of an undifferentiated whole and theft of part only is proved. For theft of part of such a larger quantity is perfectly possible.[27] In *Gilks*,[28] for instance, P paid D £117.25 in cash when, as D realised, he should have paid £10.62. It was held that D was guilty of theft of £106.63.   **2–161**

If D is charged with stealing a part of a larger unit of property, he can be convicted as charged although it is proved that he stole the whole unit. Thus, in *Pilgram v. Rice-Smith*[29] D, a shop assistant, "sold" corned beef and bacon to her friend, at 83½p below the proper price. This was theft of all the meat, not merely, as the information alleged, of meat to the value of 83½p. It was held that this fact would not prevent a conviction on the information as laid.

---

[22] *Hallam and Blackburn*, above; see also *Rader* [1992] Crim.L.R. 663.
[23] See the terms of rule 12 (above, §2–156).
[24] *Thompson* [1914] 2 K.B. 99.
[25] *Ballysingh* (1953) 37 Cr.App.R. 28.
[26] *Machent v. Quinn* [1970] 2 All E.R. 255.
[27] Smith, *Theft*, para. 2–100, citing *Tideswell* [1905] 2 K.B. 273.
[28] (1972) 56 Cr.App.R. 734. Compare *Levene v. Pearcey* [1976] Crim.L.R. 63 (below, §8–03).
[29] (1977) 65 Cr.App.R. 142.

9. ABSTRACTING OF ELECTRICITY; DISHONEST USE OF PUBLIC TELECOMMUNICATION SYSTEM

2–162   The peculiar nature of electricity necessitates special provision for its dishonest use.[30] Section 13 provides:

> "A person who dishonestly uses without due authority, or dishonestly causes to be wasted or diverted, any electricity shall on conviction on indictment be liable to imprisonment for a term not exceeding five years."

2–163   *Using electricity.* The offence does not depend upon any tampering with a meter.[31]

2–164   *Dishonesty.* The partial definition of "dishonestly" in section 2 is not made to apply for the purposes of this section (s.1(3)). So a person who believes that he has a legal right to use electricity, even without authority, or that the supplier or consumer concerned would consent if he knew of the use, is not on that account, as a matter of law, to be regarded as not dishonest (compare s.2(1)(a) and (b)). But it would be very unsatisfactory if a court or jury, although of the view that the defendant may have acted with such a belief, should nevertheless not acquit him in answer to the applicable question: was what he did dishonest by ordinary decent standards?[32]

Collins and Fox v. Chief Constable of Merseyside[33] concerned domestic use of electricity, unrecorded because the voltage link of the meter had been disconnected. It was said that dishonesty in such use required knowledge of the non-recording and an intention that the consumption should not be paid for. This statement seems too generous to the defence. In theft, a person's appropriation of property "may be dishonest" notwithstanding that he is willing to pay for it (s.2(2)); and the prevailing approach to the dishonesty issue would make it a question for the jury whether particular use is not dishonest because it is intended to be paid for.[34]

2–165   *Using public telecommunication system.* A person who dishonestly uses a public telecommunication system with intent to avoid payment is guilty of an offence under section 48 of the British Telecommunications Act 1981.[35]

---

[30] Electricity is not "property" and cannot be stolen: *Low v. Blease* [1975] Crim.L.R. 513.

[31] *McCreadie and Tume* [1992] Crim.L.R. 872.

[32] *Ghosh* [1982] Q.B. 1053 (above, §2–132); compare *Woolven* (1983) 77 Cr.App.R. 231 (below, §8–76).

[33] [1988] Crim.L.R. 247.

[34] *Ghosh*, above.

[35] Replacing an offence (under the Post Office Act 1953) created by the Theft Act 1968, Sched. 2, Pt. I, para. 8.

Chapter 3

ROBBERY

1. DEFINITION

Section 8(2) creates two offences, both punishable on conviction on indict- **3-01**
ment with life imprisonment: robbery and assault with intent to rob. They are
not triable summarily.[1]

Robbery is defined in section 8(1):

> "A person is guilty of robbery if he steals, and immediately before or at the time of
> doing so, and in order to do so, he uses force on any person or puts or seeks to put
> any person in fear of being then and there subjected to force."

Although this language (in the references to force and to putting in fear)
contains pronounced echoes of the somewhat unclear and unsatisfactory
offence that, together with certain aggravated offences, was latterly penalised by the Larceny Act 1916, it is not appropriate to resort to the old cases to
elaborate the new definition; and the Court of Appeal, indeed, has firmly
declined to flirt with "the old technicalities".[2]

2. THE DETAILS OF THE OFFENCE

"Steals"

Section 1(3) provides that "steals" is to be construed in accordance with **3-02**
the definition of theft in section 1(1). That plainly refers to the word "steals"
in section 8(1) and an offence of theft within the meaning of the the Act is
therefore an essential ingredient of robbery (and an assault with intent to rob
requires an intention to commit theft).[3] So where D uses force or the threat of
force in order to get from P property that he believes he is entitled to, he does
not steal the property he obtains and the force or threat is not used in order to
steal.[4] It is therefore a misdirection to instruct a jury on a charge of robbery
that D can rely on a belief that he was entitled to deprive P of the property
only if he also believed that he was entitled to get the property in the way he
did.[5]

---

[1] Magistrates' Courts Act 1980, Sched. 1, para. 28(a).
[2] *Dawson* (1976) 64 Cr.App.R. 170.
[3] *Shendley* [1970] Crim.L.R. 49 (alternative verdict of theft); *Guy* [1991] Criml.L.R. 462 (robbery implied theft for the purpose of the Firearms Act 1968, Sched. 1—before its amendment by
the Criminal Justice and Public Order Act 1994, Sched. 9, para. 8). The indecisiveness on this
point in *Forrester* [1992] Crim.L.R. 793 is mystifying.
[4] s.2(1)(a) (above, §2–125).
[5] *Robinson* [1977] Crim.L.R. 173 (facts at §2–128, above); compare *Skivington* [1968] 1 Q.B.
166. (He would need something like the latter belief to avoid a conviction of blackmail: s.21.)

3–03   Where D has used force on P in order to steal from him but has failed to make himself master of P's property, it may be a nice question whether D has committed a robbery or only an assault with intent to rob. This depends on whether D's acts have amounted to an appropriation of any property or only to an attempted appropriation. This distinction has been discussed in the preceding chapter.[6] In any case in which appropriation is at all doubtful it will be preferable to charge assault with intent to rob (if the assault can be proved) or attempted theft.

"Uses force on" a person

3–04   The element of force in robbery, though expressed in simple language, involves questions that have called for judicial solution. They concern the meaning of "force" itself and the requirement that force be used "on [a] person".

"Force"

In *Dawson and James*,[7] two men nudged P so that he lost his balance, and while he was off balance a third man stole his wallet. The Court of Appeal appears to have approved of the approach of the trial judge in leaving it to the jury to decide whether jostling having such an unbalancing effect amounted to the use of force. This was open to the objection that, the matter being one for uniform decision, the court should have held plainly and affirmatively on the question as a matter of law, which it certainly did not do. Subsequently, however, in *Clouden*,[8] the court interpreted *Dawson* as having so held. Perhaps what the court meant was that, as the court in *Dawson* regarded the conviction before it as not improper, it must be treated as having held that jostling causing P to lose his balance is "force". For if it is in one case, it must be in another. And presumably a jury should now be told so. If that is the position, the outcome is satisfactory.

"On [a] person"

3–05   *Clouden* also rather puzzlingly regarded *Dawson* as being an authority on a question with which it seems not to have been at all concerned: that is, the question whether force is used "on [a] person" within the meaning of section 8 when the force is used against property in order to detach the property from the person. The C.L.R.C. said on this point:

> "We should not regard mere snatching of property, such as a handbag, from an unresisting owner, as using force for the purpose of the definition, though it might be so if the owner resisted."[9]

---

[6] See §2–74, discussing *Corcoran v. Anderton* (1980) 71 Cr.App.R. 104, a robbery case.
[7] (1976) 64 Cr.App.R. 170.
[8] [1987] Crim.L.R. 56; but this brief report does not reflect some aspects of the judgment referred to in the text.
[9] *Eighth Report*, para. 65.

Just such a case was nevertheless held to be capable of being robbery in *Clouden*, where D approached P from behind and wrenched her handbag down and out of her grasp. *Dawson* was mysteriously said to "[make] it quite plain that ... the distinctions which formerly undoubtedly existed[10] between force on the actual person and force on the property which in fact causes force on the person have all gone". Whether D was guilty of robbery had been properly left to the jury, who had simply been told the terms of the statutory definition.

Three comments may be made. First, this case in its turn presumably establishes that force on property "which in fact causes force on the person" is force "on [the] person". Once again the court was content with a direction that left the point to the jury; but once again it has no doubt decided a point of law. Secondly, it ought to be held that force is not used "on" P unless D realises that P may feel the effect of the force; for otherwise the very serious offence of robbery would be an offence of strict liability in respect of its distinguishing ingredient. Thirdly, and quite simply, it is respectfully thought that the decision in *Clouden* is wrong and that a simple handbag-snatching case ought, as the C.L.R.C. intended, to be treated as one of theft only and not of force "on [a] person".

"Puts or seeks to put any person in fear..."

3–06 It is sufficient if the thief "puts or seeks to put any person in fear of being then and there subjected to force."

Although a threat of future force will not suffice for robbery, one who obtains property by such a threat will normally be guilty both of theft and of blackmail, the essence of which is the making of an unwarranted demand with menaces.[11]

The putting in fear must be "in order to [steal]". So it seems that D must intend P to be put in fear and not merely do an act (to advance the theft) that in fact puts P in fear.

The words "or seeks to put ... in fear" cover the case in which D intends to use the threat of force as a means of accomplishing his theft, but in which P remains either unconscious of the threat or unmoved by it. If there is no question but that D intended P to be fearful of the imminent use of force, there is no need for P to say, on D's trial, whether he was actually frightened—except as a matter possibly relevant to sentence.

"Any person"

3–07 There must of course be a victim of the theft (or, in the case of an assault with intent to rob, somebody who would be the victim of the theft proposed). But the victim of the use of force or of the putting, or seeking to put, in fear may be "any person"; he need not be the victim of the theft. D may use force on P, or put P in fear, in order to steal from P or from Q.

---

[10] That is, in the common law offence of robbery, as embodied in the Larceny Act 1916.
[11] s.21. See Chap. 14.

It follows that force need not be used at the scene of the theft, so long as it is used immediately before or at the time of stealing and in order to do so. The C.L.R.C. gave the example of force used on a signalman, and on no one else, in order to effect theft from a mail train.[12]

"Immediately before or at the time of the stealing"

3–08 The force, or the threat of force, must be used "immediately before or at the time of" the stealing.

It was held in *Hale*[13] that a theft is not over and done with the very moment the thief lays hands on the property. Appropriation is a "continuous", not a momentary, act. Having already taken possession of a jewellery box in P's house, the accused men tied P up in order to ensure their escape; they thereby used force "at the time of" the theft and were guilty of robbery. It is in general, according to the Court of Appeal, a question for the jury whether the appropriation was finished before the force was used; but in *Hale* itself it was "a matter of common sense" that it was not. This decision goes far (happily, it is submitted) to undo the effect of the deliberate omission from section 8 of a reference to force, or the threat of force, used "immediately after" the stealing.[14]

3–09 Cases could arise in which it would be desirable to entertain a generous conception of the period "immediately before" the stealing. Force might be used on a signalman or security guard some while before theft from a train or a warehouse actually takes place. It is thought that, if the force can realistically be regarded as an aspect of the physical accomplishment of the theft on the occasion of its occurrence, the court—or perhaps, in the light of *Hale*, the jury—will be justified in treating it as occurring "immediately before" the stealing.

"In order to" steal

3–10 The act of using force or of putting or seeking to put P in fear must be done "in order to" steal. The mere fact that violence and theft occur as ingredients of the same transaction does not justify a conviction of robbery.[15] D may, for instance, attack P and steal from him a wallet that is shaken from his pocket by the violence. If the attack was not made for the purpose of theft, D cannot be convicted of robbery.[16]

In other respects the words "in order to do so" will be read fairly liberally as meaning not only "in order to accomplish the theft" but also "in order to do so more safely, more expeditiously," and so on. It will thus be robbery if

---

[12] *Eighth Report*, para. 65.

[13] (1978) 68 Cr.App.R. 415.

[14] *Eighth Report*, para. 65. The words "or immediately after" appeared in the corresponding phrase in the old offence of robbery with violence: Larceny Act 1916, s.23(1)(b).

[15] See, *e.g. Shendley* [1970] Crim.L.R. 49; *Donaghy and Marshall* [1981] Crim.L.R. 644.

[16] On an indictment for robbery, D may be convicted of theft if force is not used, or not used at the appropriate time or in order to steal: see above, §1–08.

force is used upon someone who might discover the theft and give the alarm.[17] So if D, immediately before or at the time of the theft, uses force on a jeweller at his home, to prevent him going to his shop where he would find D's confederates opening the safe, D and any confederates who are parties to this use of force will, it is submitted, be guilty of robbery if they succeed in stealing from the safe and of an assault with intent to rob if they do not.

Participation in robbery

Where two or more persons are together involved in a theft in which force **3–11** or the threat of force is used, any of them, to be guilty of robbery, must himself either use or threaten force in order to steal or be a party to a use or threat of force, for that purpose, by a companion. D1 will be a party to D2's use or threat of force if it was understood between them that force would, or might, be used or threatened; or if he was aware of a real risk that D2 might use or threaten force in aid of their joint venture to steal.[18] A person is not guilty of robbery merely because, in stealing or being a party to theft, he takes advantage of force used for that purpose by another.[19]

---

[17] The point passed without comment in *Hale* (1978) 68 Cr.App.R. 415 (above, §3–08).
[18] Compare *Hyde* [1991] 1 Q.B. 134; *Roberts* [1993] 1 All E.R. 583 (D1 guilty of murder having been aware of risk that D2 might intentionally kill in course of joint venture of *e.g.* robbery).
[19] *Harris, The Times,* March 4, 1988.

Chapter 4

BURGLARY AND AGGRAVATED BURGLARY

1. BURGLARY

Definition and penalty; mode of trial

4–01   Burglary is defined by section 9. It is committed by one who—

(i) enters any building or part of a building as a trespasser and with intent to commit therein[1] an offence of theft, inflicting grievous bodily harm, rape or unlawful damage (subss. (1)(a), (2)); or

(ii) having entered any building as a trespasser, steals or attempts to steal anything therein or inflicts or attempts to inflict grievous bodily harm therein (subs. (1)(b)).

Where burglary is committed in respect of a building or part of a building which is a dwelling,[2] the maximum penalty on conviction on indictment is 14 years' imprisonment; in any other case, 10 years' imprisonment (s.9(3)).[3] Aggravated burglary, considered below, is punishable with life imprisonment (s.10(2)).

Section 9(1) and (2) apply to an inhabited vehicle or vessel as they do to a building; and for sentencing purposes an inhabited vehicle or vessel is treated as a building which is a dwelling (s.9(4)).[4]

4–02   Any (non-aggravated) burglary is triable either way *except* the following[5]:

(i) "burglary comprising the commission of, or an intention to commit, an offence which is triable only on indictment." The relevant offences triable only on indictment are rape (Sexual Offences Act 1956, s.1) and causing grievous bodily harm with intent (Offences against the Person Act 1861, s.18). So any burglary involving (a) entry with intent to rape, (b) entry with intent to inflict (and therefore cause) grievous bodily harm, or (c) entry and

---

[1] This wording summarises the prevailing interpretation of the section's more elaborate wording; but it is inaccurate in one minor respect: see the precise terms of s.9, and below, §4–29.

[2] This must mean: (i) in respect of a building the whole of which is a dwelling, whether what is entered as a trespasser is the building or only a part of it, or (ii) in respect of part of a building, that part being a dwelling, whether or not the building as a whole is. Compare text at n. 8, below.

[3] This is the result of an amendment by the Criminal Justice Act 1991, s.26(2). The variation in maximum penalty means that there are two offences of burglary: *Courtie* [1984] A.C. 453; *Button, The Times*, October 21, 1994. A burglar cannot be punished as for the more serious offence except on an indictment alleging that what was entered was a dwelling: compare *Button*, above (below, §6–25).

[4] For consideration of the phrase, "inhabited vehicle or vessel", see below, §4–27.

[5] Magistrates' Courts Act 1980, Sched. 1, para. 28(b), (c).

attempting to inflict (which must involve an intention[6] to cause) grievous indictment. But burglary in the form of entering as a trespasser and actually committing an offence under section 20 of the Offences against the Person Act 1861—that is, maliciously inflicting grievous bodily harm—is triable either way, the section 20 offence being itself so triable.

(ii) "burglary in a dwelling if any person in the dwelling was subjected to violence or the threat of violence." Some other cases of "burglary in a dwelling", now triable either way, were originally triable only on indictment.[7] Their description included the phrase "building containing the dwelling", language which confirmed that where a "dwelling" is part of a larger building, burglarious entry into some other part of that building is not "burglary in a dwelling."[8]

Entry as a trespasser

Burglary depends upon entry as a trespasser and therefore in part upon the **4–03** civil law of trespass to land. Trespass is a wrong committed against another's possession of land. A person enters premises as a trespasser if they are in the possession of another and he enters them without a right, by law or licence, to do so.

P's right to exclude D

A person's entry into a building, or part of a building, cannot be trespass-**4–04** ory unless someone else has a possession that entitles him to exclude the entrant from that building or part. This platitude may be important when considering the liability for burglary of, for instance, D, the owner of a house, who enters the room of P in that house with intent to steal therein. If P has exclusive possession of the room—in which case he is probably a tenant—D requires P's permission to enter it (otherwise than for limited purposes for which the agreement between them may reserve to D a right of entry); and an entry without P's permission (otherwise than under such a reserved right) will be entry as a trespasser. On the other hand, P may occupy the room without having exclusive possession of it—for example, as a lodger, as where "[D] provides attendance or services which require [D] ... to exercise unrestricted access to and use of the premises."[9] In such a case D's entry to steal P's property would not be burglary because it would not be trespassory.[10] The

---

[6] Criminal Attempts Act 1981, s.1(1); as to the intention required, see *Pearman* (1984) 80 Cr.App.R. 259.
[7] s.29(2) (repealed).
[8] J. C. Smith, *The Law of Theft* (3rd ed.), para. 417.
[9] *Per* Lord Templeman in *Street v. Mountford* [1985] A.C. 809 at 818.
[10] In *A.G. Securities v. Vaughan* [1990] 1 A.C. 417, four independent persons occupied a flat under separate agreements with the owner in circumstances making them all licensees rather than joint tenants. An unpermitted entry would not be a trespass as against such occupiers, though an entry by a stranger would be trespass as against the owner: see *per* Lord Bridge at 454.

sometimes difficult distinction between tenant and lodger is not obviously a happy one in the law of burglary.

Trespass must be knowing or reckless

4-05   What if D wrongly believes that he is not trespassing? His belief may rest on facts which, if true, would mean that he was not trespassing: for instance, he may enter a building by mistake, thinking that it is the one he has been invited to enter. Or his belief may be based upon a false view of the legal effect of the known facts: for instance, he may misunderstand the effect of a contract granting him a right of passage through a building. Neither kind of mistake will protect him from tort liability for trespass. In either case, then, D satisfies the literal terms of section 9(1): he "enters ... as a trespasser." But for the purpose of criminal liability a person should be judged on the basis of the facts as he believed them to be, and this should include making allowances for a mistake as to rights under the civil law. This is another way of saying that a serious offence like burglary should be held to require *mens rea* in the fullest sense of the phrase; D should be liable for burglary only if he knowingly trespasses or is reckless as to whether he trespasses or not.

4-06   The Court of Appeal, accepting the view stated above, supplied the required mental element in the remarkable case of *Collins*.[11] D stripped off his clothes and climbed to the window-sill of P's bedroom, intending to enter and to have intercourse with her, by force if necessary. P mistook him for her boyfriend. She beckoned or assisted him into the room and intercourse took place. The Court of Appeal quashed D's conviction of burglary, holding that:

> "there cannot be a conviction for entering premises 'as a trespasser' ... unless the person entering does so knowing that he is a trespasser and nevertheless deliberately enters, or, at the very least, is reckless as to whether or not he is entering the premises of another without the other party's consent."[12]

D may not have satisfied this test, for it was not clear on the evidence "where exactly [D] was at the moment when, according to him, [P] manifested that she was welcoming him .... It was a crucial matter."[13] At the moment of entering the room he may have believed, ignorant of her mistake, that she was consenting to his entry.

4-07   Edmund Davies L.J., giving the judgment of the court in *Collins*, was probably using the word "reckless" in a restricted sense, according to which D will be reckless as to whether he is entering premises without consent only if he realises that he may not have consent. This is suggested by the terms of his lordship's opinion in the later case of *Caldwell*,[14] in which he strongly dis-

---

[11] [1973] Q.B. 100 ("about as extraordinary a case", according to Edmund Davies L.J., "as my brethren or I have ever heard either on the Bench or while at the Bar").
[12] *ibid*., at 105.
[13] *ibid*., at 103–104. The decisive point in the case was therefore "a narrow one, as narrow maybe as the window-sill" (p. 106).
[14] [1982] A.C. 341.

sented from the attribution of a wider meaning to the same word in another context. It is true that in *Collins* he hinted that a belief on D's part that P consented to his entry must be a reasonable one if it is to protect D from conviction of burglary.[15] But this is explained by the view his lordship then held of the weight of the authorities on the defence of mistake; see his dissenting speech in *D.P.P. v. Morgan*[16] three years later. By analogy with the decision in *Morgan*, D's belief that he has consent to enter is in fact inconsistent with recklessness on that issue (in the supposed *Collins* sense), whether that belief is reasonable or not.

But D's failure to realise that he is trespassing, or his belief that he is not, may be the result of intoxication. It seems that in such a case he probably does enter as a trespasser if the truth would be obvious to him were he sober.[17]

Right to enter granted by law

A person may be entitled to enter a building by virtue of a right granted by the law. A constable, for instance, does not trespass when he enters a building to execute a search warrant. But if, armed with a warrant, he enters the premises intending to steal therein and not to search, it is clear that he trespasses. It is otherwise if he enters to execute the warrant and, after entry, steals; for in such a case his entry can only be treated as trespassory by application of the doctrine of trespass *ab initio*, which does not apply to burglary.[18] **4–08**

Licence to enter—whose licence?

To avoid trespass under the civil law, an entrant upon premises requires the licence of the occupier of the premises (the person with legal possession) or of someone acting with his authority. So where D enters P's house upon the invitation of Q, a member of P's household, D will nevertheless be a trespasser for the purposes of the law of tort if Q has no authority to permit D's entry. It was said in *Collins*[19] that such a result would be "unthinkable" in the criminal law. But would it be unthinkable? If D does not doubt Q's authority, he is innocent of burglary on another ground, established in *Collins* itself.[20] On the other hand, D may know or suspect that Q's pretended permission gives him no right to enter. Why then should it not be burglary if he enters with intent to steal (Q may, after all, be a party to that intent)? The context in *Collins* was a special one; Q was herself the intended victim of rape. Perhaps D needs the licence of the occupier (or of one acting with the occupier's authority) or of the intended victim of the ulterior offence. **4–09**

---

[15] [1973] Q.B. 100 at 106.
[16] [1976] A.C. 182 at 230 *et seq*. The case concerned the analogous problem of mistake as to the victim's consent in rape.
[17] Compare *Caldwell* [1982] A.C. 341; and, specifically as to the effect at common law of a drunken mistake, *O'Grady* [1987] Q.B. 995 (mistake and self-defence).
[18] *Collins* [1973] Q.B. 100 at 107.
[19] [1973] Q.B. 100 at 107.
[20] See above, §4–06.

Licence extending to part of building only

4–10   A licence to enter a building may extend to part of the building only. If so, the licensee will trespass if he enters some other part not within the scope of the licence. To do so with intent to commit, in that other part, one of the offences specified in section 9(2), or to do so and then to steal or attempt to steal therein or inflict or attempt to inflict grievous bodily harm therein, will be burglary.

Entry "in excess of" permission to enter

4–11   A person may enter a building with intent to commit a relevant offence (most commonly, to steal) but claim that he did not commit burglary because he had a licence to enter. This claim may be met by showing that, because of the purpose with which he entered, he entered not by licence but as a trespasser. That is to say, it may be shown that his entry was—and that he knew it was or was reckless whether it was—"in excess of" the permission he had to enter (as it was oddly expressed in the leading English case) or "for a purpose outside the scope of the permission" (to use the kind of language employed in an important Australian authority).

The English case is *Jones and Smith*,[21] in which the two appellants had entered the house of Smith's father (which Smith had a general licence to enter) for the purpose of stealing a television set. The Court of Appeal upheld their burglary convictions. The basis of the decision was that Smith's entry was "in excess of the permission that [had] been given to him." This expression appears to mean that the licence which Smith had to enter the house did not extend to an occasion on which he entered for the purpose of stealing. His father's general permission is read as subject to an unspoken limitation to this effect. Much more elaborate judgments than that in *Jones and Smith* were delivered in *Barker v. The Queen*[22] in the High Court of Australia, of which account will have to be taken in any future consideration of the relationship between licence and unlawful purpose. Particularly challenging is the view of Brennan and Deane JJ. that if a consent to enter premises is not limited, expressly or by necessary implication, by reference to the purposes for which entry may be effected, the fact that the entrant's purpose is one of which the person giving consent would not have approved does not make that entry a trespassory one.[23]

Entering a shop to steal

4–12   The decision in *Jones and Smith* seems plainly to imply that one who enters a shop on a shoplifting expedition enters as a trespasser ("in excess of" the

---

[21] (1976) 63 Cr.App.R. 47.

[22] (1983) 153 C.L.R. 338. P asked D to keep an eye on his house while he was away and told D how to gain access. D entered the house to steal furniture. This was burglary under section 76(1) of the Crimes Act 1958 (Vic.), as amended, which is in relevant respects in the same terms as section 9(1)(a) of the Theft Act.

[23] (1983) 153 C.L.R. at 357 *et seq*.

permission given to members of the public generally to enter the shop) and therefore commits burglary when he enters. The view of Brennan and Deane JJ. would not stand in the way of this result if the shopkeeper's licence to the public can be regarded as limited "by necessary implication" by reference to lawful purposes or at least to purposes which do not include theft from the shop. On that understanding, *Jones and Smith* and the learned judges' view would in most cases lead to the same result. But the application of that view seems not to be so simple. For their Honours went on to illustrate it by saying that the ordinary invitation extended by a shopkeeper to the public, though no doubt limited to particular areas of the shop and to shopping hours, is not to be taken as limited by reference to purpose so as to exclude the would-be thief.[24] This, with respect, seems to narrow remarkably the notion of limiting a licence "by necessary implication"; and it makes application of the Brennan and Deane test difficult to predict with assurance. There is much to be said for a simple rule such as that suggested by counsel for the Crown in *Barker*,[25] namely, that anyone who enters premises in the possession of another with intent to steal therein enters as a trespasser. This is no doubt intended by *Jones and Smith*. If the thief masquerading as a shopper is not a burglar, the law of burglary may be thought to be too complicated.

Fraud to obtain entry

D may obtain permission to enter a building by pretending to be someone **4–13** he is not or by falsely claiming to have a valid reason for entering. He may, for instance, claim to be the gas man come to read the meter. His entry is surely a trespass. A sufficient reason will be that the permission to enter, properly understood, does not extend to an entry made for D's secret nefarious purpose. One who obtains his licence to enter by fraud can hardly be in a better position than one whose entry is "in excess of" a permission spontaneously given.

Objections to burglary liability of one exceeding licence

The foregoing paragraphs accept the correctness of the decision in *Jones* **4–14** *and Smith*,[26] if only for the sake of avoiding excessive complexity in the law of burglary. But the case has been vigorously criticised by Professor Williams.[27] His main objections appear to be these:

(i) That the decision is not well-founded in the tort authority relied on by the court.[28] This objection may be technically sound. The case in question was

---

[24] *ibid.*, at 361–362. Nor were the other majority judges in *Barker* clear that an intending shoplifter was necessarily a burglar. And Mason J. (at 344) was not sure that *Jones and Smith* was a correct application of principle.
[25] Recorded by Brennan and Deane JJ., *ibid.* at 356.
[26] Above, §4–11.
[27] Williams, *Textbook*, pp. 847–849. See also P. J. Pace [1985] Crim.L.R. 716.
[28] *Hillen and Pettigrew v. I.C.I. (Alkali) Ltd.* [1936] A.C. 65.

not concerned with entry for an unpermitted purpose. But this does not demonstrate that *Jones and Smith* is incorrect.[29]

(ii) That the decision takes inadequate account of the language of section 9, even to the point of rendering redundant the words "as a trespasser" in section 9(1)(a). For according to the decision an intent to commit a relevant ulterior offence suffices to make the entry trespassory; yet such an intent is itself an independent requirement under paragraph (a). It is respectfully suggested that this objection is not sound. If the intent is to commit an offence against someone other than the occupier, the entry will not necessarily be trespassory; the occupier may licence the entry, acquiescing in or being indifferent to the proposed offence. Moreover, the phrase "as a trespasser" excludes from burglary a person entitled to possession of the premises entered.[30] So it does have a function independent of the ulterior intent.

4–15   (iii) That the decision is inconsistent with the case of *Collins*.[31] Collins may have believed that the girl was inviting him to enter the house. The jury's verdict nevertheless involves a finding that when he entered he intended to rape her if necessary. Entry with this intention (the argument runs) was surely entry "in excess of" the permission apparently given to him to enter. Yet his conviction was quashed. This implies that entry with a relevant criminal intention outside the terms of the licence granted does not negative that licence. Yet *Jones and Smith* holds that it does.

Two answers are available.[32] First, a distinction might be taken between an unqualified intention (that of Smith to steal) and a conditional one (that of Collins to have intercourse by force if necessary). Collins may fulfil his purpose without exceeding the licensor's purpose in admitting him; not so with Smith. This is a real distinction, but hardly a satisfying one. The second answer is simply that, for all that appears, the court in Collins did not advert to the effect upon the (supposed) licence of the ulterior intent. It may be Collins that is defective on this point.

4–16   (iv) That the decision is contrary to the purpose of the law of burglary. Burglary is aimed at the unwelcome intruder. It is not intended to deal with the entrant whose presence is expected, even welcome—such as the occupier's son (as in *Jones and Smith*), or his customer, guest or employee. The decision rests burglary on the entrant's state of mind, not on the "objective illegality" of his entry. This objection has considerable force. Burglary is a traditional category of crime, protecting premises and their occupants against invasion, against entry that is "manifestly suspicious."[33] But the

---

[29] The tort authorities are comprehensively reviewed in *Barker v. The Queen* (1983) 153 C.L.R. 338; above, §4–11.
[30] As pointed out by Mason J. in *Barker,* above, at 347.
[31] [1973] Q.B. 100; above, §4–06.
[32] Perhaps three. Because of P's apparent welcome, Collins may have abandoned even a conditional intention to rape by the time he entered: see Smith (J. C.), para. 11–06; Williams and Weinberg, *Property Offences* (2nd ed.), pp. 303–304; compare Mason J. in *Barker v. The Queen* (1983) 153 C.L.R. 338 at 345. But Collins' conviction was quashed because he may not have entered as a trespasser, not because it was unsafe to conclude that he entered with intent to rape.
[33] G. Fletcher, *Rethinking Criminal Law*, p. 128.

objection may be to the way in which section 9 was drafted, rather than to the way it has been interpreted in *Jones and Smith*.

Entry

Entry of part of the body

The question what amounts to an entry into a building for the purpose of **4–17** section 9 arose in *Brown*,[34] in which D put part of his body through a shop window and stole goods from the shop. The Court of Appeal rejected a submission that a person does not "enter" a building unless his whole body is within the building. The court approved, in the context of the case, the trial judge's suggestion to the jury that "to put a hand, or an arm, or the upper part of your body through a broken shop window, is plainly an entry into that shop." But this was strictly speaking a suggestion only and not a firm direction. The Court of Appeal said that whether there has been an entry is a question of fact for the jury, apparently meaning that whether a proved intrusion amounted to an "entry" is a question for the jury's judgment. This is open to the familiar objection that it is capable of producing a different law of burglary for each of two identical cases. If D puts his forearm through a shop window and rummages around among goods, he should be guilty of burglary as a matter of law.[35]

The court in *Brown* was attracted by the suggestion that a jury should be **4–18** directed that what is required is "an effective entry" (though failure to use such terms in the instant case was by no means a misdirection). The notion of an "effective" entry was derived from a remark of Edmund Davies L.J. in *Collins*.[36] The learned Lord Justice had said that Collins could not properly be convicted unless he had made "an effective and substantial entry" before he was caused to believe that he was entering with consent. Too much has been made of this unelaborated dictum in an extempore judgment; and the court in *Brown* happily made plain that the word "substantial" does not assist. The word "effective", with respect, is not much more helpful. It might be understood to suggest in one kind of case that it is necessary to be more or less completely in (was he "effectively" in?) and in another that it is enough if a slight degree of intrusion permits an attempt at the ulterior offence (was it "effective" to allow him to attempt theft?). The results in both cases may be sound; yet they will be achieved by giving different meanings to a word that does not appear in the statute.

Under the law of burglary and related offences replaced by section 9, the **4–19** intrusion into the building of any part of the body, however small, satisfied the requirement of an entry.[37] The court might in *Brown* have adopted the

---

[34] [1985] Crim.L.R. 212.
[35] If the point arises again, it will very likely be held that this is what *Brown* decided; compare §§3–04, 3–05, above, on points in the law of robbery.
[36] [1973] Q.B. 100 at 106; above, §4–05.
[37] *Davies* (1823) R. & R. 499.

same simple rule. It did not do so; and its judgment is explicable only on the basis that the rule has not survived.[38] If that is right, we are left in need of further authority, preferably in firm terms that will make for uniformity of decision, to supplement our understanding of the range of cases in which a person "enters" a building although part of him remains outside. It might with advantage be clearly laid down that a person has "entered" a building (or part of a building) not only when he is entirely inside the building (or part) but also (i) when he has intruded so far into the building (or part) that he may be described more properly as inside it than as outside; or (ii) when his intrusion into the building (or part) suffices to permit him to attempt the intended offence (in a case under section 9(1)(a)) or to commit a relevant attempt (in a case under section 9(1)(b)).

Entry by an innocent agent

4–20   Burglary should be no exception to the general rule that crimes can be committed through innocent agents.[39] There is no doubt that the act of appropriation or of violence needed to complete a burglary under section 9(1)(b) can be so committed.[40] It is submitted that, similarly, D "enters ... as a trespasser" within the meaning of section 9(1) when he does not himself physically enter but trespasses through the instrumentality of (for example) a child under 10, an adult without *mens rea*[41] or a well-trained animal. But this simple route to a conviction was overlooked in one case in favour of a more refined and controversial doctrine.[42]

Insertion of an instrument

4–21   There is a third category of problem cases on the meaning of entry. D may insert an instrument into the building without any part of his own body intruding. Under the old law this was an entry if the instrument was inserted for the purpose of committing a relevant ulterior offence (*e.g.* theft or causing grievous bodily harm), but not if it was inserted merely to facilitate access to the premises. Such a distinction, slightly adapted, may continue to be serviceable. The insertion of an instrument simply as a means of access need not be regarded as an entry. D has not, by that insertion, made an "effective" entry in any sense of that adjective. His act seems to be described more convincingly as an attempt to enter the building than as an actual entry by him,

---

[38] But in *Watson* (1989) 89 Cr.App.R. 211 at 214, Lord Lane C.J. (*obiter*) seemed to assume that a burglary is committed "on [D's] foot crossing the threshold or windowsill."
[39] Williams, *C.L.G.P.*, pp. 349 *et seq.*; Draft Criminal Code Bill, cl. 26(1)(c), 3(a), in *A Criminal Code for England and Wales* (Law Com. No. 177), vol. 1.
[40] As to appropriation, see *Stringer and Banks* (1991) 94 Cr.App.R. 13.
[41] Compare Hale, 1 *Pleas of the Crown*, pp. 555–556; *Paterson* [1976] 2 N.Z.L.R. 394.
[42] *Wheelhouse* [1994] Crim.L.R. 756: D, having intent to steal, procured E (an innocent dupe) to enter garage and take car; D held liable as secondary party for acts done without *mens rea* by E (applying *Cogan and Leak* [1976] Q.B. 217; *Millward* [1994] Crim.L.R. 527).

and attempted burglary can be charged if nothing further occurs. On the other hand, when D inserts an instrument into the air-space of the building he certainly does trespass; the instrument can readily be regarded as an extension of his person,[43] and if by the instrument so inserted he is able to commit or attempt to commit one of the specified offences without intrusion of his own body, he has made as effective an entry as if he had inserted an arm with the same result. But should the hooked object, by which D proposes to steal, or the gun, with which he seeks to cause grievous bodily harm, enter only slightly and not far enough for the ulterior purpose to be attempted, the case would again, it is submitted, be properly treated as attempted burglary.

Buildings and parts of buildings

"The imperfection of human language renders it not only difficult, but absolutely   **4–22**
impossible, to define the word 'building' with any approach to accuracy. One may
say of this or that structure, this or that is not a building; but no general definition
can be given. ...."[44]

The Act attempts no definition; nor need we. There must be a structure capable of being entered; it must presumably be a fairly permanent affair[45]; and further than this it is probably not safe to go. Difficulty will occur infrequently, but eventually the courts will no doubt have to decide whether a kiosk is a building; or a potting-shed; or a bandstand; and so on.[46] There is little point in trying to anticipate their decisions. Nor would it be wise to base any predictions upon decisions given on various structures under the numerous statutes in which the word "building" is used, for what is denoted by a word of this kind in a particular statute depends so much on the subject and purpose of the legislation.

The word "building" and the distinction taken by the Act between buildings and parts of buildings give rise to some tantalising problems.[47] In considering the illustrations and explanations that follow, it must be remembered that burglary is committed if D intends to commit one of a number of offences either (a) in a *building* that he enters as a trespasser, or (b) in part of a building, that *part* being entered by him as a trespasser.

---

[43] It is submitted that this consideration, if any be needed, is sufficient to distinguish the case of the hand-held instrument from that of the projected missile; compare Smith (J. C.), para. 11–04.
[44] *Per* Byles J. in *Stevens v. Gourley* (1859) 7 C.B.(N.S.) 99 at 112.
[45] It is clear that a tent is not a building. The C.L.R.C. were against giving tent-dwellers the protection of the law of burglary on the not very satisfying ground that "a tent seems too open a structure to be naturally regarded as the subject of burglary": *Eighth Report*, para. 78.
[46] Reported Crown Court decisions have concerned a large freezer container standing in a farmyard, without foundations (a "building": *B. and S.* v. *Leathley* [1979] Crim.L.R. 314); and a lorry trailer, supplied with mains electricity, used as a storehouse (not a "building": *Norfolk Constabulary v. Seekings and Gould* [1986] Crim.L.R. 167).
[47] For a valuable and ingenious discussion, see Smith (J. C.), paras. 11–13 to 11–21.

Premises 1, 2 and 3 are contiguous. If D enters 1, intending to pass from it into 2 or 3, there to steal, he is guilty of burglary if 1 and 2 or (as the case may be) 1, 2 and 3 constitute one "building".[48] This must depend on detailed facts as to structure and, perhaps, occupancy. A block of offices is surely one building. A row of terraced houses almost as surely is not; but it is possible to conceive of doubtful cases, such as that in which one large building has been converted into a row of residences with a common roof.

4–24

Here is a block of flats. D is lawfully in 1. He enters 2, intending to pass from it into 3 and to steal in 3. Assuming that the block of flats is one "building", do 2 and 3 constitute one "part", so that D enters that part as a trespasser with intent to steal therein? It is thought not.[49] In such a case, the relevant component portions of the building are clearly distinguishable; in other cases the meaning of "part" may seem less clear.

---

[48] He is also guilty of burglary if, when entering 1, he intends to do damage to 1 by damaging the wall between 1 and 2: Collins [1968] Crim.L.R. at 643–644. A similar point affects the next illustration.

[49] *Contra*, it seems, Smith (J. C.), paras. 11–18 to 11–20, who argues that for the purpose of s.9 a building has only two parts: that where D may lawfully go, and the remainder. *Sed quaere?* The reading is desirable but strained.

(a)

(b)

(c)

(d)

Each of these diagrams represents a floor of a shop. D is a customer, lawfully present in the shop.

(a) Here the prohibition imposed by the notice and the area to which it relates are clear. That area is a "part" of the building which D enters as a trespasser.

(b) A counter area is formed by three movable counters, with a till in one corner. D moves into the counter area in order to steal from the till. The jury are entitled to find that the area is a "part" of the building which members of the public are, to D's knowledge, impliedly prohibited from entering.[50] It seems that the area may be a "part" for this purpose although its boundaries cannot be exactly defined.

(c) There is "a single table" (with, say, a till on it) "in the middle of the store, which it would be difficult for any jury to find was properly a part of the building in which the licensor prohibited customers from moving."[51]

(d) D has the licence that all customers have in a shop to move from counter to counter. He has lawfully entered the shop and bought something from counter 1. He now moves to counter 2, intending to steal at it. If in doing so he is entering a different "part" of the shop, he may be guilty of burglary on the ground that his entry into that part with intent to steal is a trespassory entry.[52] But it does not seem likely that the courts will be hasty to divide buildings artificially into "parts" in the way that would be necessary to make a case of burglary out of the situation presented here.

---

[50] *Walkington* (1979) 68 Cr.App.R. 427.
[51] *ibid.*, at 434.
[52] See above, §§4–11, 4–12.

4–26

1 and 2 are distinct "parts" of a building. D is lawfully in 1 as a customer, guest, etc. He trespasses in 2 but commits no offence there. Later he comes back into 1, intending to steal therein. When he re-emerges into 1, does he enter that part as a trespasser? Applying the principle of *Jones and Smith*,[53] he probably does. Although he lawfully entered the building and has not yet left it, his re-entry into part 1 can be regarded as a distinct entry of a part of the building and as trespassory because of his intent to steal.

Inhabited vehicles and vessels

4–27   An inhabited vehicle or vessel, whether or not "the person having a habitation in it" is there at the time of the offence, is given the same protection as a building by section 9(4). Moreover, the law of burglary applies as between the parts of, *e.g.* an ocean liner as it does between the parts of a building.

Clearly a person ordinarily living in, or for the time being spending a holiday in, a caravan or a house-boat has a habitation in it; and the subsection does not cease to apply because he goes away for a few hours or days. It is not, however, so clear whether during the winter a caravan left fully equipped on a caravan site for the purpose of occasional visits during the summer is an "inhabited vehicle" within the meaning of the subsection. It is tentatively suggested that it is not; that the phrases "inhabited" and "having a habitation in it" should be understood as referring to active or regular residential use in the period in which the alleged burglary occurs; and that in each case it must be a question of degree whether P currently has a habitation in the vehicle or vessel (whether it is then "inhabited"). It is easy to see the force of a contrary argument according to which, if the primary use of the vehicle or vessel is residential, one has a habitation in it so long as it is available (and equipped?) for use as an occasional home, no matter how long the gaps between visits. But this argument seems to give insufficient force to the word "inhabited". The language of the subsection is lamentably imprecise.

Nor is it clear to what use one must put a vehicle or vessel for it to be inhabited. Its mere casual use for sleep on an isolated occasion is presumably not enough. On the other hand, must it serve as a self-sufficient home? At first sight one would suppose not; but if not, a vehicle fitted out for sleeping and for no other non-vehicular purpose might be "inhabited" and within the protection of the law of burglary when its tourist occupants are taking a meal elsewhere. There seems little need for such special protection.

---

[53] (1976) 63 Cr.App.R. 47; above, §4–11.

Two modes of burglary: entry with intent; offence after entry

It must be proved either that D intended when he entered the building or   **4–28**
part to commit one of the offences mentioned in section 9(2) (s.9(1)(a)), or
that after entry he actually stole or inflicted grievous bodily harm on any
person or attempted to do either (s.9(1)(b)). On the one hand, the only justification for the alternative provided by section 9(1)(b) is that it meets the case
where the relevant guilty intention at the time of entry cannot be proved;
there is no wider ground for making an offence more serious merely because
it is committed by a trespasser. On the other hand, paragraphs (a) and (b) of
section 9(1) are not mutually exclusive,[54] and in practice the existence of
paragraph (b) enables the normal case of entry (with intent) plus theft to be
charged as a single offence, instead of as two offences under paragraph (a)
and section 1. Paradoxically, therefore, section 9(1)(b), justified by the
exceptional (and probably bogus) defence, "I did not at the time of entering
intend to steal; prove that I did", is used for the great majority of burglaries.[55]

It seems clear that, to satisfy section 9(1)(a), an offence of theft, inflicting   **4–29**
grievous bodily harm or rape must be intended to be committed in the building that D enters as a trespasser or, as the case may be, in the very part that he
enters as a trespasser, and not elsewhere against a person or property taken
from the building or part[56]; and that the offence after entry required by section 9(1)(b) must be committed in that building or part. Where D intends to
do unlawful damage, the damage must be intended to the building he enters
or to something therein; but here there is no limitation to the part trespassed
in, if D's presence in the building itself was lawful.[57]

The specified offences

Four offences are mentioned in section 9(2). The first two, and attempts to   **4–30**
commit them, appear also, in substance, in section 9(1)(b). The four offences
are those—

(i) *"of stealing anything in the building or part of a building in question"*

There can be no intent to steal unless the accused would be guilty of theft if
the intended appropriation took place.[58] So, for example, his belief that he

---

[54] *Taylor* [1979] Crim.L.R. 649.
[55] As to conviction under paragraph (a) on an indictment for an offence under paragraph (b),
see above, §1–08.
[56] Notwithstanding doubts expressed by S. White (1986) 150 J.P.N. 37, 56. It is thought also that
the intention must relate to a thing or person in the building (or part) at the time of entry.
[57] See the precise terms of s.9(1)(b), (2).
[58] Nor, of course, an offence under s.9(1)(b) involving theft unless all the ingredients of theft are
present; but failure to direct the jury about all those ingredients is not necessarily fatal to a
conviction: *O'Sullivan and Lewis* [1989] Crim.L.R. 506 (doubtfully, but gratifyingly, distinguishing *McVey* [1988] Crim.L.R. 127).

has a right to deprive of the property the person to whom it belongs will exclude burglary as it will exclude theft. Again, theft depends upon an appropriation of "property"; and as electricity is not "property", burglary is not committed by entering a building as a trespasser and abstracting electricity therein (or entering with intent to do so).[59]

4–31   A charge under section 9(1)(a), of entering a building or part of a building as a trespasser "with intent to steal therein", without reference to particular property, is permissible.[60] On such a charge it is not necessary to prove either that D entered with intent to steal any specific thing,[61] or that anything, or anything such as he was seeking, was present in the building or part of a building in question.[62] "An intention to steal can exist even though, unknown to the accused, there is nothing to steal. . . ."[63] and even though his only intention is to steal anything that he may find worth stealing.[64] It follows that one who attempts to enter a building with such an intention can be convicted of attempted burglary.[65]

(ii) *"of inflicting on any person therein any grievous bodily harm"*

4–32   A distinction must be drawn between (a) entry with intent to inflict harm and (b) the infliction of, or an attempt to inflict, harm after entry.

(a) *Entry with intent* (s.9(1)(a)). A person charged with entry with intent to commit an offence under this head must be proved to have intended the infliction of some harm which would be regarded by a jury as "grievous"— that is, "really serious bodily harm."[66]

(b) *Infliction of, or attempt to inflict, harm after entry* (s.9(1)(b)). A "specific intent" to inflict such harm is also plainly required for an attempt, after entry as a trespasser, to inflict grievous bodily harm.[67] But the Act is obscure as to the *mens rea*, if any, required for burglary committed by entering and actually inflicting grievous bodily harm. Section 9(1)(b), unlike paragraph (a), does not in terms require the commission of any "offence."[68] On a

---

[59] *Low v. Blease* [1975] Crim.L.R. 513.
[60] *Attorney-General's References (Nos. 1 and 2 of 1979)* [1980] Q.B. 180, approving the indictment in *Walkington* (1979) 68 Cr.App.R. 427.
[61] *Attorney-General's References*, above.
[62] *Walkington*, above; *Attorney-General's References*, above.
[63] *Per* Lord Scarman in *D.P.P. v. Nock* [1978] A.C. 979 at 1000; *Attorney-General's References*, above, at 194.
[64] These obvious propositions needed to be established because a doctrine to the contrary was in vogue for a time, based on an unsatisfactory dictum in *Husseyn* (1977) 67 Cr.App.R. 131, on attempted theft.
[65] This was the specific point in the second of the *Attorney-General's References*, above.
[66] *Metharam* (1961) 45 Cr.App.R. 304 (on Offences against the Person Act 1861, s.18). For observations on what may provide evidence of such an intent, see *O'Neill and others, The Times,* October 17, 1986.
[67] Compare *Pearman* (1984) 80 Cr.App.R. 259 (on Criminal Attempts Act 1981, s.1(1)).
[68] The drafting is the result of an inept amendment: see [1983] Crim.L.R. 386–387 (comment on *Jenkins*, next note).

literal reading a trespasser could commit burglary by accident.[69] On principle, however, *mens rea* should be required. The offence to which paragraph (b) was undoubtedly intended to refer was that of maliciously inflicting grievous bodily harm under section 20 of the Offences against the Person Act 1861, which requires intention or ("subjective") recklessness as to the infliction of some, though not necessarily serious, bodily harm.[70] Thus: D trespasses in P's premises; P uses reasonable force to eject him; D resists P's force by a blow that D realises may cause a slight wound; the blow unexpectedly causes severe injury; D is guilty of burglary.

(iii) *"of raping any person therein"*

Rape, as defined by section 1(2) of the Sexual Offences Act 1956,[71]   **4–33** requires either knowledge that the other person does not consent to the sexual intercourse involved or recklessness as to whether he or she consents or not. Attempted rape requires an intent to commit rape; and it was decided in *Khan*[72] that this requirement is satisfied if D, intending to have intercourse with P, is reckless as to whether the victim consents. In the attempt context, D's state of mind concerns P's present attitude: does he or she consent to what is now being attempted? The intent to commit rape required for burglary is rather different; it is a state of mind about the (no doubt near) future. A case where, as he enters the building or bedroom as a trespasser, D has it in mind that he will have intercourse with P even if, when it comes to it, he should prove to be unsure whether P is consenting, can be imagined (with difficulty) but will surely not be encountered in practice. The rule in *Khan* is unlikely to have room for application. The nearest applicable rule is one of conditional intention: for a conviction of burglary it is sufficient if, on entry, D intends to have intercourse with P whether P consents or not.[73] If in the event P consents, or D believes that P consents, no rape or attempted rape is committed, but liability for the burglary would strictly be unaffected.[74]

(iv) *"of doing unlawful damage to the building or anything therein"*

The question will be whether what D intended would have been an offence under section 1 of the Criminal Damage Act 1971. Section 5 of that Act provides a special defence of "lawful excuse" and expressly preserves general defences.

---

[69] As apparently contemplated by the Court of Appeal in *Jenkins* (1983) 76 Cr.App.R. 313 at 318 (reversed on another ground [1984] A.C. 242).
[70] *Savage* [1992] 1 A.C. 699.
[71] As substituted by Criminal Justice and Public Order Act 1994, s.142: rape is an offence committed by a man who has sexual intercourse (whether vaginal or anal) with a woman or a man who at the time of the intercourse does not consent to it.
[72] (1990) 91 Cr.App.R. 29.
[73] The contrary was not suggested in *Collins* [1973] 1 Q.B. 100, where the point was available for decision. (The point can, of course, be generalised: for instance, an intention, if P will not make a loan, to take his money willy-nilly will be sufficient intention to steal.)
[74] *Collins (Christopher)* [1976] Crim.L.R. 249. (This case has to be read in the light of *D.P.P. v. Humphrys* [1977] A.C. 1, on issue estoppel.)

2. AGGRAVATED BURGLARY

Definition

4-34   A person commits aggravated burglary if he "commits any burglary and at the time has with him any firearm or imitation firearm, any weapon of offence, or any explosive" (s.10(1)), and this offence is punishable on conviction on indictment with imprisonment for life (s.10(2)). It is not triable summarily.[75] The C.L.R.C. regarded the offence as comparable with robbery, which also carries life imprisonment.[76]

     The terms "firearm", "imitation firearm", "weapon of offence" and "explosive" are defined or partially defined in section 10(1).

Firearm

4-35   Apart from saying that " 'firearm' includes an airgun or air pistol", the Act does not define this term. It is extensively defined in the Firearms Act 1968 for purposes of that Act[77]; but that definition does not apply for purposes of the present section.[78] Where it is doubtful whether an article carried by a burglar was a firearm it will often fall within the section in any event as a "weapon of offence".

Imitation firearm

4-36   This means:

> "anything which has the appearance of being a firearm, whether capable of being discharged or not."

The question is whether the thing that the burglar had with him had the appearance at that time of being a firearm. Two metal pipes, bound together with tape, one end being held by the burglar under his clothing or other material, may at that time have looked like a double-barrelled shotgun. It is a question for the jury.[79]

Weapon of offence

4-37   This means:

> "any article made or adapted for use for causing injury to or incapacitating a person, or intended by the person having it with him for such use."

---

[75] Magistrates' Courts Act 1980, Sched. 1, para. 28(a).
[76] *Eighth Report.*
[77] Firearms Act 1968, s.57(1), read with s.5(2).
[78] Compare *Seamark v. Prouse* (1980) 70 Cr.App.R. 236.
[79] *Morris and King* (1984) 79 Cr.App.R. 104 (decided under the Firearms Act 1968, s.18(1)).

This wording is borrowed almost verbatim from the definition of "offensive weapon" in section 1(4) of the Prevention of Crime Act 1953, section 1(1) of which penalises the possession of an offensive weapon in a public place without lawful authority or reasonable excuse. One addition to the 1953 definition, however, is the reference to incapacitation. It covers articles "such as cords for tying up, gags or pepper."[80]

There is an important distinction between two classes of articles referred to in the definition. If an article is "made or adapted for use for causing injury to or incapacitating a person"—if it is, as it is commonly put, offensive *per se*—the burglar who has it with him is guilty of aggravated burglary whether or not he intends it for such use. It need not be proved that he so intended.[81] But in the case of an article not offensive *per se* it must be proved that the burglar intended it for such use.[82]

"Made ... for use for causing injury ... or incapacitating"

An article is "made for use for causing injury" if it was originally made for   **4–38** such use.[83] The question is as to the purpose for which it was made, not that for which it may be used.[84] There are some articles of which the court will take judicial notice that they are made for the purpose of causing injury to a person, so that the matter does not have to be proved and the jury can be so directed. This was held in relation to flick-knives by the Court of Appeal in *Simpson*[85]; other articles judicially declared to be offensive *per se* have included coshes, knuckle-dusters, revolvers,[86] swordsticks,[87] bayonets and stilettoes.[88] Flick-knives are to be contrasted with sheath knives; it is not possible to declare of "every knife which may be in a sheath" that it is made for the purpose of causing injury to a person, and the question whether a particular sheath knife was so made is a question of fact for the jury to decide.[89]

---

[80] *Eighth Report*, p. 128 (Notes on draft Bill).
[81] *Davis v. Alexander* (1970) 54 Cr.App.R. 398.
[82] *Petrie* (1961) 45 Cr.App.R. 72. In *Flynn* [1986] Crim.L.R. 239; *Rowe* [1990] Crim.L.R. 344, the question was left open whether it is enough that the jury agree on the article's having been an offensive weapon without agreeing either that it was "offensive *per se*" or that D intended it for a relevant use. A negative answer is proposed, surely correctly, by J. C. Smith [1988] Crim.L.R. 335 at 338.
[83] Compare *Hubbard v. Messenger* [1938] 1 K.B. 300 at 307 ("constructed or adapted for use for the conveyance of goods").
[84] *Simpson* (1983) 78 Cr.App.R. 115.
[85] (1983) 78 Cr.App.R. 115; approving the judgment of Griffiths L.J. in *Gibson v. Wales* (1982) 76 Cr.App.R. 60.
[86] All in *Petrie*, n. 82, above.
[87] *Davies v. Alexander*, above, n. 81; *Butler* [1988] Crim.L.R. 695.
[88] *Simpson*, above, n. 84, at 791.
[89] *Williamson* (1977) 67 Cr.App.R. 35. The general statement in this case (at 38) that "in any case" it is a question for the jury to decide "whether the object ... can properly be described as an offensive weapon" must now be read subject to *Simpson*, above.

"Adapted for use for causing injury ... or incapacitating"

4–39   An article is "adapted for use for causing injury" if it has been altered so as to be apt for such use.[90] Once again it seems to be a question of purpose; examples often given are "the bottle deliberately broken in order that the jagged edge may be inserted into the victim's face"[91] and the chair leg into the end of which nails have been inserted. It need not be proved that the defendant was a party to the alteration.

"Intended by the person having it with him for such use"

4–40   Many things, however, that are not "made or adapted" to injure or incapacitate can be put to such use by one so minded: a razor, a kitchen knife,[92] a machete[93] or a rope, for instance. If such a thing is carried by a burglar as a potential weapon (a conditional intention is plainly enough), the aggravated offence is committed. It has been held that the contemplated occasion for use of the weapon need not be the burglary itself.[94]

The judge should normally avoid reference in his direction to an intention to use the article to frighten or intimidate; but in a rare case the evidence may justify a finding that the intention was to injure by shock.[95]

4–41   *Time of forming intention.* In *Kelly*,[96] D, having used a screwdriver to effect entry into a house, was surprised by the occupier in the process of stealing a television and video. He compelled the occupier to unplug these items, prodding him with the screwdriver to make him comply. The jury's verdict, in the light of the judge's direction, implied a finding that at that stage D intended, if necessary, to use the screwdriver to cause injury. The indictment alleged that D had an offensive weapon with him at the time of a burglary under section 9(1)(b). It was held that he was guilty of aggravated burglary because the screwdriver had become a weapon of offence before the burglary was committed—that is, before the theft that completed the burglary as charged[97]—

---

[90] Compare *Hubbard v. Messenger*, above, and many other cases under the Road Traffic and Vehicles (Excise) Acts; *Formosa and Upton* [1991] 2 Q.B. 1.
[91] *Simpson*, above, n. 84 at 117.
[92] *Stones* (1989) 89 Cr.App.R. 26.
[93] *Southwell v. Chadwick* (1987) 85 Cr.App.R. 235.
[94] *Stones*, above.
[95] *Rapier* (1979) 70 Cr.App.R. 17, purporting to apply *Edmonds* [1963] 2 Q.B. 142. The relevant dictum in *Edmonds* (at 151) suggests that an intention to frighten may be sufficient where "the frightening [is] ... of a sort which is capable of producing injury through the operation of shock." But D's intention to injure through shock must be proved, and not simply the fact that a frightening use of the article is "capable" of causing, or even likely to cause, such injury (see Criminal Justice Act 1967, s.8).
[96] (1992) 97 Cr.App.R. 245.
[97] This rests too much on the form of charge. No doubt the jury, if invited to do so by a charge under s.9(1)(a), would have found that D entered the building with intent to steal. If so, he surely did not commit a second burglary when he stole. The facts do not change with a change in the charge. The decision might have been (but was not) that D, by his late decision to use the screwdriver as a weapon, became armed *either* during the course of a burglary initiated on entry and thereafter continuing (see *Watson* (1989) 89 Cr.App.R. 211) *or* before a burglary first completed by the theft. That would have excluded the suggestion in the following paragraph of the text.

even though D may have formed the intention to use it to injure only after he had entered the building.

Kelly is not easy to reconcile with authority on the corresponding definition of "offensive weapon" under the Prevention of Crime Act 1953, which establishes that the intention to use the article to cause injury must be "formed before the actual occasion to use violence has arisen"[98] and not "ad hoc".[99] The Court of Appeal sought to distinguish the purposes of the two provisions: the mischief at which the 1953 Act is aimed is the *carrying* of weapons rather than their use,[1] whereas section 10, it was said, "is directed at the *use* of articles which aggravate the offence of simple burglary."[2] This distinction is very doubtful. It seems that there remains room for the application of the Prevention of Crime Act principle, consistently with the rest of the judgment in *Kelly*, in a case in which the mode of burglary alleged is that under section 9(1)(a) and the burglar has made "ad hoc" use, as a weapon, of something he is carrying.

"Has with him"

When does a person have a thing "with him"?

In what range of circumstances will a person "have with him" a firearm or other weapon? The most nearly relevant English cases concern section 18(1) of the Firearms Act 1968, under which it is an offence for a person "to have with him a firearm ... with intent to commit an indictable offence."

In *Kelt*,[3] D was arrested in his kitchen, in which was found a holdall containing a robber's kit including a sawn-off shotgun. His conviction of the Firearms Act offence was quashed because the judge had failed to explain to the jury the distinction between a person's possessing a thing and his having it with him. A person may, it is true, have a gun "with him" although he is not carrying it, so long as it is "immediately available to him". But whether D had the shotgun "with him", as opposed to possessing it, was a question of fact and degree for the jury's decision and they had been inadequately directed. The Court of Appeal spoke in this case of a need for "a very close physical link and a degree of immediate control over the weapon."

In *Pawlicki and Swindell*,[4] however, the same court, to judge by its response to the facts of the case, seems to have expanded the meaning of "have with him." The appellants, who had entered premises with intent to commit robbery, were held to have had with them, while in those premises, guns that they had left some 50 yards away in a locked car outside the premises. It was contended on appeal that at this distance the guns were not "immediately available" to the appellants; and it is certainly not easy to

4–42

---

[98] *Ohlson v. Hylton* [1975] 1 W.L.R. 724; [1975] 2 All E.R. 490 (*per* Lord Widgery C.J. at 729 and 497 respectively).
[99] *Humphreys* [1977] Crim.L.R. 225.
[1] *Ohlson v. Hylton*, above; *Bates v. Bulman* (1978) 68 Cr.App.R. 21.
[2] *Kelly* (1992) 97 Cr.App.R. 245 at 248. (Emphasis supplied.)
[3] (1977) 65 Cr.App.R. 74.
[4] (1992) 95 Cr.App.R. 246.

discern a "very close physical link" in this case. But the court declined to read *Kelt* as laying down a criterion of "immediate availability" in substitution for the statutory language; and, although propinquity was an element to be considered,

> "the emphasis must be not so much on exact distances between criminals and their guns but rather on the accessibility of these guns, judged in a commonsense way in the context of criminals embarking on a joint enterprise to commit an indictable offence."

The appellants' guns had been readily accessible to them when they were about to commit the robbery. This case, as a considered interpretation of *Kelt*, must be taken to have superseded that decision to the extent that the two may seem to conflict.

4–43   The question then arises: how far are these cases relevant to aggravated burglary? In *Pawlicki* the court took an avowedly purposive approach to the statute it was considering. It remains possible to argue that the purpose of section 10 is to provide an additional sanction against one who enters premises "with" a weapon or has a weapon on premises during a burglary. The burglar is not (as in the case of the Firearms Act offence) intending to commit an offence; he is engaged in it. He is intended to be guilty of the aggravated offence only if he is "armed" while he is committing it. This is the view that has been taken in the Court of Criminal Appeal of Northern Ireland of an offence very similar to aggravated burglary—the offence of one who "while he has a firearm with him, ... enters or is in any building or part of a building as a trespasser."[5] A burglar who left his pistol in his car on the road opposite the house he was burgling would not, said Lord MacDermott L.C.J., commit this offence; to be guilty "he must enter or be on the premises as an armed man."[6] It is submitted that this is correct. But it was said before the English Firearms Act decisions, the relevance of which in the present context remains uncertain.

The requirement of knowledge

4–44   The phrase "has with him" can properly mean only "knowingly has with him".[7] So a burglar who is ignorant that he has a firearm in his pocket is not guilty of the aggravated offence.[8] The point is more likely to arise when two or more persons commit burglary together and one of them has physical possession of an article within s.10(1). Then only such of them as know of the

---

[5] Firearms Act (Northern Ireland) 1969, s.18(1).
[6] *Murphy, Lillis and Burns* [1971] N.I. 193.
[7] Compare *Cugullère* (1961) 45 Cr.App.R. 108.
[8] One who has forgotten what he formerly knew is ignorant for this purpose: *Russell* (1985) 81 Cr.App.R. 315.

article can be guilty of aggravated burglary.[9] In one case, indeed, something more than knowledge of the article's presence is necessary. This is the case in which the article (not being a firearm, imitation firearm or explosive) is a "weapon of offence" only because D1 intends to use it for causing injury. For D2 then to be guilty of aggravated burglary he must know of D1's intention or have that intention himself.

"At the time has with him"

Whether a person is guilty of aggravated burglary depends on whether he **4–45** has with him a weapon or other article within section 10 "at the time" he commits burglary.

Burglary contrary to section 9(1)(a) is committed at the time of entering a building or part of a building with intent to commit a relevant offence; D must therefore have the offending article with him when he enters if he is to be guilty of aggravated burglary. Burglary contrary to section 9(1)(b), on the other hand, is committed only when D steals (or commits another offence satisfying the paragraph) within the building or part that he entered as a trespasser; so that aggravated burglary depends on D's having the offending article with him at the time of the theft (or other offence). If by that time he has abandoned a weapon with which he entered, he is guilty of simple burglary only.[10]

There remains the question whether one who enters a building without a **4–46** weapon, arms himself with a heavy candlestick when inside and then steals can be convicted of aggravated burglary. On the face of it he can; he was armed when his burglary under section 9(1)(b) was committed. This natural reading of the section has been confirmed.[11]

---

[9] Compare *Webley and Webley* [1967] Crim.L.R. 300. It would seem that a burglar whose companion, as he anticipates, carries a weapon into the building has that weapon "with him" during the burglary, so as to be guilty of aggravated burglary as a principal offender; and it was so ruled in *Jones* [1979] C.L.Y. 411 (Judge Solomons).

[10] *Francis* [1982] Crim.L.R. 363.

[11] *O'Leary* (1986) 82 Cr.App.R. 341, rejecting an argument to the contrary rehearsed in earlier editions of this book: see 5th ed., §4–42.

Chapter 5

REMOVAL OF ARTICLES FROM PLACES OPEN TO
THE PUBLIC

1. INTRODUCTION

5–01   The clause that eventually became section 11 of the 1968 Act acquired the popular name "the Goya clause" while the Bill was before Parliament. This is because the need for the clause was suggested in particular by the notorious removal of Goya's portrait of the Duke of Wellington from the National Gallery. The portrait was returned after four years. Despite evidence that he had tried to make the Gallery buy the portrait back by paying a large sum to charity (which was certainly evidence that at the time he took it he intended to deprive the Gallery permanently, and would now be evidence of the same intention for the purposes of theft), the taker was acquitted of larceny of the portrait. There had been some other recent cases of the temporary removal of articles from public buildings—among them the removal of the Stone of Scone from Westminster Abbey. Art galleries, cathedrals and other places housing famous treasures are no doubt particularly vulnerable to temporary deprivation at the hands of eccentrics, exhibitionists and people with causes that can be brought to the public notice by removal of public property.

On balance, having considered arguments for and against the creation of a new offence, the C.L.R.C. decided[1] that there should be special provision for the protection of articles kept in places open to the public. But they included no such provision in the draft Bill, preferring to recommend the consideration of special legislation for the purpose. A first version of "the Goya clause" nevertheless appeared in the Bill presented to Parliament; and section 11 represents that clause in a much revised form.

5–02   Section 11 renders it an offence in certain circumstances to remove an article from a place to which the public have access. The offence is punishable on conviction on indictment with imprisonment for five years (subs. (4)).

A person guilty of this offence is, of course, quite likely to be guilty of the full offence of theft. Most people who remove valuable articles from art galleries, museums and stately homes no doubt intend to deprive their owners permanently of them and can pretend to no right to do so. What section 11 does is to provide for two classes of case: those where there is in fact no intention of permanently depriving; and those in which that intention, though it may well have existed, cannot be proved. There is no provision for a conviction, on a charge of theft, of an offence under section 11. So where an article has been removed from a place within section 11 and there is any doubt about

---

[1] See *Eighth Report*, para. 57(ii).

the offender's intention or any doubt about proving it, it will often be expedient to include in the indictment a count charging an offence under section 11.

The section is drafted with a complexity disproportionate to the importance of the offence. The reader is referred to the text of the section in Appendix 1. What follows here is a statement of the conditions of the offence, with such commentary or explanation as seems to be required.

2. THE DETAILS OF THE OFFENCE

The offence under section 11 is committed if, and only if, the following conditions are satisfied[2]:   **5–03**

(i) There must be *a building to which the public have access.*

We shall see (in (iv), below) that the section protects articles in the grounds of a building within the section as well as in the building itself. But the fact that the public has access to the grounds of a house in order to see its gardens and model railway is not enough to bring the section into operation if the public are not also admitted to the building itself for the purpose mentioned in (ii), below.

> "It is immaterial ... that the public's access to a building is limited to a particular period or particular occasion" (subs. (2)).

A "building" must probably have a roof; and if so, an exhibition staged in the ruins of Tintern Abbey or Coventry Cathedral would not be protected.

(ii) The public must have access to the building *in order to view the building or part of it, or a collection or part of a collection housed in it,* including a collection or part of a collection "got together for a temporary purpose."   **5–04**

A trial judge has ruled that the question whether the public has access "in order to view" depends on the purpose of the occupier in giving access rather than on that for which people come in.[3] This is no doubt true; but the principle can only be sensibly applied if the known motives of visitors are allowed to affect the description of the occupier's purposes. If a vicar knows (as surely he must) that many visitors to his church will come in just to look round, he must be construed, it is submitted, as giving access to the public "in order to view", although the primary reason for leaving the church door open is to enable people to enter for devotional purposes.

(iii) If the public have access to a building in order to view a collection   **5–05**

---

[2] All conditions, and qualifications of them, stated in the following account are justified by subs. (1), unless otherwise stated.
[3] *Barr* [1978] Crim.L.R. 244 (vicar's evidence that his church was open only for devotional purposes and that the cross and ewer taken were displayed simply as aids to devotion; held, no case to answer).

rather than the building, the *collection* must be one *not "made or exhibited for the purpose of effecting sales or other commercial dealings."*

Where an artist's work is collected and put on show for sale, the application of the section to the collection may depend upon the nature of the building in which the collection is to be viewed. If the works are shown in a shop, there is little doubt that the collection must be regarded as made "for the purpose of effecting sales" even though an interested but impecunious public are welcome to view the collection with no idea of buying. On the other hand, if the collection is exhibited in a building which happens itself to be on show to the public or which contains some other collection which the public come to view and which is not excluded from the section by the motive of sale, the works exposed for sale fall within the section as it were parasitically. A familiar intermediate case is that of the educational institution which puts on a short-term exhibition of the work of a local artist. The public are invited to view the collection for their own pleasure; but the works are priced and the artist hopes to sell them as a result of the public's visits. From one point of view this is a collection "made or exhibited for the purpose of effecting sales"; and it may be safer to treat this contributory purpose as sufficient to prevent the section from applying.

5–06   (iv) There must be *a removal of the whole or part of an article from the building or its grounds.*

If the article is in the building the offence will be complete if it is removed from the building and, for example, hidden in the grounds. But a removal of an article from one part of the building to another or from one part of the grounds to another is not enough.

The word "grounds" is pleasantly untechnical. It could in an exceptional case cause difficulty. D is a gardener employed in the park of a great house to which the public have access, and he lives in a cottage within the park. He removes an article displayed outside the house and places it in the garden of his cottage, or in the cottage itself. Liability here is not as clear as it ought to be. It might not be improper to say that the gardener lives "in a cottage in the grounds of the great house", and that the article has therefore not been removed from the grounds.

5–07   (v) The *article* removed must be one *displayed or kept for display to the public in the building* (or in the part of it that the public come to view) *or in its grounds.*

The point, of course, is that the private belongings of the family who live in the great house, the overcoats and umbrellas of visitors to the museum, the bibles and hymn-books lying around the church, are not accorded special protection against unlawful "borrowing" merely because they happen to be within a building to which the section applies. It seems that an article is "displayed ... to the public" only if the purpose, or one of the purposes, of its display is that it may be seen by those who are admitted to view the building or a collection housed in it—only if it is, in effect, "exhibited".[4]

An article within the protected class need not at the time of removal be actually on show. It is enough if it is "kept for display"; so an offence is committed by removing from a workshop within an art gallery an old master in the process of being cleaned but intended for exhibition in the gallery.

(vi) *The removal must in some cases be on a day when the public have* **5–08**
access to the building (subs. (2)), but in most cases the time of removal
is immaterial.

This condition as to the time of removal applies when the thing removed is not in the building or grounds as part of a collection intended for permanent exhibition to the public and is not on loan for exhibition with such a collection. The distinction intended is that between "a place, such as the National Gallery, which conducts a permanent exhibition ..." and "a place such as a stately home which is open only occasionally to the public...."[5] The purpose of making this distinction is to limit an anomaly. A servant or trespasser in an ordinary home not opened to the public view never commits an offence if he temporarily removes an article from it, however precious or priceless the article. By contrast, a servant or trespasser in a stately home sometimes open to the public may commit an offence if he takes something displayed to the public; yet his taking of the article may be quite unconnected with the fact that the public are granted access to the house—that is to say, it may not be an abuse of the privilege that that access constitutes, whereas the abuse of that privilege is the mischief intended to be penalised by the section. This anomaly is to some extent limited by providing, in effect, that if the thing removed is not on permanent exhibition it must be removed on a day when the public have access to it or there will be no offence.

In *Durkin*,[6] D removed from an art gallery owned by a local authority a **5–09** painting forming part of the authority's permanent collection. This painting, like other works in the collection, was not continuously on display; different parts of the collection were exhibited at different times. The painting nevertheless formed part of "a collection intended for permanent exhibition to the public" since the collection was intended to be permanently available for such exhibition, that intention being sufficiently manifested by the authority's settled practice of periodically displaying this and other pictures in the gallery. D was guilty of an offence under section 11(1), although he had taken the painting on a Sunday, when the gallery was closed.

(vii) The removal must be *without lawful authority*. **5–10**
(viii) The remover must act *without the belief that he has lawful authority for*
the removal or that he would have it if the person entitled to give it knew
of the removal and the circumstances of it (subs. (3)).[7]

---

[4] *Barr*, above.
[5] H.C. Standing Committee H, June 25, 1968: Official Report, col. 56.
[6] [1973] Q.B. 786.
[7] Compare s.12(6), the remarks on which at §6–21, below, apply equally to s.11(3).

Chapter 6

TAKING A CONVEYANCE WITHOUT AUTHORITY AND AGGRAVATED VEHICLE-TAKING

6–01   The unauthorised use of vehicles has long been a social mischief requiring penal sanctions. The conduct to be controlled may vary in gravity between a thoughtless adolescent joy-riding prank and the use of a handy car for a serious criminal purpose. At either extreme the temporary loss of the vehicle can seriously inconvenience its owner,[1] while the public are in danger from the uninsured use of the vehicle by an often reckless or immature driver. In many cases the police may rightly suspect the taking of a vehicle to be theft but be unable to prove the necessary intention of permanently depriving the owner. In such cases the provable wrong is better described as an unauthorised taking of the vehicle than as a theft of the petrol consumed by its use, which was all that could be charged before the taking of the vehicle was made an offence in itself.

6–02   Section 12 amends, and extends to all "conveyances", an offence of taking and driving away a motor vehicle that was first created in 1930. The main purpose of the extension was to provide for yachts, boats and pedal cycles.[2]

Section 12A was added by the Aggravated Vehicle-Taking Act 1992, a hasty government response to a fashionable, and mainly juvenile, practice of reckless exhibitionist driving in cars taken for the purpose.

1. TAKING A CONVEYANCE WITHOUT AUTHORITY

Taking a conveyance other than a pedal cycle

6–03   Section 12(1) deals with conveyances other than pedal cycles. It creates an offence in what may conveniently be called primary and secondary forms:

(i) The primary form of the offence is that of taking a conveyance for one's own or another's use without having the consent of the owner or other lawful authority.
(ii) The secondary form occurs where a person, knowing that a conveyance has been taken without authority, drives it or allows himself to be carried in or on it.

The offence was formerly triable either way but was converted by the

---

[1] But this inconvenience does not itself justify a unique "theft of use" offence in the case of vehicles where there is none in the case of other property (*e.g.* industrial plant).
[2] *Eighth Report*, para. 83.

122

Criminal Justice Act 1988, s.37(1), into a summary offence,[3] punishable with a fine not exceeding level 5 on the standard scale, or up to six months' imprisonment, or both.[4] An effect of the 1988 Act was the abolition of the offence of attempting to commit an offence under section 12(1), for the Criminal Attempts Act 1981 applies only to attempts to commit indictable offences. But interference with a motor vehicle with the intention that an offence under section 12(1) shall be committed is an offence under section 9 of the 1981 Act (vehicle interference).

An offence under subsection (1) is an arrestable offence (as is an offence of **6–04** conspiring to commit, or of inciting, aiding, abetting, counselling or procuring the commission of, an offence under the subsection).[5] The powers of arrest without warrant provided by the Police and Criminal Evidence Act 1984, s.24(4)–(7), therefore apply; and one who does an act with intent to impede the apprehension or prosecution of an offender may be convicted under section 4(1) of the Criminal Law Act 1967.[6] That offence is punishable with imprisonment for three years on conviction on indictment[7]—a fact possibly overlooked when the offences under section 12(1) were downgraded.

The ingredients of the offence under section 12(1) will be considered under four heads.

(1) *"Conveyance"*

Section 12(1) does not apply to pedal cycles (subs. (5)) or to any convey- **6–05** ance constructed or adapted for use only under the control of a person not carried in or on it (subs. (7)(a)); but it applies to any other "conveyance constructed or adapted for the carriage of a person or persons whether by land, water or air ...", and the word "drive" is to be construed accordingly (subs. (7)(a)). It is clear that any vehicle, vessel or aircraft which, as originally constructed or by virtue of subsequent alteration,[8] makes physical provision for its "driver" to be carried in or on it is within the definition of "conveyance." If it were otherwise the section would not protect, for example, a goods van without a passenger seat.

---

[3] But inclusion in an indictment of a count charging such an offence is possible in certain circumstances: Criminal Justice Act 1988, s.40(1), (3)(b). The offence is then tried as if it were an indictable offence; but the Crown Court may deal with the offender only as a magistrates' court could have done: *ibid.*, s.40(2). A person charged on indictment with theft may be convicted of an offence under s.12(1) and, again, is liable to the same penalties as on summary conviction: subs. (4), as amended by the 1988 Act.

[4] A person convicted of an offence in respect of a motor vehicle may be disqualified for holding or obtaining a driving licence: Road Traffic Offenders Act 1988, Sched. 2, Pt. II.

[5] Police and Criminal Evidence Act 1984, s.24(2)(d) and (3).

[6] By virtue of Criminal Law Act 1967, s.4(1A) (added by the Police and Criminal Evidence Act 1984, Sched. 6).

[7] *ibid.*, s.4(3)(d).

[8] Compare *French v. Champkin* [1920] 1 K.B. 76; *Hubbard v. Messenger* [1938] 1 K.B. 300; *Taylor v. Mead* [1961] 1 W.L.R. 435; *Flower Freight Co. Ltd. v. Hammond* [1963] 1 Q.B. 275.

A horse is not a "conveyance".[9] The section is "directed towards artefacts rather than towards animals."[10]

(2) *The prohibited conduct*

6–06   (i) The *primary offender* is he who "takes any conveyance for his own or another's use." The word "takes" will be satisfied by any movement intentionally[11] caused (*e.g.* by pushing, by lifting or by releasing a hand-brake). But some movement there must be. It appears that a "taking" for the purposes of the section has two ingredients: (a) an assumption of possession or control, and (b) movement. The Court of Appeal in *Bogacki*[12] said that before a person can be convicted of this form of the offence it must be shown

> "that there was an unauthorised taking of possession or control of the [conveyance] by him adverse to the rights of the true owner or person otherwise entitled to such possession or control, coupled with some movement, however small … of that [conveyance] following such unauthorised taking."

6–07   *"Taking" a conveyance already possessed.*[13] Several cases hold that a person may "take" a conveyance within the meaning of section 12(1) even though he already has possession of it as the owner's servant or bailee. This was first revealed in *Wibberley*,[14] decided under the Road Traffic Act 1960, s.217(1) (the predecessor of s.12). In that case D was employed to drive a truck. At the end of his day's work he should have returned it to one of his employer's yards. Instead he drove it to his home and, later that evening, used it for his own purposes. His conviction of taking and driving away was upheld. He was in no better position than if he had returned the truck to the yard and later taken it from there without consent.[15] A stronger case than this is *McKnight v. Davies*,[16] in which, again, D's duty was to return his lorry to his employer's depot when he had completed his round of deliveries. Instead he drove to a public house for a drink, drove around elsewhere for his own purposes, and parked the lorry for the night near his home. He returned it to the depot early the next morning. The Divisional Court held that an employed driver can be regarded as "taking" his vehicle

> "if in the course of his working day … he appropriates it to his own use in a manner

---

[9] *Neal v. Gribble* (1978) 68 Cr.App.R. 9.

[10] *ibid.*, at 11.

[11] *Blayney v. Knight* (1975) 60 Cr.App.R. 269 (movement caused by accidental pressure on accelerator; no "taking").

[12] [1973] Q.B. 832 at 837; see also *Marchant and McCallister* (1984) 80 Cr.App.R. 361 (where the full offence was plainly committed although the conviction was of attempt only).

[13] Smith (A.T.H.), paras. 9–24 *et seq.*; Glanville Williams and A. T. H. Smith (1984) 148 J.P.N. 115; J. Dine, *ibid.*, 277.

[14] [1966] 2 Q.B. 214.

[15] *ibid.*, at 219. It seems that D's employer would not have complained if D had parked the truck outside his home until next morning.

[16] [1974] R.T.R. 4.

which repudiates the rights of the true owner, and shows that he has assumed control of the vehicle for his own purposes."[17]

Applying such a test the court held that D "took the vehicle when he left the first public house."[18]

In so deciding *McKnight v. Davies*, the Divisional Court rejected the pre- **6–08** Act authority of *Mowe v. Perraton*[19] as being inconsistent with *Phipps and McGill*,[20] which the court preferred. The latter case was in one respect a stronger one still, for it involved not an employee, traditionally conceived as having mere custody of his employer's property,[21] but a person in possession as bailee. On condition that he would be back by 9.30 p.m., D borrowed P's car at Dagenham in order to drive to Victoria Station. He did not return that night, but drove the car next day to Hastings. His conviction was upheld. The direction to the jury, that "as from the time he decided not to return the car and drove it off on his own business . . . , if he did not have [P's] permission, he took it and drove it away", was "perfectly proper and accurate" and "supported by . . . *Wibberley*."[22]

The word "takes" is thus read as embracing the notion of entering upon an **6–09** unauthorised use other than that for which D has custody or possession. The reading is questionable on a number of grounds. First, its artificiality is at odds both with the principle of the strict construction of penal statutes and with the courts' own preference for the normal meanings of "ordinary words".[23] Secondly, it is not clear that the reading brings within the offence any mischief for which the section was intended to provide. Where a motor vehicle is concerned, the unauthorised use can often be prosecuted as an uninsured use; it is doubtful whether any other penal sanction is called for in a case where a conveyance has not been taken "without any reference to the owner."[24] Thirdly, there is an embarrassing discordance between the cases on use beyond the consent given (penalised as "taking") and those on use sanctioned as a result of fraud (not penalised because not "without . . . consent").

---

[17] *ibid.*, at 8.
[18] *ibid.* Thus the court avoided the unhappy conclusion that every driver who deviates from his route for the sake of a drink on his way back to base comits an offence unless he thinks that his employer would consent if he knew (see s.12(6)). More generally: "Not every brief, unauthorised diversion from his proper route . . . in the course of his working day will necessarily involve a 'taking' of the vehicle for his own use" (p. 8).
[19] (1952) 35 Cr.App.R. 194. This case had been somewhat painfully distinguished in *Wibberley*, above.
[20] (1970) 54 Cr.App.R. 301.
[21] On this conception see Williams and Smith, *op. cit.*, n. 13, above, at 117.
[22] (1970) 54 Cr.App.R. at 304.
[23] "If the defendant initially gained possession with the consent of the owner how then can it be said that he *took* the vehicle without the owner's consent?": *Singh v. Rathour* [1988] 1 W.L.R. 422 at 428; [1988] 2 All E.R. 16 at 21 (May L.J., citing Hobhouse J. as trial judge).
[24] See *Peart* [1970] 2 Q.B. 672 at 675; compare *Whittaker v. Campbell* [1984] Q.B. 318 at 328.

The conflict, which will be demonstrated when the fraud cases are discussed,[25] should be resolved in favour of the latter.

6–10   *"For his own or another's use."*[26] The taking by D must be "for his own or another's use." In *Bow*,[27] the Court of Appeal accepted a submission that this involves "that the conveyance should have been used as a conveyance, *i.e.* as a means of transport."[28] So if D, indulging his sense of humour, pushes P's car round a corner in order that P may think it has been stolen,[29] or releases its handbrake so that it runs away down a hill, the offence is not committed unless someone is in (or, presumably, on) it while it moves. But where, as in *Bow* itself,[30] D moves the conveyance "in a way which necessarily involves its use as a conveyance",[31] it is immaterial that his motive in doing so is one to which that use is entirely subservient.

6–11   Notwithstanding the language of *Bow* quoted above, the Court of Appeal held in *Marchant and McCallister*[32] that the offence may be committed by taking control of, and moving, the conveyance (as by pushing it) with the intention that it shall be used as a conveyance later, although it is not so used at the time of the taking. In so deciding the court restored the authority of *Pearce*,[33] a decision which had seemed to be called into question by *Bow*. In *Pearce*, D took a dinghy, placed it on a trailer and towed it away. His conviction under section 12 was upheld. The case was understood in *Marchant and McCallister* as one in which D's purpose was to use the dinghy as a conveyance. The case of a boat "towed away to be used later" was certainly intended to be brought within the scope of this section by the removal of the words "and drives away" during the passage of the Bill.[34]

6–12   *Aiding and abetting.* Aiding and abetting this offence, like any other, requires full *mens rea*. D must be found to have been knowingly a party to the taking of the conveyance (that is, its removal from its original position). His mere voluntary presence when E takes the conveyance is not in itself participation in the taking; nor does his subsequently allowing himself to be carried in the conveyance necessarily establish that participation.[35] To be guilty of aiding and abetting, D must, on general principles, either assist or encourage the taker in the commission of the offence.

---

[25] Below, §6–17.
[26] This phrase is elaborately discussed by S. White [1980] Crim.L.R. 609.
[27] (1976) 64 Cr.App.R. 54. A gamekeeper used his Land Rover as an obstruction to prevent D, a suspected poacher, from making an escape. D sat in the driving seat of the vehicle and ran the vehicle downhill by releasing the handbrake. His only purpose was to remove the obstruction. Held, a taking "for his own use."
[28] (1976) 64 Cr.App.R. 54 at 57.
[29] *Stokes* [1982] R.T.R. 59.
[30] See n. 27, above.
[31] (1976) 64 Cr.App.R. 54 at 58.
[32] (1984) 80 Cr.App.R. 361.
[33] [1973] Crim.L.R. 321.
[34] H.L. Deb., vol. 291, col. 106.
[35] *C (a minor) v. Hume* [1979] Crim.L.R. 328 (where the secondary form of the offence—see text following—could have been, but was not, charged).

(ii) The *secondary offender* is he who knows that the conveyance has been **6–13** taken without authority and "drives it or allows himself to be carried in or on it." The secondary form of the offence has three elements.

First, the conveyance must in fact have been taken without authority. There must be admissible evidence of this offence. D's confession that he was told of it by a person claiming to have committed it is not admissible for this purpose.[36]

Secondly, D must drive the conveyance or allow himself to be carried in or **6–14** on it.

The word "drives" has been considered in many cases under the Road Traffic Acts, including cases under the present section's predecessors. Although the word has to be allowed a wide meaning, the alleged driver of a motor vehicle "must be in the driving seat, or in control of the steering wheel and ... his activities are ... not to be held to amount to driving unless they come within the ordinary meaning of that word."[37]

A motor vehicle can be driven without starting the engine,[38] but it cannot be driven by merely pushing it while controlling the steering wheel with one hand from the outside.[39] A person in command of the steering wheel and brakes of a vehicle on tow is driving it.[40] If there is any doubt as to whether a person drove a conveyance for the purpose of section 12(1) he can normally be charged with having allowed himself to be carried in or on it. The word "drive" has to be understood as referring to appropriate modes of controlling conveyances generally, and not just those in relation to which the word is normally used.[41]

A person does not "allow himself to be carried" in or on a conveyance merely by being present in or on it, even in anticipation of its being moved. There must be some actual movement.[42]

Thirdly, D must know that the conveyance has been taken without auth- **6–15** ority. The taking may in fact have amounted to theft; and D may know this or may simply know that it has been taken without authority. In either case he is within the section.[43] If he boards the conveyance without knowledge and learns the truth while being carried, he cannot presumably be guilty of the

---

[36] *Francis* [1982] Crim.L.R. 694 (Judge Jolly); compare the proof of theft in a case of handling (below, §§15–07 *et seq.*).

[37] *MacDonagh* [1974] Q.B. 448 at 452, referring to *Roberts* [1965] 1 Q.B. 85 at 88. A merely accidental occurrence cannot be an act of driving: *Blayney v. Knight* (1975) 60 Cr.App.R. 269 (above, §6–06).

[38] *Saycell v. Bool* [1948] 2 All E.R. 83; *Floyd v. Bush* [1953] 1 W.L.R. 242.

[39] *MacDonagh* [1974] Q.B. 448.

[40] *McQuaid v. Anderton* [1980] 3 All E.R. 540; *Caise v. Wright* [1981] R.T.R. 49.

[41] s.12(7)(a) (where the reference to "drive" is rather obscurely expressed, and can be read as also restricting the meaning of the word to "control by a person in or on the conveyance").

[42] *Miller* [1976] Crim.L.R. 147; *Diggin* (1980) 72 Cr.App.R. 204.

[43] *Tolley v. Giddings* [1964] 2 Q.B. 354. Smith (A. T. H.), para. 9–47, considers whether the original taker can be guilty a second time—or even repeatedly—by subsequently driving the vehicle or otherwise acting as a secondary offender. It is suggested not; compare the one-theft-only rule: above, §2–94.

offence unless he remains on board after he has had a realistic opportunity of disembarking; he must, knowing the truth, "allow" himself to be carried.

(3) *The absence of consent or other lawful authority*

6–16   The taking must be without the consent of the owner of the conveyance or other lawful authority. In the case of a conveyance on hire or hire-purchase, "owner" means the hirer (see subs. (7)(b)), and the fact that the taker does not have the consent of the legal owner is immaterial.[44] The reference to other lawful authority will cover such cases as the removal of a vehicle under statutory power by the police[45] or by a local authority.[46]

The consent required to exclude the offence is a consent actually given, not simply the consent that, as it may later transpire, the owner would have given had he been asked.[47]

6–17   *Consent obtained by fraud.* The use of fraud to obtain the owner's consent to the taking of a conveyance does not impair the effectiveness of that consent so as to found an offence under section 12. In *Whittaker v. Campbell*[48] D, who had no driving licence, obtained a van on hire from P by presenting to P the licence of one X and pretending to be X. The Divisional Court held that D did not take the van "without having the consent of [P]." The court declined to base this decision on the narrow ground that D and P did business face to face, so that P's mistake induced by the fraud was not as to the identity of the person he was dealing with but only as to one of his attributes (his holding a driving licence). No distinction, it seems, is to be drawn between mistakes as to fundamental and collateral matters respectively, or between mistakes preventing and those not preventing the formation of binding contracts. The mischief against which the section is directed does not require any such subtle inquiry. Where P has, in "commonsense terms", consented to part with the possession of his conveyance, but has done so as a result of D's fraud, the offence (if any) properly to be charged is one involving deception, which is the gravamen of D's conduct.[49] An earlier case in which fraud did not affect P's consent was *Peart*,[50] where P allowed D to borrow P's car, being induced to do so by D's lie about the nature of the journey he proposed to take. D committed no offence when he drove the car away; he did not take without consent.

---

[44] *Tolhurst and Woodhead* (1961) 106 S.J. 16.
[45] See Road Traffic Regulation Act 1984, s.99, and regulations thereunder.
[46] See Refuse Disposal (Amenity) Act 1978, s.3.
[47] *Ambler* [1979] R.T.R. 217. A dictum of Woolf L.J. to the contrary in *Singh v. Rathour* [1988] 1 W.L.R. 422 at 430; [1988] 2 All E.R. 16 at 22, seems to be a slip.
[48] [1984] Q.B. 318.
[49] See especially [1984] Q.B. at 328-329, *per* Robert Goff L.J. Where a hiring is fraudulently induced an offence of obtaining services by deception contrary to the Theft Act 1978, s.1, is plainly committed; compare *Widdowson* [1986] Crim.L.R. 233 (obtaining goods on hire-purchase). No deception offence is available, however, in a case of gratuitous borrowing such as *Peart* (text following).
[50] [1970] 2 Q.B. 672.

The principle of these cases seems to collide with that of a group of cases   **6–18**
(considered above)[51] which hold an offence under section 12 to be committed
when a person lawfully in possession of a conveyance enters upon a use
which has not been authorised. The unsatisfactory state of the law appears
most clearly when the cases of *Peart* and *Phipps and McGill*[52] are placed side
by side. In *Peart* D's original journey was quite different from that which P
had permitted, but the taking effected by driving off on this journey was held
to be with P's consent. In *Phipps and McGill* D's original journey was the one
authorised; but when he embarked on a further journey not authorised by P,
he "took" the car without consent. It therefore appears that if one proposes
to use another's vehicle for two purposes, one of which he might not consent
to, it is safer to lie to him about both purposes than to be harmlessly truthful
about the first and silent about the second. This can hardly be better law than
sense.[53]

Taking obtained by force or duress. It seems that if the owner of a convey-   **6–19**
ance is induced by force or duress to part with possession of it, his act may be
regarded as one of submission rather than consent and an offence under section 12 can be found.[54]

(4) *Relevant states of mind; the relevance of intoxication*

The primary form of the offence requires no "specific intent." In particu-   **6–20**
lar, it does not require actual knowledge that the taking is without the owner's consent or other lawful authority. So conviction cannot be avoided by
evidence that D was too drunk to form any intent or to know that he was
taking without consent.[55] By contrast, knowledge that the conveyance has
been taken without lawful authority is an express requirement of the secondary form of the offence—driving or allowing oneself to be carried; and evidence of intoxication is clearly admissible in relation to this issue.

Section 12(6), on the other hand, provides equally for both offences a   **6–21**
limited form of "honesty" defence:

---

[51] §§6–07, 6–08.
[52] (1970) 54 Cr.App.R. 300.
[53] It is not suggested that any deception was in fact practised by the accused in *Phipps and McGill*. Note that in *Peart* "no issue was left to [the jury] as to whether ... there could have been a fresh taking ... of this particular van at some time after it was originally driven away" ([1970] 2 Q.B. 672 at 675); the conviction was quashed because of a misdirection on the only issue left to the jury, namely, whether there was at the outset an effective consent to the taking of the van. It seems to be suggested that on a direction canvassing "a fresh taking" a conviction might have been proper. But if there was evidence of only one journey, it is difficult to see at what point a new "taking" (without consent) could be identified; and even if D made, and all along intended to make, two distinct journeys, it would be highly artificial to regard a consent obtained by deception as applying only to the first.
[54] Compare *Hogdon* [1962] Crim.L.R. 563; *Whittaker v. Campbell* [1984] Q.B. 318 at 328 (without deciding the point).
[55] *MacPherson* [1973] R.T.R. 157. But S. White [1980] Crim.L.R. 609 argues that the phrase "for his own or another's use", correctly understood, renders the offence in its primary form one of specific intent.

"A person does not commit an offence under this section by anything done in the belief that he has lawful authority to do it or that he would have the owner's consent if the owner knew of his doing it and the circumstances of it."

D, of course, can rely on this defence only if he adduces, or can point to, evidence tending to show that he held a positive belief within the subsection.[56] But if there is such evidence, the question will be whether the tribunal of fact is satisfied beyond reasonable doubt that D did not so believe; the persuasive burden rests on the prosecution.[57] And the question is simply as to D's belief, not as to whether D had lawful authority or whether the owner would have consented.[58]

It is submitted that D may rely on a belief within section 12(6) even if it is the result of self-induced intoxication. A close analogy exists in the form of authority on a provision to similar effect in the Criminal Damage Act.[59]

Taking a pedal cycle

6–22   It is a summary offence, punishable with a fine of £500,[60] to take a pedal cycle for one's own or another's use or to ride a pedal cycle knowing it to have been taken without such authority (s.12(5)). The exception for honesty provided by subsection (6) applies here also. The offences created by subsection (5) are not, of course, arrestable offences.

A difficulty may arise as to the correct classification of a motor-assisted pedal cycle. This was a motor vehicle for the purpose of the replaced offence of taking and driving away a motor vehicle, for which substantial penalties were provided. That offence could be committed by pedalling away such a cycle without using the motor[61]; but when the motor could not be used because of the absence of vital working parts, the vehicle was not a "motor vehicle" within the meaning of that phrase as defined in the Road Traffic Acts.[62] Perhaps a similar distinction can be drawn under section 12 as a means of identifying vehicles which at the relevant time are mere pedal cycles.

2. AGGRAVATED VEHICLE-TAKING

The offence

6–23   The Aggravated Vehicle-Taking Act 1992, s.1(1), added section 12A to

---

[56] *Gannon (Kevin)* (1987) 87 Cr.App.R. 254.
[57] *MacPherson*, above; *Gannon*, above. A failure to refer to this question on trial on indictment may, of course, be fatal to a conviction. But *Briggs* [1987] Crim.L.R. 708 is a surprising illustration: the Court of Appeal seemed to contemplate that the jury, though satisfied that D knew the motorcycle had been taken without lawful authority, might have thought that he possibly believed that he had lawful authority to drive it. The decision should be confined to its own facts.
[58] *Clotworthy* [1981] Crim.L.R. 501.
[59] *Jaggard v. Dickinson* [1981] Q.B. 527, decided on Criminal Damage Act 1971, s.5(2).
[60] Originally £50; thus, level 2 on the standard scale (Criminal Justice Act 1982, ss.37, 46) and currently £500: Criminal Justice Act 1991, s.17(2).
[61] *Floyd v. Bush* [1953] 1 W.L.R. 242.
[62] *Lawrence v. Howlett* [1952] 2 All E.R. 74.

the Theft Act 1968. This created the offence[63] of aggravated vehicle-taking. D is guilty of this offence if—

(i) [64] he commits an offence under section 12(1) (a "basic offence") in relation to a mechanically-propelled vehicle—that is to say (in the language adopted in the first part of this chapter) he commits *either* the primary form of the basic offence, by himself taking such a vehicle without consent or other lawful authority, *or* the secondary form, by driving or allowing himself to be carried in or on such a vehicle, which he knows has been taken without authority; and

(ii) [65] at any time after the vehicle is unlawfully taken[66] and before it is recovered,[67] the vehicle is driven, or injury or damage is caused, in one or more of the following circumstances[68]:

    (a) the vehicle is driven dangerously[69] on a road or other public place;

    (b) owing to the driving of the vehicle, an accident occurs by which injury is caused to any person;

    (c) owing to the driving of the vehicle, an accident occurs by which damage is caused to any property, other than the vehicle;

    (d) damage is caused to the vehicle.[70]

Defences

It will be observed that there is no requirement that the dangerous driving **6–24** be done, or that the accident or damage be caused, by D or by anyone subject to his control. Section 12A creates a remarkable kind of vicarious liability. This is to a degree limited by subsection (3), which enables D to escape liability by proving (a) that the driving, accident or damage occurred before he committed the basic offence, or (b) that he was neither in, nor on, nor in the immediate vicinity of, the vehicle when the driving, accident or damage occurred.

Penalties; mode of trial; conviction of basic offence

Section 12A in fact creates two offences, because different maximum **6–25**

---

[63] Strictly speaking, two offences: see below, §6–25.
[64] s.12A(1)(a).
[65] s.12A(1)(b).
[66] Whether by the person himself, if he committed the primary form of the basic offence, or by another.
[67] That is, before it is restored to its owner or to other lawful possession or custody: s.12A(8). "Owner" has the same meaning as in s.12: *ibid.*; see above, §6–16. For restoration to "other lawful possession or custody," see below, §15–13.
[68] Set out in s.12A(2).
[69] That is, (a) it is driven in a way which falls far below what would be expected of a competent and careful driver, and (b) it would be obvious to a competent and careful driver that driving in that way would be dangerous: s.12A(7).
[70] This includes damage caused by D in trying to get out of the vehicle: *Dawes v. D.P.P.* [1995] 1 Cr.App.R. 65 (D locked in police "rat-trap" vehicle).

punishments are provided for different factual situations.[71] The maximum term of imprisonment on conviction on indictment is in general two years; but it is five years in a case where, in circumstances falling within section 12A(2)(b), the accident caused the death of any person.[72] A person cannot be punished as for the more serious offence simply because a death is proved to have occurred; its occurrence, as a result of a relevant accident, must be alleged in the indictment.[73]

The offences are triable either way,[74] except that if the only circumstance in section 12A(2) that is alleged is that the vehicle and/or other property was damaged, and the total value of the damage alleged to have been done does not exceed £5,000, the offence must be tried summarily.[75]

The offences carry obligatory driving disqualification and endorsement and attract 3–11 penalty points.[76]

A person who is found not guilty of an offence under section 12A but is proved to have committed a basic offence may be convicted of the latter offence.[77]

---

[71] *Button, The Times*, October 21, 1994, applying *Courtie* [1984] A.C. 463.
[72] s.12A(4).
[73] *Button*, above.
[74] Aggravated Vehicle-Taking Act 1992, s.1(2)(b), confirming the application of Magistrates' Courts Act 1980, Sched. 1, para. 28.
[75] Magistrates' Courts Act 1980, s.22(1) (as amended by Criminal Justice and Public Order Act 1994, s.46(1), as to the "relevant sum"), and Aggravated Vehicle-Taking Act 1992, s.2(1)(2). But the lower maximum penalties applying in similar criminal damage cases (1980 Act, s.33(1)(a)) do not apply (*ibid.* s.33(3), added by Aggravated Vehicle-Taking Act 1992, s.2(3)).
[76] Road Traffic Offenders Act 1988, Sched. 2, Part II, as amended by Aggravated Vehicle-Taking Act 1992, s.3(1). The fact that a person convicted of an offence under s.12A did not himself drive the vehicle in question at any particular time or at all is not to be regarded as a special reason for the purposes of the 1988 Act, s.45(1): s.45(1A), added by the 1992 Act, s.3(2).
[77] s.12A(5). If this is in the Crown Court, the court has the same powers and duties as a magistrates' court would have had upon such a conviction: subs. (6).

Chapter 7

INTRODUCTION TO THE FRAUD OFFENCES

The Theft Acts, by a variety of offences to be considered in Chapters 8 to   **7–01**
12, make an important contribution to the armoury of the criminal law in its
fight against fraud. These offences require a general introduction, for two
reasons. First, an unassisted reader examining the relevant provisions, while
readily understanding each individually, would very likely be baffled as to
why they take the form they do. The first part of this chapter explains the
origins of the various provisions. Secondly, to study only the offences considered in the following chapters would be to receive a misleading impression
of the range of important fraud offences. The second part of the chapter
refers briefly to the most significant of the other offences alongside which the
Theft Act offences stand. The chapter concludes with a brief observation on
the state of the law.

1. OFFENCES IN THE THEFT ACTS

The 1968 Act

In the *Eighth Report*, the C.L.R.C. canvassed arguments for and against   **7–02**
some alternative schemes to provide for offences of deception.[1] Had the
scheme that the Committee favoured been accepted, there would have been
three main provisions. The first, to replace the offence of obtaining by false
pretences,[2] would have dealt with obtaining property by deception; this was
accepted and is now embodied in section 15, which is the subject of Chapter 8.
The second would have been an improved and extended version of the
offence of obtaining credit by fraud[3]; this was in itself uncontroversial. The
third and highly controversial proposal was for a provision making it an
offence, dishonestly and with a view to gain, to induce a person by deception
to do or refrain from doing any act. This was included in the Bill but foun-
dered in the House of Lords. It was felt that it would effect too wide and
vague an extension of the criminal law. Instead, in place of the second and
third of the offences originally proposed, section 16 (obtaining certain kinds
of "pecuniary advantage" by deception) was hurriedly devised to cover
obtaining credit by deception together with so much of the rejected general
offence as was felt to be acceptable. The remnants of section 16, after its
partial repeal by the 1978 Act (as explained below), are examined in Chapter
11. They deal with a variety of specialised transactions that ought not to
require individual mention in a well-drafted code.

---

[1] *Eighth Report*, paras. 97–100.
[2] Larceny Act 1916, s.32(1).
[3] Debtors Act 1869, s.13(1).

7–03 Sections 17, 19 and 20 contain modified versions, as recommended by the C.L.R.C., of some other pre-existing fraud offences. They are considered in Chapter 12. It would appear that the Committee desired to retain the substance of any offences in the replaced legislation that had anything distinctive to offer to the control of fraud.[4] The most important of these, undoubtedly, was falsification of accounts[5]—now re-enacted in modern guise as false accounting in section 17. Section 20(2) contains the only other offence meriting mention here. Procuring by deception the execution of a valuable security, which replaced a pre-existing offence of false pretences,[6] has proved more useful to prosecutors than its predecessor was.[7]

The 1978 Act

7–04 The most important case of the offence created by section 16 of the 1968 Act was that committed, under subsection (2)(a), by one who by deception dishonestly obtained the reduction, or the total or partial evasion or deferment, of a debt or charge for which he made himself liable or was or might become liable. Happily it was not necessary to wrestle for many years with the obscurities of this provision and with the difficult case law it generated. Section 16 was before long described as having created "a judicial nightmare"[8] and it was clear that subsection (2)(a) must be replaced. Proposals for amending legislation were made by the C.L.R.C. in 1977 in its *Thirteenth Report* (with a draft Bill appended).[9] The outcome was the Theft Act 1978, which repealed section 16(2)(a) and created three new offences.

7–05 There are two ways of expressing simply what the C.L.R.C. was seeking to achieve by clause 1 of its draft Bill. First, to use the language of the offence which had been replaced by section 16(2)(a), the aim was to penalise the obtaining of credit by deception—more precisely, the obtaining of credit in respect of the payment of money.[10] But the Committee was not in favour of employing the term "credit" in the drafting of the offence.[11] Secondly, the clause might be said to be aimed at the obtaining by deception "of services on which a monetary value is placed."[12] For an obtaining of credit in respect of a supply of property was already covered by section 15 of the 1968 Act, at least where an intention of permanently depriving P of the property existed; and what needed to be dealt with, to supplement section 15, was the use of decep-

---

[4] *Eighth Report*, paras. 102 *et seq.*
[5] Falsification of Accounts Act 1875, s.2.
[6] Larceny Act 1916, s.32(2).
[7] See below, §12–14.
[8] *Per* Edmund Davies L.J. in *Royle* (1971) 56 Cr.App.R. 131 at 136.
[9] The Report was preceded by a Working Paper published in August 1974. An excellent account of the genesis of s.16 and of its history in the courts is provided in Appendix 2 to the Report.
[10] Working Paper, para. 25.
[11] *Thirteenth Report*, para. 8.
[12] *ibid.*, para. 9.

tion to obtain on credit other valuable benefits such as a hiring of goods, the provision of labour or the grant of a licence—benefits that might collectively be called "services". But the C.L.R.C. preferred not to employ the term "services" in the drafting of the offence.[13] Instead it offered in clause 1 an offence of dishonestly inducing another by deception to act on any person's promise of payment. This formula, attended by an adequate apparatus of definition, would have achieved the objects described above.

When the Bill was considered by the House of Lords, clause 1 was criti- **7–06** cised as too complex and a new clause was substituted, penalising the obtaining of services by deception. After the Bill had passed the Lords, the new clause was hurriedly referred to the C.L.R.C., which recommended instead the further version that was enacted as section 1 of the 1978 Act. The essential contribution of the Committee at this final stage was to provide a definition of "services" so as to ensure that the offence would be limited, as all along intended, to an obtaining of services "on which a monetary value is placed." On the other hand, the offence that emerged was drafted so as not to be limited to deception as to the prospect of payment; nor, indeed, need credit be involved at all. Moreover, section 1 does not (as the Lords amendment did) require the offender to have acted "with a view to gain or an intent to cause loss." The result is an offence not only of completely different design from that originally proposed, but also substantially wider in scope. It is examined in Chapter 9.

Section 2 (evading liability by deception) is considered in Chapter 10. **7–07** Whereas section 1, at least as originally drafted, was designed to control the deceptive obtaining of credit "at the outset of a transaction"[14] (that is, when a liability to pay for services is originally incurred), section 2 is mainly concerned with the obtaining by deception of relief from some existing liability. But it also covers the obtaining by deception of an exemption from, or abatement of, liability to make a payment, which includes some cases of fraud committed before liability is incurred. Section 2 completed the task of replacing section 16(2)(a) of the 1968 Act.

The opportunity was taken at the same time to create, by section 3, a gen- **7–08** eral offence of making off without payment in a situation in which payment "on the spot" is expected. This deals with the mischief of "bilking", which was only partially, accidentally and artificially covered by sections 1, 15 and 16 of the 1968 Act.[15] The offence is examined in Chapter 13. Deception is not an ingredient of this offence.

2. OTHER OFFENCES

There follows a brief review of the more important fraud offences outside **7–09**

---

[13] *ibid.*, para. 7.
[14] *ibid.*, para. 13.
[15] As explained below, §§13–03 to 13–05.

the Theft Acts. The intention is to indicate, without treating in detail, the larger context in which the Theft Act offences require to be viewed, whether for the practical purpose of the selection of charges or as a basis for assessing the condition of this department of the criminal law.[16] The offences can conveniently be divided into four groups: general offences; offences involving companies; offences for the protection of investors; and fraud on the public revenue and social security fraud.

General offences

7–10   *Conspiracy to defraud.* The Criminal Law Act 1977 in principle limited conspiracy to agreements for the commission of crime.[17] The common law offence of conspiracy to defraud (which is not so limited) was nevertheless preserved, by section 5(2) of the 1977 Act, pending further consideration by the Law Commission of the steps that would need to be taken, to avoid unacceptable gaps in the criminal law, if it were abolished.[18] It now carries a maximum of 10 years' imprisonment.[19] Section 5(2) was amended in 1987 to ensure that an agreement to defraud that amounts also to a statutory conspiracy to commit an offence may be prosecuted either at common law or under the statute.[20]

7–11   This is not the place for detailed consideration of conspiracy to defraud. It is sufficient to say that it is wide enough to embrace, not only agreements to commit many offences under the Theft Acts (including theft and most of the offences to be studied in the immediately following chapters), but also any other dishonest[21] agreement to act to the prejudice of the proprietary rights or economic interests of another or others[22]:

---

[16] For more comprehensive surveys, see Smith (A. T. H.) and Arlidge and Parry, *passim.*
[17] Criminal Law Act 1977, ss.1(1), 5(1).
[18] Law Commission Working Paper No. 56, *Conspiracy to Defraud* (1974); *Conspiracy and Criminal Law Reform*, Law Com. No. 76 (1976), paras. 1.14–1.16. The Law Commission has since recommended that the offence be preserved for a further period, while a general review of dishonesty offences is undertaken: *Conspiracy to Defraud*, Law Com. No. 228 (1994).
[19] Criminal Justice Act 1987, s.12(3). (This is the same maximum as for conspiracy to obtain property by deception.)
[20] Under s.5(2) in its original form, as surprisingly interpreted, an agreement on a course of conduct amounting to or involving the commission of a substantive offence, even of fraud (such as obtaining property by deception), could be charged only under s.1 of the Criminal Law Act 1977 as a conspiracy to commit that offence, and not as a conspiracy to defraud (though if the agreement involved additional fraudulent conduct, not amounting to a substantive offence, this aspect of the agreement could be charged as a conspiracy to defraud): *Ayres* [1984] A.C. 447 (as explained in *Cooke* [1986] A.C. 909); *Tonner* (1984) 80 Cr.App.R. 170; *Grant* (1985) 82 Cr.App.R. 324. This inhibition continues to apply to agreements made before July 20, 1987 (and not subsisting on that date: *Boyle and Mears* (1991) 94 Cr.App.R. 158). But on that date s.12 of the Criminal Justice Act 1987 came into force, removing the inhibition (subs.(1)) and appropriately amending s.5(2) of the 1977 Act (subs. (2)).
[21] *Landy* (1981) 72 Cr.App.R. 237. The requirement of dishonesty is governed by the principles in *Ghosh* [1982] Q.B. 1053 (see above, §2–132).
[22] *Scott v. Metropolitan Police Commissioner* [1975] A.C. 819; *Allsop* (1977) 64 Cr.App.R. 29; *Wai Yu-tsang v. R.* [1992] 1 A.C. 269.

"[I]t is enough that ... the conspirators have dishonestly agreed to bring about a state of affairs which they realise will or may deceive the victim into so acting, or failing to act, that he will suffer economic loss or his economic interests will be put at risk."[23]

So long, therefore, as two or more persons are involved, conspiracy to defraud substantially supplements the Theft Act offences. Deception need not be an intended means of effecting the fraud[24]; and the offence does not require an intention to obtain any of the specific benefits with which the Theft Act offences are concerned (property belonging to another; services; the execution of a valuable security; a pecuniary advantage; or the evasion of a liability).

Forgery is the offence committed by one who "makes a false instrument,   **7–12** with the intention that he or another shall use it to induce somebody to accept it as genuine, and by reason of so accepting it to do or not to do some act to his own or another person's prejudice."[25] Another offence is that of using a false instrument, knowing or believing it to be false, with the intention of inducing somebody to accept it as genuine and thereby to act to his or another's prejudice.[26] The former offence is, of course, often preparatory to the commission of a Theft Act or other fraud offence that will occur when somebody is induced to act to his prejudice. Using a false instrument is commonly an attempt to commit such an offence. But "prejudice" is very widely defined,[27] and there is no requirement of dishonesty.[28] So forgery and using a false instrument somewhat extend the reach of the criminal law.[29]

Offences involving companies

Fraudulent trading. Section 458 of the Companies Act 1985 provides that   **7–13** "[i]f any business of a company is carried on with intent to defraud creditors of the company or creditors of any other person, or for any fraudulent purpose", a person is guilty of an offence, carrying a maximum of seven years' imprisonment, if he is "knowingly a party to the carrying on of the business in

---

[23] *Wai Yu-tsang v. R.*, above, *per* Lord Goff of Chieveley at 280. But defrauding is not limited to the sphere of economic interests: *Welham v. D.P.P.* [1961] A.C. 103 (deceiving person into acting contrary to public duty); *Wai Yu-tsang v. R.*, above, *per* Lord Goff at 277, considering *Welham*.

[24] *Scott v. Metropolitan Police Commissioner*, above.

[25] Forgery and Counterfeiting Act 1981, s.1. For making a copy of a false instrument, see *ibid.*, s.2. For the meaning of "instrument" and "false", see *ibid.*, ss.8 and 9(1).

[26] *ibid.*, s.3. For using a copy of a false instrument, see *ibid.*, s.4.

[27] *ibid.*, s.10.

[28] *Horsey v. Hutchings, The Times*, November 8, 1984.

[29] See also the Computer Misuse Act 1990, s.2. This makes it an offence to cause a computer to perform any function with intent to secure unauthorised access to any program or data held in any computer (an offence under s.1), with the further intent to commit or facilitate an offence punishable with five years' imprisonment. The conduct so penalised may be conduct preparatory to fraud, or to forgery (of a "device on or in which information is recorded or stored by ... electronic ... means": see 1981 Act, s.8(1)(d)), or of false accounting in aid of, or to conceal, fraud (see below, §12–01).

that manner."[30] This offence was once capable of being prosecuted only in the course of the winding up of the company, because of the appearance of the offence in the same section as a provision providing for the civil liability of persons knowingly party to fraudulent trading that emerged "in the course of the winding up."[31] But the dependence of the offence upon a winding up was abandoned in 1961.[32] In consequence, the notion of carrying on the business of a company "for any fraudulent purpose" is now understood in its widest sense (and not, as it formerly was, as limited to frauds on existing creditors).[33] The offence is thus one of considerable utility. It can be used, for example, where it is desired to lay a single fraud charge (rather than to rely on specific obtaining offences) against a person who, working alone but through his company, has conducted a sustained course of obtaining property or services by deception. Nor need the "fraudulent purpose" involve an intention to commit offences. As it has been well expressed, "prosecutors sometimes use this type of charge as a kind of one-man conspiracy to defraud."[34]

7–14   *Other offences.* Numerous other offences capable of being committed specifically by companies or their officers have, taken together, a great deal to contribute to the control of fraud.[35] Many involve the making of misleading, false or deceptive statements or the falsification of accounts; others are directed at the misuse of company assets in fraud of the company itself, its shareholders or creditors.

Offences for the protection of investors

7–15   *Misleading statements, etc.* The protection of investors and others against deceptive inducements to risk their money is the special concern of important offences under section 47(1) of the Financial Services Act 1986 (investment generally); under section 133 of the same Act (contracts of insurance); and under section 35 of the Banking Act 1987 (the making of deposits). These provisions, which carry maximum prison terms of seven years, are all drafted on the same model: they penalise the making of a statement, promise or forecast known to be misleading, false or deceptive, or the dishonest concealment of any material facts, or the reckless making (dishonestly or otherwise) of a statement, promise or forecast which is misleading, false or deceptive, for the purpose of inducing, or being reckless whether it may induce, another person to (in particular) enter into an investment contract or a contract of insurance or to make a deposit. A less serious offence, but one punishable with two years' imprisonment on conviction on indictment, is that

---

[30] Companies Act 1985, s.458, Sched. 24. In spite of the high maximum penalty on conviction on indictment, the offence is triable either way.
[31] Companies Act 1948, s.332(1) and (3); *D.P.P.* v. *Schildkamp* [1971] A.C. 1.
[32] Companies Act 1967, s.96.
[33] *Kemp* (1988) 87 Cr.App.R. 95.
[34] Arlidge and Parry, para. 12.45.
[35] See, in particular, Companies Act 1985, ss.110(2), 114, 143(2), 151(3), 342(1)(2), 393, 450(1)(2); Insolvency Act 1986, ss.206–211 (and compare ss.353–359 for offences connected with bankruptcy). See also s.19 of the Theft Act 1968.

(under section 70(1) of the Companies Act 1985) of authorising the issue of a company prospectus which includes an untrue statement.

Creation of false market. Section 47(2) of the Financial Services Act 1986 **7–16** provides an offence (punishable with imprisonment for up to seven years) of creating a false or misleading impression as to the market in, or the price or value of, any investments (very broadly defined)[36] for the purpose (in effect) of inducing investment decisions based on that impression. Until the creation of this statutory offence such conduct could be prosecuted only as a conspiracy to defraud and therefore only if two or more persons could be shown to be involved.[37]

Insider dealing. This offence, formerly contained in the Company Securi- **7–17** ties (Insider Dealing) Act 1985, has been re-created in much extended form by Part V of the Criminal Justice Act 1993. It is designed to control the behaviour of persons having privileged price-sensitive information relating to particular securities or to securities issued by particular issuers.[38] A person has information as an "insider" if it is, and he knows it is, "inside information"[39] and he has it, and knows that he has it, from an "inside source"—that is, (a) through being a director, employee or shareholder of an issuer of securities or through having access to information by virtue of his employment, office or profession, or (b) directly or indirectly from a person within (a).[40] Such a person commits an offence (subject to defences made available by section 53) by dealing[41] in such securities,[42] or by encouraging another to do so,[43] or by disclosing the information, otherwise than in the proper performance of the functions of his employment, office or profession, to another person.[44]

Frauds on the public revenue and social security fraud

Cheating at common law. The old common law offence of cheating was **7–18** abolished by the Theft Act 1968 "except as regards offences relating to the public revenue."[45] According to modern decisions, the exception preserves a

---

[36] By s.1(1) and Sched. 1, Pt. I.
[37] *Scott v. Brown, Doering, McNab & Co.* [1892] 2 Q.B. 724.
[38] Part V applies to a wide range of "securities": s.54 and Sched.2; Insider Dealing (Securities and Regulated Markets) Order 1994 (S.I. 1994, No. 187).
[39] See s.56.
[40] s.57.
[41] More precisely, dealing (see s.55) in circumstances that involve an acquisition or disposal on a regulated market (see s.60(1); S.I. 1994, No. 187, above) or a person's dealing in reliance on, or as, a professional intermediary (see s.59): s.52(3).
[42] s.52(1).
[43] "knowing or having reasonable cause to believe that the dealing would take place in the circumstances mentioned in [s.52(3)]" (see n. 41, above): s.52(2)(a).
[44] s.52(2)(b). See also Companies Act 1985, s.323(1) (prohibition on directors dealing in share options).
[45] s.32(1)(a). The existence of the offence of cheating the revenue has been repeatedly confirmed in modern times, most recently in *Mulligan* [1990] Crim.L.R. 427.

broad offence of great utility, available to deal with any conduct intended to defraud the revenue, whether consisting of positive act—as, for example, the understating of income, profits or assets attracting tax, the overstating of expenses or the claiming of fictitious allowances—or of omission.[46] There are no maximum penalties for the offence, since it is punishable at common law. But a person may be convicted of it although there exists a statutory offence with limited penalties specially provided for such conduct as is proved against him—as, for example, an offence specifically concerned with failure to meet VAT liability.[47]

7–19   *Offences under revenue legislation.* The most important statutory offences relating to the public revenue occur under the Customs and Excise Management Act 1979,[48] the Value Added Tax Act 1983[49] and the Income and Corporation Taxes Act 1988, s.561(10) and (11).[50]

7–20   *Offences under the general law.* Fraud on the Inland Revenue is not, in general, the subject of offences under tax legislation, but is left to be dealt with under the general criminal law. Obvious available offences, apart from common law cheating, are a number under the Theft Acts (most obviously obtaining property by deception, evasion of liability by deception and false accounting) and the Forgery and Counterfeiting Act 1981. And the Perjury Act 1911 provides in section 5 an offence of knowingly and wilfully making (otherwise than on oath) a statement, false in a material particular, in a document (such as a tax return) required to be made by any public general Act of Parliament.

7–21   *Social security fraud* is the subject of a special offence under section 55(1) of the Social Security Act 1986. This renders liable to a fine not exceeding level 5 on the standard scale or to imprisonment for up to three months, or to both, a person who, "for the purpose of obtaining any benefit or payment under any of the benefit Acts, or for any other purpose connected with any of

---

[46] *Mavji* [1987] 1 W.L.R. 1388; [1987] 2 All E.R. 758 ("The common law offence of cheating does not require a false representation, either by words or conduct. Cheating can include any form of fraudulent conduct which results in diverting money from the revenue and in depriving the revenue of money to which it is entitled."); *Redford* (1988) 89 Cr.App.R. 1. Actual loss to the revenue need not be proved: *Hunt*, May 5, 1994, C.A. no. 93/4189/W2.

[47] Cases in last note.

[48] See in particular ss.50(2) (improper importation of goods: one variety of this offence involves an intent to defraud Her Majesty of chargeable duty), 167 (untrue declarations, etc.), 168 (counterfeiting documents, etc.), 170(1)(2) (fraudulent evasion of duty, etc.).

[49] s.39, as amended by the Finance Act 1985, s.12, Sched. 6. (One amendment made in 1985 was the raising of the maximum sentence of imprisonment from two to seven years, thus removing one ground for resort to the common law offence of cheating: see above, text at n. 47.) Compare the Car Tax Act 1983, s.1(4), Sched. 1, para. 8.

[50] These provisions are concerned with frauds involving the obtaining or misuse of certificates and vouchers required for exemption from the special deduction of tax (under s.559(4)) from payments made to sub-contractors in the construction industry ("the lump"). The offences are punishable on summary conviction with a fine not exceeding £5,000.

those Acts—(a) makes a statement or representation which he knows to be false; or (b) produces or furnishes, or knowingly causes or knowingly allows to be produced or furnished, any document or information which he knows to be false in a material particular." But the policy in relation to relatively small frauds is to avoid prosecution in favour of warning and the recovery of benefit wrongly obtained (commonly by deduction from future benefits).[51] Offences under the general criminal law, notably obtaining property by deception, are likely to be used for the more serious cases that require prosecution.

3. COMMENT

No one wanting to construct a rational, efficient law of criminal fraud **7–22** would choose to start from the present position. The law sketched in the preceding parts of this chapter is in a very untidy and unsatisfactory condition. The various offences are not so framed and related to each other as to cover, in a clearly organised way and without doubt or strained interpretation, the range of fraudulent conduct with which the law should be able to deal. And the offence of theft, as stated in sections 1–6 of the 1968 Act and interpreted by the courts, has accumulated a number of serious defects. It is no surprise, therefore, that the Law Commission should have announced, in November 1994, a decision to undertake a comprehensive review of dishonesty offences.

The only general offence available to catch wrongdoers who might slip through the mesh of other offences is conspiracy to defraud, which suffers from three vices: it requires two or more parties; it is a common law offence; and it may consist of an agreement to do something that is not an offence if done by one person (that is why it can catch those who might otherwise escape). An obvious solution, if it could be achieved, would be to create a general offence, capable of being committed by an individual, based on an appropriately broad concept of fraud—perhaps such a concept as that employed in the conspiracy offence. But a satisfactory definition of a general offence, that does not rest its whole weight effectively on a vague adverb such as "fraudulently" or "dishonestly",[52] has proved hard to devise. We may in the end have to be content with a rationalisation, and any necessary specific supplementation, of existing offences of fraud and dishonesty (including those to be studied in the following chapters). Meanwhile, it seems, pending the outcome of the Law Commission's general review, conspiracy to defraud will be preserved, despite its defects of principle, for the sake of its interim pragmatic virtues.[53]

---

[51] See comments of Lord Lane C.J. in *Stewart* [1987] 1 W.L.R. 559; [1987] 2 All E.R. 383.
[52] This vice disqualified a form of general offence canvassed in Law Commission Working Paper No. 104, *Conspiracy to Defraud* (1987).
[53] See above, n. 18.

Chapter 8

OBTAINING PROPERTY BY DECEPTION

1. THE OFFENCE

8–01   The dishonest obtaining by deception of property belonging to another with the intention of permanently depriving the other of it is an offence punishable on conviction on indictment with up to 10 years' imprisonment (s.15(1)).

"For the purposes of this section a person is to be treated as obtaining property if he obtains ownership, possession or control of it ..." (s.15(2)). "Property" and "belonging to another" have much the same large meanings as they have in the law of theft (s.34(1)). "Deception" is defined (s.15(4)) so as to include any deliberate or reckless deception as to a matter of fact or law, however effected.

These definitions combine to produce a very wide offence—one distinctly wider than that of obtaining by false pretences which it replaced.[1] The main limitations of that offence were: that it applied only to the obtaining of any chattel, money or valuable security; that it applied only when ownership and not merely possession of property was obtained; and that the pretence had to be as to some present or past fact, not including the alleged offender's intentions as to the future.

8–02   All the conditions of liability are stated in section 15(1). In a case of obtaining a social security benefit by deception it was argued that no offence could be proved in the absence of an adjudicator's decision that the defendant was not entitled to benefit. This remarkable argument, effectively making an administrative adjudication an ingredient of the offence, inevitably failed.[2]

The Court of Appeal has also had occasion to declare irrelevant the tendency of the victim's trading policy, sought to be circumvented by the deception charged, to contravene European community law. The use of the criminal law is concerned with the dishonest deception charged, not with support for the victim's policy.[3]

2. "OBTAINS PROPERTY BELONGING TO ANOTHER"

Property belonging to another

"Property"

8–03   The definition of "property" in section 4(1)[4] is made to apply generally for

---

[1] Larceny Act 1916, s.32(1).
[2] *Lally* [1989] Crim.L.R. 648.
[3] *Dearlove and Drucker* (1988) 88 Cr.App.R. 279.
[4] " 'Property' includes money and all other property, real or personal, including things in action and other intangible property."

142

purposes of the Act by section 34(1), so that the offence under section 15 can be committed in respect of any kind of property. There are no provisions, as there are in the case of theft, limiting the circumstances in which land can be the subject of the offence. Whatever can be transferred by one person to another as property is in practice within section 15, for deception can induce its transfer. So, for instance, a beneficial interest in property under a trust is, it is submitted, itself property within the phrase "things in action and other intangible property", and to induce the assignment of such an interest is therefore to obtain property.

If D, by deception, induces P to pay him more money than he would have paid but for the deception, there is an obtaining of property within the section and D may be convicted even though the precise amount of the excess cannot be specified.[5]

"Belonging to another"

The property obtained must be property "belonging to another".[6] The **8–04** wide definition of this phrase in section 5(1)[7] is also made to apply here by section 34(1). It is desirable to notice the force of this in conjunction with the provision that "a person is to be treated as obtaining property if he obtains ownership, possession or control of it" (s.15(2)). The result is that there is an obtaining within section 15 if the effect of D's fraud is that he obtains ownership, possession or control of any property which P owns, possesses or controls or in which P has any proprietary right or interest.[8]

Of course, the normal case will be that in which D induces P to part with property of which P is the owner. It will be enough if D obtains ownership only or possession only. For instance, if D by deception induces P to agree to sell him specific goods in a deliverable state so that, as prima facie occurs in such a case,[9] the property in the goods passes to D on the making of the contract, D is guilty even if he never acquires possession.[10] Conversely, D may deceive P into lending or hiring goods to him, D's intention being to deprive P permanently of them, and here D is guilty although he does not acquire ownership.

---

[5] *Levene v. Pearcey* [1976] Crim.L.R. 63 (taxi driver telling passenger that normal route is blocked, using longer route and obtaining larger fare).

[6] A mistake in the information or indictment as to the person to whom the property belonged will be immaterial if the defendant nevertheless has enough information to know the nature of the charge; if the victim's identity is material, an error on the point can be cured by amendment: *Etim v. Hatfield* [1975] Crim.L.R. 234.

[7] " 'Property' shall be regarded as belonging to any person having possession or control of it, or having in it any proprietary right or interest (not being an equitable interest arising only from an agreement to transfer or grant an interest)." Other provisions of s.5 are not made to apply for purposes of s.15.

[8] With one immaterial exception: see the parenthesis in s.5(1) (preceding note).

[9] Sale of Goods Act 1979, s.18, r. 1.

[10] By obtaining ownership, D puts himself in a position to pass ownership to a third person, who may buy in good faith and obtain a valid title as against P: Sale of Goods Act 1979, s.23; *Eighth Report*, para. 90.

8–05   Alternatively, D may himself be the owner and still commit the offence. Two obvious examples are the following:

(i) P contracts to sell goods to D, D using no deception to induce the contract. The circumstances are such that the property in the goods passes before delivery. P retains possession and is entitled to do so until D pays or tenders the price. D by deception induces P to part with possession (*e.g.* he gives P a cheque that he knows to be worthless).
(ii) D pledges goods with P. By deception he induces P to redeliver the goods to him.

Again, neither D nor the person deceived need be the owner. P may have possession or control of Q's goods. If D induces P to part with the goods, intending to deprive both P and Q of them, either P or Q can be named in the indictment as the person to whom the goods belong. It will no doubt be convenient to name P.

Obtaining a thing in action

8–06   The requirement that what is obtained be "property belonging to another" seems to be inept in its application to some important kinds of case in which what D obtains by his deception is a thing of action. There is no problem where P is induced to assign to D an existing thing (such as a debt); what D obtains in such a case is the very property that P parts with. An apparent difficulty arises, however, in any case in which what D obtains is a thing in action created by the transaction itself—a thing in which, by definition, P has had no prior proprietary interest. How then can D be said to obtain property "belonging to another"? The point is not attractive in terms of merit; and it is perhaps partly for that reason that the Court of Appeal, in a succession of cases, has either overlooked it or swept it aside in judgments somewhat lacking in argumentative rigour. Two kinds of situation must be separately considered.

8–07   (i) *Obtaining the issue of a cheque.* (a) *The problem.* D deceives P into drawing a cheque in favour of D or E. When the cheque is delivered to the payee it has the quality of a thing in action—it embodies a right of the payee or subsequent holder to be paid the amount for which it is drawn. That is not something that formerly belonged to the drawer; indeed, it is a right enforceable against the drawer himself. Viewing the cheque as a thing in action,[11]

---

[11] The problem discussed here ought not to arise in practice. A prosecutor can avoid it by charging the obtaining by deception of the piece of paper on which P wrote the cheque (as to the requirement of an intention of permanently depriving P of the property so described, see below, §8–71). A charge of procuring by deception the execution (the signing) of the cheque as a valuable security (s.20(2); below, §12–14) seems even less problematic. There seems also to be an offence of theft of the cheque (viewed as a piece of paper), applying *Gomez* [1993] A.C. 442; above, §2–80.

what does D or E obtain that will satisfy section 15(1)?[12] (b) *The judicial response*. An answer was attempted in *Pyman*,[13] in which the Court of Appeal was concerned with mortgage loan cheques obtained by deception. The court relied in the first place on section 5(4): that is, it regarded the cheques (got by mistake induced by D's fraud), or their proceeds, as property belonging to the drawer because D was obliged to "make restoration of" the cheques, their proceeds or their value. This was plainly an error; it appears not to have been noticed that section 5(4) does not apply for the purposes of the section 15 offence but only for the purposes of theft.[14] The court's alternative analysis was that the deceived lender had in any case a "proprietary interest" within the meaning of section 5(1)—applying the doctrine in *Chase Manhattan Bank N.A. v. Israel-British Bank (London) Ltd.*[15] that a person who pays money under a factual mistake retains an equitable interest in it. As a reason for rejecting the argument that the cheque *as a thing in action* never "belonged to" the drawer, this implies the conception (not spelt out in the judgment) that at the very moment D obtains his claim against the deceived drawer on the cheque, the drawer acquires (and thus "retains") an equitable interest in that claim against himself. This is a conception that needs some defending. The language of the unreserved judgment is casual[16] and the decision is not an impressive one; but the case is the only explicit Court of Appeal authority on the point under discussion.

(ii) *Obtaining credit in a bank account*. (a) *The problem*. D procures the   **8–08** crediting of his own, or E's, bank account with a sum, in a transaction that involves the corresponding debiting of P's account with his bank. Here the thing in action obtained by D or E—a right against his bank[17]—is a new thing and not, on the face of it, property that formerly belonged to another; it is not the same thing as P's pre-existing right against his bank. Such an obtaining has occurred at the expense of P and ought no doubt to be within section 15; but it seems on the face of it not to be within the section as drafted. What does D or E obtain that will satisfy section 15(1)? (b) *The judicial response*. In some cases convictions have been upheld without the point apparently being

---

[12] The transaction does not effect an assignment to the payee of the debt to the drawer represented by the credit in his account: Bills of Exchange Act 1882, s.53(1). A variant of the problem occurs in the case of an obtaining by deception (*e.g.* by disguised multiple applications) of shares issued on flotation direct to the public. Such shares (as opposed to relevant documents— letters of allotment, share certificates—transferred by the company) are "things in action [or] other intangible property" existing for the first time as the propety of the person to whom they are allotted.

[13] May 24, 1994, no. 93/3689/Z4.

[14] See ss.1(3), 34(1).

[15] [1981] Ch. 105.

[16] It was said that, because P "retained . . . an equitable interest in that *money*, it cannot be said that at the time [D] received *the cheque* . . ., he was the only and exclusive owner of *the property*." (Emphasis supplied.)

[17] See §2–146, above. Even if the credit merely goes to reduce D's overdraft, there is presumably for a fraction of time property that can be said to have been obtained by D.

noticed.[18] But the Court of Appeal addressed the problem in *Preddy, Slade and Slade.*[19] The case concerned the fraudulent obtaining of mortgage loans, which were made by telegraphic or electronic transfer having the effect of crediting the account of the solicitor acting for both parties and debiting the account of the lender. Each transaction was described in the indictment as the obtaining of "an advance by way of mortgage in the sum of [£x] with the intention of permanently depriving [the lender] thereof". The property obtained,[20] the court asserted, was not a thing in action but "other intangible property" within the meaning of section 4(1).[21] So what is obtained is not, after all, either the pre-existing credit in the lender's account (which is *pro tanto* destroyed by the transaction[22]) or the resulting credit in the solicitor's account, for both of these *are* things in action; and thus the difficulty presented by the words "belonging to another" is side-stepped. What is left entirely obscure is the nature of the intangible property—variously called "funds" and an "asset"—referred to. It is easy to see that the lender has lost and the borrower has gained; it remains difficult to see just what "property", formerly "belonging to" the lender, has been "obtained" by the borrower.

"Obtains"

8–09   For purposes of section 15:

(a) "a person is to be treated as obtaining property if he obtains ownership, possession or control of it." The flexibility that this gives to the offence has been illustrated above.

(b) "'obtain' includes obtaining for another or enabling another to obtain or to retain." The following are examples:

(i) *Obtaining for another.* P has a lien on E's goods and D on E's behalf persuades P to give up possession to him (D) by promising to discharge E's debt. (Note that, as P is the only person whom D intends to deprive, he alone can be named as the person to whom the property belongs.)

(ii) *Enabling another to obtain.* In a similar situation, D prevails on P to deliver the property direct to E. In *Duru,*[23] D deceived P into making

---

[18] See *Davies* (1981) 74 Cr.App.R. 94 (D presented for payment a cheque drawn by P that he (D) had stolen from the payee; he was convicted both of stealing the cheque and of obtaining "the sum of £10,000 belonging to P"); *Thompson* (1984) 79 Cr.App.R. 191 (D by fraud induced P bank to transfer funds to a bank in England for the credit of D's account; he was convicted of obtaining "£x the property of P bank"). The court did not comment on the language of the indictments in these cases, as to which see above §2–17, at n. 34.

[19] August 8, 1994, no. 93/5211/Y5.

[20] By the solicitor, but that was immaterial: see s.15(2) (below, §8–09).

[21] This had previously been suggested, *obiter*, in *Williams and Crick*, July 29, 1993, C.A. no. 91/3265/W3 (*sub nom. Crick and another*, July 29, 1993, C.A. no. 91/3265/W3 (*sub nom. Crick and another, The Times*, August 18, 1993). Compare *King* [1992] 1 Q.B. 20 (below, §12–18), treating a CHAPS order for the transfer of funds between bank accounts as "a document ... transferring ... [a] right ... over property" within the meaning of s.20(3).

[22] D's act, intentionally effecting this destruction, appears to be a theft.

[23] (1973) 58 Cr.App.R. 151.

a loan to F, which P did by sending a cheque to F's solicitor, E. D had "enabled [E] to obtain" possession or control of the cheque; and it was irrelevant that E was not himself a party to the deception.

(iii) *Enabling another to retain.* E is in possession of P's goods. D deceives P into leaving them with E rather than claiming their return.

It is odd that enabling another to retain is obtaining within the section, but that enabling oneself to retain is not.

3. DECEPTION

Statutory definition

Section 15(4) provides a partial explanation of the term "deception":   **8–10**

> "For purposes of this section 'deception' means any deception (whether deliberate or reckless) by words or conduct as to fact or as to law, including a deception as to the present intentions of the person using the deception or any other person."

The purpose of this subsection is not to provide a definition in the full sense, but rather to make clear that the term "deception" used in this Act does not share some of the limitations of the term "false pretence" in the Larceny Act offence replaced by section 15.[24] In particular, it was not formerly an offence to obtain property by making a promise that the maker had no intention of keeping or by otherwise deliberately misrepresenting an intention. It was therefore thought desirable to single out fraudulent statements of intention for express reference. Section 15(4) is one of those provisions designed as important messages for the pre-Theft Act practitioner in particular.[25]

The parenthesis, "whether deliberate or reckless", may conveniently be reserved to a discussion of the whole of the fault element of the offence.[26] The rest of the subsection requires extensive consideration at this point.

Deception requires a deceiver and a deceived

Towards the end of section 15(4) occurs the phrase "the person using the   **8–11**
deception". This might suggest that deception is something employed (a lie or other tricking device) rather than something practised (a lie or trick having an effect upon a victim). But the C.L.R.C., in the course of justifying the choice of the word "deception" in place of the old phrase "false pretence", said that the new expression has

> "the advantage of directing attention to the effect that the offender deliberately

---

[24] Obtaining any chattel, money or valuable security by any false pretence: Larceny Act 1916, s.32.
[25] Others are ss.3(1) and 4(1).
[26] See §§8–60, 8–61.

147

produced on the mind of the person deceived, whereas 'false pretence' makes one think of what exactly the offender did in order to deceive"[27];

and it is certainly true that there can be no deception without a deceived party. This part of the chapter—like section 15(4)—will be concerned only with the deceptive practice used by D; but it must not be forgotten that one element of a deception is P's being in some sense misled by that practice. In what sense he must be misled will be considered hereafter.

"Deceiving" a machine

8–12   It appears now[28] to be universally accepted that a deception offence cannot be committed by obtaining an advantage through misuse of a machine (whether a computer or a mechanical device) without the intervention of a deceived human being.[29] The terms of two of the deception offences seem to confirm this view. Sections 1 and 2 of the Theft Act 1978 (obtaining services by deception; evasion of liability by deception) are both worded in a way which assumes the existence of a person who is not merely the victim of the offence but is also personally affected by the deception.[30] It would be odd if the offence of obtaining property, but not that of obtaining services, could be committed by feeding a false coin into a machine. The oddity would be compounded by the fact that where property is obtained, as from a vending machine, the transaction can perfectly aptly be prosecuted as theft.

8–13   The Law Commission has several times considered whether the need for a human object of deception leaves a gap in the law of fraud that ought to be filled.[31] The tendency of its discussions has been that, although there is a case for law reform, the gap is only a small one, because the dishonest manipulation of machines almost always involves the commission of some other offence, often theft. But the gravamen of many transactions will be the actual dishonest obtaining of an advantage (otherwise than by theft) that a conviction of an offence such as forgery[32] or false accounting will only imperfectly reflect. If the 1978 offences survive the current review of dishonesty offences, they should be amended to cover the deception of machines.

Deception by words or conduct

8–14   Section 15(4) explains that "deception" embraces "any deception ... by

---

[27] *Eighth Report*, para. 87.
[28] The point was left open in *Davies v. Flackett* [1973] R.T.R. 8.
[29] There has been at least one ruling to this effect in the context of false VAT returns (*Moritz*, 1961, unreported), with consequent amending legislation: Value Added Tax Act 1983, s.39(2C) (added by Finance Act 1985, s.12(5)).
[30] s.1(2): " ... the other is induced to confer a benefit"; s.2(1)(b): " ... induces the creditor ... to wait for payment."
[31] Working Paper No. 56, *Conspiracy to Defraud* (1974), paras. 61–63; Working Paper No. 104, *Conspiracy to Defraud* (1987), paras. 4.9–4.14; *Computer Misuse*, Law Com. No. 186 (1989), paras. 2.4–2.7; *Conspiracy to Defraud*, Law Com. No. 228 (1994), paras. 4.40–4.46.
[32] See Forgery and Counterfeiting Act 1981, ss.8(1)(d), 10(3)).

words or conduct." A conventional way of saying much the same thing is to say that one person may deceive another by either an express or an implied representation which is false; he represents something to be the case which is not. But it has been observed that some kinds of deception cannot properly, or at least without artificiality, be analysed as involving the making of representations.[33] Although this may be true, the conventional language remains useful. In every case of deception the victim will in some sense[34] be led to suppose that which is not; and in this chapter "that which is not" will be referred to as that which is "falsely represented" to be the case.

Adherence to this conventional usage in a general discussion does not imply that similar language is obligatory or even appropriate in the drafting of particular charges. What matters in charging is that the substance of the allegations should be clear to the defendant and to the court. It may or may not, depending on the type of case, be accurate and informative to assert that the defendant implied a particular false proposition (or "represented" something) by his conduct.

Deception as to fact or law

Law

The reference in section 15(4) to a deception "as to law" is included for the avoidance of doubt.[35] It was not settled whether a false statement as to a matter of law was a false pretence under the old law. There was no need for similar uncertainty under the present Act.   **8–15**

Fact and opinion; implied fact

A "deception ... by words ... as to fact" involves the making of an untrue statement as to some past or present fact: that the car being sold was first registered in a particular year; that the fire giving rise to an insurance claim destroyed the mink coat; and so on. Usually it is easy enough to identify a fact falsely asserted by the words used. But difficulties can occur where the defence is in a position to argue that the statement made was one of opinion rather than of fact; or where the prosecution need to argue that what was false was something implied by a true statement of fact or an apparent expression of opinion.   **8–16**

(i) *Fact and opinion.* In criminal law, as in civil law, liability does not normally derive from the giving of an unjustified or exaggerated opinion. A statement of opinion is not a statement of fact. A person seeking to make a sale is not penalised for over-praising his goods so long as he confines himself to statements as to value and quality. But he cannot with impunity assert that the goods have some attribute that is no mere matter of opinion and which it can be demonstrated that they do not have. The difference has been happily   **8–17**

---

[33] Arlidge and Parry, paras. 2.06 *et seq.*; Williams, *Textbook*, pp. 780–782.
[34] See below, §§8–45 to 8–49.
[35] *Eighth Report*, para. 101(ii).

expressed as that "between saying that something is gold and saying that something is as good as gold."[36]

8–18   (ii) *Implied fact.* There may be deception "by words ... as to fact" although no untrue fact is expressly stated. The assertion of one fact, for example, may be such as to imply the non-existence of some other fact which the maker of the assertion knows to exist and which might affect the mind of the person to whom the statement is made. For instance, a statement about the past fortunes of a business for sale may assert that the average turnover of the business during the past 10 years has been of a certain satisfactory order. This assertion may be literally true; but if the turnover has consistently decreased over the 10 years, so that the volume of business now being done is disastrously small, the concealment of this material fact should certainly involve potential liability for "deception ... as to fact."[37] A neat example of an implied fact is provided by a case in which a car dealer turned back the odometer of a car and displayed a notice saying that the mileage reading "may not be correct". He thereby falsely represented, as the indictment alleged, "that he had no reason to disbelieve" the reading.[38]

8–19   (iii) *Expression of opinion implying fact.* A statement that is, in form, one of opinion may likewise imply some fact that can be shown to be untrue. To say that Mr Smith is "a most desirable tenant" is to seem to assert at least that there are no facts known to the speaker that would justify the view that Mr Smith does not deserve this description.[39] Similarly, the statement that the shares of a company would be a worthwhile investment is in form a value judgment; but it would surely be falsified by proof that the company was unable to pay its creditors and had no apparent means of achieving solvency. Another way of discovering a statement of fact in such cases is to say that D is asserting that he holds the opinion he expresses when in fact he does not hold that opinion at all. An indictment would accurately charge that D falsely represented that he "was of the opinion" or "believed" that such-and-such was the case.

Deception as to intention

8–20   The reference in section 15(4) to "a deception as to ... present intentions" makes clear that the doctrine of *Edgington v. Fitzmaurice*[40] operates in the criminal law as well as in the civil. D's statement that, for example, he intends to use for a particular purpose money that P is thereby induced to invest in

---

[36] Smith and Hogan, *Criminal Law* (1st ed.), p. 410, comparing (*inter alia*) *Bryan* (1857) Dears. & B. 265 (opinion; but an unsatisfactory case) and *Ardley* (1871) L.R. 1 C.C.R. 301 (fact).
[37] Compare *Kylsant* [1932] 1 K.B. 442, decided on the wording of the Larceny Act 1861, s.84 ("statement ... false in any material particular").
[38] *King* [1979] Crim.L.R. 122. In *Banaster* (1978) 68 Cr.App.R. 272 a minicab driver told a passenger at London Airport that he was an "airport taxi". The jury, it was held, were rightly told that his words implied that it was "all official"; and his conviction of obtaining the fare paid by the deception that it was "the correct fare" was upheld.
[39] Compare *Smith v. Land and House Property Corporation* (1884) 28 Ch.D. 7.
[40] (1885) 29 Ch.D. 459.

D's enterprise is a deception if D does not then have that intention. The definition refers, of course, to "the present intentions of [D] or any other person." So D's statement that E, or the limited company that D represents, intends to do something in the future is also within the definition, if E or the company has not that intention and D either knows this fact or does not believe his statement to be true.

Promises

The statement "I promise to do such-and-such" is in effect a statement of **8–21** intention; for after all a person may be taken to imply an intention to keep his promise. So with the enactment of the Theft Act 1968 it became an offence to obtain property by a false promise—that is, a promise which, at the time he makes it, the maker does not intend to keep.[41] Under the former law of obtaining by false pretences there were situations in which, although the essential wrongdoing was the making of a false promise, a conviction had to rest on the discovery of some pretence as to a fact other than intention. Thus, if D obtained money from P by promising to marry her, he could formerly be convicted of obtaining the money by false pretences only if he was not free to marry her and then only upon the ground that he had asserted that he was. He may now be convicted if, and because, he did not intend to marry P. But it is vital to stress that the criminal law has not become a vehicle for the enforcement of promises. What must be proved is that at the time of the obtaining D did not have the intention that his words or conduct could be taken to assert. It is neither necessary nor sufficient to prove that he later decided not to keep his promise (though the fact that he did not keep it may be evidence in favour of the conclusion that he never intended to do so).

Deception by conduct

The following are some standard examples of different kinds of fraud **8–22** depending upon deception by conduct.

(i) A person who sells property is normally taken to imply by his conduct that he has a right to do so. If he has not (and knows that he has not or does not believe that he has), he employs a deception which is likely to influence his buyer; for the buyer would be unlikely to buy if he knew that the seller had no title. If the buyer is so influenced, what he pays for the property is obtained by deception by conduct.[42]

(ii) The fraud perpetrated by one who wears a uniform to which he is not entitled has long been a classic of the textbooks because of the direction of Bolland B. in *Barnard* in 1837[43]:

---

[41] For important observations as to statements of present intention, expectation or belief implied by the making of promises or forecasts, see cases decided under the Trade Descriptions Act 1968: *Sunair Holidays Ltd.* (1973) 57 Cr.App.R. 782; *British Airways Board v. Taylor* (1975) 62 Cr.App.R. 174.
[42] Compare *Edwards* [1978] Crim.L.R. 49 (squatter "letting" a room).
[43] (1837) 7 C. & P. 784.

"If nothing had passed in words, I should have laid down that the fact of the prisoner's appearing in the cap and gown would have been pregnant evidence from which a jury should infer that he pretended he was a member of the university . . . ."

There is no reason why this popular illustration of an implied pretence should not survive as a simple example of deception by conduct.

8–23　　(iii) A similar example is that of the fraud committed by establishing the outward appearance of a genuine business or enterprise and thereby inducing people to supply goods that will not be paid for, or to pay for non-existent goods, or to invest money in a worthless undertaking. Frauds of this kind are often large-scale operations in which several people are involved. They are commonly prosecuted as conspiracies—either to commit offences (as obtaining property by deception) or to defraud[44]—or as fraudulent trading.[45]

(iv) A person who enters a restaurant and orders a meal impliedly represents that he intends to pay for the meal (and, in the ordinary case, that he intends and has the means to pay before leaving the restaurant).[46]

Cheques, cheque cards and credit cards

8–24　　The representations involved in the use of cheques, cheque cards and credit cards have been considered by the House of Lords in two cases.

(i) *Cheques.* Professor Kenny long ago identified a number of representations as implied by "the familiar act of drawing a cheque."[47] (a) The first implied statement was "that the drawer has an account with [the] bank" upon which the cheque is drawn. There is no doubt that this statement is implied; and it is a convenient representation to allege where the drawer has no such account. (b) The second implied statement was "that [the drawer] has authority to draw on [the account] for [the] amount" for which the cheque is drawn. This implication, it has now been suggested, is incorrect. "A customer needs no authority from his banker to draw a cheque on him; it is the banker who needs authority from the customer to pay it on presentment."[48] It is in any case redundant, being, like the first statement, embraced by the third.[49] (c) In *Metropolitan Police Commissioner v. Charles*[50] the majority of their Lordships[51] accepted Kenny's third representation, namely:

---

[44] See above, §7–10.
[45] See above, §7–13.
[46] See *D.P.P. v. Ray* [1974] A.C. 370 (§8–34, below)—where there was no offence under s.15, because the intention not to pay was formed after the food had been consumed.
[47] *Outlines of Criminal Law*—see now 19th ed. (1966), p. 359. Kenny cited *Hazelton* (1874) L.R. 2 C.C.R. 134, and his analysis was adopted by the Court of Appeal in *Page* [1971] 2 Q.B. 330n.
[48] *Per* Lord Diplock in *Metropolitan Police Commissioner v. Charles* [1977] A.C. 177 at 182; see also *per* Viscount Dilhorne at 185.
[49] *ibid.*, at 190–191 (Lord Edmund-Davies).
[50] [1977] A.C. 177.
[51] Lord Diplock (at 182) restated the drawer's representation to be that "the cheque is one which the bank on which it is drawn is bound, by an existing contract with the drawer, to pay on presentment or, if not strictly bound to do so, could reasonably be expected to pay in the normal course of dealing."

"... that the present state of affairs is such that, in the ordinary course of events, the cheque will on its future presentment be duly honoured."[52]

Kenny went on to point out that the drawing of the cheque

"does not imply any representation that the drawer now has money in this bank to the amount drawn for, inasmuch as he may well have authority to overdraw, or may intend to pay in (before the cheque can be presented) sufficient money to meet it"

—or, it may be added, may expect the account to be sufficiently fed by some other person. Indeed, the cheque may be considerably postdated; yet the same representation will be implied.[53] This does not mean that the drawer's act simply implies a representation as to the future, a prediction; this would not satisfy the requirement of a "deception ... as to fact."[54] Rather it implies a statement as to the existence of a "state of affairs" (to repeat Kenny's words) which includes the drawer's present intention or expectation. Nevertheless, it is certainly less pedantic to express it in Viscount Dilhorne's pithy terms: "a man who gives a cheque represents that it will be met on presentment."[55]

Withdrawal from D's account. The transaction contemplated by Kenny is **8–25** that where D uses a cheque to obtain property from the payee. When he demands cash from his own bank against his account he thereby represents that the state of his account (no doubt including uncleared effects[56] and overdraft facilities) is such that he is entitled to draw that amount.[57]

(ii) *Cheque cards and credit cards.* In *Charles*, D obtained gambling chips **8–26** at a club by giving 25 cheques for £30 each, supported by a cheque card. The use of the card in accordance with specified conditions created an undertaking by D's bank to honour the cheques. So the representation involved in giving the cheques was true; the cheques would undoubtedly be met, whatever the state of D's account. The House of Lords held, however, that when the drawer of a cheque presents a cheque card by way of guarantee, he represents to the payee that he has the bank's authority to use the card in relation to that cheque so as to create a contractual relationship between

---

[52] This was in fact Kenny's explanation of another statement by which he no doubt sought to express the same notion: "that the cheque, as drawn, is a valid order for the payment of that amount." But this can be read as referring to the future; so that the version quoted in the text, which is a representation as to existing fact, is now preferred: see *per* Robert Goff L.J. in *Gilmartin* [1983] Q.B. 953 at 960–961.
[53] *Gilmartin*, above.
[54] See *per* Robert Goff L.J. in *Gilmartin*, above, at 960.
[55] *Charles* [1977] A.C. 177 at 186. Compare *per* Lord Reid in *D.P.P.* v. *Turner* [1974] A.C. 357 at 367.
[56] In *Christou* [1971] Crim.L.R. 653, D paid in for the credit of his account cheques which were worthless, as he knew they were or might be. He then drew on the account before those cheques were presented. This was one indivisible deceptive practice.
[57] *Hamilton* [1990] Crim.L.R. 806: by withdrawal slips requesting cash from accounts into which he had paid forged cheques, D falsely represented that the bank owed him the amounts requested.

bank and payee. If the cheque is one which would not be met but for the use of the cheque card, he will lack that authority. The use of the card will then involve a misrepresentation.

In *Lambie*,[58] D selected goods in a shop and proposed to pay by Barclaycard. That is to say, she was using the card as a credit card. The shop had the usual agreement with D's bank that the bank would honour a voucher signed by the holder of a current card for a transaction within an agreed limit. D's transaction was within that limit. The shop manageress accepted this form of payment. The House of Lords held, applying its decision in *Charles*, that D had represented (falsely, on the facts) that she had authority to contract with the shop on the bank's behalf that the bank would honour the voucher signed by D.

A person dishonestly using a cheque card or credit card is guilty of an offence involving deception only if the payee is deceived by the cardholder's misrepresentation into accepting the cheque or voucher concerned. This aspect of deception is considered below.[59] The discussion may be anticipated by saying that convictions were confirmed in both *Charles*[60] and *Lambie*.[61]

8-27   The representations found in *Charles* and *Lambie* have attracted much criticism.[62] The gist of the criticism is that resort to the notion of the cheque card or credit card holder as agent of the issuer of the card is not necessary to explain the existence of a contract between the issuer and the payee or supplier; card-holders do not, on a true analysis, act as agents[63] and a dishonest card-holder cannot properly be interpreted as asserting an authority which no card-holder has. Moreover, it is said, the payee or supplier with whom the card-holder deals is not interested in whether the latter has the bank's authority. He is interested only in whether the conditions that will entitle him to payment (by guarantee of a cheque or by payment against a voucher) are satisfied. This criticism asserts, in effect, that it is inept to identify a representation on which the representee cannot truly be said to rely.

A strong case has undoubtedly been made that the language of agency in *Charles* and *Lambie* is inappropriate. The House of Lords might rather have said quite simply that the user of a cheque card or credit card impliedly represents that he is entitled as between himself and the bank to use the card for the transaction in question. This way of expressing the matter would, of

---

[58] [1982] A.C. 449.

[59] §§8–45 *et seq.*

[60] What was obtained in *Charles* was a pecuniary advantage in the form of D's being "allowed to borrow by way of overdraft" (see below, §8–58 and §11–12) and D was convicted accordingly under s.16(2)(b).

[61] The conviction in *Lambie* was under s.16(2)(a), since repealed. It might have been under s.15—and should have been: [1982] A.C. 449 at 456.

[62] Williams, *Textbook*, pp. 778–780; F. Bennion (1981) 131 New L.J. 1041 (on *Lambie*); P. Paulden (1981) 145 J.P.N. 708.

[63] That this, however, is not the view of the courts seems to be confirmed by the civil case of *First Sport Ltd. v. Barclays Bank plc* [1993] 1 W.L.R. 1229; [1993] 3 All E.R. 789.

course, still be open to the objection that such a representation is of no interest to the third party—a point that will be referred to again below.

Overcharging

A common mischief which may involve an offence under section 15 is that   **8–28**
of serious overcharging for work done—as, for instance, domestic building repairs. An example was before the Court of Appeal in *Silverman*.[64] D was known to two elderly sisters because of work that he or his employers had done for their family over a long period. He charged them grossly excessive sums for work done on their property. He was held to have been rightly charged under section 15 with obtaining the sums by impliedly representing them to be "a fair and proper charge." The court interpreted the situation as being one of "mutual trust"—thus, it seems, referring to the trust likely to have been reposed in D by the sisters. The question was whether he had taken advantage of them "by representing as a fair charge that which he, but not [they], [knew] to be dishonestly excessive." He had; "his silence on any matter other than the sums to be charged was as eloquent as if he had said that he was going to make no more than a modest profit." Although liability on such facts may be supportable, its proper basis needs careful consideration if section 15 is not to be misused in cases of this kind. There is a world of difference between fraud (with which the section is concerned) and exploitation (with which it is not).

What kind of representation? The first question is: what is the substance of   **8–29**
the deception? The suggested implied statement, "My charge is fair and proper" (or "My profit is only modest") looks like a statement of opinion rather than of fact, unless "fair and proper" can be understood as referring to an objective yardstick. The only yardstick available, it is submitted, is "the going rate for the job". To convert the alleged deception into a "deception . . . as to fact", conduct such as Silverman's must be interpreted as carrying some such implication as: "The price I am quoting or charging is within the range of prices likely to be quoted for the same services by other tradesmen (with similar overheads)."[65] This is a clumsy kind of implication to spell out in an information or indictment; but it is submitted that the defendant (and the tribunal of fact) should know that what is in substance alleged is that such an assertion was implied in the circumstances and that the victim paid the price in reliance upon it. It would be helpful, at any rate, if in a future case the

---

[64] (1987) 86 Cr.App.R. 213. The convictions in this case were quashed on a separate ground.
[65] The alternative, "*I hold the opinion that* my price is reasonable" or "fair and proper" (which, like any statement about one's state of mind, is a statement of fact) means little until translated into a claim to hold an opinion about the price relative to the market; and once that translation is made, the simpler interpretation, "It is the case that . . ." seems permissible and preferable. (Silverman's victims thought that they were paying a "normal" or "standard" charge (86 Cr.App.R. at 215), not that Silverman was of that opinion.) A related interpretation, "Other tradesmen would think my price reasonable", recalls the likely meaning of "proper" in s.21(1)(b) (blackmail): see below, §14–30.

phrase "fair and proper" could be explained, whether or not along the lines suggested here.[66]

8–30   *When is such a representation to be implied?* Clearly such a representation cannot be implied whenever a quotation for work is given or payment for work is demanded. The judgment in *Silverman*, which was concerned with rather special facts, does not go far to identify the circumstances that will justify the implication. It is submitted that it is helpful to refer in this context to the fact that deception, as explained in section 15(4), must be "deliberate or reckless". So D cannot be guilty of obtaining his price by deception unless he realises[67] that P may understand him to be implying the propriety (as above explained) of his price and may employ him, or pay him, on the strength of that understanding. If D does so realise, it must become relatively easy to find a false representation (once granted that overcharging can ever found a conviction under section 15). D's knowledge of P's innocence and inexperience may be relevant; or his knowledge that P is likely to trust him on the strength of prior transactions or social connections (as in *Silverman* itself). Such knowledge may combine tellingly with the fact (no doubt a feature of most cases attracting the concern of prosecutors) that D has spontaneously approached P to propose the transaction and is not tendering in a competitive situation initiated by P.

8–31   *Deception or extortion?* The grosser the overcharging, the greater the temptation may be to allege that a deception has occurred. But the more grossly excessive D's price is, the more hopelessly innocent and trusting P must be (and be thought to be) if he is to suppose D to be asserting the propriety of the price (and if D is to anticipate his reliance on such an assertion). Some people, indeed—as, apparently, the victims in *Silverman*—are astonishingly gullible and a claim to have supposed that even an absurdly exorbitant price was a normal price may compel belief. But, paradoxically, the greater the price, the more critically considered must be the suggestion that P was deceived into paying it. If deception is not the explanation, however, there must be some other. One possibility, where D announces the price of work already done, is that P feels under pressure to pay what D demands because the very demand for so excessive a sum carries a quality of menace. In a sufficiently clear case (and certainly where menaces are expressly used) the appropriate charge will be blackmail or theft rather than obtaining by deception.

---

[66] *Jones, The Times*, February 15, 1993 (C.A. no. 3650/Y3/91), was a simpler case. D over many years supplied P, his friend of long standing, with milk to be sold in P's shop. Every week D told P what the milk bill was and P paid the amount stated without question or calculation. In fact D regularly charged double the normal wholesale price and well over the price at which P could sell the milk. The discovery of a representation that P had received milk to the stated value hardly needed the support of the court's reference (citing *Silverman*) to the relationship of trust between D and P.

[67] See below, §8–60.

Conduct to conceal facts

An interesting situation is presented by conduct of D which is intended to **8-32** work a deception but of which, if the deception is to succeed, P must remain in ignorance. For instance, D may intercept a letter warning P of a fact that would be likely, if known to P, to make him refuse a proposed transaction; or D may hide physical evidence of the fact, that P would otherwise see. It would appear to be open to a court to say that such conduct amounts to deception within section 15. A clearer case would be that where D conceals (as by filling in and painting over) a serious defect in goods, the goods then being examined by P. In this case the result of the work of concealment would be visible to P.[68]

Silence as conduct

In some situations D may be thought to have a moral duty (and may for **8-33** other purposes have a legal duty) to reveal to P some fact which might affect P's mind in relation to a proposed transaction. Suppose that, after forming his intention that P shall be misled by his own ignorance, D does nothing active but pursues his dishonest purpose by maintaining silence. If a transaction then ensues in which D obtains property from P, the question may arise whether he has obtained that property by deception.[69]

Before considering particular examples of situations of this kind, the following general observations may be offered. First, the question for present purposes is not whether D had a duty to reveal facts but only whether he appeared to assert or deny them. But if D is not, according to the law of contract or of tort, under a duty to reveal a fact known to him, it is the more difficult to interpret his silence as a denial of that fact; and this consideration contributes to ensuring that the criminal law is not in practice more demanding than the civil. Secondly, there may in fact be no situation in which mere silence, mere inaction, alone can work a deception within the meaning of the Act. It may be necessary at least to find some other conduct of D in association with which his silence may be interpreted as making a representation.

The main relevant authority under the Act is *D.P.P. v. Ray*.[70] D entered a **8-34** restaurant intending to pay for the meal he was to eat. The representation implied by his conduct (that he intended to pay) was therefore true. After he had eaten his meal he decided not to pay and sat at his table until the waiter was out of the room. He then made his escape without paying. The House of Lords held by a majority that he had obtained by deception the evasion of his obligation to pay,[71] either because the initial representation made on enter-

---

[68] Compare under the Trade Descriptions Act 1968, *Cottee v. Douglas Seaton (Used Cars) Ltd.* [1972] 1 W.L.R. 1408 at 1417; [1972] 3 All E.R. 750 at 758, *per* Milmo J.
[69] See *Eighth Report*, para. 101(iv); J. C. Smith, *The Law of Theft* (4th ed.), paras. 170–172; Arlidge and Parry, paras. 2.44 *et seq.*; A. T. H. Smith [1982] Crim.L.R. 721 at 729–731.
[70] [1974] A.C. 370. See also *Nordeng* (1975) 62 Cr.App.R. 123, and commentary by J. C. Smith [1976] Crim.L.R. 196.
[71] Contrary to s.16(2)(a), since repealed. The diner who makes off without payment will now be prosecuted under the Theft Act 1978, s.3: see Chap. 13.

ing and ordering the meal was "a continuing representation which remained alive and operative" and had become false,[72] or because by remaining at the table after forming his dishonest intention he continued to make from moment to moment, but now falsely, the representation that he intended to pay.[73] A corresponding case under section 15 would be provided by the diner who forms his decision not to pay for his food between the time of ordering it and the time of its being served.

8–35   *D.P.P. v. Ray* illustrates the situation where D makes an assertion to P which is true when made but which becomes untrue before the relevant obtaining. Three other situations may be briefly considered. The first is where D makes an assertion which he believes to be true but which is not. Before he obtains any property from P, D learns that his assertion was false. He does not correct it. He may probably be interpreted as now falsely representing that he believes his original assertion to be true, or as continuing to make (but now falsely) that same assertion. The second situation is that where P makes clear to D that he assumes some fact to be true which is material to a negotiation between them. D knows the assumption is false but, though he does not actively confirm it, he does nothing to disabuse P. It is unlikely that a court would hold D's silence to be "conduct" within the meaning of section 15(4). The third situation is even clearer. D simply refrains from mentioning to P a fact, known to D, that might affect P's mind in the transaction proposed between them. The fact that it will usually be impossible to identify a clear statement to be inferred from D's silence should suffice to exclude liability, quite apart from all other considerations, including the consideration that no civil liability normally arises from simple nondisclosure.

Identifying a representation: whose function?

8–36   The scope of deception offences (cases of express falsehood apart) depends upon the readiness of courts to read into the behaviour of defendants the making of relevant false representations—that is, to interpret their conduct or what they have said or written as implying statements that are untrue. It can be argued that this dependence on interpretation by the courts should not be necessary. For strictly speaking the only questions relating to

---

[72] *Per* Lord MacDermott at 382.
[73] See *per* Lord Pearson at 391; and compare *per* Lord Morris of Borth-y-Gest at 385–386. (The latter explanation may be necessary if the decision is to apply where the waiter allegedly deceived is one who was not present until after the meal was served: see S. White (1986) 37 N.I.L.Q. 255 at 258.) Lords Reid and Hodson dissented. Lord Reid (at 379): "Deception, to my mind, implies something positive. It is quite true that a man intending to deceive can build up a situation in which his silence is as eloquent as an express statement. But what did the accused do here to create such a situation? He merely sat still." Lord Hodson (at 389): "Nothing he did after his change of mind can be characterised as conduct which would indicate that he was then practising a deception."

deception that should require answer are: (i) whether P understood D's words or conduct to imply some proposition that was false, and (ii) whether D intended that P should, or knew that P would, or realised that P might, understand him as implying that proposition and (if so) whether he knew that proposition to be false or did not believe in its truth.[74] If all of this is the case, it would appear that P has been affected by a "deliberate or reckless" deception. On this view of the matter it should be unnecessary for anyone to attempt to say whether, in some objective sense, D's words or conduct "in fact" implied the proposition in question.

But this view does not represent actual practice. For in practice the prosecution will allege that D actually made this or that false representation, by words or conduct; and the court in its turn will say whether that representation was actually made, and not merely whether it was understood by the alleged victim to have been made. This is understandable, for two reasons. First, it is not likely to be accepted, and will rarely be thought worth alleging, that P understood D, and that D intended or foresaw P's understanding him, to be asserting something that he is not reasonably to be interpreted as asserting. And secondly, many successful allegations of deception, as will be seen, are based on plausible interpretations of D's behaviour that will not in truth have been present to P's mind. Courts are concerned, rather, to satisfy themselves that P would not have acted as he did if he had known that what D plainly implied was not the case.[75]

There being, then, a task of interpretation for the courts, who is to perform   **8–37** that task—the judge or the jury? There is, of course, at least a threshold question for the judge to answer: is D's conduct or language or the document made by him reasonably open to the interpretation suggested by the prosecution? That question being answered affirmatively, it seems on principle to be for the jury to say whether D made the alleged representation; and this principle has been expressly asserted in some recent cases. In one case the trial judge had erred in not leaving it to the jury to say whether, by his answers to questions on a form of application for car hire, D had implied that he had never been disqualified from driving[76]; in another (a case of alleged fraudulent trading), the judge had rightly left it to the jury to decide whether a representation as to the underwriting of an issue of shares was conveyed by the language of a prospectus inviting subscriptions for those shares.[77]

---

[74] Compare commentary by Sir John Smith on *Adams* [1993] Crim.L.R. 525, at 527.
[75] See below, §8–46.
[76] *Adams* [1993] Crim.L.R. 525. "Where the central question is whether the defendant has made a representation or not, and, if so, whether it is false, then both aspects of that question are questions of fact for the jury. This is clearly so where the alleged representation is oral. It must equally be so in our judgment where the representation is contained in writing." The appeal against conviction was dismissed because the meaning of the document was so obvious that, properly directed, the jury would have been bound to convict.
[77] *Morris*, November 26, 1993, C.A. no. 93/1363/Z2. In this case *Clowes (No. 2)* [1994] 2 All E.R. 316 (see above, §2–33) was distinguished as a case concerning contractual documents, whose interpretation is for the judge. But the issue in that case was as to the legal effect of the documents in question (did they create "proprietary interests" under a trust?)—surely a question for the judge whatever the material on which it had to be decided.

In some contexts, however, the judges themselves have laid down that particular types of conduct imply particular representations of fact. For example, as seen above, the House of Lords has explained what representations are implied by the tendering of a cheque or a credit card in payment, or by the use of a bank's cheque card to support a cheque drawn on the bank.[78] Perhaps the distinction is between situations of common occurrence, which require an established understanding to be imposed as a matter of law, and situations with special facts and particular documents, where the meaning of what D has done, or written, looks more like a question of fact and within the jury's province. But the distinction is not convincing.

The falsity of the representation

8–38 The representation that D makes by words or conduct must be false if there is to be a deception. It is not enough that he thinks he is telling a lie. If "quite accidentally and, strange as it may sound, dishonestly",[79] he tells the truth, he cannot be convicted of an offence requiring deception. He may, however, be convicted of an attempt, even if he obtains what he sets out to obtain.[80]

Falsity of representation as to law

8–39 When D is charged with an obtaining effected by a "deception as to law", it must be up to the judge to direct the jury as to the truth or falsity of the representation said to have been made. The representation may be an implied one, as where D is alleged to have obtained the price of property he had no right to sell. Whether he had such a right will usually turn on matters of pure fact. Exceptionally, however, where it depends upon the legal consequences of background events, those consequences are for the judge to declare.[81]

A problematic illustration

8–40 An illustration of the need to prove the falsity of the precise representation alleged is provided by *Wheeler*.[82] D, a market stall-holder, one morning sold a stolen medal to P; but, as was the custom between them, D kept the medal for P to collect and pay for in the afternoon. Meanwhile D learnt from the police that the medal was stolen property.[83] P, when he returned, and having heard of the police visit, asked D whether the medal was on the police's list of stolen property; and D falsely said that it was not. P paid for the medal. D was charged with dishonestly obtaining the price by falsely representing "that he was the lawful owner of [the medal] and entitled to sell it."

---

[78] See above, §§8–24, 8–26.
[79] *Deller* (1952) 36 Cr.App.R. 184, *per* Hilbery J. at 191.
[80] Criminal Attempts Act 1981, s.1(2)(3); *Shivpuri* [1987] A.C. 1.
[81] See, *e.g. Walker* (1983) 80 L.S.Gaz. 3238; [1984] Crim.L.R. 112 (above, §1–21).
[82] (1990) 92 Cr.App.R. 279.
[83] It had to be assumed that D did not know this earlier; he was acquitted of handling the medal and other stolen property.

This wording, read as meaning that at the time of the contract of sale D impliedly represented his good title, was understandable; D had, after all, been prosecuted as a handler. But it was not proved that the alleged representation in this sense was false to D's knowledge. An alternative sense was that D had represented his ownership and right to sell in the afternoon (presumably by asserting that the medal was not on the stolen list). The Court of Appeal accepted that, even thus understood, the charge was not made out; the argument was that, since P had obtained a good title to the medal in the morning,[84] when the property in the medal passed to him by virtue of the contract of sale,[85] D could not in the afternoon have represented himself to be the owner.

The case admits of the following doubts. First, why did the fact that P was **8–41** already the owner (a legal consequence not necessarily appreciated by him)[86] entail D's inability to represent that he himself was? D and P may have been equally ignorant of sale of goods law; and there would seem to have been a genuine issue as to the meaning of D's behaviour at the afternoon meeting. Secondly, is the decision not unduly literalist? D's actual statement, answering a question in these terms, was that the medal was not stolen property; and the representation alleged might reasonably have been treated as an inept translation of that statement. P may well not have wanted, for whatever reason, to pay for stolen property; and the jury seem to have found that he was deceived into doing so.[87]

Proving a negative

Where the burden of proving the falsity of the representation involves **8–42** proving a negative, there is in common sense a limit to the quantity of evidence that the prosecution can be expected to adduce on the issue. If D has asserted that such-and-such is the case (*e.g.* the goods he sells cost eight times as much in the big shops), it is enough for the prosecution to speak of limited unsuccessful efforts to verify his assertion (seeking the goods at higher prices in a few shops). Reasonable efforts of that kind having been reported, it is not wrong for the judge to observe to the jury that the defence might be expected to give positive evidence, if it can be given, tending to support the representation.[88]

---

[84] Under the law of market overt: Sale of Goods Act 1979, s.22 (now repealed: Sale of Goods (Amendment) Act 1994).
[85] Sale of Goods Act 1979, s.18, r. 1.
[86] See 92 Cr.App.R. 279 at 281.
[87] The court (at p. 282) doubted whether rescission of the contract would be ordered on P's application; but the relevance of this to the question whether P was misled into paying is not clear. The decision is also questioned by Smith (A. T. H.): see paras. 4–27 (n. 75), 5–77, 17–90 (n. 67).
[88] *Mandry and Wooster* (1972) 58 Cr.App.R. 27, from which the illustrative facts in the text are taken.

Multiple representations

8–43   It may be alleged that D induced P to act as he did by making a number of false statements. In such a case there may be a conviction only if the jury agree that D was so induced by at least one particular statement as to which they (or a sufficient majority)[89] are all satisfied. This is an application of the general proposition that:

> "where a number of matters are specified in [a] charge as together constituting one ingredient in the offence, and any one of them is capable of doing so, then it is enough to establish the ingredient that any one of them is proved; but ... any such matter must be proved to the satisfaction of the whole jury."[90]

4. RELATION BETWEEN THE FALSE REPRESENTATION AND THE OBTAINING

The deception must precede the obtaining

8–44   This proposition should be too obvious to need stating. But it was the sole reason required for the quashing of the conviction in *Collis-Smith*.[91] D had petrol put in the tank of his car at a petrol station. He then falsely stated that he was using the car for business purposes and that his firm would pay for the petrol. This was the substance of the deception charged and his appeal against conviction was rightly allowed; the petrol was not obtained by this deception.

The prosecution argued in *Collis-Smith* that after possession of property had been obtained D might, by a deception then made, obtain ownership, and that such a transaction would satisfy the section. This argument, it is submitted, was clearly correct in principle (though the court, seemingly anxious to protect criminal courts from "difficult points under the Sale of Goods Act", was not prepared to acknowledge this); but it was equally clearly inapplicable in the instant case, in which the property in the petrol must have passed on its being put into the tank.

---

[89] Juries Act 1974, s.17. The same majority, of course, would need to be satisfied as to all other elements of the offence.
[90] *Brown* (1983) 79 Cr.App.R. 115 at 119 (distinguishing, and effectively explaining away, *Agbim* [1979] Crim.L.R. 171). For general consideration of the problem of "satisfying the jury", see J. C. Smith [1988] Crim.L.R. 335. *Brown* asserted the need, where multiple allegations are made, for a direction to the jury based on the principle stated in the case; and see *Day, The Times*, October 3, 1991; *Gray*, October 9, 1992, C.A. no. 90/3462/Z3. But in other cases it has been said that such a direction is necessary only where there is a real risk that the jury may disagree as to the particular ingredient on which a verdict of guilty may be based and may not appreciate (despite the judge's general direction on the need for unanimity: see *Price* [1991] Crim.L.R. 465) that they must all be agreed on the same ingredient—such occasions being said to be "comparatively rare": *More* (1988) 86 Cr.App.R. 234 at 244 (C.A.; no opinion expressed by H.L.); *Mitchell* [1994] Crim.L.R. 66 (reviewing the authorities, and stressing the need to avoid confusing the jury unnecessarily); *Keeton, The Times*, July 21,1974.
[91] [1971] Crim.L.R. 716.

The effect of the representation on P [92]

Need P believe the representation?

"To deceive is, I apprehend, to induce a man to believe that a thing is true   **8–45**
which is false." This well-known statement by Buckley J. in *Re London and
Globe Finance Corporation*[93] was cited with approval in *D.P.P. v. Ray.*[94] It
appears at first sight to state the obvious and to require no elaboration. Yet
there is, on reflection, a good deal of uncertainty attaching to the notion of
"believing that a thing is true"; and there has been no judicial consideration
of what amounts to "believing" for this purpose.[95] It is submitted that, if
indeed "believing" is an appropriate word in this context, it should not be
understood only in the sense of firmly accepting the truth of the statement in
question. The deception offences can hardly be limited to cases in which P is
induced to hold a strong positive belief. P may be well aware that he does not
know D, that there are rogues and liars abroad and that D may be one of
them. He may act "on the strength" of D's assertion and in reliance upon it,
but without in any positive sense either believing or disbelieving it. If D is
lying, P is surely "deceived" for the purposes of section 15. It may in fact be
better to abandon the word "believe" and to say that to deceive is to induce a
person to act in reliance upon a false representation.[96]

The test of whether P has been so induced is whether he would have acted   **8–46**
as he did if he had known that the representation made by D was false. This
question (and not whether P believed D, or why P acted as he did) is therefore the question to which evidence should be directed. This appears from
the decisions of the House of Lords in *Metropolitan Police Commissioner v.
Charles*[97] and *Lambie*,[98] which have already been mentioned for another
purpose.[99]

In *Charles*, P accepted D's cheques because they were backed by a cheque
card. He would not have done so if he had known that D had no authority to

---

[92] For criticism of modern developments, see A. T. H. Smith [1982] Crim.L.R. 721.
[93] [1903] 1 Ch. 728 at 732.
[94] [1974] A.C. 370.
[95] The authorities on obtaining by false pretences largely avoided reference to any particular
state of mind that the pretence must bring about. It was variously said that it must be proved that
by his statement D "did so act on the mind of the prosecutor as that he did thereby obtain money,
etc. . . . [and] if in fact the prosecutor was not . . . persuaded [by D's statement] . . . , the charge is
not supported" (*Aspinall* (1876) 2 Q.B.D. 48 at 57, *per* Brett J.A.); that the offence was committed if "the property was parted with on the faith of the false pretence" (*Jones* (1884) 50 L.T. 726);
that it must be shown that P was "influenced by the false pretence and would not have transferred [the goods] but for his reliance on it" (*Russell on Crime* (12th ed.), p. 1184; compare
Seagrave (1910) 4 Cr.App.R. 156, as to reliance); that P must have been "induced by" the false
statement to part with the property (*Smith* (1915) 11 Cr.App.R. 81). References to P's "believing" D's statement were rare; but see *Grail* (1944) 30 Cr.App.R. 81; *Sullivan* (1945) *ibid.*, 132.
[96] This paragraph was approved by the Court of Appeal in *Lambie* (1980) 71 Cr.App.R. 350
(reversed on another ground, [1982] A.C. 449).
[97] [1977] A.C. 177.
[98] [1982] A.C. 449.
[99] Above, §8–26.

use the card. D's conviction under section 16 of obtaining a pecuniary advantage by deception[1] was upheld. It is quite clear from the evidence that P was at best agnostic on the question of D's right to use the cheque card. Their Lordships, in asserting that P "believed" that D was authorised to use it,[2] must, on the facts, have been using "belief" to stand for ignorance of the truth plus reliance on the representation of authority; firm acceptance of the truth of that representation was not in question.[3] In *Lambie*, the manageress was not asked in evidence whether she would have completed the transaction had she known that the customer was acting dishonestly *vis-à-vis* the bank, having no authority to use the credit card. But the House of Lords held that the manageress's answer "No" to that question could be assumed.[4] On that basis *Charles* was regarded as indistinguishable and the customer's conviction of a deception offence was confirmed.[5]

"Acting in reliance": need P be aware of the representation?

8–47   It is natural enough to describe a deceived person as "believing" the truth of what he is told; that is no doubt the standard effect of a successful lie. But positive belief is not required; so the typical victim may instead be described (as for convenience he is in this chapter) as acting, even agnostically, "in reliance on" what he is told. Yet even this language—or any expression suggesting that D's representation must have some effect on P's mind—is not perfectly appropriate for many cases. Although the victim of a deception by words will be exactly aware of the representation made by D, this is not necessarily the case with deception by conduct. There must be many cases in which the relevant implication of D's conduct (that which a court will recognise[6] and a well-drawn indictment will allege) is not present to P's mind at all. Some kinds of conduct, indeed, are said to imply representations that are no doubt beyond the conception or comprehension of many of their asserted victims.[7]

---

[1] For the pecuniary advantage, see below, §§8–58, 11–12.

[2] [1977] A.C. 177 at 183, 193.

[3] For analysis of the facts, see J. C. Smith at [1977] Crim.L.R. at 618–619.

[4] [1982] A.C. 449 at 460. It is assumed, that is to say, that she would not have been prepared to testify that, had she known the truth, she might have been willing to participate in a fraud on the credit card company. (But the reason cannot be—*pace* Lord Roskill—that an affirmative answer to the hypothetical question would have made her a party to the fraud.) See further, §8–53, below.

[5] For elaborate criticism of *Charles* and *Lambie*, see J. C. Smith at [1977] Crim.L.R. 617–621 and at [1981] Crim.L.R. 713–717. The essential argument may perhaps be summarised thus: that the payee in a cheque card or credit card case (as witness the evidence in *Charles* and *Lambie*) has no interest in the state of the card-holder's account with his bank, for the very point of the card is to guarantee payment whatever the state of that account; that this is as much as to say that the payee has no interest in whether the user has authority to use the card; that a representation cannot be said to deceive one who is indifferent as to its truth; that the question whether the payee would have accepted payment by means of the card had he actually known of the lack of authority is improperly hypothetical; and that dishonest misuse of a cheque card or credit card in a transaction with a third party should not be held to be an offence of deception. See also A. T. H. Smith [1978] J.B.L. 129, especially at 135–136.

[6] See above, §8–36.

[7] See above, §8–26 (cheque cards and credit cards).

Presumably it rarely occurs to a railway passenger that the steward serving   **8–48**
him in the buffet car may be engaged on a fraud on his employers, selling his
own food rather than theirs, intending to keep the purchase price and
defraud his employers of the profit they should make. But cases on this kind
of fraud make clear that if, knowing the truth, the customer would not buy
the steward's food, the price he pays in ignorance of the truth is obtained
from him by deception.[8] Such a victim is deceived although, almost inevitably, the relevant implication of the deceiver's conduct ("This is my
employer's food") never crosses his mind. This seems to confirm that, so far
as concerns the relationship between D's conduct and P's act, the sufficient
questions are: Did D's conduct imply a particular statement? And did P act in
response to D's conduct in a way in which he would not have acted if he had
known the contrary of the statement? References in this chapter to P's "rely-
ing" on what is implied by D's conduct must be understood in this sense.

Suppose the case of a competition in which only one entry is permitted   **8–49**
from each competitor. D puts in two entries in different names. The judge
considers one of D's entries and awards it a prize. It seems plain that D has
obtained consideration of the entry, and perhaps[9] a prize, by deception even
though it did not occur to the judge that the entry might be one of two or more
entries submitted by the competitor, still less that its submission implied that
it was a unique entry. This example is stimulated by the surprising reason
reported for the failure of a prosecution for the obtaining by deception of an
allotment of shares by disguised multiple applications: "the prosecution
could not prove that the shares were issued in the belief that this was the only
application."[10] It is submitted that the prosecution were expected to prove
too much.

P's knowledge of falsity or indifference to truth

If D makes a false statement of fact to P, intending thereby to induce P to   **8–50**
lend him money or sell him property, and P knows that the statement is false
but nevertheless lends the money or sells the property, D is not, despite himself, guilty of obtaining by deception. He may, however, be convicted of an
attempt.[11]
   Another possibility is that P is misled by D's statement but is indifferent to
the matter about which the statement is made and therefore transfers property without reliance on it; he would act in the same way even if he knew the
truth. Here again, though D may have committed an attempt, he has not
committed an offence under section 15.
   On the other hand, if D's representation is a factor operating on P's mind

---

[8] Especially *Doukas* (1977) 66 Cr.App.R. 228; *Cooke* [1986] A.C. 909. The cases concern the
offence of going equipped to cheat (s.25) and are discussed below, §16–10.
[9] Acknowledging a possible argument about causation.
[10] *Best, The Times*, October 6, 1987. The obtaining charge having failed, there was a conviction of
attempt. *Sed quaere?* Was the defendant proved to have intended to induce the "belief" that he
failed to induce?
[11] Compare *Hensler* (1870) Cox C.C. 570; *Edwards* [1978] Crim.L.R. 49.

as an inducement to part with his property, the offence is complete. It is irrelevant that other factors also operated on his mind.[12]

Evidence of effective representation

8–51   To prove that P was induced to part with his property by the particular false representation charged, the prosecution are normally obliged to adduce P's evidence to this effect. There are two points here.

(a) First, it is *necessary to charge and prove the representation that operated on P* as the relevant inducement. This was not done in *Laverty*.[13] D, having acquired a stolen car, registration number JPA 945C, put different number plates on it—DUV 111C. He sold the car to P. He was charged with obtaining the price from P by the false representation that the car "was the original motor car DUV 111C". There was no evidence that P bought the car in reliance upon the representation that it was the car for which that registration number was originally issued. Nor could it safely be inferred that he would not have bought the car if he had known that its number had been changed. His evidence was that he bought it because he thought that P was its owner. The representation charged should have been that D was entitled to sell. D's conviction was quashed.

8–52   (b) Secondly, it is *normally necessary for P to give evidence of the inducement*.[14] The obtaining by the deception charged must, after all, be proved beyond reasonable doubt. P's reliance on the particular representation may, however, be a matter of irresistible inference from other proved facts; and if that is so and P's evidence on the point "is not and cannot reasonably be expected to be available", that reliance may be found as a fact.[15] P should nevertheless be produced as a witness unless his absence can be explained.[16]

8–53   The conviction in *Lambie* depended, as has been seen,[17] on the confidence of the House of Lords that the manageress, had she been asked, would have said that she would not have accepted Ms Lambie's credit card voucher if she had known that Ms Lambie lacked authority to use the card. But the case can hardly establish an irrebuttable presumption that one who is aware that his customer no longer has a right to use his credit card or cheque card will refuse to accept payment involving its use.[18] The point arises, of course, in a hypothetical way. In practice, P will not have known the truth; he will justifiably

---

[12] Compare, *e.g. Lince* (1873) 12 Cox C.C. 451.
[13] (1970) 54 Cr.App.R. 495.
[14] *Laverty* (1970) 54 Cr.App.R. 495.
[15] *Lambie* [1982] A.C. 449 at 460–461; applying *Sullivan* (1945) 30 Cr.App.R. 132; and see *Tirado* (1974) 59 Cr.App.R. 80; *Etim v. Hatfield* [1975] Crim.L.R. 234.
[16] *Tirado*, above (P not able to be brought to this country). In *Etim v. Hatfield*, above, post office counter clerks were understandably not called to give evidence about particular giro cheque transactions, which presumably they would not recollect.
[17] Above, §8–46.
[18] Compare *Cooke* [1986] A.C. 909 at 921: would railway passengers necessarily refuse to buy from staff engaged in a restaurant car fiddle?

have regarded the card as guaranteeing payment whatever the position as between D and his bank.[19] But it may not be impossible to persuade P to admit that, had he known the truth, he might have been unscrupulous and still accepted that mode of payment. He ought therefore to be available for cross-examination.

The problem of causation

Intervening events and transactions

Suppose that, by deception, D induces P to buy goods or services from him.   **8–54** D delivers the goods or renders the services and P pays D's price. Obviously the fact that the payment may from one point of view be described as motivated by D's performance of his contract is not necessarily inconsistent with the conclusion that D has obtained P's payment by the original deception. The transaction must be viewed as a whole; and an act may have more than one cause.

In the leading modern case, *King and Stockwell*,[20] it was said that "the question in each case is: was the deception an operative cause of the obtaining of the property? This question falls to be answered as a question of fact by the jury applying their common sense." The defendants posed as representatives of a known firm of tree surgeons and persuaded P that trees in her garden urgently needed removing, work which they would do for £470. She agreed. The fraud was uncovered before any money was paid. It was held that there was ample evidence to justify convictions of attempting to obtain money by deception—that is, money that "would have been paid over by P as the result of the lies told to her".[21] The Court of Appeal declined to found any general proposition on an influential, though unreported, case from 1922 that was cited to it. This was *Lewis*,[22] in which a schoolteacher who had obtained her appointment by misrepresenting her qualifications was acquitted of obtaining her salary by this pretence, "on the ground that she was paid because of services she rendered, and not because of the falsehood".[23] This case was not said to have been wrongly decided. Indeed, given the role accorded to the jury on the causation question, it can only be regarded as representing a particular answer to the "question of fact": was the deception "an operative cause" of the obtaining?

Abstract language such as *"an operative cause"* is hardly appropriate, it   **8–55** may be thought, to express the crucial question for a lay tribunal. But at least,

---

[19] See n. 5, above.

[20] [1987] Q.B. 547.

[21] *ibid.*, at 554. A striking example occurred in the old case of *Martin* (1867) L.R. 1 C.C.R. 56. D by false pretences induced P to contract to build him a vehicle. P built the vehicle and delivered it to D although in the meantime D had countermanded the order. A conviction of obtaining the vehicle by false pretences was upheld.

[22] Referred to in *Russell on Crime* (12th ed.), p. 1186n.

[23] This case was the reason for the enactment of part of s.16(2)(c), making it an offence to obtain by deception the opportunity to earn remuneration or greater remuneration in an office or employment.

as the judge can explain to the jury, the phrase acknowledges that an action can have more than one cause; and it can be interpreted for the jury as requiring a judgement as to whether P, when he or she made the payment or transferred the property, was still acting in reliance on D's earlier falsehood. It is alarming to note, however, that the Court of Appeal has not remained faithful to this language. In *Miller*,[24] the question that the jury had to answer was expressed as having been: "what was *the effective cause*[25] of the transfer of this money?" The passage quoted above from *King and Stockwell* was cited, in a manner suggesting that "an operative cause" and "the effective cause" may have been regarded as interchangeable. But the former appears to be wider than the latter; and the latter, it is thought, is even less suitable than the former as language in which to express a jury question.

Payment by P who realises he has been deceived

8–56   In *Miller*,[26] D picked up foreign passengers at airports, falsely representing by his conduct that he was a taxi-driver and that he would charge fair and reasonable sums for journeys. Some of his passengers realised by the time they came to pay his outrageous charges that D's car was not a taxi and that the charges were excessive. One victim paid him to avoid trouble or because he thought he was obliged to; another because of D's manner and her fear for her luggage, which was in the car. D was convicted of obtaining the fares by deception. He was refused leave to appeal. It was argued that money is not obtained by deception unless the victim continues to believe the lie at the time of payment. But the court insisted that it was

> "not legitimate to isolate the moment when the money is handed over from the rest of the story. If on the whole of the story it can legitimately be said that the various deceptions alleged in the indictment were the cause for the money being handed over, it is, or may be,[27] irrelevant that at the final moment the victim suspected or even believed that he or she had been swindled."[28]

The jury were entitled to find that D's false representations were the effec-

---

[24] (1992) 95 Cr.App.R. 421; below, §8–56.

[25] Emphasis supplied. The phrase was used in *Clucas* [1949] 2 K.B. 226, in which the Court of Criminal Appeal held that one who induced a bookmaker to accept a large bet by falsely pretending to be a commission agent acting on behalf of a number of persons did not obtain *by the pretence* the sums paid when the horse won; the backing of the winning horse was "the effective cause" of the payment. (This led to the enactment of part of s.16(2)(c): obtaining by deception the opportunity to win money by betting.) Another language used has been that of remoteness: in *Button* [1900] 2 Q.B. 597 D, an able runner, obtained a big handicap in a race by pretending to be E, a runner with a poor record. D won the race and claimed the prize. He was convicted of attempting to obtain the prize by false pretences. Matthew J. (at 600) described the original pretence as "not too remote." The decision must now be understood as justifying the leaving of a "question of fact" to the jury.

[26] (1992) 95 Cr.App.R. 421.

[27] Perhaps this phrase is intended to acknowledge the ultimate role of the jury.

[28] At 424.

tive cause of the payments. This decision is easy to sympathise with.[29] But it is somewhat weakened by the puzzling use that the court made of authorities that seem not to have been in point.[30]

Critique

It is respectfully thought to be regrettable that the authorities reviewed in this section should, in characteristic English criminal law fashion, down-grade what is essentially a question of law into a so-called "question of fact" and pass it in that guise to the jury in unsuitable terms. If two defendants in different cases behave like King and Stockwell, or like Miller, they should both be guilty or both innocent of obtaining by deception, the outcome being determined by a general solution of the causation problem raised by the language of the Act. The genuine questions of fact for the jury are questions about conduct and states of mind and perhaps, in the *Miller* situation, about the victim's motivation. The jury ought to be told that, given certain answers by them to such questions, the defendant is, or is not, guilty, according to the law (that is, the Act properly interpreted) as the judge understands it to be. As it is, they may be asked to apply a language of "effective cause" without effective help. In a case like *Miller* they would no doubt disappoint the Court of Appeal if they decided that *the* effective cause for the victim's payment was her fear of D or her concern for her luggage. Worse still, they might run away from a question framed according to the Court of Appeal's prescription and take refuge in the question: "Is this a rogue whom we should like to convict?" **8–57**

Deception of P, obtaining from Q

D may deceive P and thereby obtain property from Q or a pecuniary advantage at Q's expense. If there is "a causal connection"[31] between the deception and the obtaining D may be convicted under section 15 or section 16, as may be appropriate. The phrase "causal connection" is rather vague and the scope of the principle may at some time need to be more closely determined. The following are examples of the operation of the principle: **8–58**

  (a) *Property*. An insurance agent by deception induces P to insure with Q company and may be convicted of thereby obtaining commission from the company in respect of the policy.[32]
  (b) *Pecuniary advantage*. D wrongfully uses a cheque card to induce P to accept his cheque. D's bank is thereby obliged to honour the cheque

---

[29] The court was possibly influenced by the consideration that, if D was not guilty of obtaining the money by deception, he would have had no answer to a charge of attempt. But this would not be true in a case in which, by the time he does an act more than merely preparatory to his obtaining, the rogue knows that his victim has detected the deception.

[30] See the commentary on the case at [1992] Crim.L.R. 745.

[31] *Kovacs* (1973) 58 Cr.App.R. 412 at 416; approved in *Metropolitan Police Commissioner v. Charles* [1977] A.C. 177; *Clarkson* [1987] V.R. 962 at 980 (Supreme Court of Victoria).

[32] *Clegg* [1977] C.L.Y. 619 (Judge Beaumont).

so that his bank account is to that extent overdrawn. D may be convicted of obtaining by deception the pecuniary advantage of being "allowed to borrow by way of overdraft" (s.16(1) and (2)(b)).[33]

5. THE MENTAL ELEMENT

8–59   There are three strands in the mental element of the offence under section 15. D cannot be convicted of the offence unless it is proved:

  (i)   that his deception was "deliberate or reckless";
  (ii) that he obtained the property "with the intention of permanently depriving [P] of it"; and
  (iii) that he obtained the property "dishonestly".

"Deliberate or reckless" deception[34]

8–60   "Deception" means "any deception (whether deliberate or reckless) ..." (s.15(4)). "Deception" is, as it were, a two-sided word; it involves both the making of a deceptive statement and the effect of that statement upon the person to whom it is made. Conformably with the nature of the word they qualify, the words "deliberate" and "reckless" also do double duty. There are two senses, that is to say, in which D may deliberately or recklessly deceive P. He may know or be reckless as to the falsity of the statement; and he may make the statement intending to deceive P or being reckless whether P is deceived. There is no doubt that both of these senses of the compressed expression "deception (whether deliberate or reckless)" must be satisfied. On the other hand it would seem that recklessness in both of the relevant respects will suffice. So D is guilty of deception if (a) by words or conduct he makes to P a statement which is false, and (b) he is at least reckless as to its falsity, and (c) he is at least reckless as to its misleading P and (d) it does mislead P. But he is not guilty of deception if, though he makes a false statement, he genuinely believes that P will not be misled by it—if, for instance, he believes that P knows it to be untrue.

Deliberate deception

8–61   Deliberate deception appears to require an intention on D's part to make, by words or conduct, the representation that deceives P; knowledge that that representation is false; and an intention to deceive someone thereby, or an awareness that someone will (or at least may) be deceived. A finding that D was aware of the falsity of his representation may exceptionally require a decision as to whether he knew the technical meaning, in context, of what he asserted. In one case D obtained local authority repair and improvement

---

[33] Cases cited at n. 31, above. Also *Smith v. Koumourou* [1979] R.T.R. 355. And see *Beck* (1984) 80 Cr.App.R. 355 (procuring execution of valuable security); although discredited on another ground (see below, §12–21), the case can stand as an illustration of the present point.
[34] See *Eighth Report*, para. 101(i).

grants in respect of certain houses on the strength of certificates that he intended each house to be available for "letting as a residence". The houses were not so available within the meaning of the relevant legislation; but D could not be convicted unless the jury were satisfied that D knew what was meant by the phrase and therefore knew that, in that meaning, what he had certified was untrue.[35]

Reckless deception

A question arises as to the meaning of "reckless". The House of Lords has **8–62** held that in some other modern criminal statutes the word includes failing to advert to a risk that ought to be obvious—in effect a case of gross negligence.[36] It can be argued that the word has the same meaning in section 15 and that the present offence is committed by one who makes a statement that he crassly fails to recognise may be false and who dishonestly obtains property as a result. This is in fact an unlikely case. One who dishonestly obtains by deception (as section 15 requires) is almost bound to have deceived dishonestly; he will have realised that his statement might be false and might mislead.

The House of Lords decisions mentioned above did not specifically refer to offences of dishonesty or to existing authority requiring more than mere negligence for reckless deception.[37] It is submitted that deception requires at least indifference to the truth of the representation.[38] This would keep the criminal offence in line with House of Lords authority on the tort of deceit.[39]

It would be unfortunate if the above discussion were to give the impression **8–63** that the issue of recklessness arises routinely in deception cases. On the contrary; as the Court of Appeal has observed, it will rarely be necessary "to embark on an investigation of recklessness in the context of section 15."[40] In the great majority of cases attention can be directed to the question whether D was guilty of "deliberate" deception and thereby dishonestly obtained the property in question.

"With the intention of permanently depriving the other of it"

If D deceives P into lending him a chattel or letting it to him on hire, intend- **8–64**

---

[35] *Parker, The Times*, March 11, 1994.
[36] *Caldwell* [1982] A.C. 341 (Criminal Damage Act 1971, s.1); *Lawrence* [1982] A.C. 510; *Reid* [1992] 1 W.L.R. 793 (reckless driving—no longer an offence).
[37] *Staines* (1974) 60 Cr.App.R. 160; *Royle* (1971) 56 Cr.App.R. 131; and see *Waterfall* [1970] 1 Q.B. 148, where the point is expressed to relate to the requirement of dishonesty rather than to that of deception.
[38] Compare *Large v. Mainprize* [1989] Crim.L.R. 213 (on "recklessly furnishing false information").
[39] *Derry v. Peek* (1889) 14 App.Cas 337. Common law fraud is committed by one who makes a false statement "(1) knowingly, or (2) without belief in its truth, or (3) recklessly, careless whether it be true or false": *per* Lord Herschell at 374. Lord Herschell observed that "(3)" is really only an instance of "(2)".
[40] *Feeny* (1991) 94 Cr.App.R. 1 at 6.

ing to return it when the period of the loan or hiring is over (or even intending to return it at some future time[41]), he commits no offence under section 15. (In the case of the hiring, however, he commits the offence of obtaining services by deception.[42]) It is necessary, however, to distinguish carefully between a loan of money and a loan of other property. When D, pretending to be down on his luck, persuades P to lend him £10 in cash, he intends to deprive P permanently of the particular notes and coins handed to him; and, so far as this aspect of the mental element of the offence is concerned, his conduct is within the section although he may intend to repay his debt.[43]

8–65   D has the necessary intention for the purpose of section 15 if he intends to deprive P entirely of whatever interest P has in the property. As has been seen,[44] P need only have possession or control of the property or any proprietary right or interest in it, in order to be the victim of this offence. So, for example, if P has a lien on D's goods, and D by deception induces P to deliver the goods to him, intending to defeat the lien, the offence is committed. Similarly, D may trick P into parting with possession of property which P is entitled to possess for a short while only, and this will be an offence under section 15 even if D intends to return the property to its owner (for whom, indeed, he may have practised the fraud).

Application of section 6 for section 15 purposes

8–66   It will be remembered that the expression "with the intention of permanently depriving the other of it" is partially defined for the purpose of theft by section 6.[45] By section 15(3) that section is made to apply also for purposes of section 15 "with the necessary adaptation of the reference to appropriating." Section 6 is therefore to be read for purposes of section 15 as though for the word "appropriating" in section 6(1) there were substituted the words "obtaining by deception". There are obviously some difficulties involved in applying a section that is sufficiently obscure in its primary context to another offence for which it is, in a number of places, even less happily worded.

8–67   (a) Cases in which D obtains ownership of P's property by deception "without meaning [P] permanently to lose the thing itself", yet intending "to treat the thing as his own to dispose of regardless of [P's] rights", must be rare indeed.[46] We may construct one, admittedly unlikely, case by way of example. D is hard up. By deception he induces P to sell him a valuable article at a very low price. He merely wants to raise money on the article. He pawns it for a large sum and sends the pawn ticket to P with an apologetic letter.[47]

---

[41] Compare *Warner* (1970) 55 Cr.App.R. 93 (theft).

[42] Theft Act 1978, s.1; see below, §9–07.

[43] The point is illustrated in *Halstead v. Patel* (1972) 56 Cr.App.R. 334. It applies, of course, to any other fungible property of which D intends to restore the equivalent.

[44] Above, §§8–04, 8–05.

[45] See above, §§2–104 *et seq.*

[46] See below, §8–71, for the specialised case of obtaining a cheque.

[47] Compare situation (iii) in §2–105.

(b) It is easier to imagine cases in which section 6 might be relevant where D by deception obtains possession but not ownership of the property in question. Suppose that D dishonestly deceives P into giving him possession (not by way of loan) of some property other than land.[48] The effect of section 6 is that if, though he does not mean P permanently to lose the thing itself, D intends to treat it as his own to dispose of[49] regardless of P's rights, the mental element of the present offence, as of theft, is satisfied. The reader is invited to consider the three situations suggested in §2–105 and to suppose that possession in each situation is obtained by deception. In each case D will on the altered facts have committed an offence under section 15.

(c) D may induce P by deception to lend him property. If he intends to **8–68** return it, but only when it is "in such a changed state that all its goodness or virtue has gone",[50] his borrowing is "equivalent to an outright taking" and he may be said to be treating it as his own to dispose of regardless of P's rights. His intention so to treat it is regarded as an intention of permanently depriving P of it.

(d) If D obtains property by deception, intending to lend it to E for a period and in circumstances making the lending equivalent to an outright disposal, he will be regarded as intending to deprive P permanently (s.6(1)). So also if he obtains the property intending for his own purposes to part with it under a condition as to its return which he may not be able to perform (s.6(2)). It must be doubtful whether such cases, though provided for by the terms of section 6 as applied to section 15, ever actually arise.

(e) In some of the situations dealt with above, D may be guilty both of **8–69** obtaining property by deception and of theft. But this is not possible if the property is land: you cannot by the same transaction obtain land by deception and also steal it.[51] It is clear, however, that an offence under section 15 can be committed by a deception which obtains an existing interest in land (by the assignment of a lease, for example). But suppose that D by deception induces P to grant him a lease. In this case what D "obtains" must be the land, by obtaining possession of it (s.15(2)); it is the land which is "property belonging to [P]".[52] The question that might arise is whether a fraudulent lessee can ever be described as intending to deprive a lessor permanently of the land the subject of the demise. What, in particular, if D obtains a very long lease? Leaving aside section 6 for the moment, is there any point short of the assignment of P's whole interest at which the quality of temporariness ceases

---

[48] As to land, see (e), below.
[49] But not simply to use, however dishonestly and to P's disadvantage: *pace* Judge Fricker Q.C. in *Harkinder Atwal* [1989] Crim.L.R. 293 (obtaining credit card and charge cards); compare above, §2–108.
[50] *Lloyd* [1985] Q.B. 829 at 836; above, §2–109.
[51] See s.4(2), which limits the circumstances in which land can be stolen, but which does not apply to s.15 (s.1(3)).
[52] The leasehold interest carved out of P's estate in the land does not exist before it is created by the lease and it never belongs to P. It cannot itself, therefore, be the subject-matter of an offence. Compare *Chan Wai Lam* [1981] Crim.L.R. 497.

and that of permanence takes over? If D obtains a lease for 99 years or more it is certainly tempting to say that he intends to deprive P permanently of the land. It cannot be confidently predicted that the courts would yield to this temptation without the aid of section 6: it is sufficient here to hint at the possibility of their doing so. But suppose that P's age and the length of the lease permit D a plausible claim that he did not intend to permanently deprive P personally (let alone his successors in title) of the land. Does D nevertheless intend, within the meaning of section 6(1), to treat the land as his own to dispose of regardless of P's rights? It would not seem so, unless the taking of the lease can be treated as "a borrowing ... for a period and in circumstances making [the borrowing] equivalent to an outright taking." In *Chan Wai Lam v. The Queen*,[53] where deception induced a government grant of a sub-lease expiring (in 1997) three days before expiry of the head lease, the Court of Appeal of Hong Kong considered questions raised in this paragraph and concluded, no doubt correctly, that an offence under the local equivalent of section 15 could be committed only where D intends to deprive P of the whole of his interest.

Nor does the Act cater in clear terms for the case—surely not a fanciful one—of the person who by deception obtains a tenancy or short lease, intending, when his contractual right is determined by notice or effluxion of time, to claim security of tenure under relevant legislation.

Obtaining drawing and delivery of cheque

8–70   The case in which D obtains by deception the drawing and delivery by P of a cheque in favour of himself or E requires special treatment. The case is not problematic in practical terms; it admits of two simple statements:

(i) When D by deception dishonestly induces P to sign a cheque as drawer (or as indorser), he thereby by deception procures the execution of a valuable security and commits an offence under section 20(2). Viewed in this light the case presents no difficulty whatever.

(ii) And the Court of Appeal has consistently held that obtaining a cheque from a deceived drawer may be prosecuted under section 15. Convictions are routine.

8–71   The case presents some difficulties of analysis, however; and the authorities are not well reasoned.[54]

(a) *The cheque as thing in action.* In two cases the Court of Appeal has (at least in part) explained D's having the intention of permanently depriving P of the cheque in terms appropriate to the cheque considered as a thing in action.[55] The difficulty of considering the cheque in that capacity as property

---

[53] Above.
[54] For fuller analysis and criticism, see Smith (J. C.), para. 2–132 and the same author's elaborate commentary on *Mitchell* [1993] Crim.L.R. 788 at 789.
[55] *Duru* (1973) 58 Cr.App. R. 151 at 160: D intended that "the cheque ... should be presented and paid, thereby permanently depriving [P] of the cheque in its substance as a thing in action"; *Mitchell*, above: the cheque would return physically to P's bank, but would by that time, as D knew, "no longer be a negotiable instrument, but worthless."

"belonging to" the deceived drawer has been considered earlier in this chapter.[56] The difficulty was not adverted to in one of the two cases (*Duru*); in the other (*Mitchell*) the court saw no need to resolve it.

(b) *The cheque as a piece of paper.* The alternative rationalisation of a conviction under section 15 involves viewing the property obtained merely as a piece of paper. The Court of Appeal may be understood as taking this view of the case when, somewhat as an afterthought, it acknowledges section 6(1) as a basis for a finding of the requisite intention.[57] No doubt D, when he induces P to issue the cheque, does not mean P to lose "the thing itself" (for the cheque, when cleared, will become available to P by returning to his bank); but he intends "to treat the thing as his own to dispose of regardless of [P's] rights", for he will not allow P thus to recover it except upon payment. The rights of P of which D is "regardless" can only be the rights P had in the piece of paper before the issue of the cheque. It is a curiously trivial basis for conviction of a serious offence.

"Dishonestly"

Dishonesty and deception are separate issues

Dishonesty and deception, although they have often been confused or telescoped in the cases,[58] are separate issues. So far as reckless deception is concerned, this was a sufficient basis for quashing the conviction in *Feeny*,[59] in which the judge's direction may have led the jury to understand that conviction could be based on a finding of recklessness alone. The Court of Appeal insisted that there must be a finding of "dishonesty in relation to the obtaining" in addition to one of "recklessness in relation to the deception."[60] The same no doubt holds true as a matter of law in relation to "deliberate" deception.[61] But evidence which proves deception will in most cases tend to establish dishonesty. One proved to have deliberately deceived another in order to obtain property, if he is to have any hope of avoiding conviction, is virtually bound to give evidence either of an actual or supposed claim to the property or of his honest intention in relation to the overall transaction (such as evidence of an intention to avoid ultimate loss to the victim). If such evidence is tendered it cannot be excluded as irrelevant.[62]

8–72

---

[56] Above, §8–07.
[57] The court in *Duru*, above, said that it would have held s.6(1) to apply if it had thought it necessary to refer to it. The court's final observation on the point in *Mitchell*, above, was that D "intended to treat the cheques as his own to dispose of regardless of [P's] rights" because "he intended to deprive [P] of each of the cheques unless value was given for it." Compare the "ransom" cases: above, §2–105.
[58] Examples may be found in *Waterfall* [1970] 1 Q.B. 148 (see (1970) 33 M.L.R. 217); *Potger* (1970) 55 Cr.App.R. 42; *Halstead v. Patel* (1972) 56 Cr.App.R. 334; *Green and Greenstein* (1975) 61 Cr.App.R. 296; *Lewis* (1975) 62 Cr.App.R. 206; *Ravenshad* [1990] Crim.L.R. 398.
[59] (1991) 94 Cr.App.R. 1.
[60] *ibid.*, at 6.
[61] See, however, the citations in n. 71, below.
[62] *O'Connell* (1991) 94 Cr.App.R. 39.

Questions for the jury

8–73   The word "dishonestly" qualifies the phrase "obtains property"; it is the obtaining that must be dishonest. Guilt depends upon affirmative answers to the two *Ghosh*[63] questions:

>   (i) was what D did dishonest according to the ordinary standards of reasonable and honest people? and
>   (ii) must D have realised that it was dishonest according to those standards?

These are matters for decision by the jury; but they need not be troubled with question (ii) unless there is some evidence to suggest that D believed that what he did was honest by ordinary people's standards.[64]

8–74   This double test for dishonesty has been fully discussed in the chapter on theft.[65] General explanation and comment need not be repeated here; but it is of interest to note that in relation to deception offences the *Ghosh* test contradicts earlier Court of Appeal and Divisional Court authorities without explicitly overruling them. For it had been held that as a matter of law it could be no defence that one had intended to repay a loan obtained by deception[66] or a sum of money obtained across a post office counter by a cheque drawn on an empty giro account.[67] These authorities were silently overturned when the leading theft case of *Feely*[68] (the source of question (i), above) was applied[69]

---

[63] [1982] Q.B. 1053. (The case concerned offences under ss.15 and 20(2).)
[64] See above, §2–133. In *Lightfoot, The Times*, November 3, 1992, D was charged with attempting to commit an offence under s.15 by using E's credit card which, at E's invitation, he had signed in E's name. After a *Ghosh* direction, the jury asked whether ignorance of the law was a defence. It was held that simply to say that it was not, without repeating that D must appreciate that he was doing something dishonest, was a misdirection.
[65] Above, §§2–134 *et seq.*
[66] *McCall* (1970) 55 Cr.App.R. 175.
[67] *Halstead v. Patel* (1972) 56 Cr.App.R. 334. In *Potger* (1970) 55 Cr.App.R. 42, the Court of Appeal had said that the word "dishonestly" had a "wider ambit" than the phrase "intent to defraud" used in the old law of false pretences. This suggested that a number of situations which under that law were cases of intent to defraud were now as a matter of law to be classified as cases of dishonesty: see especially *Naylor* (1865) L.R. 1 C.C.R. 41; *Carpenter* (1911) 22 Cox C.C. 618; and, as to conspiracy to defraud, *Allsop* (1976) 64 Cr.App.R. 29.
[68] [1973] Q.B. 530.
[69] By *Green and Greenstein* (1975) 61 Cr.App.R. 296; and then, with the gloss of question (ii), by *Ghosh* itself. In the former case D applied for shares being issued to the public. He knew that the issue would be oversubscribed and that shares would be allotted to applicants in proportion to the size of their applications. Cheques had to be sent with applications; an applicant allotted less shares than he applied for would be sent a "return" cheque for the change with the letter of allotment. D applied for very large amounts of shares, sending cheques which could not possibly be met on first presentation without the help of the proceeds of the issuing houses' own return cheques (which he knew could be speedily cleared). Granted that D obtained the letters of allotment by deception, the question was whether this method of conducting a "stagging" operation was "dishonest". This was the first prosecution to test the question. The question was held to be for the jury to decide, a remarkable allocation of law-making power to the jury. Speculation is justified as to the kind of precedent the jury's decision constituted: D. W. Elliott [1976] Crim.L.R. 707 at 715. The jury convicted.

to deception offences.[70] That application was not perhaps quite inevitable, for, except in cases where D believes he has a legal right to the thing obtained, it might have been possible to hold that D's deception itself supplies a sufficient element of dishonesty.[71] But it is hardly surprising that the principle that the jury should apply their own understanding of the meaning of the word "dishonestly" was regarded as valid in all contexts if valid in one.

Belief in legal entitlement

There is no provision (corresponding to s.2(1)(a) in relation to theft) **8–75** declaring that a person does not obtain property dishonestly if he believes that he is entitled in law to obtain it. Nor are the jury to be directed to that effect. The expectation appears to be that, with the benefit of an ordinary *Ghosh* direction, the jury will achieve the right result.[72] If the right result is inevitably an acquittal, it is surely preferable that the jury be told so; their function should merely be to say whether he may have believed as he claims. If the right result is not inevitably an acquittal, there is a strange inconsistency between theft and other offences: although (by virtue of s.2(1)(a)) I am innocent of theft if by no matter what unlawful force I induce P to give me what I wrongly think I have a claim to,[73] I may (depending on the view of the jury) be guilty under section 15 if by lying I induce him to do the same.[74] It is submitted that there should be no question of a conviction if D by deception obtains property in any of the following cases:

(a) D believes that the property belongs to him and that P is not entitled to retain it.

(b) D believes that the property belongs to E, for whom he is obtaining it, and that P is not entitled to detain it from E.

(c) D believes, or it is the case, that P owes D or E money; and he believes that the obtaining of the property in question from P is a proper way of enforcing his or E's claim against the defaulting debtor.[75]

6. LIABILITY OF COMPANY OFFICERS, ETC.

Any director, manager, secretary or other similar officer of a body corpor- **8–76** ate, or any person who was purporting to act in any such capacity, may be proved to have consented to or connived at an offence under section 15 committed by the body corporate. If so, such a person is also guilty of the offence (s.18(1)).[76]

---

[70] The point was confirmed, specifically in respect of *McCall* (above, n. 66), in *Melwani* [1989] Crim.L.R. 565.

[71] Compare, at least as to "deliberate" deception, *Potger* (1970) 55 Cr.App.R. 42; *Ghosh* [1982] Q.B. 1053 at 1060, where Lord Lane C.J. is tempted by the point but does not pursue it; *Cooke* [1986] A.C. 909, *per* Lord Mackay at 934.

[72] *Woolven* (1983) 77 Cr.App.R. 231.

[73] See above, §2–128.

[74] This unbecoming distinction does not exist in Victoria: *Salvo* [1980] V.R. 401.

[75] Compare *Williams* (1836) 7 C. & P. 354; Williams, *C.L.G.P.*, pp. 330–331.

[76] As to bodies corporate managed by their members, see s.18(2).

An officer of a company who actively encourages or participates in the offence will be liable on ordinary principles independently of this provision. Indeed, depending on his status and function in the company, it may be his acts and states of mind which render the company itself guilty of the offence together with him.

Section 18 therefore strikes at the officer who is not guilty as an ordinary principal or accessory party to the offence. It assumes, that is to say, that the company has committed the offence by the conduct of some other officer or officers, but treats as fully liable the officer who inactively acquiesced in what was done. The section therefore (in common with many similar provisions in other legislation) involves a striking example of criminal liability for omission.

Connivance on the part of a company officer seems to consist in (i) knowing that the offence in question is being or will be committed, or at least realising that this may be the case, and (ii) intentionally failing to take steps that he might take to prevent the offence.[77] It is difficult to believe that in practice consent can involve anything less, for consent can hardly be manifested except by active participation or encouragement (for which the section is not needed) or by deliberate passivity.

---

[77] See *Codification of the Criminal Law* (Law Com. No. 143), para. 11.18; Draft Criminal Code Bill, cl. 31(1)(a), in *A Criminal Code for England and Wales* (Law Com. No. 177), Vol. 1.

Chapter 9

OBTAINING SERVICES BY DECEPTION

1. THE OFFENCE

Section 1(1) of the Theft Act 1978 provides: **9–01**

"A person who by any deception dishonestly obtains services from another shall
be guilty of an offence."

The offence carries the following penalties: on conviction on indictment, up
to five years' imprisonment[1]; on summary conviction, up to six months'
imprisonment and/or a fine not exceeding, for the time being, £5,000.[2]

The background to the creation of this offence has been described in
Chapter 7.[3]

Liability of company officers, etc.

Section 18 of the 1968 Act applies in relation to the offence as it does in   **9–02**
relation to section 15 of the 1968 Act (1978 Act, s.5(1)).[4]

2. "BY ANY DECEPTION DISHONESTLY OBTAINS"

"By any deception"

The word "deception" has the same meaning here as in section 15 of the   **9–03**
1968 Act—namely, the meaning stated in section 15(4) of that Act (1978 Act,
s.5(2)). The discussion of the word in that context may therefore be referred
to.[5] So may the discussion, in connection with the section 15 offence, of the
necessary relationship between the false representation and the relevant
obtaining.[6]

It should be noted that the present offence may be committed by means of
any deception. The C.L.R.C.'s original draft clause limited their proposed
offence to deception "going to the prospect of payment being duly made."

---

[1] s.4(2)(a).
[2] s.4(3); Magistrates' Courts Act 1980, s.32(9), as amended by Criminal Justice Act 1991,
s.17(2)(c).
[3] See especially, §§7–05, 7–06.
[4] s.18 is discussed at §8–76.
[5] §§8–11 *et seq*. and §§8–60 to 8–63.
[6] §§8–44 *et seq*.

179

But under section 1 as eventually enacted "services" may be obtained by deception as to any matter, which may or may not be concerned with the question of payment.

"Dishonestly"

9–04 The obtaining of services must be achieved "dishonestly". There is no need to repeat here what has already been said of the same element in the offence of obtaining property by deception under section 15 of the 1968 Act.[7]

3. "OBTAINS SERVICES FROM ANOTHER"

"Services"

9–05 "It is an obtaining of services where the other is induced to confer a benefit by doing some act, or causing or permitting some act to be done, on the understanding that the benefit has been or will be paid for" (subs. (2)).

It was important that the notion of "services" should be broadly understood; hence the explanation in terms simply of the conferring of a benefit by the doing of any act or by causing or permitting any act to be done. But purely gratuitous services (such as lending a lawn-mower or "lending a hand") ought to be excluded; hence the need for a benefit conferred "on the understanding that [it] has been or will be paid for."

It seems clear that "services" is established by the definition as a term of art and that anything falling within the definition ought to be treated as "services" for the purposes of the offence, even something not generally thought of as "services" or "a service". But the Court of Appeal has not consistently understood the legislative technique of the section in this way, as will appear below.[8]

"Confer a benefit"

9–06 There are two competing approaches to the reference to P's being induced to "confer a benefit". According to the first approach, the reference imports a limiting requirement into the section. It is understood to mean that there are some acts beneficial to D (or to a third party) and some non-beneficial, and that an offence is committed only if deception is used to include the doing, causing or permitting of an act of the former class.[9] It is thought that this approach is erroneous. It renders the offence too vague at its outer edge and promises the introduction of an unsatisfactory and unnecessary issue into prosecutions under the section. The alternative approach may be introduced

---

[7] §§8–72 *et seq.*
[8] §9–08.
[9] See J. R. Spencer [1979] Crim.L.R. 24 at 27 ("To some extent as yet uncertain ... the use of the word 'benefit' cuts down the extreme wideness of the phrases which follow it."); Smith (J. C.), paras. 4–74 *et seq.* (suggesting the exclusion from the class of benefits of some criminal and some unlawful acts).

by observing on the difficulty that would have attended the drafting of the end of section 1(2) if some such notion as that of conferring a benefit had not been employed earlier in the subsection. Some word or short phrase was apparently needed to stand for the thing that "has been or will be paid for." It is thought that "to confer a benefit by [doing, etc.]" is simply a drafting device that makes the phrase "the benefit" available for this purpose. The device need not be understood as modifying the sense of the subsection. Precisely because someone is understood to be prepared to pay for an act or a permission to do an act, the doing or causing of that act or the giving of that permission is perfectly sensibly described as the conferring of a benefit on him.[10] Who else is to be the judge of the matter? If it were not a benefit to him he would not pay for it.

"Doing some act, or causing or permitting some act to be done"

P may perform, or cause his employee to perform, some professional service, for example, or some work such as driving, building or repairing. Or he may give permission to D (or to E, for whom D uses the deception) to do some act (*e.g.* permission to use equipment, as when D hires a car[11] or the use of a computer, or an amenity such as a tennis court). Many benefits will involve P in both the doing or causing of acts and the giving of permission (*e.g.* the provision of hotel accommodation).　　　　　　　**9–07**

Loans; savings accounts

One who makes a loan which will have to be repaid with interest seems to confer a benefit upon the borrower by doing an act on the understanding that the benefit will be paid for. There seems to be no reason, therefore, why the obtaining of a loan by deception should not amount to an offence under section 1. Yet in *Halai*,[12] the Court of Appeal held that "a mortgage advance cannot be described as a service"; obtaining such an advance by deception was not caught by section 1. The hint of an explanation is given in the observation that a mortgage advance is "a lending of money," so that obtaining an advance by deception "can properly be charged under section 15 of the 1968 Act, if the facts support it." But the explanation is inadequate. There is no reason why the transaction should not amount to an offence under both sections; and in any case section 15 may not always be available on the facts of the case.　　　　　　　　**9–08**

Halai has been a troublesome impediment to the prosecution of mortgage fraud. It should always be possible to prosecute such fraud under section 1 of the 1978 Act. Faced with *Halai*, however, prosecutors have had to resort to sections 15 (obtaining property by deception) and 20(?) (procuring the execution of a valuable security) of the 1968 Act; or to conspiracy to　　　**9–09**

---

[10] Compare the convenient use of the same wording in the *Thirteenth Report*, para. 9.
[11] Or takes goods on hire-purchase: *Widdowson* [1986] Crim.L.R. 233.
[12] [1983] Crim.L.R. 624.

defraud, if the guilty involvement of two or more people can be proved. Whether section 15 or section 20(2) can be used depends upon the mechanics of the making of the mortgage advance; it must have involved the obtaining of "property belonging to another" or the "execution" of a "valuable security". There are technical difficulties in these requirements[13] that a resort to section 1 should be capable of avoiding in every case. It is clear that the Court of Appeal has become aware of the damage done by its own decision, which has been discredited by Lord Lane C.J.'s description of it as having "all the hallmarks of a decision *per incuriam*."[14] This might have been taken as an invitation to a bold prosecutor to use section 1 once again against mortgage fraud.[15] But it seems that it has not been so interpreted. And there is indeed some room for doubt as to whether *Halai* was technically *per incuriam* rather than simply erroneous: it was not achieved through oversight of any binding authority[16]; and it is not clear that it can be regarded as proceeding from the kind of "manifest slip or error"[17] that is required for a precedent to be, exceptionally, disregarded. The error of *Halai* should be corrected by legislation, as the Law Commission has recommended.[18]

9–10 The court was on firmer ground in *Halai* in holding that a building society's act in opening a savings account for an investor was not "services" because it was not an act that would be paid for. The further reason, that the opening of a building society or bank account when the customer pays money in is not, in ordinary parlance, the conferring of a benefit on the customer, is, with respect, questionable. It is, in ordinary parlance, a benefit to have a bank account; in any case, it is doubtful, as argued above, whether the reference to the conferring of a benefit need be regarded as a limiting factor in section 1[19]; and the fact that the act in question would not normally be called a service should be irrelevant.[20]

Agreements; omissions

9–11 An offence under section 1 is not committed merely by inducing P's agreement to confer a benefit. He must actually confer a benefit by doing, or causing or permitting to be done, an act that has been or is to be paid for. It is submitted that this is not P's act of agreement but some act that he will do, or cause or permit to be done, in performance of the agreement. Partial

---

[13] See in particular, §8–06, above, and §§12–17 and 12–20, below.
[14] *Teong Sun Chuah* [1991] Crim.L.R. 463; see also *Williams and Crick*, July 29, 1993, C.A. no. 91/3265/W3; *sub nom. Crick and another*, *The Times*, August 18, 1993.
[15] With a view to a formal reconsideration of *Halai* on an appeal against conviction or on a reference by the Attorney-General.
[16] See *Morrelle Ltd. v. Wakeling* [1955] 2 Q.B 389.
[17] See *Rickards v. Rickards* [1990] Fam. 194.
[18] *Conspiracy to Defraud*, Law Com. No. 228 (1994), para. 4.76, and draft Theft (Amendment) Bill.
[19] §9–06.
[20] Above, §9–05.

performance should be enough where P abandons performance after discovering the deception or where D, perhaps anticipating detection,
disappears and thus frustrates further performance. If detection occurs
before anything is done under the agreement, the inducing of the agreement
may, of course, depending on the circumstances, be enough to constitute an
attempt.

It seems clear that neither P's forbearance to act (as by not enforcing a debt
or realising a security) nor his causing an omission (as by instructing his
employee not to retake possession of hired goods from D) is "doing some
act" within the meaning of section 1(2).

Obtaining services for another

Section 1(2) does not specify that the act be one that is done for, or permit-   **9–12**
ted to be done by, the person using the deception. So D may commit an
offence under section 1 by obtaining services for E.

"On the understanding that the benefit has been or will be paid for"

The reference to an "understanding" as to payment should rarely cause   **9–13**
difficulty. The alleged deception will normally relate to the question of payment and will induce P's "understanding" about the matter; and this will suffice. In an exceptional case, however, where the alleged deception relates to
something other than payment, P's understanding that the benefit will be
paid for ought surely to be a well-founded understanding. It should be
necessary to prove a transaction on the strength of which a reasonable
observer would share P's understanding.

The section is no doubt mainly directed to deception relating to payment   **9–14**
or the prospect of payment. Consideration of such deception may, indeed,
have influenced the wording of subsection (2). But the subsection does not
provide, as it might easily have done, that P's "understanding that the benefit
has been or will be paid for" must itself be induced by deception, or even, for
that matter, that the understanding must be false. Despite the way in which
the final words of subsection (2) were introduced in Parliament,[21] those
words do nothing to limit the range of relevant deceptions. They simply re-
strict the benefits that are to be regarded as "services" to benefits for which
payment is required. It seems, therefore, that there will be an obtaining of
services by deception even where P does an act that D will in fact pay for,
being induced to do the act by the deception, for example, that he is dealing
with somebody other than D (where it is known that he is unwilling to deal
with D) or that D was first-comer among a number of persons seeking the
benefit.[22]

---

[21] Mr Brynmor John explained that the words "are there to cover two possibilities: ... the giving
of a dud cheque ... [and] the deception which persuades the victim that he has already been
paid" (Standing Committee D, June 27, 1978: Official Report, cols.4–5).
[22] Compare J. Parry (1978) 128 New L.J. 663. (The equivalent point may be made, of course,
about the offence of obtaining property by deception.)

Transactions contrary to law or unenforceable

9–15   It does not matter that the transaction is one in respect of which the victim of the deception could not in any case enforce payment. A man may be convicted under the section if he obtains the services of a prostitute without intending to pay her; or if he similarly obtains services which it is positively a criminal offence for his victim to provide.

The wording of the section seems, however, to exclude gaming and wagering contracts. If D bets with a bookmaker on credit, he may perhaps be said to induce the bookmaker to confer a benefit on him by doing an act—namely, by recording the bet. But even if this is so, the act is done on the understanding, not that the benefit "will" be paid for, but only that it "will in a certain event" be paid for. Such a case is, however, within section 16(2)(c) of the 1968 Act.[23]

No view to gain or intent to cause loss is necessary

9–16   If D's deception need not concern the fact or prospect of payment, it is remarkable that he is not required to act with a view to gain or an intent to cause loss. As it is, if the above analysis of subsection (2) is correct, the offence may be committed by a person who pays or will pay the proper price for the services he will obtain. A 15-year-old who misrepresents his age in order to gain admission to a cinema showing a film with an "18" classification appears to commit the offence, so long as his obtaining of admission is regarded as dishonest.[24]

---

[23] Below, §11–16.
[24] Compare Parry, *loc. cit.*, n. 21, above. For an attempted justification of the omission of any reference to gain or loss, see H.L.Deb., Vol. 394, col. 1647: the omitted phrase produces "inconsistent results when applied to services". The examples given do not, with respect, explain the difficulty.

Chapter 10

EVASION OF LIABILITY BY DECEPTION

1. THE OFFENCE[1]

Section 2 of the Theft Act 1978 penalises a range of conduct originally **10–01** covered or intended to be covered by section 16(2)(a) of the 1968 Act. (The background to the 1978 Act has been described in the first part of Chapter 7.) Section 2 deals with deception that secures the remission of an existing liability, or induces an existing creditor to wait for payment or to forgo payment, or obtains exemption from or abatement of a liability. The offence created by the section attracts the same penalties as the offence under section 1: on conviction on indictment, up to five years' imprisonment[2]; on summary conviction, up to six months' imprisonment and/or a fine not exceeding, for the time being, £5,000.[3]

Liability of company officers, etc.

Section 18 of the 1968 Act applies in relation to this offence as it does in **10–02** relation to section 15 of the 1968 Act (1978 Act, s.5(1)).[4]

2. "BY ANY DECEPTION"; "DISHONESTLY"

"By any deception"

The word "deception" has the same meaning here as in section 15 of the **10–03** 1968 Act—namely, the meaning stated in section 15(4) of that Act (1978 Act, s.5(2)). The discussion of the word in that context may therefore be referred to.[5] So may the discussion, in connection with the section 15 offence, of the necessary relationship between the false representation and its relevant effect.[6]

"Dishonestly"

A person charged with an offence under this section must be proved to **10–04** have acted "dishonestly". Reference may be made to the discussion of this word in the context of section 15 of the 1968 Act.[7]

---

[1] For criticism, see J.R. Spencer [1979] Crim.L.R. 24 at 34–35.
[2] s.4(2)(a).
[3] s.4(3); Magistrates' Courts Act 1980, s.32(9), as amended by Criminal Justice Act 1991, s.17(2)(c).
[4] s.18 is discussed at §8–76.
[5] §§8–10 et seq. and §§8–60 to 8–63.
[6] §§8–44 et seq.
[7] §§8–72 et seq.

10–05   (i) As under section 15, so here, the word "dishonestly" contributes to limiting "reckless" deception to cases in which D is indifferent to the truth of his statement and not merely negligent in making it.[8] Only if he does not believe in the truth of his representation is that representation "dishonest".[9]

(ii) Under section 15 the word "dishonestly" qualifies "obtains", so that the obtaining of property must be dishonest. Here it qualifies "secures", "induces" or "obtains" (s.2(1)(a)(b) and (c) respectively) with the like effect. It is possible, therefore, though cases must be rare, that a deceptive evasion of liability otherwise falling within section 2 may not be an offence because D believes that he (or, as the case may be, E, for whose benefit he acts) is legally entitled to the advantage secured or is legally entitled to use the advantage as a means of enforcing a right against P.[10]

(iii) Under section 15 there is, of course, the need for an intention to deprive P of the property obtained by the deception. The present section does not in terms require an intention to secure whatever relevant advantage derives from the deception, but "dishonestly" performs the corresponding function. D does not by deception dishonestly induce P to wait for payment, for example, unless his object in using the deception is that P shall be so induced.[11]

3. "LIABILITY TO MAKE A PAYMENT"

10–06   Each part of section 2(1) refers to some existing or prospective "liability to make a payment". Such liability may have a contractual, delictual or restitutionary basis. It may arise in equity, as under a trust. Or it may exist as a matter of public rather than private law. The C.L.R.C. gave as an example of the application of section 2(1)(c) the case of a ratepayer who makes a false statement in order to obtain an abatement of his liability to pay rates.[12]

"Liability" means "legally enforceable liability"

10–07   The section is concerned only with "legally enforceable liability" (subs. (2)). So, for example, no offence under the section can be committed against a bookmaker or other party to a gaming transaction, against a prostitute, or against a person conducting an unlicensed consumer credit business in respect of a regulated agreement unenforceable by virtue of the Consumer Credit Act 1974, s.40(1). But an agreement which, because of non-compliance with a statutory requirement, is by statute "enforceable on an order of the court only", the court having power to deny enforcement, does give rise to a "legally enforceable liability".[13]

---

[8] See above, §8–62.
[9] *Waterfall* [1970] 1 Q.B. 148; *Royle* (1971) 56 Cr.App.R. 131.
[10] Compare above, §8–75.
[11] Compare *Locker* [1971] 2 Q.B. 321 (decided under s.16 of the 1968 Act).
[12] *Thirteenth Report*, para. 15; for further examples, see Appendix 2 to that Report, para. 7.
[13] *Modupe* [1991] Crim.L.R. 530 (Consumer Credit Act 1974, s.65: improperly-executed consumer credit agreement).

There is a partial inconsistency between sections 1 and 2. D may induce P by deception to perform a service for an abated price. If the contract for the service is illegal or *contra bonos mores*, D cannot be convicted under section 2(1)(c) but is liable to conviction under section 1.

A liability is presumably not "legally enforceable" (although it may poss-   **10–08** ibly be enforceable by lawful means other than action) if action to enforce it is statute-barred, or if it arises under a contract of guarantee unenforceable by action for want of a note or memorandum of it signed by or on behalf of the guarantor.

Liability for wrongful act or omission

P may claim to have a right to compensation from D in respect of an   **10–09** alleged tort or other "wrongful act or omission". So long as D has not "accepted" liability and P has not "established" it, no deception used by D to induce P to abandon his claim or reduce his demand can found an offence under the section (subs.(2)). Once D has accepted liability, however, it seems that he may commit an offence by some deception affecting the determination of quantum.[14] It is not clear whether liability may be "accepted" for this purpose even though its admission occurs in negotiations that are properly described as being "without prejudice". It is thought that it may be. The test, it is submitted, should be whether it is clear, from a statement made by D or on his behalf, that liability is not in dispute.

Meaning of "existing liability"

The "existing liability" required by section 2(1)(a) and (b) must, it is sug-   **10–10** gested, be an actual, and not merely a potential or contingent, liability (*debitum in praesenti*), though payment may be due only in the future (*solvendum in futuro*). The fact that liability to pay under an existing contract may be conditional upon performance by the other party should not prevent the liability's being "existing" for this purpose. If P has agreed to deliver goods next week against D's promise to pay within the month, D has an "existing liability". But an insurer or a surety would seem to have only a potential and not an "existing" liability until the occurrence of the insured risk or the default of the primary obligee.

4. SECURING REMISSION OF EXISTING LIABILITY

Section 2(1)(a)

A person commits an offence under section 2(1) who   **10–11**

---

[14] Compare *Thirteenth Report*, para. 16.

"... by any deception—

> (a)   dishonestly secures the remission of the whole or part of any existing liability to make a payment, whether his own liability or another's ...."

This is the case of the debtor who persuades his creditor by a lying hard-luck story to let him off the debt altogether; or that of the purchaser of goods or services who, some time after the bargain is concluded (so that there is an "existing liability"), falsely claims to belong to an association to whose members the supplier customarily gives a discount, with the result that a percentage is knocked off the bill. It is equally an offence if D induces P to remit E's liability rather than some liability of his own.

What mainly distinguishes paragraph (a) of section 2(1) from paragraph (b) is that under paragraph (a) the creditor intends an extinction (in whole or in part) of the debtor's *liability*, whereas what is affected under (b) is merely the creditor's attitude to the prospect of *payment*—he resigns himself to its deferment or to its never occurring. It must, under paragraph (a), be immaterial that the creditor's agreement to the extinction of liability is not binding on him, because it was obtained by fraud, and that the debtor whose fraud is uncovered may in the result, like the paragraph (b) offender, gain temporary relief only.[15]

Meaning of "remission"

10–12   A "remission" of liability seems to require knowledge on the creditor's part of what is being remitted. It is submitted that the following case is not within section 2(1)(a). D hires a car from P. The sum that D must pay at the end of the hiring depends in part on the extent to which he has used the car. Before returning the car to P, D tampers with the odometer so that its reading is lower than it should be. P therefore charges a smaller sum than is actually due. This, it is submitted, is not a "remission" of liability. (It may be an "abatement" of liability within the meaning of section 2(1)(c).)

It is further submitted that "remission" of liability also requires knowledge that the liability exists. So where P is persuaded that D has already paid him, he does not "remit" D's liability.[16] (He is induced to "forgo payment" within the meaning of paragraph (b).)

It has been held that a person who pays a debt by using a stolen credit card is guilty of an offence under paragraph (a).[17] The creditor certainly regards

---

[15] Compare Smith (A. T. H.), para. 20–35; [1971] Crim.L.R. 259 at 262–263. Smith (J. C.), paras. 4–83 to 4–86, argues that a "remission" requires an agreement effective in law to destroy the debt, at least in part (as in the case of a composition by D with his creditors); but it does not seem credible that s.2(1)(a) should be as narrow as this view would make it.

[16] Smith (J. C.), para. 4–86, agrees. *Contra*, G. Syrota [1978] Current Law Statutes Annotated, and (1979) 42 M.L.R. 301 at 304–306; and it must be acknowledged that the C.L.R.C. seem to have intended "remission" to be understood in a wider, but surely inadmissible, sense: *Thirteenth Report*, para. 16.

[17] *Jackson* [1983] Crim.L.R. 617.

the use of the card as effectively discharging the debtor's liability; but the decision somewhat stretches the language of the paragraph in treating the acceptance of a form of payment as the "remission" of liability to pay.

5. INDUCING CREDITOR TO WAIT FOR OR FORGO PAYMENT

Section 2(1)(b)

A person commits an offence under section 2(1) who   **10–13**

" ... by any deception— ...

> (b)   with intent to make permanent default in whole or in part on any exist-
> ing liability to make a payment, or with intent to let another do so, dis-
> honestly induces the creditor or any person claiming payment on behalf
> of the creditor to wait for payment (whether or not the due date for
> payment is deferred) or to forgo payment .... "

Liability of D or of another?

There are two ways, under this paragraph, of committing the offence: **10–14**
(i) inducing a creditor to wait for, or to forgo, payment of one's own debt,
with intent to make permanent default on one's liability (*i.e.* never to pay);
(ii) inducing a creditor to wait for, or to forgo, payment of the debt of
another, with intent to let that other make permanent default on his liability.
The absence of words such as "whether his own or another's" after "with
intent to make permanent default ... on any existing liability ...", and the
inclusion of the alternative, "or with intent to let another do so", confine the
"default" referred to in the first phrase to "a default by the party whose liability it is."[18] Where D, a hotel manager, used deception to induce creditors to
wait for payment of debts incurred by the owner of the hotel before his
appointment, and was charged in terms of the first part of the paragraph, it
was a misdirection to tell the jury that the only issue was whether D's conduct
was dishonest and that it was irrelevant whose liability was involved.[19]

Inducing creditor to wait for payment

This is a controversial case. The stalling debtor is not in general guilty of a   **10–15**
criminal offence, and there is a strong argument that his use of deception
should not be distinguished from, say, keeping deliberately out of the creditor's way. At the other extreme it is contended that one who deceives his
creditor into waiting for payment should be guilty of an offence even if he
intends to pay at some time. The present provision is a compromise between
these views. Deceiving the creditor into waiting for a payment is an offence
only if the debtor intends never to pay. This solution effectively brings para-

---

[18] *Attewell-Hughes* (1991) 93 Cr.App.R. 132 at 137.
[19] *Attewell-Hughes*, above.

graph (b) into line with paragraphs (a) and (c): remission, exemption or abatement will inevitably be secured by one who intends to avoid payment altogether. It does not follow that the solution is a virtuous one.[20]

The creditor who cannot choose but wait

10–16   The requirement that P be induced by deception to wait for payment does not seem to imply that P need have any alternative. Suppose that D has decided not to pay P. He puts P off most easily by pretending that he is short of ready funds. P says: "Oh, very well; but you must pay next week". This acquiescence means that what P would do if D simply refused to pay him is never put to the test. Probably he could not avoid waiting for payment (though he might promptly resort to litigation and would no doubt refuse credit for further transactions).

P may be induced by deception to wait for payment even if the fact is that D could not in any case pay now. This kind of situation was familiar from the case law on section 16(2)(a) (now repealed). D owes P money. He induces P to accept a cheque. P is thereby "induced to wait for payment", as is expressly provided by section 2(3). D knows that there is no prospect of the cheque's being met. He has induced P to take the cheque by deception.[21] If he intends to make permanent default and is dishonest, he is guilty of the offence— even, it seems, if he has no present means of paying cash.[22]

D may give his creditor a cheque in accordance with credit terms agreed between them. Even if the cheque is known by D to be worthless, it seems that in such a case the creditor is not induced by deception to take the cheque in payment or, therefore, to wait for payment (despite the terms of s.2(3)).[23]

Inducing creditor to forgo payment

10–17   The C.L.R.C. did not explain the difference between remitting liability (paragraph (a)) and forgoing payment. A parliamentary request for an explanation received an unconvincing reply.[24] It has already been suggested[25] that a "remission" of liability requires an intention to extinguish a liability of the existence of which the creditor is aware. If this is correct, "remission" does not cover two types of case:

(i) P is induced to give up a claim to payment by being induced to accept that D has no liability. D pretends, for example, that he has paid already[26]; or that he has a set-off; or that the goods P sent did not arrive or were worthless.

---

[20] See Professor Glanville Williams' powerful Note of Reservation to the *Thirteenth Report* (para. 5 at p. 20); Smith (A. T. H.), para. 20–28; J. R. Spencer, *loc. cit.*, n. 1, above, at 34.
[21] See above, §8–26.
[22] *D.P.P. v. Turner* [1974] A.C. 357.
[23] *Andrews and Hedges* [1981] Crim.L.R. 106 (Mr. Recorder Sherrard Q.C.).
[24] See H.L.Deb., Vol. 389, col. 265. The example of "remission" given on behalf of the Government is an example of "forgoing" according to the distinction suggested in the text, and not one of "remission". But it would be one of "remission" according to the C.L.R.C.: see n. 16, above.
[25] Above, §10–12.
[26] As in *Holt and Lee* (1981) 73 Cr.App.R. 96.

(ii) P is induced to abandon any hope of payment. He does not agree to the extinction of liability; but he goes further than merely agreeing to wait for payment, for in the circumstances as represented to him he expects never to see it—he writes off the debt.

Both types of case must be taken to be covered by the phrase "induces [P] … to forgo payment", though the language is not ideal.

6. OBTAINING EXEMPTION FROM OR ABATEMENT OF LIABILITY

A person commits an offence under section 2(1) who   **10–18**

" … by any deception—

    (c)   dishonestly obtains any exemption from or abatement of liability to make a payment";

and for this purpose he "obtains" any such exemption or abatement if he obtains it for another or enables another to obtain it (subs.(4)).

Unlike paragraphs (a) and (b), this paragraph does not require an "existing liability".[27]

"Exemption"

An "exemption" most obviously occurs where a creditor or potential   **10–19** creditor grants that a liability that would ordinarily arise shall not arise in the circumstances represented by D to exist—as where D obtains a service free by representing that he belongs to class of persons (*e.g.* P's employees) whom P does not charge. But the decisions to be mentioned in the following paragraphs allow the word a wider scope; they extend it to cases where (i) the creditor makes no charge because he is not aware of a liability, rather than because he grants an "exemption" in the usual sense of that word, or (ii) the creditor thinks that the relevant liability has already been discharged.

In *Firth*,[28] a consultant did not tell a hospital that patients whom he   **10–20** referred for treatment were private patients. There was held to be a deception constituted by this "omission", as a result of which the patients were treated without charge under the National Health Service. But the act of referring the patients to the N.H.S. hospital, nothing being said about their status, seems to be positive conduct implying that they are N.H.S. patients. So far as the hospital knows, no liability arises. Any stretching of the notion of "exemption" that is involved in upholding the consultant's convictions under paragraph (c) can be interpreted as filling what would otherwise be a gap in the legislation. The consultant obtains a "benefit" that ought to be paid

---

[27] *Firth* (1989) 91 Cr.App.R. 217.
[28] Above.

for, without, however, "an understanding that the benefit . . . will be paid for"; and such a benefit is not "services" within section 1.

10–21   In *Silbartie*,[29] D, at a London Underground interchange station, waved at a ticket inspector a season ticket that did not cover the whole of either part of a journey that he was taking on two lines. This attempt to persuade the inspector that he had a ticket covering his journey was held to be an attempt to obtain exemption from the balance of his liability. The inclination to uphold D's conviction is understandable; but here the notion of "exemption" is surely stretched too far. One does not "exempt" another from a liability that one thinks has been discharged.

"Abatement"

10–22   Other examples of the offence occur where D by deception obtains a service at a reduced rate; or where by a false statement, he procures a lower assessment to tax than would otherwise have been made on him (or on his principal). It could be objected that D's fraud does not, strictly speaking, affect his liability to pay but only affects the other party's demand.[30] This objection would destroy paragraph (c) almost entirely. It is submitted that the words of the section cannot be understood in their strictest sense.[31]

"Abatement" is not limited to an arrangement at the outset of a transaction. It will cover a case where D persuades P that his existing liability is smaller than P would otherwise have thought; indeed, a false return of income for tax purposes might be such a case. Paragraph (c) therefore overlaps paragraph (b) (as to forgoing payment). It also overlaps section 1; for many cases of obtaining an abatement of liability by deception will involve an obtaining of services by deception.

7. RELATIONSHIP BETWEEN THE PARAGRAPHS OF SECTION 2(1)

10–23   It is one thing to acknowledge that there is a degree of overlap between the paragraphs of section 2(1), as the Court of Appeal has indeed contemplated more than once.[32] It would be quite another thing to conclude that the paragraphs may be "simply different ways of describing the same end result"—a view which presented itself to Lawton L.J. in *Holt and Lee*[33] as at least a possibility. His Lordship went so far as to state that "the differences between

---

[29] [1983] Crim.L.R. 470. Para. (b) would have been an apter home for this case: see text at n. 26, above.
[30] See Smith (J. C.), para. 4–89.
[31] See *Thirteenth Report*, para. 15.
[32] *Silbartie* [1983] Crim.L.R. 470; *Jackson* [1983] Crim.L.R. 617.
[33] (1981) 73 Cr.App.R. 96.

the offences relate principally to the different situations in which the debtor-creditor relationship arises." There is surely no warrant for this view. The section mainly concerns existing liability and events which can affect it. One and the same debt might be the subject of a remission by the creditor, a decision by the creditor to wait for payment or to forgo payment, an abatement (a reduction in the amount required by the creditor) or, on the court's own interpretation, an exemption. Such events, though they overlap, are on the whole distinct; indeed, there must be a strong presumption that Parliament intended every part of the subsection to makes its own contribution to the control of the mischiefs with which the 1978 Act was concerned. So the dicta in *Holt and Lee* ought not to carry weight. Moreover, prosecutors and courts might be a little more critical of the precise choice of charge than they have sometimes been.

Chapter 11

OBTAINING A PECUNIARY ADVANTAGE BY DECEPTION

1. THE OFFENCE

11–01   Section 16(1) of the 1968 Act provides:

"A person who by any deception dishonestly obtains for himself or another any pecuniary advantage shall on conviction on indictment be liable to imprisonment for a term not exceeding five years."

Section 16(2) sets out "[t]he cases in which a pecuniary advantage within the meaning of this section is to be regarded as obtained for a person." Those "cases" were originally three in number; but the first, prescribed by the notorious section 16(2)(a), was despatched to a welcome oblivion by the Theft Act 1978, as explained above in the first part of Chapter 7.[1] All that remains is the limited group of cases specified in section 16(2)(b) and (c), which are examined below.

"Pecuniary advantage"

11–02   It was rightly said in *D.P.P. v. Turner* that "we do not have to consider what is meant by pecuniary advantage"[2]—plainly because, by telling us in what cases "a pecuniary advantage ... is to be regarded as obtained", subsection (2) establishes its whole meaning for the purpose of the section.[3] Yet, to deal with the argument (in a case under subs. (2)(a)) that a person with no means could gain no pecuniary advantage by evading a debt, Lord Reid further held that the phrase "is to be regarded as obtained" also means "is to be deemed to have been obtained even if in fact there was none"[4] (that is, no pecuniary advantage). This involves treating the phrase "pecuniary advantage" in the section as having both only a technical meaning (*i.e.* the meaning, and only the meaning, allowed by subs. (2), read as a definition) and also a "natural" meaning (*i.e.* what you would look for by way of pecuniary advantage if subs. (2), read as a deeming provision, did not render this unnecessary)! This is a small miracle of syntax.

Liability of company officers, etc.

11–03   Section 18 applies to offences under section 16. Reference may be made to the text of section 18 in Appendix 1 or to the discussion at §8–76, above.

---

[1] §7–04.
[2] [1974] A.C. 357 at 364.
[3] *Waites* [1982] Crim.L.R. 369.
[4] [1974] A.C. 357 at 365.

2. "BY ANY DECEPTION"; "DISHONESTLY"

"By ... deception ... obtains for himself or another"

(i) *"Deception."* Section 16(3) provides that for the purposes of the section **11–04** "deception" has the same meaning as it has in section 15. It is therefore sufficient to refer to the definition of "deception" in section 15(4) and to the discussion of that definition in the treatment of the offence of obtaining property by deception.[5]

(ii) *"Obtains."* The obtaining of the pecuniary advantage must be a consequence of the deception; once again reference may be made to the discussion of the corresponding point in relation to the offence under section 15.[6]

(iii) *"For himself or another."* The result of the words "for another" is that D may commit the offence by, for example, obtaining by deception for E the granting of an overdraft facility by E's bank (subs.(2)(b)) or an opportunity for E to earn remuneration (subs. (2)(c)).

"Dishonestly"

A person charged with an offence under section 16 must be proved to have **11–05** acted "dishonestly." Reference may be made to the discussions of this word in the context of section 15[7] and of the Theft Act 1978, s.2.[8]

3. OVERDRAFTS, INSURANCE POLICIES AND ANNUITY CONTRACTS

Section 16(2)(b)

A pecuniary advantage is to be regarded as obtained for a person **11–06**

"where— ... (b) he is allowed to borrow by way of overdraft, or to take out any policy of insurance or annuity contract,[9] or obtains an improvement of the terms on which he is allowed to do so ... " (s.16(2)(b)).

"Is allowed to borrow by way of overdraft"

Borrowing by way of overdraft

A person borrows "by way of overdraft" by drawing upon a bank account **11–07**

---

[5] See above, §§8–10 *et seq.* and 8–60 to 8–63.
[6] Above, §§8–44 *et seq.*
[7] Above, §§8–72 *et seq.*
[8] Above, §10–04.
[9] Even a policy or contract void because of the mistake induced by the deception: *Alexander* [1981] Crim.L.R. 183.

that is not in credit[10] when the drawing is effective—that is, when the account is debited. He thus borrows from the bank, becoming its debtor to the extent of the overdrawing. The transaction is to be distinguished from a bank loan, which is typically made by the bank's crediting the customer's account with the amount of the loan and correspondingly debiting a separate loan account.[11] The wording of section 16(2)(b) is very specific and ought to be strictly construed as referring to the former kind of transaction only.

11–08   Take, for example, the following case of "documentary advances". Under a facility agreed with P (a bank), D discounts with P bills of exchange drawn on E for 90 per cent. of their value, the discounted sum being credited to D's current account and the full value of the bills being debited to a "discount account". The "advance" with interest will be repaid when the bills are paid on maturity; but if the bills are not paid the current account will be debited with their full value. In fact D by deception induces P to discount further bills, the discounted value of which keeps his account apparently in balance. In spite of a confident dictum to the contrary,[12] it is submitted that the deception cannot found liability under section 16. No borrowing "by way of overdraft" results from such deception. As a result of the deception the current account is credited, not debited. The "advance" against the fresh bills is debited to the discount account, which is not an account to be drawn upon. Nor, by the same token, is the overall facility—allowing D to discount bills for "advances" up to a stated limit—an overdraft facility.

11–09   Section 16(2)(b) no doubt specifies a borrowing by way of overdraft because such a borrowing will not normally involve the obtaining by D of property[13]; he merely becomes P's debtor. Other modes of borrowing, however, will usually involve the transfer of property—either money or documents creating rights to money.[14] When such a transfer occurs as a result of deception, an offence under section 15 will commonly be committed.[15] Moreover, the borrower seems to obtain services within the meaning of section 1 of the Theft Act 1978; but the puzzling case of *Halai*[16] denies this, as has been seen in Chapter 9.

Being "allowed to borrow by way of overdraft"

11–10   An obvious case within section 16(2)(b) is that where by deception D

---

[10] Or not in credit to the extent of the drawing.

[11] See Ellinger, *Modern Banking Law*, pp. 475–476.

[12] *Golechha* (1989) 90 Cr.App.R. 241 at 249. No offence under s.16 was charged. Nor any under s.2 of the Theft Act 1978, which the Court of Appeal also thought apt. The reference is presumably to inducing P to wait for payment (s.2(1)(b)); but this needs an "intent to make permanent default". For the issue with which the court was concerned, see below, §12–06.

[13] *Pace* Judge Paul Clarke in *Watkins* [1976] 1 All E.R. 578 at 579.

[14] If the latter, s. 20(2) is also available.

[15] For an apparent difficulty where the transfer is effected by the crediting of a bank account, see above, §8–08.

[16] [1983] Crim.L.R. 624; above, §9–08.

induces his bank manager to sanction an overdrawing (or further overdrawing) of his account. A trial judge has ruled that the offence is complete when the overdraft facility is granted.[17] This ruling is supported, as the judge observed, by the phrase beginning "or obtains an improvement", which also points to the time when the arrangement is made. The same is true of the reference to the taking out of an insurance policy or an annuity contract.

Paragraph (b) seems not to cover the case where D by deception induces   **11–11**
his bank not to call in an existing overdraft. The case is within section 2(1)(b) of the Theft Act 1978, but only if D acts "with intent to make permanent default."

Misuse of cheque card. It seems to have been accepted without argument in   **11–12**
the leading case of *Metropolitan Police Commissioner v. Charles*[18] that D, a bank's customer with a cheque card and an overdrawn account, obtains a pecuniary advantage when, having no right to overdraw further, he uses the card to guarantee a cheque drawn on the account. The bank has to honour the cheque and D's overdraft increases. Argument in *Charles* concentrated on the deception (of the payee) and its effect in obtaining the advantage.[19] Strangely, a plausible objection to conviction was neither advanced in argument nor faced by the House of Lords: that, although D does "borrow" by way of overdraft, it is hardly convincing to describe him as "allowed to borrow"; for the bank is merely unwillingly obliged to honour its guarantee and may actually (as in *Charles*) have prohibited further drawing against the account. The Court of Appeal has subsequently ratified the decision in *Charles* thus: by using the guaranteed cheque D impliedly requests the advance by way of overdraft[20]; and the bank, however constrained by its guarantee to the payee, meets the cheque voluntarily (by "an act of will"); it thus "reluctantly agrees" to the request and "allows" the borrowing.[21] The somewhat desperate character of this explanation suffices to cast doubt on the application of section 16(2)(b) where the deception is not practised on the bank itself.

4. OPPORTUNITY TO EARN REMUNERATION OR TO WIN MONEY BY BETTING

Section 16(2)(c)

A pecuniary advantage is to be regarded as obtained for a person   **11–13**

---

[17] *Watkins* [1976] 1 All E.R. 578.
[18] [1977] A.C. 1; approving *Kovacs* (1974) 58 Cr.App.R. 412.
[19] See above, §8–26 and §8–46.
[20] Compare *Cuthbert v. Robarts Lubbock & Co.* [1909] 2 Ch. 226 at 233.
[21] *Bevan* (1986) 84 Cr.App.R. 143. See also *Waites* [1982] Crim.L.R. 369; by issuing the card the bank gives D the "power" to borrow. But this "allowing" is not obtained by the deception (of the payee) in question.

"where— ... (c) he is given the opportunity to earn remuneration or greater remuneration in an office or employment, or to win money by betting" (s.16(2)(c)).

There is no doubt why this paragraph is included. A person was understood to be not guilty of an offence of obtaining money by false pretences under the old law (1) if he obtained employment by deception (as by falsely claiming certain qualifications) and then drew his salary; the salary was regarded as paid because of the work done and not because of the deception[22]; or (2) if by a false pretence he induced a bookmaker to accept a bet on a race and then collected the winnings when his horse won.[23] Paragraph (c) ensures that in each case D will commit an offence, if not in obtaining the remuneration or winnings, at least in obtaining the opportunity to do so; it will, of course, be irrelevant whether D is actually paid.

It may be felt that the wording of paragraph (c) sticks over-closely to the particular cases that revealed the mischief to be remedied. The paragraph certainly has an oddly narrow and selective appearance.

"The opportunity to earn remuneration ... in an office or employment"

11–14 *Remuneration "in an office."* One who is appointed to a directorship or to a public position that is rewarded with pay will earn remuneration "in an office". But a person to whom a brewery grants the tenancy of a public house will not hold "an office". Nor will he be in the "employment" of the brewery.[24]

11–15 *Remuneration "in ... employment."* The Court of Appeal has adopted a distinctly purposive approach to this part of the paragraph. It has held that an independent contractor who is employed to do work for reward has thus the opportunity "to earn remuneration ... in ... employment". This is the effect of *Callender*,[25] in which a self-employed accountant who misrepresented his qualifications in order to obtain freelance work was held to have committed an offence under the paragraph. The court acceptably regarded the accountant as "employed" to do the work and overrode doubts that had been expressed[26] as to whether he could properly be said to earn his fees "in" an employment. The paragraph is carelessly drafted; the interpretation it has received is correspondingly robust; and the outcome is satisfactory: there is no policy ground for distinguishing the office-holder or employee from the independent contractor.

"The opportunity to win money by betting"

11–16 The opportunity to win money by betting is distinguished in the case law

---

[22] *Lewis* (1922), unreported; see above, §8–54.

[23] *Clucas* [1949] 2 K.B. 226; see above, §8–55, n. 25.

[24] *McNiff* [1986] Crim.L.R. 57. Nor is his power as tenant to apply for a justices' licence (an "office" leading to "remuneration"?) an opportunity to earn remuneration: *ibid*.

[25] [1993] Q.B. 303.

[26] As in previous editions of this book.

from the opportunity to win a prize by competing in a contest. The fraudulent punter was not guilty of obtaining his winnings by false pretences[27]; but the runner fraudulently procuring an excessive handicap was guilty of that offence if he obtained the prize.[28] But even if the distinction between the two cases subsists for the purpose of section 15, it does not follow that they should be distinguished for the purpose of the present section. Perhaps the explanation for the exclusion of the dishonest runner from paragraph (c) lies in the fact that to have included him would have meant creating a different unjustifiable distinction—namely, that between the runner who competes for a money prize and the runner who competes for something other than money. Section 16 is concerned with pecuniary advantages and paragraph (c) is drafted accordingly.

---

[27] See above, §11–13 at n. 23.
[28] *Button* [1900] 2 Q.B. 597; above, §8–55 at n. 25.

Chapter 12

OTHER FRAUD OFFENCES

1. FALSE ACCOUNTING

Introduction

12–01   Section 17 creates two offences—in short, the falsifying of accounts and the use of false or deceptive accounts. Both offences are punishable on conviction on indictment with seven years' imprisonment. The section supplements both the law of theft and deception and the law of forgery and using false instruments.

If D fraudulently doctors a cash-book or destroys copy invoices and other sales records, he may not obtain or intend to obtain any property thereby. His conduct may rather be designed to cover up offences already committed. But the particular crime concealed by the false accounting may be hard or impossible to identify; or, though it may be clear, for instance, that D has systematically "milked" an enterprise of which he is a member or an employee, it may not be possible to frame an indictment for theft or to rely solely on a charge of theft.[1] For such reasons as these, the criminal law is provided with a weapon which strikes at the falsification of the accounts rather than at the dishonest gain that those accounts assist or conceal.

Again, the destruction or falsification of a document or record under section 17(1)(a) may, in truth, be merely an act of *preparation* for a criminal purpose yet to be accomplished; or the use of a deceptive account under paragraph (b) may be an *attempt* to commit some other offence, very likely one of the offences discussed in the preceding four chapters. In this respect offences under section 17 are akin to forgery and using a false instrument, which they considerably overlap. The fabrication or use of false documentation is regarded as a sufficient commitment to the criminal purpose to have the status of a distinct substantive offence. Within the narrow accounting field, section 17 covers conduct not caught by the Forgery and Counterfeiting Act 1981 and is an important ally of that essentially preventive statute.

Falsifying accounts (s.17(1)(a))

12–02   A person commits an offence under section 17(1)(a) if, dishonestly and with a view to gain for himself or another or with intent to cause loss to

---

[1] Where it is clear that over a period D has stolen money amounting in total to not less than a certain sum, he can be convicted on an indictment charging the theft of that amount between specified dates: see above, §2–159. But such a charge, alleging a "general deficiency", may not be available. It may not be possible, for instance, to prove whether D stole goods in the shop he managed or money from the till. For observations on the use of "twin" counts charging theft and false accounting, see *Eden* (1971) 55 Cr.App.R. 193.

another, he destroys, defaces, conceals or falsifies any account[2] or any record or document made or required for any accounting purpose.

It was held in *Attorney General's Reference (No. 1 of 1980)*[3] that a document may be "required" for an accounting purpose if its recipient will in certain events use it for such a purpose, although the maker (who is charged with falsifying it) makes it solely for a non-accounting purpose. The case concerned false statements in a personal loan proposal form addressed by a would-be borrower to a finance company. If the proposal were accepted, the company would use the form for an accounting purpose. But ought not the maker at least to know of the intended use? The decision does not require such knowledge. Moreover, a reading of the section which extends it to the making of false statements about such matters as personal and financial circumstances is surprising. The maker will no doubt have a view to gain or an intent to cause loss by the making of such statements, but not by the use of the document as an accounting document, which is surely what the section contemplates.

"Falsifying"

Section 17(2) provides that a person is to be treated as falsifying an account or other document if he **12–03**

(i) makes or concurs in making in it an entry which is or may be misleading, false or deceptive in a material particular, or
(ii) omits or concurs in omitting a material particular from it.[4]

In *Edwards v. Toombs*,[5] a turnstile operator at Tottenham Hotspur's ground omitted to record on the turnstile meter the passage of paying spectators into the ground. This was a "falsifying" of a "record" within the meaning of subsection (1)(a). The argument that the record was not "an account or other document" within the meaning of subsection (2), which alone expressly refers to the omission of particulars as a mode of falsification, was rejected as misconceived. It was held that subsection (2) does not provide a definition but is merely a deeming provision, so that if there was a conflict between subsection (1)(a) and subsection (2), the latter could be ignored.

Another liberal reading of the section was employed to sustain convictions in *Shama*.[6] A British Telecom operator did not record international calls

---

[2] The word "account" has its meaning in normal English usage: *Scot-Simonds* [1994] Crim.L.R. 933. An entirely false set of accounts is an "account" within the meaning of the section: *ibid.*
[3] (1980) 72 Cr.App.R. 60.
[4] It seems that a particular omitted from a document is not a material particular if there was no duty to enter it in the document: see, *e.g. Keatley* [1980] Crim.L.R. 505 (public house manager; no duty to enter in employer's books details of transactions conducted on his own account in breach of his contract of employment: Judge Mendl).
[5] [1983] Crim.L.R. 43. See also *Levitz, The Times,* June 1, 1989, for the view that wiring a "meter mute" to a telephone, causing calls not to be metered, would be false accounting.
[6] (1990) 91 Cr.App.R. 138.

made through him by his grandmother. He failed to fill in forms (or "charge tickets") in a pile of forms provided for the purpose. He was held to have falsified documents required for an accounting purpose—namely, the forms (any in the pile) that he *ought* to have used. This is a robust decision. The ill-drafted section appears on its face to refer only to the omission of particulars from identifiable documents and to leave untouched the more thorough-going default of not creating a document at all in the case of an accounting system that happens to use separate documents for individual transactions rather than a composite document for transactions of a class. The Court of Appeal found itself able to read the section in a way that avoided that absurdity.

"Dishonestly"

12–04   Little needs to be said here about the requirement of dishonesty, which is discussed above in relation to other offences.[7] The falsification may be dishonest although it does not conceal a separate dishonest transaction, as where D makes a false entry in an account in order to conceal a muddle and to put off the evil day of having to sort out the muddle and make good the resulting loss.[8]

"With a view to gain or an intent to cause loss"

12–05   The requirement of a view to gain or an intent to cause loss is to be understood in the light of the definitions of "gain" and "loss" in section 34(2)(a). Gain and loss "in money or other property" are alone relevant, but the intended gain or loss may be only temporary. So D may, for example, falsify an account in order to facilitate an intended unlawful borrowing from the funds of his employers; and he may be guilty of the offence although he intends to replace what he takes.

12–06   *"With a view to gain"*. " 'Gain' includes a gain by keeping what one has, as well as a gain by getting what one has not" (s.34(2)(a)(i)). There is some authority in the context of blackmail for the proposition that a view to "a gain by getting what one has not" includes a view to obtaining what one is entitled to—such as payment of a debt.[9] But this simple basis for a conviction was not employed by the Privy Council in *Lee Cheung Wing v. R.*[10] Employees of a company dealing in futures contracts abused their positions in order to operate their own accounts with the company in the name of a friend. They were charged with falsifying documents required to make withdrawals against

---

[7] See especially, §§2–120 *et seq.*, 8–72 *et seq.*, 10–04.
[8] *Eden* (1971) 55 Cr.App.R. 193.
[9] See below, §14–35, para. (i).
[10] (1992) 94 Cr.App.R. 355; decided under the corresponding provisions of the Hong Kong Theft Ordinance.

their accounts. They argued that they were merely withdrawing what belonged to them; but it was held that, as they were bound to account for profits made in breach of their duty to the company, the withdrawals could have been refused if the company had known who was making them. In seeking payments to which they were not, therefore, entitled, they had "a view to gain". It is not clear what significance attaches to the fact that the shorter route to conviction mentioned above was not adopted.

In *Golechha*,[11] D discounted trade bills with P (a bank). The question arose   **12–07**
whether a falsification practised with a view solely to inducing P to forbear from enforcing its rights under the bills would be a falsification "with a view to gain." It was held not; P's forbearance to enforce D's indebtedness is not a gain "in money or other property" to D. "Property" is defined in section 4(1) to include things in action; but "the [thing] in action represented by the debt is owned by the creditor." D neither obtains nor retains from P's forbearance anything "on which he can draw or which he can convert into cash or goods."
The full implications of this decision are not clear. On the one hand, the court expressly forbore to pass judgment on the trial judge's interpretation of section 17, which appears in effect to have treated an intention to make an indirect gain as "a view to gain."[12] It is thought that that interpretation is correct. If, for example, D's purpose in falsifying documents is to preserve a business relationship that will produce future profits, it appears that he acts "with a view to gain."[13] *Golechha* does not plainly undermine this submission. On the other hand, the quite general proposition in that case that a debtor has no "view to gain" when he intends to induce a forbearance to sue in his creditor seems to rule out as "a view to gain" an intention to gain indirectly by "keeping what one has" as the result of not having to satisfy a (judgment) debt. Perhaps this implication was not intended.

"With intent to cause loss." "'Loss' includes a loss by not getting what one   **12–08**
might get, as well as a loss by parting with what one has" (s.34(2)(a)(ii)). So an intention to induce a creditor not to sue ought to be "an intent to cause loss", for by not suing the creditor will not get what he might get (at least in a case where the debtor has assets against which a judgment might be enforced); but again *Golechha* gives rise to doubt.

Use of misleading, false or deceptive accounts (s.17(1)(b))

Section 17(1)(b) strikes at the production or use of an account, or of a   **12–09**
record or document made or required for an accounting purpose, which, to

---

[11] (1989) 90 Cr.App.R. 241.
[12] *ibid.*, at 247–248.
[13] See *Stringer and Banks*, March 22, 1991, C.A. no. 89/1885/W3 (not reported on this point at (1991) 94 Cr.App.R. 13). So also if his purpose is to obtain, or preserve an existing, employment for the sake of the salary. This was the opinion of the C.L.R.C.: *Eighth Report*, para. 96.

the knowledge of the producer or user, is or may be misleading, false or deceptive in a material particular. Such production or use in furnishing information for any purpose is an offence if committed with the same *mens rea* as that required under section 17(1)(a), just discussed. The material particular need not be directly connected with the accounting purpose for which the document is made or required; it is sufficient if the document is misleading, false or deceptive in a particular that is material for the purpose for which it is being produced or used—that is, the purpose for which information is being furnished.[14]

This offence is similar to those of uttering a forged document under the Forgery Act 1913, s.6 (now repealed) and using a false instrument under the Forgery and Counterfeiting Act 1981, s.3. A person "uttered" a forged document when he "used" it.[15] The forgery authorities on "uses" may accordingly be relevant for the interpretation of the phrase "makes use of" in the present paragraph.[16]

A document may offend section 17(1)(b) notwithstanding that every statement or entry in it is individually true. It may omit facts material to the purpose for which the information is furnished, so as to be effectively false or so that it may mislead those who will rely upon it.[17] If D knows of or suspects the omission and knows that because of it the document may be misleading in some material respect, he is as guilty as if the document contained a positive lie.

Liability of company officers, etc.

12–10   Section 18 applies to offences under section 17. The reader may refer to the text of section 18 in Appendix 1 or to the discussion at §8–76, above.

2. FALSE STATEMENTS BY COMPANY DIRECTORS, ETC.

12–11   If a company director, intending to deceive members or creditors of the company about its affairs, is party to the publication of a written statement or account which to his knowledge is or may be misleading, false or deceptive in a material particular, he is guilty of an offence carrying seven years' imprisonment on conviction on indictment. Section 19, which so provides, applies in fact to all officers of bodies corporate or of unincorporated associations and to all persons purporting to act as such.

3. SUPPRESSION OF DOCUMENTS. PROCURING EXECUTION OF VALUABLE SECURITIES

12–12   Section 20 preserves, with certain amendments desirable to achieve con-

---

[14] *Mallett* (1978) 67 Cr.App.R. 239.
[15] Forgery Act 1913, s.6(2).
[16] See in particular *Harris* [1966] 1 Q.B. 184 ("use" by posting a copy).
[17] Compare *Kylsant* [1932] 1 K.B. 442; *Birshirgian* (1936) 25 Cr.App.R. 176.

formity with other provisions in this part of the Act, offences formerly found in the Larceny Acts of 1861 and 1916. These offences are best regarded as supplementary to offences already considered, as will be indicated in the descriptions of them which follow. The reader is referred to the text of the Act in Appendix 1 for the full terms of the section. The offences created by it are punishable on conviction on indictment with imprisonment for seven years.

Suppression, etc., of certain documents

Section 20(1) concerns the destruction, defacement or concealment of **12–13** certain classes of document—namely:

(i) any "valuable security"; this phrase is defined in very wide terms by subsection (3)[18];
(ii) any will or other testamentary document;
(iii) any original document of, or belonging to, or filed or deposited in, any court of justice or any government department.

The *mens rea* of the offence is the same as that required for an offence of falsifying accounts under section 17(1)(a), and the discussion in that context need not be repeated. Indeed the two offences have very much in common. The destruction or concealment of a deed or a will, like that of an accounting document, may be a mere act of preparation with a view to the eventual accomplishment of a fraudulent purpose.

Procuring execution of a valuable security

Section 20(2) renders it an offence, dishonestly and with a view to gain or **12–14** with intent to cause loss, by any deception to procure the execution of a valuable security.

This is a version of an offence first invented in the mid-nineteenth century.[19] Probably the C.L.R.C. thought the offence of little importance, in view, particularly, of its recommendation that Parliament should enact a broader offence (which would have included this one) of dishonestly, with a view to gain, by deception inducing a person to do or refrain from doing any act.[20] The Committee would have dispensed with the present offence in the event of the proposed offence's being given a sufficiently large maximum penalty. This may help to explain the seemingly casual way in which an offence as clumsily worded as that in section 20(2) came to be included in the Act, without benefit of analysis or defence from the Committee.[21] In the result the Committee's wider offence was not enacted; and, as things have

---

[18] See below, §12–16.
[19] 21 & 22 Vict. c. 47, which became s.90 of the Larceny Act 1861 and subsequently s.32(2) of the Larceny Act 1916.
[20] cl. 12(3) of the Draft Bill; see above, §7–02.
[21] See *ibid.*, para. 107. The Law Commission has drawn attention to "the unsatisfactory terms in which the offence is formulated": Law Com. No. 180, para. 3.22.

turned out, section 20(2) has acquired an altogether unexpected importance. This is particularly the case in connection with mortgage fraud. For the offence of obtaining services by deception, which ought to be available whenever a mortgage advance has been fraudulently obtained, has been neutered for this purpose by the remarkable decision in *Halai*[22]; and the appropriateness of a conviction of obtaining property by deception is not always beyond argument.[23]

12–15   Section 20(2) supplements other offences in two ways.

(i) First, it strikes at conduct analogous to obtaining property or services, or evading liability, by deception. The aim of a fraud within section 20(2) will commonly be the imposition of some liability upon the victim or a third person[24] (as when D procures P's signature to a deed, a cheque or a guarantee) or the extinction of some liability of D or a third person (as when D by deception induces P to cancel a bill of exchange of which he is the holder). Such a fraud may or may not involve another offence under the Acts. Where it does not, section 20(2) enlarges the range of the Acts.

(ii) Secondly, the ultimate aim of one who by deception procures the execution of a valuable security may in fact be the obtaining of property or of some other advantage by use of the security. Section 20(2) therefore makes a separate substantive offence out of conduct which may be merely preparatory to commission of one of the offences discussed in earlier chapters.

12–16   *"Deception"* has the same meaning in this context as in the offence of obtaining property by deception (subs.(3)).[25] The procuring must be *by* the deception; the discussion of the relation between a false representation and the obtaining of property required for an offence under section 15 applies here with necessary modifications.[26] The *mens rea* of the offence is the same as that required under section 17(1)(a); reference may be made to the earlier discussion.[27]

"Valuable security"

12–17   "Valuable security" is defined by subsection (3) to mean:

"any document creating, transferring, surrendering or releasing any right to, in or over property, or authorising the payment of money or delivery of any property, or

---

[22] [1983] Crim.L.R. 624; see above, §9–08.

[23] See in particular, above, §8–08.

[24] Compare *Thornton* [1964] 2 Q.B. 176 at 182.

[25] See above, §§8–10 *et seq.*

[26] See above, §8–44 *et seq.* In *Beck* (1984) 80 Cr.App.R. 355, it was accepted that the deception of one person might procure the execution of a valuable security by another; compare above, §8–58.

[27] Above, §§12–04 to 12–08.

evidencing the creation, transfer, surrender or release of any such right, or the payment of money or delivery of any property, or the satisfaction of any obligation."

This language obviously applies to cheques and other bills of exchange, and to receipts for money and other property. The words "transferring ... any right ... over property" have been read as, in effect, equivalent to "transferring any property"[28]; and it may indeed be the case that written transfers or assignments of property are, in general, valuable securities. But a transfer executed by the fraudulent party, although for the purpose of a transaction induced by the fraud, of course does not qualify, the execution not having been procured by deception.[29]

Documents involved in transfers of bank funds. Mortgage fraud cases have   **12–18** obliged the Court of Appeal to consider a number of ways in which mortgage advances are made without the use of cheques or banker's drafts (which, of course, are valuable securities). A telegraphic transfer of funds[30] and the print-out of a telex message between banks requesting that funds be made available[31] have both been denied the character of valuable securities. In each case the absence of any relevant signature or other mark by way of "execution" would seem to be a crucial disqualifying factor.

By contrast, in *King*,[32] the court accepted as a valuable security a "CHAPS order"[33]—an internal bank document, signed by or on behalf of a customer, directing a transfer of funds by electronic means between the customer's account and the account of a payee in another bank. The instructions on the document being completed, the order is counter-signed by officials of the bank; and this, in the court's surprising view, amounts to "execution" of the order. The court in *King* regarded the CHAPS order as a document transferring to the payee a right over the property represented by the credit in the paying customer's account; but that property—the customer's claim against the bank—is surely destroyed by the transfer.[34] Another objection to the decision is that, in the transaction analysed in detail in the judgment, the "property" in question was the property of the person practising the fraud; for the CHAPS order directed the transfer of funds from the account of one of the defendants with the victim bank to an accomplice's account. The bank had earlier been induced by the deception charged to advance that sum for

---

[28] *King* [1992] 1 Q.B. 20; see below, §12–18.
[29] *Dhillon and Dhillon*, June 19, 1992, C.A. no. 91/4682/Y2; the point does not appear in the report at [1992] Crim.L.R. 889. The suggestion of Woolf L.J. in *Bolton* (1991) 94 Cr.App.R. 74, at 78, that an offence under s.20(2) may be based on procuring the execution of a mortgage deed, must be viewed with caution.
[30] *Manjdadria* [1993] Crim.L.R. 73.
[31] *Johl* [1994] Crim.L.R. 522. It was also held that a letter from the paying bank confirming that payment had been made was not a valuable security.
[32] [1992] 1 Q.B. 20.
[33] A clearing house automated payment system order.
[34] Compare above, §8–08.

the purpose of a mortgage—whether by execution of a valuable security does not appear. It was surely then, if at any time, that an offence was committed. It is very doubtful whether s.20(2) was intended to stretch as far as it was made to do in this case.

12–19   *Documents creating contractual rights*. It was held in *Benstead*[35] that the definition of "valuable security" embraces an irrevocable letter of credit (notwithstanding that the liability created by such a document is conditional upon acts to be performed by the seller). The document creates a thing in action in favour of the beneficiary and therefore a "right . . . in . . . property". It has been objected that this phrase should be understood to refer only to rights in existing property and not to property created by the document itself; for otherwise all written contracts, since they create things in action, would appear to be valuable securities, which can hardly be intended.[36] But it seems that the courts are prepared to go this far; for it has been held, following *Benstead*, that a "sale agreement", under which P agreed to buy certain equipment from D's company and to lease it back to the company, was a valuable security.[37]

"Execution"

12–20   The word "execution" is a shorthand expression for an extensive range of acts spelt out in section 20(2) itself, which provides that the subsection

> "shall apply in relation to the making, acceptance, indorsement, alteration, cancellation or destruction in whole or in part of a valuable security . . . as if that were the execution of a valuable security."

The words "making, acceptance, indorsement, alteration, cancellation or destruction" are all peculiarly apt to describe acts in connection with bills of exchange and other negotiable instruments. The need to make a criminal offence of the fraudulent obtaining of a drawee's acceptance of a bill drawn upon him was revealed by a case in 1857[38]; and the gap in the law was remedied by legislation soon replaced by section 90 of the Larceny Act 1861. That section (subsequently the Larceny Act 1916, s.32(2)) made it an offence to fraudulently cause or induce a person to "execute, make, accept, endorse, or destroy" a valuable security. The present Act has added some items to that list. It is plain from the history, and from the very particular list in which the term occurs, that "acceptance" has here its technical meaning in the law relating to bills of exchange. That is, it refers to the drawee's act of writing on the bill, and signing, his assent to the order of the drawer.[39]

12–21   The correctness of this view of the extended definition of "execution" was

---

[35] (1982) 75 Cr.App.R. 276.
[36] J. C. Smith [1982] Crim.L.R. 457.
[37] *Moffat and McCaffer*, September 15, 1992, C.A. no. 91/3373/Z2, unreported.
[38] *Danger* (1857) 7 Cox C.C. 303.
[39] Bills of Exchange Act 1882, s.17.

confirmed by the House of Lords in *Kassim*.[40] D, using a false name and address, opened a number of accounts with P bank and obtained cheque books and a credit card. Charges under section 20(2) concerned cheques which D had drawn on those accounts and a credit card voucher. The House of Lords (overruling the Court of Appeal decision in *Beck*,[41] on the strength of which D had been convicted) held that the cheques and the voucher were not "executed" within the meaning of section 20(2), and in particular were not "accepted", when payment was made against them. Lord Ackner, in a speech in which other Lords concurred, asserted the "narrower technical meaning" of "acceptance" and continued:

> "It is ... also clear from the legislative history of section 20(2) that 'execution', which is deemed to cover the various activities detailed in the subsection, has as its object a wide variety of documents including bills of exchange and other negotiable instruments. The subsection contemplates acts being done to or in connection with such documents. It does not contemplate and accordingly is not concerned with giving effect to the documents by the carrying out of the instructions which they may contain, such as the delivery of goods or the payment out of money."[42]

"Execution" (s.20(2) also provides) includes   **12–22**

> "the signing or sealing of any paper or other material in order that it may be made or converted into, or used or dealt with as, a valuable security ...."

The purpose referred to by the words "in order that" may be that of D alone and not that of the person deceived into signing; indeed, a typical deception which the subsection certainly covers is a deception as to the very nature of the document being signed.[43] Nor, according to old authority, need the "valuable security" into which the document is intended to be converted be one which will in fact be valid if put to use.[44]

"Procuring" execution

In *Beck*,[45] D used forged travellers' cheques and a stolen credit card; and in   **12–23**
due course the bank and the credit card company, although not legally bound to do so, honoured the cheques and the credit card vouchers by paying those whom D had defrauded. The court mistakenly[46] viewed these payments as

---

[40] [1992] 1 A.C. 9.
[41] (1984) 80 Cr.App.R. 355. In *Nanayakkara* (1986) 84 Cr.App.R. 125, the same court loyally accepted the erroneous view of "execution" in *Beck*; but it correctly held (see *Kassim* [1992] 1 A.C. 9, *per* Lord Ackner at 18) that stolen U.S. Treasury social security orders delivered to a bank, to be cleared before crediting of the amounts to an account with the bank, were not "accepted" by the bank within the meaning of s.20(2).
[42] [1992] 1 A.C. 9 at 18.
[43] Compare *Graham* (1913) 8 Cr.App.R. 149.
[44] *Graham*, above.
[45] (1984) 80 Cr.App.R. 355.
[46] See above, §12–21.

the "execution" of the cheques and vouchers. On that view the question arose whether D had "procured" the payments. It was held that he had done so. The word "procure", it was said,[47] was one which "a jury can be relied on safely to understand"; they will understand it, it seems, to mean "to cause or to bring about". Notwithstanding the invocation of the jury as interpreters of "a word in common usage", this seems to be a judicial interpretation. Its correctness is doubtful. It rejects the well-known definition of "procure" by Lord Widgery C.J. (in the context of secondary liability) as involving a person's purpose to bring about an action or event.[48] Moreover, it was implicitly contradicted by the House of Lords in *Kassim*.[49] For it had been argued in that case that, if payment of the cheques D had drawn was not "execution" of them, he had nevertheless procured their ultimate "cancellation" or "destruction" (two other varieties of "execution") in the ordinary course. But this argument was rejected, as "confus[ing] consequences with intention". D had set out to make a gain for himself. Payment, not the cheques' cancellation or destruction, was the means by which he intended to achieve this. It seems that "procure" means "produce by endeavour" after all.

---

[47] (1984) 80 Cr.App.R. 355 at 360.
[48] *Attorney-General's Reference (No. 1 of 1975)* [1975] Q.B. 773 at 779: "To procure means to produce by endeavour. You procure a thing by setting out to see that it happens and taking the appropriate steps to produce that happening."
[49] [1992] 1 A.C. 9 at 19; applied in *Johl* [1994] Crim.L.R. 522.

Chapter 13

MAKING OFF WITHOUT PAYMENT

1. THE OFFENCE. POWER OF ARREST

An offence is committed by   **13–01**

"a person who, knowing that payment on the spot for any goods supplied or service done is required or expected from him, dishonestly makes off without having paid as required or expected and with intent to avoid payment of the amount due" (Theft Act 1978, s.3(1)).

The offence is punishable on conviction on indictment with up to two years' imprisonment (s.4(2)(b)), and on summary conviction with up to six months' imprisonment and/or a fine not exceeding, for the time being, £5,000.[1]

The change in the law effected by section 3

Criminal law sanctions are not generally provided against the dishonest   **13–02** debtor. Section 3 makes an exception for one who, by physically removing himself from the scene at which his obligation arises, may effectively put himself beyond his creditor's grasp. The mischief is commonly termed "bilking". Only certain examples of it were formerly subject to control. Section 3 provides a comprehensive sanction. The following paragraphs explain the change in the law effected by the section.

(i) *Theft or no theft.* If D dishonestly makes off without paying for goods   **13–03** supplied to him, he is not guilty of theft if the property in the goods has already passed to him and the supplier has ceased to have possession or control of them.[2] The present section, therefore, apart from extending the law, avoids nice questions of civil law even in a case where it may in fact be possible to prove theft.

(ii) *Original or supervening dishonesty.* When D runs out of a restaurant   **13–04** without paying for his meal, conviction under section 15 of the 1968 Act requires proof that his intention not to pay was formed before he obtained the food, so that it may be found that he obtained it by deception as to his intention to pay.[3] Exactly the same point applies under section 1 of the 1978 Act, as to obtaining services by deception. Under the present section there is

---

[1] s.4(3); Magistrates' Courts Act 1980, s.32(9), as amended by Criminal Justice Act 1991, s.17(2)(c).
[2] See above §2–57. It is assumed that D has not got the goods by the supplier's mistake in circumstances bringing the case within s.5(4) of the 1968 Act (above, §2–48). No one, in any case, wants to rely on s.5(4) if something simpler will do.
[3] See above, §8–20.

211

no need to prove that a prior deception induced the supply of goods or the rendering of the service.

13–05   (iii) *Making off achieved by deception or otherwise.* Where prior deception cannot be proved (and property in the goods, if any, has passed) D may still be guilty under section 2 of the Theft Act 1978 of evading his liability to pay if by deception he induces his creditor to wait for payment. The corresponding offence before 1978 was that under section 16(2)(a) of the Theft Act 1968 (now repealed) of obtaining the evasion of a debt by deception (as a form of "pecuniary advantage"). As a result of the decision of the House of Lords in *D.P.P. v. Ray*,[4] D might be convicted of this offence if, having decided to make off from a restaurant, garage forecourt or barber's shop without paying, he waited until P (a person aware of his transaction) had turned his back and then fled. P was to be treated as relevantly deceived and D's evasion as being effected by the deception. It is doubtful whether *D.P.P. v. Ray* can be adapted to the 1978 evasion offence; but even if it can, the extensive notion of deception upon which it rests and the distinction between the situations it would catch and those it would not are equally disreputable. There should be an offence in all of these situations or in none. Section 3 provides an offence in all of them.

Power of arrest

13–06   Unlike the offences created by sections 1 and 2 of the 1978 Act, which carry a maximum penalty of five years' imprisonment, this offence is not an arrestable offence within the meaning of the Police and Criminal Evidence Act 1984, s.24(1). A special power of arrest without warrant is therefore provided in respect of anyone who is or, with reasonable cause, is suspected to be, committing or attempting to commit the offence (s.3(4)). This is a so-called "citizen's arrest" power; the waiter, hotel receptionist or petrol pump attendant may arrest the customer who is "making off" or attempting to do so.

    The arrest must be made while the offender is still "making off"; there is no power to arrest a person who is, or who is suspected of being, "guilty of the offence"[5] but who is no longer (suspected to be) "committing" it. The problem of determining when the "making off" ends can therefore arise.[6] It is not one that can be resolved by a general formula.[7]

---

[4] [1974] A.C. 370; above, §8–34.
[5] Compare Police and Criminal Evidence Act 1984, s.24(5) and (6).
[6] Compare "the course of the stealing" in s.22(1) of the 1968 Act.
[7] Compare *Moberley v. Alsop, The Times*, December 13, 1991 (Divisional Court) (alighting passenger who had not shown a ticket at exit barrier failed to produce one on request in ticket hall and refused name and address; arrest at that point lawful) and *Drameh* [1983] Crim.L.R. 322 (Judge Pickering) (arrest at home half an hour after making off from taxi; unlawful).

2. THE DETAILS OF THE OFFENCE

There must be some "goods supplied" or "service done"

Goods supplied

The section is particularly designed to cover the kind of sale transaction   **13–07**
under which property in the goods inevitably passes before payment is
expected—the transfer of petrol from pump to fuel tank, for example, or the
service of a meal to a diner who will pay after eating. But it will also apply to a
delivery of goods in anticipation of the passing of property. A common case is
that of the wrapping and pricing of goods at a supermarket food counter, the
goods being handed to the customer to be paid for at the cashier's desk. It is
submitted that these goods are "supplied" at the food counter although they
are not yet "sold"; so that if the customer dishonestly leaves without paying,
he commits the present offence, which is thus an alternative to a charge of
theft. This does not mean that the standard case of shoplifting is necessarily
an offence under section 3; goods simply exposed for sale (except, perhaps, in
a self-service shop[8]) are not "goods supplied" when they are lifted from the
display.

"Goods" has the meaning stated in section 34(2)(b) of the 1968 Act
(s.5(2)).

Service done

The definition of "an obtaining of services" by section 1(2) is not matched   **13–08**
by a definition of "service done" in section 3(1). Nor is the shift from "services" to "[a] service" explained. It is submitted, however, that "service
done" should be liberally interpreted, as "obtains services" is broadly
defined. For example, permitting a person to use a tennis court in a public
park or a rowing boat on a private lake should be regarded as the doing of a
service, even though nothing is done apart from the giving of permission to
use the amenity. But something in the way of permission (if only a permission
to be inferred from deliberate inaction) appears to be necessary. The section
does not cover a making off from a cinema or dance hall that has been clan-
destinely entered through a back door or window. An amenity thus involun-
tarily provided is not a "service done."[9]

"Service done" must cover the letting of goods on hire (which is, however,
more obviously a supply of goods),[10] as it will also cover the letting of a room
in a guest house or hotel.

---

[8] See Smith (J. C.), para. 5–03 and n. 2, questioning the view formerly taken in the present work.
[9] See *Thirteenth Report*, para. 21. For an argument to the contrary, see Smith (A. T. H.) para.
20–83.
[10] Compare *Cahaine v. Croydon L.B.C.*, *The Times*, March 20, 1985 (Trade Descriptions Act
1968, s.1).

Transactions contrary to law or unenforceable

13–09   Making off without having paid is no offence if the supply of goods or the doing of the service was contrary to law or if the service done is such that payment is not legally enforceable (s.3(3)).

The contract under which the goods are supplied or the service done may itself be "contrary to law".[11] Thus, it may be an offence to supply the goods in question (*e.g.* a flick knife) or to do the service; or to conduct the sale in a particular manner (*e.g.* in contravention of the Mock Auctions Act 1961); or to supply the goods to the particular customer served (*e.g.* intoxicating liquor to a minor).

13–10   The supply of goods or the doing of the service may be "contrary to law" because of some breach of the law committed in carrying out the transaction.[12] All depends upon the correct construction of the statutory provision that is contravened: is it intended to affect the contract in performance of which the contravention occurs, or does it merely impose penalties for the contravention?[13] A new jurisprudence on this difficult question could well arise from the present section. It will merely be observed here, by way of example: (a) that the lack of a necessary licence—*e.g.* a street trader's or hackney carriage driver's licence—will very probably take the transaction outside section 3; (b) that a serious breach of the Motor Vehicles (Construction and Use) Regulations may render the doing of a service "contrary to law"[14]; but (c) that it can hardly be intended that a relatively trivial breach of the same Regulations should render a taxi-driver's contract with his passenger "contrary to law" so that he cannot in theory sue for his fares or in practice arrest the passenger for an offence under section 3.[15]

13–11   Services for which payment is not legally enforceable include, most obviously, services under contracts void by statute (*e.g.* gaming contracts) or as being contrary to public policy (*e.g.* the services of a prostitute or other "immoral" services).

D must know that "payment on the spot is required or expected"[16]

13–12   *"On the spot."* The expression "on the spot" is a somewhat colloquial way of saying that payment is required contemporaneously with the doing of the service."[17] Payment "on the spot" is payment "then and there"—that is, before leaving the place at which the goods are on that occasion supplied or

---

[11] See this heading in Treitel, *An Outline of the Law of Contract* (4th ed.), pp. 152 *et seq.*
[12] The topic is not suitable for full treatment here. See Chitty, *Law of Contracts* (26th ed.), Chap. 16, especially at paras. 1242 *et seq.*
[13] *St. John Shipping Corporation v. Joseph Rank Ltd.* [1957] 1 Q.B. 267.
[14] As in *Ashmore, Benson, Pease & Co. Ltd. v. A. V. Dawson Ltd.* [1973] 1 W.L.R. 828 (overloading lorry).
[15] Compare *St. John Shipping Corporation v. Joseph Rank Ltd.*, above, at 281.
[16] See Smith (A. T. H.), paras. 20–70 *et seq.*, for an elaborate discussion.
[17] *Per* Pill J. in *Moberly v. Alsop, The Times*, December 13, 1991.

the service is on that occasion done; or at the termination of a service—as on passing through the exit barrier of a station at which a passenger alights after having travelled without a ticket.[18] It also includes "payment at the time of collecting goods on which work has been done or in respect of which service has been provided" (s.3(2)). It does not matter that the car has been repaired on an earlier day or that the clothes have been dry-cleaned off the premises from which they are being collected.

"Payment." The word "payment" here seems to refer to any transaction **13–13** that would discharge the debtor's obligation. The establishment that welcomes card-holders[19] and the restaurant that accepts luncheon vouchers are plainly protected by the section although they do not expect cash.

"Required or expected." The transactions covered by the section are **13–14** mainly of an informal type, and the language of the section is correspondingly informal at this point. The terms governing payment will rarely be express; if they are, payment on the spot may be expressly "required". The obligation to pay on the spot will much more often derive from common usage; such payment will be "expected" as a matter of common understanding.

Knowledge. The debtor must know of the requirement or expectation. If **13–15** he thinks that he enjoys credit terms, he cannot be guilty of the offence, however dishonest he may be. If, conversely, he has in fact been served on credit terms, but believes that payment on the spot is required or expected, again he cannot commit the offence (although he may technically be guilty of an attempt); for one cannot "know" what is not the case.

"Makes off"

The words "makes off" do not stand alone—the making off must be dis- **13–16** honest. This being so, the words can be applied "in their ordinary natural meaning". A person "makes off" when, quite simply, he departs from the spot where payment ought to be made.[20] (If he is stopped before he passes that spot, so that he does not achieve such a departure, he may be guilty of an attempt to commit the offence.[21]) No particular mode of departure is required, such as stealth or haste. The departure may occur with the knowledge and assistance of the creditor or his staff, as where a cool customer calls for his hat and coat, requests that a cab be summoned for him and sends his compliments to the chef.

---

[18] *Moberly v. Alsop*, above.
[19] For payment by credit card as discharge of the customer's obligation, see *Re Charge Card Services Ltd.* [1989] Ch. 497.
[20] *Brooks and Brooks* (1982) 76 Cr.App.R. 66. The making off need not be from the "spot" on which payment was known to be expected; D and his creditor may have moved from that spot before D makes off, as in *Aziz* [1993] Crim.L.R. 708.
[21] *McDavitt* [1981] Crim.L.R. 843 (Mr. Recorder M. Mann Q.C.); approved in *Brooks and Brooks*, above.

It has been argued that the mischief struck at by the section is "leaving in a way that makes it difficult for the debtor to be traced".[22] But if the implication of this view is that no one can "make off" if his identity and address are perfectly well known to the creditor, it produces a very strange reading of the section. Moreover, it is doubtful whether it hits the whole of the mischief. Some typical creditors in whose interests the offence was created depend entirely on payment then and there, their debts being far too small to warrant pursuing.

Deception to achieve departure

13–17   There has been controversy as to whether a person can be said to "make off" where by deception he induces the creditor to consent to his departure. It is thought that he can.[23] It is, of course, agreed that "the creditor's consent to the fetching by a person of the means of payment is not to be treated as consent to his departure"[24] (P the taxi-driver waits while D will—so he pretends—"just pop indoors to find the fare"). The problem is with other kinds of deception. Does D "make off" when he gives counterfeit coin to the flower-seller in pretended payment or misleads the restaurateur into believing that he has paid the waiter? The preferable solution, it is thought, is to say that he does, following the Court of Appeal in the view that "makes off" simply means "departs". Discrimination between cases can then turn on whether D has departed "without having paid as required or expected".

"Without having paid as required or expected"

13–18   It is suggested that a person "makes off without having paid as required or expected" if he leaves without doing what he ought to do to discharge his obligation. One who leaves foreign coins in the news vendor's tray or gives forged banknotes for his petrol does not "pay". Giving stolen money is a different case, however; the innocent creditor acquires a good title to stolen currency that is passed to him, so that the debtor's obligation is discharged.

Some difficulty is caused, however, by the case of one who gives in purported payment a cheque that he realises will not be met on presentment. One view of this case is that it involves no "making off"[25]; but that view has been criticised above. Assuming now that there is a "making off", it would seem odd to describe as "payment" the giving of a worthless cheque. On the other hand, it is precisely for such a case that section 2(3) is at pains to provide, for purposes of section 2(1)(b), that the creditor who is given a cheque is

---

[22] J. R. Spencer [1983] Crim.L.R. 573.
[23] Smith (J. C.), para. 5–02, in general agrees (though he is wrongly credited with the opposite opinion in *Brooks and Brooks*, above, at 68); but he yields to the persuasion of J. R. Spencer, *loc. cit.* above, to the extent of accepting that one "who leaves a worthless cheque with his true name and address" does not "make off" because, being traceable, he is outside the mischief of the offence. For argument to the contrary, see Smith (A. T. H.), paras. 20–93 *et seq.*
[24] F. Bennion [1983] Crim.L.R. 205, elaborating his argument at [1980] Crim.L.R. 670 in favour of a narrow interpretation of "makes off".
[25] Bennion and Spencer, *loc. cit.* above; *Hammond* [1982] Crim.L.R. 611 (Judge Morrison).

not to be treated as being paid but as being induced to wait for payment.[26] The silence of section 3 on this point may possibly imply that the contrary is intended for purposes of that section; and it has indeed been argued that one who gives a cheque that is sure to bounce nevertheless "pays" by making a conditional payment.[27] It was at one time widely thought that section 3 did not require an intention to avoid payment permanently. If this were true, the section might have been employed in a deception case in which section 2(1)(b) would not be available for want of an "intent to make permanent default." Now that the contrary has been held,[28] the point discussed above ought to be academic; there will be no advantage in charging under section 3 and no room for argument if section 2 is used, as surely it should be. In case section 3 should be used, however, it is suggested that common sense provides the preferable solution: one who leaves a worthless cheque does not "pay".

"With intent to avoid payment of the amount due"

There must be an "amount due"

The supply of goods, or doing of a service, must obviously be such as to give **13–19** rise to a payment obligation. If the supplier has earned no money (perhaps because of breach of contract or because he has not completed performance of his own obligations), there is no "amount due". If the supplier's breach of contract or failure to complete performance discharges the customer from obligation under the supply contract, the customer commits no offence if he departs.[29] It is otherwise, however, if it is the customer who, by his very departure, prevents completion of the supply. In such a case the supplier becomes entitled to the value of his performance so far.[30] If the customer's making off is with intent to avoid payment even of that amount, he ought to be guilty of the offence. This has to be secured by treating the amount as "due" because the very act of making off makes it so. The slight paradox is supportable.

D must intend never to pay

It was for a time a widely held view that the phrase "intent to avoid pay- **13–20** ment", read in its context and in the light of the contrast with section 2(1)(b), clearly meant an intention to avoid the on-the-spot payment known to be required, and that an intention never to pay was not necessary. The contrary, however, was held by the House of Lords in *Allen*.[31] D left the hotel where he had been staying, without paying his bill. It was held that his defence, that he had been prevented from paying the bill by temporary financial difficulties

---

[26] See above, §10–16.
[27] G. Syrota [1980] Crim.L.R. 413.
[28] See below, §13–20.
[29] In *Troughton v. Metropolitan Police* [1987] Crim.L.R. 138, a conviction was quashed on the basis of such an interpretation of the facts.
[30] *Planché v. Coburn* (1831) 8 Bing. 14.
[31] [1985] A.C. 1029.

but expected to be able to do so from the proceeds of certain business ventures, should have been left to the jury. The arguments which prevailed with the House of Lords[32] were: (1) that the phrase "with intent to avoid payment" would add nothing to the other ingredients of the offence if it merely meant "with intent to avoid payment on the spot", for anyone leaving dishonestly without paying must have that intent; and (2) that there were other and preferable ways of drafting section 3(1) if that was the meaning to be conveyed.

13–21   The decision concludes the point and it would not be justifiable to devote much space to an attempt to counter these arguments. Suffice it to observe: (1) that the first doubtfully assumes that every phrase in a statutory provision must have an entirely independent function, a proposition that an eminent draftsman has contradicted, by chance referring to this very provision as an example of the "technique of overlap"[33]; and (2) that it would equally have been easy to insert the word "permanently", as in some other provisions, if that was what was meant.

What is more important is the outcome; section 3 turns out not to do the whole of the job that it ought to do. In the case of sellers and suppliers of services who undertake very small transactions on the basis of immediate payment, the mischief to be controlled is the very act of making off; and, as Lord Hailsham suggested,[34] there may well now be a case for the creation of a summary offence of making off with intent to avoid the on-the-spot payment required. In the meantime the decision in *Allen* threatens an increase in the number of contested cases as bilkers run bogus, but possibly just plausible, defences of "I was going to go back and pay later".

Where D believes that nothing is due

13–22   D may think that payment has already been made, by himself or a companion. In this case, not knowing there is an "amount due", he cannot be said to intend to avoid payment of it.

A similar defence may be made by a customer who pays or tenders less than the sum charged on the ground that the sum is excessive. He may claim that the price (not notified or negotiated in advance) is unreasonable; or that defects in the goods or service reduce what he is legally obliged to pay. His contention in either case is that what he pays or tenders is the whole "amount due" and that his making off is not, therefore, with intent to avoid payment of that amount.

Defences such as those just discussed equally, of course, deny dishonesty.

"Dishonestly"

13–23   The general principle[35] is that it is for the jury or the magistrates as judges

---

[32] They were those of Boreham J. for the Court of Appeal: see *ibid*., at 1034.
[33] Bennion, *Statute Law* (2nd ed.), p. 176. (The example is not repeated in the 3rd ed.)
[34] [1985] A.C. 1029 at 1035.
[35] See above, §2–132.

of fact to say whether the accused's conduct was "dishonest" within the meaning of that word as "an ordinary word of the English language", applying for this purpose "the current standards of ordinary decent people".[36] If it was, a further question arises (if, at least, there is evidence capable of raising a doubt about it[37]): must the defendant have realised that what he did was dishonest according to those standards?[38]

---

[36] *Feely* [1973] Q.B. 530.
[37] See §2–133.
[38] *Ghosh* [1982] Q.B. 1053.

Chapter 14

BLACKMAIL

1. INTRODUCTION

14–01   Before the passing of the Act, the term "blackmail" was not a term of art in English law. The word had been used by lawyers as a convenient way of referring to a number of offences contained in the Larceny Act 1916, ss.29–31, where, however, the word did not appear. By laymen it was understood to mean the obtaining of some advantage by the use of improper threats, especially threats to make use of information discreditable to the victim. The layman's use of the word was naturally looser than the lawyer's; but layman and lawyer were not far apart in their understanding of what amounted to blackmail, and they both regarded the kinds of conduct they had characteristically in mind as among the most serious criminal or moral offences.[1]

14–02   The complex statutory provisions replaced by section 21 of the present Act have been aptly described as "an ill-assorted collection of legislative bric-a-brac which the draftsman of the 1916 Act put together with scissors and paste."[2] There was a considerable number of offences, carrying widely different maximum penalties. These offences, by their own terms and still more by virtue of their interpretation at the hands of the courts, overlapped to a perplexing and unsatisfactory degree. The overlap was, if anything, rendered more serious by the fact that the most important of the provisions were so drafted as to involve fundamentally different approaches to one of the central problems of this part of the law. The problem, shortly expressed, is this: from what point of view, in considering the lawful or unlawful character of a demand with menaces, is the propriety of or justification for the relevant conduct to be judged? Should the fact that what D demands is rightly due to him be relevant? If it should, should it be relevant that, though what D demands is not something to which he has a valid claim, yet he thinks it is? If

---

[1] The worst cases of extortion, or attempt to extort, by threats to commit legal wrongs (and *a fortiori* threats to commit serious crimes) are uncontroversially bad offences. But a substantial literature is devoted to puzzled attempts to resolve the alleged "paradox of blackmail". The offence typically embraces cases in which D threatens to do what he is legally, and perhaps morally, entitled to do (even, in some cases, what he ought to do, such as report a crime) if P does not do what he (D) is perfectly at liberty to request (and may be entitled to demand). The paradox was neatly stated by Glanville Williams [1954] Crim.L.R. at 163: "two things that taken separately are moral and legal whites together make a legal black". A fascinating range of theories about blackmail is collected in a symposium in (1993) 141 U. Pa. L.Rev., Part 5; and several are reviewed by J. Lindgren (1984) 84 Col. Law Rev. 670. For elaborate discussion from a liberal perspective, with implications for the narrowing of the offence, see Joel Feinberg, *Harmless Wrongdoing (The Moral Limits of the Criminal Law*, vol. 4), pp. 238–276.
[2] B. Hogan [1966] Crim.L.R. 474.

blackmail can be committed even by demanding something to which D is (or believes he is) entitled, by what criterion is the propriety of his using a particular threat to support his demand properly to be judged—by his own subjective opinion, or by an objective standard, whether represented by the terms of a statute or by the opinion of a court or jury? To these questions the Larceny Act, as interpreted, afforded no clear or consistent answers.

Questions of the kind mentioned in the preceding paragraph may be plausibly answered in a number of different ways. The Act provides a unified and tolerably coherent solution. In order to achieve this solution and a general simplification of the law, the C.L.R.C. largely dispensed with the language of the repealed provisions. The only words of importance preserved from the Larceny Act are the words "demand" and "menaces", which reflect the language of the Larceny Act 1916, ss.29(1)(i) and 30. Apart from the use of these two words, the offence created by section 21 of the Theft Act 1968 was new in form and in approach, as well as in name. It proceeded from the necessity that the C.L.R.C. felt "to go back to first principles and to consider as a matter of policy what kind of conduct should amount to blackmail."[3]   **14–03**

The problem of policy was answered thus. Any demand with menaces should, prima facie, be condemned, and it should be caught by the Act if its purpose is a property gain or loss. But honesty should win exemption; the Act does not strike at the conscientious mind. One should be entitled to plead, in effect, "I thought my demand was justified and my pressure acceptable"; such language comes as close as the subject-matter allows to the notion of honesty. This solution inevitably proved controversial.[4]

2. DEFINITION OF BLACKMAIL. GENERAL OBSERVATIONS

The statutory definition

There are three ingredients of the crime of blackmail: **14–04**

(i) D must make a "demand with menaces."
(ii) The demand with menaces must be "unwarranted"; and it will be unwarranted unless D makes it "in the belief—(a) that he has reasonable grounds for making the demand; and (b) that the use of the menaces is a proper means of reinforcing the demand."

---

[3] *Eighth Report*, para. 115.
[4] For the controversy, see *Eighth Report*, paras. 108 *et seq*.: Sir Brian McKenna [1966] Crim.L.R. 467; B. Hogan, *ibid.*, at 474; H.L.Deb., Vol. 289, cols. 212 and 230 (debate on Second Reading of the Bill); *ibid.*, Vol. 290, col. 524 (clause considered in Committee); *ibid.*, Vol. 291 (clause considered on Report); H.C.Deb., Vol. 763, col. 1435 (debate in Second Reading Committee); and consideration of clause in Standing Committee H, June 25 and 27, 1968: Official Report, cols. 77 and 81.

(iii) D must make the demand "with a view to gain for himself or another or with intent to cause loss to another."

The crime is thus defined in section 21(1). Some slight assistance in the interpretation of "demand" and "menaces" is afforded by subsection (2). Subsection (3) provides a maximum penalty of fourteen years' imprisonment on conviction on indictment. Blackmail is not triable summarily.[5]

General observations

14–05   The ingredients of the offence require to be separately considered. First, however, some general observations may be helpful.

Only rarely is the application of section 21 likely to cause difficulty, or its policy to give rise to possible concern. Most of the cases for which provision is required and for which the section will in practice be used can readily be seen to fall within its terms. D threatens to publish discreditable details about P's private life unless P pays him for silence; a corrupt policeman threatens to lay a fictitious charge against P but suggests that the charge may be avoided by a suitable payment; a thug offers his "protection" to a club or cafe proprietor while two or three large demi-thugs lounge in the doorway; a shop proprietor is told that a bomb has been hidden on his premises and will be allowed to go off unless he hands over a stated amount in cash: in cases like these the fact that a crucial issue in the offence of blackmail is cast in subjective terms will have a splendid irrelevance. The worst cases that ought to be blackmail are clearly blackmail.

Even if what D threatens is something that may be lawfully done (or that he thinks may be lawfully done), this is never by itself enough to protect him if his threat to do it is a means of reinforcing a demand. D is perfectly entitled, as a matter of law, to tell P's wife of P's adultery, and there may be circumstances in which he may regard it as the morally correct thing to do. Further, he may properly warn P that he proposes to tell P's wife of the adultery. What he cannot do is to invoke these liberties as a sufficient ground for using them as a means of extortion.

14–06   Only when D claims that what he demands is in some way his due does the subjective test adopted in the section begin to affect the matter. Only when D can plausibly say something like: "I thought the sum I named was properly due to me," and "I thought my threat was a proper way of getting it"—only then can his demand with menaces escape the condemnation of the section. Very occasionally a person of low moral standards, holding or claiming to hold unusually liberal views as to the means which it is permissible to use to obtain what seems to be his due, may escape a conviction that he would have suffered had an objective criterion been embodied in the section.[6] There is a converse possibility—that a person of unusually high moral standards and veracity on oath may suffer a conviction merely because he has failed to live

---

[5] Magistrates' Courts Act 1980, Sched. 1, para. 28(a).
[6] But see §14–30, below.

up to his own standards and has made a demand with menaces not "warranted" by his own understanding of what is proper! But this is surely an academic rather than a real-life possibility.

A more important limitation of the scope of blackmail than the use of the   **14-07**
subjective test of propriety is the requirement that D's demand be made with a view to gain or with intent to cause loss. Gain and loss mean only "gain or loss in money or other property" (s.34(2)(a)). So it is not blackmail (though it may be some other offence) to demand, with whatever supporting threats, the custody of a child, the victim's sexual favours, a release from lawful custody or the withdrawal of evidence proposed to be given in support of a prosecution. Differing views may be held as to the propriety of excluding all such demands from the offence. The point is stressed here because it is one that it is desirable to have in mind throughout a consideration of the other aspects of blackmail.

3. THE MAKING OF A DEMAND WITH MENACES

It must be clear from the circumstances that D is demanding something   **14-08**
(some act or omission) from P. But it is not necessary that he should actually use language such as invariably carries the force of a demand. "It is not necessary that the language should be explicit", observed Lord Reading C.J. in *Studer*[7]; "it may be in language only a request." He might have added, with the facts of that case in mind, that it may on its face be only a suggestion made for P's benefit. D told P that £250 was the sum he would need from P in order that he might induce a detective to withdraw an otherwise inevitable charge against P; but D was guilty of demanding money with menaces, for the detective and the alleged charge were both fictitious. D was menacing P with talk of a supposed peril and demanding £250 as the price of its evasion. The case was but a subtle and unusual version of the more familiar transaction of which *Collister and Warhurst*[8] is an example. There police officers threatened to bring a bogus charge against P but made it clear that he could avoid the charge by a payment. Although their demand was not express, it was implicit in their words and conduct,[9] and they too were guilty of demanding money with menaces.

---

[7] (1915) 11 Cr.App.R. 307; see also *Robinson* (1796) 2 Leach 749.
[8] (1955) 39 Cr.App.R. 100.
[9] The threat was to arrest P on a charge of importuning. One of the accused said to P: "This is going to look very bad for you." A meeting was arranged for the following day, and it was made clear to P that a report on his alleged conduct would be typed but would be used only if P failed to keep the appointment. When he met the accused the next day, P was asked if he had brought anything with him. Pilcher J.'s direction to the jury (39 Cr.App.R. 100 at 102), approved on appeal (*ibid.*, at 105), remains of value on the meaning of a demand: it was enough if the jury were satisfied "that, although there was no express demand ..., the demeanour of the accused and the circumstances of the case were such that an ordinary reasonable man would understand that a demand ... was being made upon him ...."

14–09   Words, in fact, are not necessary at all, so long as D's conduct conveys a demand. If D holds a gun at the head of P's sleeping child and points at a safe of which P alone knows the combination, D's conduct is as eloquent as words could be and there is a strong prima facie case of blackmail. (If the gun were pointed at P himself or at his waking child, so that P or the child were put in fear, the natural offence to charge would be assault with intent to rob. There is a clear overlap between that offence and blackmail.)

The act or omission demanded

14–10   Section 21(2) expressly provides that "the nature of the act or omission demanded is immaterial." This provision was included in the draft Bill "in order to avoid any argument that, because the offence depends on the demand being made with a view to gain or with intent to cause loss, the thing demanded must be property."[10]

Some examples of demands for different kinds of act and omission will be given in the last part of this chapter.[11]

The making of the demand

14–11   Section 21 requires only that a demand with menaces be made, not, of course, that it be complied with. But equally, if the demand is complied with, the offence is nonetheless committed.

A question which may occasionally arise, and which on one set of facts has reached the House of Lords, is whether the full act of making a demand with menaces involves the effective communication of the demand to P. A letter sent to P may miscarry; a message may remain undelivered; P may not hear D's words or observe his gestures. The question is whether the posting of the letter, the entrusting of the message, the speaking of the words or the making of the gestures, amounts to the making of the demand which it is D's purpose to convey.

Posting of a letter

14–12   In *Treacy v. D.P.P.*[12] the House of Lords, by a majority, held that a demand conveyed by a letter is made when the letter is posted, so that the act of posting in England a letter addressed to a victim abroad had completed an offence of blackmail within the jurisdiction.[13] Lord Hodson's opinion to this effect (in which Lord Guest concurred) depended mainly on the consideration that the act of posting would formerly have constituted a complete offence under the Larceny Act 1916, s. 29(1)(i).[14] That offence, however, was one of "uttering" a letter or writing demanding property with menaces; and

---

[10] *Eighth Report*, p. 131 (notes on draft Bill).
[11] Below, §14–35.
[12] [1971] A.C. 537; discussed by P. J. Pace (1971) 121 New L.J. 242.
[13] This decision is unaffected by the provisions on jurisdiction in the Criminal Justice Act 1993. As to demands sent from abroad, see below, §17–06.
[14] [1971] A.C. 537 at 557–558.

"uttering" was an old technical expression that embraced a wide range of actions in relation to documents, including posting. Lord Diplock applied what he conceived to be the linguistic sense of "ordinary literate men and women": a man in ordinary conversation, he thought, would say "I have made a demand" as soon as he had posted a letter containing a demand.[15]

Lords Reid and Morris of Borth-y-Gest dissented. Their linguistic sense was not, apparently, what Lord Diplock would have supposed. Each gave a number of examples of factual situations illustrating the proposition that "[a] demand is not made until it is communicated."[16] This proposition would seem to be true at least of the case of a message entrusted by D to E for delivery to P, whether the message is oral or in writing. The effect of *Treacy* may be to make a special rule for the case of communication by post, although the majority did not expressly rely on any peculiarity of the post as a means of transmission.

Ineffective utterances

If words intended to communicate a demand are incapable of being heard   **14–13** by the intended victim, however acute of hearing he may be, it is submitted that no demand is made.[17] But if D shouts "Your money or your life!" at P, D probably does, as a matter of language, "make a demand with menaces" even if P is stone deaf. In any event, it would be unsatisfactory to have one rule for words which P does not hear and another for words which he does not understand, and it seems clear that if P does hear the words but does not understand their demanding or threatening implications, D has made a demand with menaces so long as an ordinary person in P's position would have understood what D was intending to convey.[18]

Attempted blackmail

If a blackmailing demand is "made" as soon as it is spoken or dispatched   **14–14** beyond recall, the possibility of a case of attempted blackmail is limited to fanciful situations such as those where D is affected by a stammer or interrupted in the act of posting.[19] In fact there is some authority for the doubtful proposition that there cannot be an attempt to demand,[20] blackmail being itself "in substance an attempt to obtain money."[21]

---

[15] *ibid.*, at 565. See also *Austin v. The Queen* (1989) 166 C.L.R. 669 at 674–675.

[16] [1971] A.C. 537 at 556, *per* Lord Morris of Borth-y-gest.

[17] J.LL.J. Edwards (1952) 15 M.L.R. at 346, puts the case of the loudspeaker, concealed in P's house, that fails to function when D seeks by means of it to convey a demand to P; surely a mere attempt. (But if the words are heard by an unintended victim and affect him as a demand with menaces, the offence will be complete.)

[18] See to the same effect John Stephenson J. in *Treacy* in the Court of Appeal: [1971] A.C. 537 at 543.

[19] And see n. 17, above.

[20] *Moran* (1952) 36 Cr.App.R. 10 at 12 (criticised by J.LL.J. Edwards (1952) 15 M.L.R. at 346; by J. C. Smith [1961] Crim.L.R. at 445; and by Williams, *C.L.G.P.*, p. 615, n. 9); *Treacy* in the Court of Appeal: [1971] A.C. 537 at 554; and in the House of Lords, *per* Lord Hodson, *ibid.*, at 558 (the proposition is "correct as a general rule").

[21] [1971] A.C. 537 at 545, *per* John Stephenson J.

The menaces

14–15   Under the Larceny Act 1916, ss. 29(1)(i)[22] and 30,[23] the word "menace" was given a wide meaning. In the leading case of *Thorne v. Motor Trade Association*,[24] Lord Wright said:

> "I think the word 'menace' is to be liberally construed and not as limited to threats of violence but as including threats of any action detrimental to or unpleasant to the person addressed. It may also include a warning that in certain events such action is intended."

There is no doubt that the word is intended to have a wide meaning in section 21 also. The possible varieties of menace are innumerable. Apart from threats of physical violence (to P or to some other person), of prosecution or of the revelation of criminal conduct or sexual misbehaviour (whether real or pretended), all of which have already been referred to in this chapter, we may add a few examples suggested by important cases under the old law: a threat to publish attacks on a company calculated to lower the value of its shares[25]; a threat to reveal that P has not honoured a debt[26]; a threat to place P on a trade association's "stop list" unless he pays a fine imposed by the association for breach of its rules[27]; a threat not to give evidence in an action.[28] These are but illustrations thrown up by the chances of earlier litigation.

Trivial threats and common sense

14–16   Although menaces may take many forms, not every trivial threat will satisfy the section. The C.L.R.C. in fact chose the word "menaces" in preference to "threats" because they regarded the former word as the stronger of the two.[29] "Give me £50 or I shall tickle you with this feather" is not, on the face of it, a threat strong enough for blackmail even if P is known to be ticklish.[30] In one case[31] a student had offered shopkeepers, for a modest contribution to charity, copies of a poster guaranteeing protection from rag activities that might inconvenience them. The jury were directed that as a matter of common sense no "menaces" were involved.

---

[22] The offence was that of uttering a letter or writing "demanding of any person with menaces, and without any reasonable or probable cause, any property or valuable thing".

[23] The offence was committed by one who "with menaces or by force demands of any person anything capable of being stolen with intent to steal the same".

[24] [1937] A.C. 797 at 817.

[25] *Boyle and Merchant* [1914] 2 K.B. 339.

[26] *Norreys v. Zeffert* [1939] 2 All E.R. 187.

[27] *Thorne v. Motor Trade Association* [1937] A.C. 797.

[28] *Clear* [1968] 1 Q.B. 670.

[29] *Eighth Report*, para. 123. This view was "notwithstanding the wide meaning given to 'menaces' in *Thorne*'s case" (above, at n. 24).

[30] Contrast the case put below, §14–20.

[31] *Harry* [1974] Crim.L.R. 32.

No "definition" needed in straightforward cases

It is indeed in most cases a matter of common sense whether proved con-   **14-17**
duct amounted to the use of "menaces." "It is an ordinary word of which the
meaning will be clear to any jury", so that only rarely will a judge need to
embark on anything in the way of a "definition."[32] The kind of elaboration
that may be necessary in an exceptional case is calculated merely to confuse
the jury in a straightforward case—typically one in which there is no evidence
that the victim was anything other than (in the language favoured by the
courts) "an ordinary person of normal stability and courage"[33] or that his
response to the defendant's conduct differed from the response to be
expected of such a person. In the straightforward case, definition (or, more
accurately, explanation) is best avoided.

Some cases requiring special direction

In *Garwood*, a case of physical threats, the Court of Appeal identified two   **14-18**
kinds of situation about which the jury may need a special direction.[34]
(i) The first is that in which "the threats might affect the mind of an ordinary person of normal stability [so as to accede unwillingly to the demand[35]]
but did not affect the person actually addressed." If these are the facts that
the jury may find, they should be told that that would be a case of "menaces,"
even though the menaces had no effect.
(ii) The other exceptional situation is "where the threats in fact affected
the mind of the victim, although they would not have affected the mind of a
person of normal stability." On these facts there would be a case of "menaces" if, but only if, the defendant "was aware of the likely effect of his
actions upon the victim"; so the jury would have to be told that they could
convict only if they were satisfied of this further fact.

"Menaces": a suggested general principle

It is important not to read the valuable judgment in *Garwood* as though it   **14-19**

---

[32] *Garwood* (1987) 85 Cr.App.R. 85; *Lawrence and Pomroy* (1971) 57 Cr.App.R. 64.
[33] The phrase originated in *Clear* [1968] 1 Q.B. 670 (see n. 35, below), before which the courts
tended to refer to persons of "ordinarily firm mind": *Tomlinson* [1895] Q.B. 706; *Boyle and
Merchant* [1914] 3 K.B. 339. The jury in *Garwood*, above, were understandably mystified by
"normal stability", but seem to have settled for regarding it as duplicating "normal courage";
they thought the victim in their case to be "probably rather timid, *i.e.* not normally stable (whatever that is)": note to trial judge, quoted (1987) 85 Cr.App.R. at 87.
[34] (1987) 85 Cr.App.R. 85 at 88. The headnote to this report derives from the case a complex form
of direction that would cater at once for the two different situations identified by the court. It is
hardly possible to conceive of a case in which the whole of this direction would be appropriate.
[35] It seems desirable for the sake of clarity to supply these words from a passage in the pre-
Theft Act case of *Clear* [1968] 1 Q.B. 670, at 679, that the trial judge in *Garwood* had quoted to
the jury and the Court of Appeal plainly had in mind. In *Clear* the court had referred to
"threats and conduct of such a nature and extent that the mind of an ordinary person of normal
stability and courage might be influenced or made apprehensive so as to accede unwillingly to
the demand . . . ."

lays down general principles exactly applying to all kinds of blackmail. In the context of physical threats it is reasonable, when concerned with the relevance of the victim's response, to refer to a standard of "normal stability and courage" (abbreviated in *Garwood* to "normal stability"). That language is less appropriate, however, in other kinds of cases. Some threats are clearly "menaces" although "stability and courage" hardly describes the qualities relevant to resisting them. An example is a threat to prosecute for a serious offence. Of course the jury can hardly ever require special assistance on the word "menaces" in such a case. More important is the case of the extortionate demand made of a person who is specially vulnerable to pressure, not because of temperament but by reason, for example, of past misdeeds, social position or medical condition. If in any such case a direction on "menaces" is necessary, the language used in *Garwood* seems at least to need adaptation. But that case would also be misleading if it were thought to imply either that a threat must have "in fact affected the mind" of a specially vulnerable person or that the person using the threat need not know of the vulnerability.

14–20   The judgment in *Garwood* is of general importance in deprecating unnecessary direction on a word which ought to give no difficulty in most cases. But it does not preclude the search for a general principle to which resort may be made in deciding in other kinds of cases whether the jury need help to protect them from error. It is suggested that the following propositions are justified: (a) a threat may amount to "menaces" within the meaning of section 21 if, on all the facts known to D, including the nature and circumstances of P, it is a threat that might be capable of reducing P's ability to resist the demand; and (b) if D knows nothing special about P, P may for this purpose be taken to be a person neither by nature nor by reason of circumstances unusually susceptible to pressure from such a threat. Applying proposition (a), if P were known to be dangerously allergic to feathers, a threat to tickle him with one, made to reinforce a demand for money, should after all be "menaces", whatever his response.

The source of the threatened evil

14–21   To be guilty of blackmail, D must make or be party to the making of a demand with menaces; but "it is . . . immaterial whether the menaces relate to action to be taken by the person making the demand" (s.21(2)). An example of a menace relating to action to be taken by another has already been seen in the case of *Studer*[36] (though in that case the circumstances were extreme in that both the threatened action and the person who would take it were fictitious).

---

[36] Above, §14–08. Compare *Smith* (1850) 1 Den. 510.

4. THE DEMAND WITH MENACES MUST BE "UNWARRANTED"

It is as well to set out the relevant part of section 21(1) again. Blackmail **14–22** depends upon the making of an unwarranted demand with menaces;

> "and for this purpose a demand with menaces is unwarranted unless the person making it does so in the belief—
> (a) that he has reasonable grounds for making the demand; and
> (b) that the use of the menaces is a proper means of reinforcing the demand."

Burden of proof and evidential burden

The passage quoted above from section 21(1) is merely a part of the defi- **14–23** nition of blackmail. It has nothing to say about the incidence of the burden of proof in relation to any ingredient of the offence. The section says that a demand with menaces is unwarranted unless D has certain beliefs when he makes the demand. It does not say that he shall be presumed not to have had those beliefs unless he affirmatively proves that he did. The unwarranted nature of the demand is one of the ingredients of the crime of blackmail—an ingredient in respect of which, as with any other, the prosecution bear the burden of proof. The jury, in order to convict, must be satisfied that D did not hold the relevant beliefs.[37] This does not mean that it will always be necessary for the prosecution to take special steps for the purpose of satisfying the jury on the issue. The prosecution need not negative the existence of a belief of which there is no evidence. The effect of the section is to place on D an evidential burden. Unless he introduces evidence, worthy of consideration, to the effect that he held the beliefs required by the section, the jury will be bound to find that the demand with menaces was unwarranted. Accordingly no direction to the jury on the topic will be required.[38]

This, at any rate, is the position in most cases; it is not certain that it is the **14–24** position in all. There may occasionally be a case in which, having heard the prosecution evidence, the jury are of the opinion not only that D did have reasonable grounds for making the demand (this may well be undisputed), but also that the use of the menaces was a proper means of reinforcing the demand. Strictly speaking, the jury's view of the justice of the demand and the propriety of the menaces is irrelevant under the section. Yet if the jury

---

[37] Yet see the *Eighth Report*, para. 121, where the C.L.R.C. consider whether, under the new law, persons in the position of accused persons in two cases decided under the Larceny Act "would establish" the beliefs required by s.21. (Italics supplied.) It is assumed that the word "establish" (and similar language in the same passage) was used *per incuriam*.

[38] *Lawrence and Pomroy* (1971) 57 Cr.App.R. 64; *Harvey* (1980) 72 Cr.App.R. 139 at 142 (no "live issue").

take a view favourable to the accused on both matters, are they not entitled to suppose that he took the same view himself when he made the demand?[39]

Belief in reasonable grounds for making the demand

14–25   D's belief that he has reasonable grounds for making the demand may be justified on any view. If P owes him money or ought to pay him compensation for a tort, it is reasonable for D to demand payment of the debt or of a reasonable sum by way of compensation, and D's belief that he had reasonable grounds for making his demand follows almost automatically from the fact that such grounds existed.

Difficulty arises only when D did not in fact have reasonable grounds for making his demand (or cannot give credible evidence to the effect that he did) or when there is room for doubt as to whether he had such grounds.

Grounds of different kinds

14–26   The section draws no distinction between the different kinds of grounds that D may believe to exist for the making of his demand. He may believe, wrongly as a matter of fact, that what he demands is due (he believes P owes him money, but P has in fact paid him). He may believe, but be wrong in his opinion, that a certain sum constitutes reasonable compensation for P's tort (actual or supposed). He may believe, wrongly as a matter of law, that P is bound to pay him a certain sum. He may believe, but be, in the opinion of others, wrong in his moral judgment,[40] that he is entitled to demand the act or omission that he demands of P. Any of these types of belief, if genuinely held, will be within the section.

D's view of the precise demand made

14–27   To escape liability D must have believed that he had reasonable grounds

---

[39] Even so, once a demand with menaces has been proved (and assuming evidence of a view to gain or an intent to cause loss), a submission that the accused has no case to answer may not ever be technically correct, because of the way in which s.21(1) is worded. But the jury might at the end of the prosecution case be invited to stop the case if they take a view of D's conduct strongly favourable to him.

[40] Contrast s.2(1)(a), under which, for the purposes of theft, an appropriation of property is not to be regarded as dishonest if D believes that he has in law the right to deprive P of the property. A moral "claim of right", even if it would not be an answer to a charge of theft, will provide a partial answer to a charge of blackmail. So, for instance, D may claim that he thought himself morally entitled to demand a rise in wages, without alleging that he had any contractual right to a rise. And a person in the position of the defendant in *Bernhard* [1938] 2 K.B. 264 (referred to in the text, below) would not be reduced, as she was under the Larceny Act 1916, s.30, to claiming that as a result of an error of law she thought she had an enforceable claim against P for money promised to her for a past immoral consideration; she would now say that she thought she was morally justified in pressing her claim.

for making the particular demand that he made. If the sum demanded is disproportionate to the claim asserted or to the interest that D is seeking to protect, the likelihood that D believes himself entitled to make the demand naturally diminishes. The point may be illustrated by reference to a question litigated under the old law. The question was whether it was lawful for a trade association to demand from one of its members or from some other person the payment of a fine for a breach of the association's rules, the demand being supported by a threat to place the member or other person on the association's "stop list" if he did not pay the fine. Under the Larceny Act 1916, s.29(1)(i), the legality of such a demand depended on whether it was made with "reasonable . . . cause". It was ultimately held that it was so made if the sum demanded was a reasonable sum having regard to the legitimate business interests of the association.[41] The test was purely objective. Under section 21 the question becomes whether D himself (perhaps the secretary of the association) believes the sum is a reasonable sum to demand, or at least believes that the association's decision to impose the fine renders it lawful and reasonable for him to demand it on behalf of the association (for this would be quite consistent with his personally considering that the sum is too great).

Unreasonable belief

There is no requirement that D's belief be reasonable. In holding the belief **14–28** that he holds, D may reveal himself as eccentric or unusually stupid or grossly careless or deficient in moral sense; but this will be quite irrelevant. The test applied to determine whether the demand with menaces is "unwarranted" is entirely subjective.

The unreasonableness of D's alleged belief goes only to its credibility. His suggestion that he acted under a particular belief may strain credulity too far. The jury may take the view that no one could have believed that the law was as D asserts he believed it to be. Or they may consider that D's demand for compensation was so plainly extortionate that D cannot have believed he was entitled to so large a sum. In these cases D will be convicted because of the jury's utter disbelief and not because of their disapproval. That at least is the theory upon which a conviction of blackmail should rest. In practice, of course, the jury's own standards are likely to be important in conditioning their willingness to give credence to D's evidence; and in that sense their disapproval is not completely irrelevant.

Belief in the propriety of using the menaces

It will commonly be much harder for D to allege with any plausibility that **14–29** he believed the use of the menaces to be a proper means of reinforcing his demand than it will be to allege a belief in reasonable grounds for making the demand. "I thought that P owed me money" or "I thought the sum I demanded was reasonable compensation" will often enough be convincing

---

[41] *Thorne v. Motor Trade Association* [1937] A.C. 797.

statements. But D's evidence obviously becomes less attractive at the point where he has to add: "and I thought it proper to seek to make P pay by threatening to reveal that as a solicitor he had misappropriated his client's money."

The prevailing view (and that of the jury) may be that a threat to expose P's fraud, or to bring criminal proceedings, or to announce to the world that he defaults on his debts of honour, is not a proper means of reinforcing a demand—even where what is demanded is due or believed to be due. But the general view is irrelevant—except to the extent that it provides a standard whereby to judge whether D himself may genuinely have believed the use of menaces to be "proper". The question of D's own belief must be left to the jury.[42] In assessing the genuineness of D's alleged belief, both the nature of the demand and the precise threat used must of course be taken into account:

> "A threat to do some harm disproportionate to the amount of a disputed claim would be strong evidence of the absence of any belief in the propriety of the threat."[43]

Meaning of "proper"

14–30   There has as yet been little in the way of authoritative elucidation of the word "proper" in this context. The C.L.R.C. suggested that the word "directs the mind to a consideration of what is morally and socially acceptable."[44] With this in mind it has been argued that whether D believed his use of the menaces to be "proper" requires reference to his understanding of "the standards of English society generally." Did he believe that it was "morally and socially acceptable" by those standards?[45] According to this test the question would be, not whether D took an indulgent view of his own conduct (the argument assumes that he always would), but whether he thought that other people would do so. He might genuinely think that they would; he might, in the jury's view, be wrong; and in such a case, but only in such a case, the subjective character of the offence would operate in his favour.

The suggested test is attractive. It seems, however, to need an amendment. D can hardly be intended to have to rely on a belief that all respectable people would find his conduct acceptable. That would not cater for the case that should most obviously be catered for, where the matter is close to the moral borderline. It is in such a case that, although the prosecution is a credible one, D may most plausibly claim that he thought his use of menaces "proper". He should be protected against a conviction of blackmail by a belief that a significant body of respectable opinion would not disapprove. The test need not postulate, or require D to conceive of, a single prevailing standard or a uniform body of general opinion.

---

[42] *Harvey* (1980) 72 Cr.App.R. 139.
[43] *Eighth Report*, para. 121.
[44] *ibid.*, para. 123.
[45] Smith (J. C.), paras. 10–24 to 10–27; see also Law Commission Working Paper No. 61, *Offences relating to the Administration of Justice*, para. 82. Compare the second limb of the test for dishonesty in *Ghosh* [1982] Q.B. 1053 (above, §2–132).

A somewhat similar criticism has been offered of a generalisation in **14–31** *Harvey*,[46] the only relevant appellate decision so far. The case was one of dishonour among villains. P had promised the appellants a large quantity of cannabis and they had paid their share of the price. No cannabis was forthcoming. The appellants kidnapped P's wife and child and threatened to commit serious criminal offences (murder, rape or maiming) against them if P did not restore what he had been paid. The Court of Appeal understandably took the view that no jury could have accepted that the appellants might have believed in the propriety of their menaces. The generalisation offered by the court was that no act known by D to be unlawful can be believed by him to be "proper" (even though he may himself hold it to be "justified"). This statement goes some way towards vindicating the test discussed above. But it has been criticised as being untrue of some acts that, though "unlawful", are less heinious than threats to kill and rape.[47] It must be agreed that there are some unlawful threats which the person making them may in special circumstances believe to be "morally and socially acceptable" (at least to some), let alone find acceptable to himself. So the reference in *Harvey* to what is known to be unlawful seems to need cautious interpretation in the light of the facts of the case.

Illustrations from pre-Act cases

The C.L.R.C., to test the likely operation of the section, took the situations **14–32** in the famous cases of *Bernhard*[48] and *Dymond*.[49] In the former case a Hungarian woman demanded money that had been promised to her in consideration of her past services as P's mistress. She threatened that if he did not pay her she would expose him to his wife, and to the public by means of a newspaper advertisement. In *Dymond*, D claimed payment (of an unspecified amount) from P for an alleged indecent assault upon her. Her threats were that P would "gett summons" and that she would "let the town knowed all about your going on." The C.L.R.C. anticipated that under the new law "Dymond probably (assuming the facts were as the defence wished to prove) and Bernhard certainly, would easily establish that they believed that they had reasonable grounds for making the demand."[50] This would clearly be to achieve the easier half of their tasks. Each would now have to allege further that she believed her threats were a proper means of reinforcing her demand for payment. Each, in her righteous indignation, may conceivably have

---

[46] (1980) 72 Cr.App.R. 139. In the only other reported case (*Lambert* [1972] Crim.L.R. 422) the jury were told that D's guilt or innocence depended upon "his own opinion as to whether he was acting rightly or wrongly". Such a direction can produce a striking acquittal, as the case itself suggests. D told P, whom he suspected of having an affair with his wife, that £250 would buy D's rights to the wife; if P would not pay, D would tell P's wife and employer of his suspicions. D was acquitted of blackmail.
[47] Williams, *Textbook*, p. 837.
[48] [1938] 2 K.B. 264.
[49] [1920] 2 K.B. 260.
[50] *Eighth Report*, para. 121.

believed so; but she would find it a harder matter to give satisfactory evidence on this point than on the other.

14–33 Whether D will succeed on this issue may depend in part on such matters as his standard of education, his intelligence and his social environment. Miss Dymond's illiteracy and Mrs Bernhard's foreign extraction might be material to support the suggestion that they did not have an accurate sense of what was "proper". Conversely, if D is in business in the City, he may find it hard to assert a belief in the propriety of threatening to publish among P's social circle the fact that P had not paid a trading debt. He, though not Miss Dymond, would know that such a thing is not "done", and he would probably himself believe that a threat to do it is an improper way of seeking to recover the debt.

5. A VIEW TO GAIN OR AN INTENT TO CAUSE LOSS

"With a view to gain ... or with intent to cause loss"

14–34 A demand with menaces is not blackmail unless made with a view to gain for oneself or another or with intent to cause loss to another.[51] " '[G]ain' and 'loss' are to be construed as extending only to gain or loss in money or other property."[52] But both words are given artificially wide meanings. By section 34(2)(a)(i), " 'gain' includes a gain by keeping what one has, as well as a gain by getting what one has not." By sub-paragraph (ii), " 'loss' includes a loss by not getting what one might get, as well as a loss by parting with what one has."

A person may have a view to gain property even if he will at the same time gain another's services in the supply of that property; and the "property" may take the form of a drug to be supplied directly into his body. In *Bevans*,[53] D demanded an injection of morphine at the point of a gun and was rightly convicted of blackmail.

14–35 Blackmail covers much more than simply demands for the transfer of money or other property. The following demands seem all to be among those capable of being blackmail:

(i) A demand that P pay a debt that he owes D. A payment of money (or a transfer of other property) to D is no less a "gain" to him because he is entitled to it. This view accords with the intention of those who framed the Act.[54] The gravamen of the offence of blackmail is the use of menaces, not conceived by D to be "proper", to reinforce a demand; and "the nature of the

---

[51] For consideration of this language in the context of offences under s.17 (false accounting), see above, §§12–05 *et seq.*
[52] s.34(2)(a); but they extend "to any such gain or loss whether temporary or permanent".
[53] (1987) 87 Cr.App.R. 64.
[54] *Eighth Report*, para. 119.

act or omission demanded is immaterial" (s.21(2)). Even a just demand should not be so supported.[55]

(ii) A demand that P give D a job, in which D will earn a salary. D has a view to gain.[56]

(iii) A demand that P permit D to take indecent photographs of her, D's purpose being to sell prints of the photographs. Here too D has a view to gain.

(iv) A demand that P abandon a claim to property that he is making against D. If D's aim is to keep particular property, he has a view to gain for himself, as well as an intent to cause loss to P by P's not getting that property. But it may be that particular property must be identifiable as that which D will preserve and which P will not get. For P's mere forbearance to sue to enforce a financial obligation has been held not to involve a "gain" to D[57]; and it could be held to follow that it does not involve a "loss" to P.

(v) A demand by D that P deceive Q into abandoning a claim to specific property against E. The section does not require the intended loss to be a loss to the person of whom the demand is made; and a view to gain "for another" is sufficient.

(vi) A demand that P destroy letters written by D to P. P will suffer "a loss by parting with what [he] has."[58]

---

[55] The point appears to have passed *sub silentio* in *Lawrence and Pomroy* (1971) 57 Cr.App.R. 64; it has been the subject of an express Crown Court ruling in *Parkes* [1973] Crim.L.R. 358. Unusual facts were before the court in *Helal* (1980) 2 Cr.App.R. (S.) 381, in connection with sentencing: executrix's demand for property belonging to testator. (The harassment of contract debtors by, *inter alia*, demands accompanied by alarming threats may be prosecuted summarily under the Administration of Justice Act 1970, s.40.)

[56] Compare, in a very different context, *Wines* (1953) 37 Cr.App.R. 197. But a demand that P appoint D to an honorary office will not be blackmail.

[57] See *Golechha* (1989) 90 Cr.App.R. 241, above, §12–07.

[58] Compare *Eighth Report*, para. 117.

Chapter 15

HANDLING

1. DEFINITION

15–01   Section 22(1) defines the offence of handling stolen goods:

> "A person handles stolen goods if (otherwise than in the course of the stealing) knowing or believing them to be stolen goods he dishonestly receives the goods, or dishonestly undertakes or assists in their retention, removal, disposal or realisation by or for the benefit of another person, or if he arranges to do so."

Section 22(2) provides a maximum penalty of imprisonment for 14 years on conviction on indictment.

The word "handling" is a term of art. The offence may be committed without physically touching the stolen goods; and one may physically handle them, even with guilty knowledge, without committing the offence. Under the Larceny Act 1916, s.33, the corresponding offence was limited to the "receiving" of goods. The offence was extended by the Criminal Law Act 1967, s.4(7), so as to be almost as wide as the present offence. The word "handling" was introduced by the Theft Act merely as the name of the offence; it ought not to be regarded as having any other significance.[1]

2. STOLEN GOODS

There must be stolen goods

15–02   Section 22(1) begins: "A person handles stolen goods if ..." and goes on to describe a variety of acts that may be done in relation to "them". The offence therefore depends upon the existence of "stolen goods" at the time of an act of handling. One example of the offence occurs when a person "believing them to be stolen goods ... dishonestly receives the goods" or does one of a number of acts in relation to them. This wording does not render guilty of handling a person who deals with goods which he wrongly believes to be stolen at the time of his act.[2] (But he may be guilty of attempted handling.[3]) Another variety of handling is that committed by one who arranges to receive stolen goods or, for instance, to dispose of them for the benefit of another person. For this purpose the goods must be stolen before the

---

[1] It does not (*pace Smythe* (1980) 72 Cr.App.R. 8 at 13) represent a "new concept" or lend itself to interpretation. For a powerful critique of the handling provisions, see I. D. Elliott (1977) 26 I.C.L.Q. 110 at 135–144.

[2] *Haughton v. Smith* [1975] A.C. 476.

[3] Criminal Attempts Act 1981, s.1(1)(2)(3) (in this respect reversing *Haughton v. Smith*); see *Shivpuri* [1987] A.C. 1 (House of Lords; declaring to have been wrong the decision of the House to the contrary in *Anderton v. Ryan* [1985] A.C. 560).

arrangement is made.[4] (But an arrangement relating to goods to be stolen in the future may constitute a conspiracy to handle stolen goods[5]; and one person may be guilty of inciting another to commit handling although there are no relevant goods at the time of the incitement.[6])

"Stolen"

Section 2(4) gives an extended meaning to the word "stolen". Its effect is   **15–03** that, for the purpose (among others) of the offence of handling, goods are to be regarded as stolen, not only if they have been the subject of theft as defined in section 1, but also if they have been obtained by blackmail or by deception (that is, by an offence under section 15).[7] Moreover, references in the relevant provisions of the Act to stolen goods include the proceeds of dealings with such goods by a thief or handler, as is mentioned immediately below. Throughout this chapter, therefore, as in those provisions, the words "steal", "stolen", "theft" and "thief" are all to be understood in correspondingly wide senses.

The theft need not have occurred in England and Wales, nor since the commencement of the Act. It is sufficient if (a) the goods were appropriated or obtained anywhere and at any time by a transaction satisfying the definition of theft in section 1, of obtaining property by deception in section 15 or of blackmail in section 21, and (b) that transaction was an offence when it was committed in the country where it was committed.[8]

"Goods" and their proceeds

"[Goods] ... includes money and every other description of property   **15–04** except land, and includes things severed from the land by stealing" (s.34(2)(b)). Handling can therefore be committed in respect of everything except land.

There is a complicated provision (s.24(2)) to secure that the taint of the theft may apply to the proceeds of stolen goods and that the offence of handling shall extend to proceeds so tainted as well as to the original goods. The reader is referred to the text of this provision in Appendix 1. The following are some illustrations of its effect[9]:

---

[4] *Park* (1988) 87 Cr.App.R. 164.
[5] *ibid.*, at 173.
[6] Compare *McDonough* (1963) 47 Cr.App.R. 37.
[7] See, *e.g. Dabek* [1973] Crim.L.R. 527 (goods obtained on credit by deception as to matters relevant to the giving of credit: "stolen" goods).
[8] s.24(1)(4). This, if not formally admitted, requires proof; there is no presumption that foreign law is the same as English law in any relevant respect or that conduct which is unequivocally criminal in English law is also an offence under the relevant foreign code: *Ofori and Tackie (No. 2)* (1993) 99 Cr.App.R. 223. Questions of foreign law are for the judge to decide: Administration of Justice Act 1920, s.15; *Hammer* [1923] 2 K.B. 786.
[9] See also n. 62, below. In *Solomon v. Metropolitan Police Commissioner* [1982] Crim.L.R. 606, Milmo J. invoked s.24(2) in dismissing a thief's civil claim in relation to the proceeds of her theft.

15–05   (a) A steals goods.
    (i)   He sells them for £1,000 in *cash*. Both the goods and the cash are now "stolen goods". B receives part of the £1,000 knowing that it represents stolen goods. He is guilty of handling.
    (ii) With the rest of the £1,000 A buys a *car*. This too is "stolen". C, knowing the truth, undertakes to dispose of the car for A. He is guilty of handling. So is D, who buys the car, if he has guilty knowledge, for the car "at [one] time represented the stolen goods in the hands of the thief" (s.24(2)(a)).
    (b) A steals £1,000 in £10 notes.
    (i)   A owes B £500 and pays him with £500 of the stolen money. B knows it is stolen and is therefore a handler. If B buys *goods* with the £500, these goods are "stolen", as will be *money* he receives on a resale of those goods.
    (ii) A pays the remaining £500 to C for services rendered. C does not know the money is stolen and is therefore not a handler. C buys *goods* with his £500. Those goods are not "stolen", for they do not represent "stolen goods in the hands of a handler" (s.24(2)(b)).

15–06   (c) A, by deception, obtains a cheque for £1,000 from his employer. Being so obtained, the cheque is "stolen".
    (i)   A pays the cheque into his bank account. The *bank balance* (as a thing in action and therefore "goods" within the meaning of section 34(2)(b))[10] may be goods representing the cheque in the hands of A as being the proceeds of his disposal or realisation of them; if so, it is "stolen".[11]
    (ii) A draws £300 *cash* from the account and pays it to B. B may thus receive "stolen goods". There is no difficulty about this if the bank account has been fed only by stolen cheques or consisted only of the proceeds of stolen goods.[12] But in the case of an account fed by both "stolen" and "honest" money, the prosecution must be able to prove, by reference to the history of the account, that the cash was capable of representing stolen goods. This may perhaps be possible even if honest money in the account could alone cover the withdrawal; but it would need to be shown that A intended to withdraw stolen rather than honest money.[13]
    (iii) A gives C *a cheque for £300* drawn on the account. C may cash this cheque or the cheque may be collected for the credit of his

---

[10] *Attorney-General's Reference (No. 4 of 1979)* (1980) 71 Cr.App.R. 341 at 348. The bank balance must be a credit balance for this analysis to be sound.
[11] Unless the victim of the theft has ceased, because of a mixing of funds, to have a right to restitution: see the discussion by Smith (J. C.), para. 13–19, referring to s.24(3) (below §15–15).
[12] *Attorney-General's Reference*, above, at 348.
[13] *ibid.*, at 349. B's intention to receive stolen money or his belief that it was stolen is no evidence as to its stolen character: *ibid.*; see below, §15–07.

bank account. If so the discussion in (ii) above applies to the cash or to the resulting debt owed to C by his bank as it applies to the cash considered in (ii). But it is not clear that it applies to the cheque itself. To be "stolen" the cheque must "represent ... [the original cheque] in the hands of [A] as being the proceeds of [a] disposal or realisation ... of ... [the bank balance] representing [the original cheque]": s.24(2)(a). But the cheque now drawn by A is surely not the *proceeds* of such a disposal or realisation but rather the means of effecting one.[14]

Proof that the goods are stolen

On a charge of handling, then, the prosecution must prove that the goods   **15–07**
were stolen within the above extended sense of the word. Sometimes they will be able to show clearly how the goods were stolen and by whom. Sometimes the fact that they were stolen will be established by the evidence of the person to whom they belong as to the manner in which they were lost,[15] though without necessarily identifying the thief. Exceptionally, the fact that they are stolen may be the proper inference from evidence that establishes the identity neither of the victim nor of the thief. In particular, the circumstances in which the alleged handler acquired the goods (at a gross undervalue, for example, in a place where such goods are not normally sold) may be fairly capable of only one interpretation as to their history.[16] The court may know of those circumstances from the reported statements of the accused himself, which are of course admissible against him.[17] But his account of what he was told about the goods is mere hearsay and inadmissible even against him.[18] Nor, it has been held, is his own belief or conclusion that they were stolen admissible to prove that they were—even if his conclusion seems "fair and safe to rely upon".[19]

Yet it has been said that "whether a belief has any evidential value must   **15–08**

---

[14] But see the court's tentative view on the point, *ibid.*
[15] As to evidence by statutory declaration in proceedings for handling goods stolen in the course of transmission, see s.27(4).
[16] *Sbarra* (1918) 13 Cr.App.R. 118 (by a side door during the night); and cases in next note.
[17] *Overington* [1978] Crim.L.R. 692; *Hulbert* (1979) 69 Cr.App.R. 243 (clothing in quantity bought for low prices in pubs); *McDonald* (1980) 70 Cr.App.R. 288 (television set bought for £90 from unidentified man in betting shop); *Korniak* (1983) 76 Cr.App.R. 145 (jewellery bought for £100 from stranger originally asking £2,000); *Barnes* [1991] Crim.L.R. 132 (over £10,000 received from cohabitee, a man with convictions for stealing large sums).
[18] *Hulbert*, above; and see *Marshall* [1977] Crim.L.R. 106.
[19] *Hulbert*, above (the words quoted are from p. 247); *Overington*, above; *Attorney-General's Reference (No. 4 of 1979)* (1980) 71 Cr.App.R. 341; *De Acetis, The Times*, January 22, 1982; and see Crown Court rulings in *Porter* [1976] Crim.L.R. 58; *Hack* [1978] Crim.L.R. 359. Cases in which the stolen character of goods has been inferred from D's conduct (*e.g.* hiding them, as in *Young v. Spiers* (1952) 36 Cr.App.R. 200) must now be treated with caution to the extent that such conduct may reflect hearsay or D's belief: A. T. H. Smith [1977] Crim.L.R. 517 at 521–523; but the seminal case of *Fuschillo* [1940] 2 All E.R. 489 is perhaps unaffected in this respect.

depend upon the facts of the case"[20]; and on the strength of this dictum it is still perhaps open to argument in a suitable case that D's own experience in the relevant trade renders his opinion effectively that of an expert and admissible on that account as evidence of the character of the goods.[21] Some authorities,[22] moreover, have been said to suggest that a defendant's bare informal admission (not expressed to be based on hearsay) that the goods were stolen is admissible as the basis of a possible inference that they were, unless he explains in evidence that his admission merely reflected what he had been told (or, presumably, what he surmised).[23] But there seems to be no ground for treating "It is stolen"[24] as prima facie meaning "I saw it stolen" rather than "I was told it was stolen" or "I concluded or assumed so"—quite the contrary; and, if there is not, the suggested rule simply creates an obligation to give evidence out of a remark no doubt left incautiously incomplete because of its maker's ignorance of the hearsay rule.[25]

15–09   An inference of theft should not be too lightly drawn from circumstances of suspicion. The unknown "thief" may have believed he had a right to the goods[26]; furtive behaviour and false explanations may conceal some other sinister truth than that the goods were stolen. Or it may be that the goods were indeed stolen, but by the accused himself; in which case a conviction of handling would only rarely be proper.[27]

Acquittal or conviction of another person for theft

15–10   For the purposes of a prosecution under section 22, the fact that the goods were stolen has to be proved against D, the alleged handler, not against the thief.

An *acquittal* of C, the alleged thief, is not necessarily inconsistent with D's conviction of handling.[28] On a trial together of C and D, there may be evidence admissible against D (most obviously, a statement of his own about the theft) that is not admissible against C. If C is tried first and acquitted, a later prosecution of D may succeed because evidence of the theft is available that was not available on the earlier trial. More strikingly, the same evidence that failed to persuade C's jury that C stole the goods might satisfy D's jury of that fact. C's acquittal is not admissible in D's favour.

---

[20] *McDonald,* above, *per* Lawton L.J. at 290.
[21] See David Stone (1979) 129 New L.J. 1018 at 1019, citing *Gibbons* [1971] V.R. 79; and compare, as to the identity of drugs, *Chatwood* (1979) 79 Cr.App.R. 39.
[22] *Korniak,* above; *Gibbons,* above.
[23] A. J. Ashworth and R. Pattenden (1986) L.Q.R. 292 at 306.
[24] Or (in *Korniak,* above), "You'll just have to do me for receiving stolen property."
[25] This objection should not be taken to imply any attachment to the application of the hearsay rule in this context.
[26] See above, §2–125. In *Farrell* [1975] 2 N.Z.L.R. 753, the supposed thief had been acquitted of theft on the ground of insanity; in *Walters v. Lunt* (1951) 35 Cr.App.R. 94, he was under the age of criminal responsibility.
[27] See below, §§15–45 to 15–49.
[28] *Close* [1977] Crim.L.R. 107 depends upon this proposition but is a very puzzling application of it on the facts.

By contrast, the fact of C's prior *conviction*[29] for the theft of the goods[30] is admissible as evidence against D that C stole the goods, the latter fact being relevant to an issue in the proceedings against D.[31] C is to be taken to have committed the offence—and hence, the goods are to be taken to have been stolen—unless the contrary is proved.[32] If it is established that C's conviction relates to the goods that D is charged with handling[33] and D wishes to dispute that they were stolen, he "will have to prove on a balance of probabilities ... that [C's] conviction was wrong."[34]

When goods cease to be stolen goods

Section 24(3) refers (rather clumsily) to events after which goods, al- **15–11** though they may be proved to have been stolen, shall not "be regarded as having continued to be stolen goods". If such an event occurs before D's alleged act, that act is not an offence of handling. There are two categories of case.

Restoration of goods to victim or to other lawful possession or custody

The first is that in which, before the handling, the goods "have been **15–12** restored to the person from whom they were stolen or to other lawful possession or custody."

Restoration to the person from whom the goods were stolen may be taken to mean a return to his possession or to that of his agent. An act by or on behalf of the victim of the theft falling short of a deliberate exercise of control over the goods will not suffice to amount to a restoration of them. So, for example, cartons of cigarettes stolen from a company by an employee and placed by him in the company's lorry were not "restored" to the company by the acts of the company's security officer in initialling the cartons for the purpose of identification and of police officers in following the lorry to where the cigarettes were sold by the thief to D; they were still "stolen" when D bought them.[35]

The phrase "the person from whom they were stolen" is somewhat casual, since property may be stolen from a variety of persons having disparate interests in it.[36] Whether the phrase refers to the person, if any, specified as the

---

[29] "by or before any court in the United Kingdom or by a Service court outside the United Kingdom."

[30] Or, exceptionally, his conviction of other offences. In *Barnes* [1991] Crim.L.R. 132 D had received from her cohabitee a large sum of money whose precise source could not be proved. Evidence of the dishonesty convictions of the cohabitee and of D's brother, who had also been involved in the transaction, was admissible as relevant to proof that the money was stolen.

[31] Police and Criminal Evidence Act 1984 s.74(1).

[32] *ibid.*, s.74(2).

[33] As to evidence to identify the facts upon which C's conviction was based, see *ibid.*, s.75.

[34] Criminal Law Revision Committee, 11th Report, *Evidence (General)* (Cmnd. 4991), para. 219(i); for discussion of authorities on the corresponding provisions of the Civil Evidence Act 1968, s.11, see Phipson, *Evidence* (14th ed.), p. 917.

[35] *Greater London Metropolitan Police Commissioner v. Streeter* (1980) 71 Cr.App.R. 113; contrast *Villensky* [1892] 2 Q.B. 597.

[36] s.1(1) read with s.5; s.15(1) read with s.5(1).

victim in the indictment or to any person who might have been so specified is rendered less important than it might have been[37] by the additional reference to other lawful possession or custody.

15–13   Goods are "restored" to lawful possession or custody (notwithstanding the inappropriateness of the verb) if they are "taken by a police officer in the course of his duty and reduced into possession by him."[38] The principle that such restoration will deprive the goods of their "stolen" status can therefore embarrass police operations. For instance, police officers seize goods in the hands of the thief. The thief then co-operates with them to trap D, an intending receiver. D receives the goods from the thief and is promptly arrested. If it can be proved that D's arrangement to receive the goods was made after the goods were stolen[39] and before they came into the hands of the police, D can be convicted of handling on an indictment carefully drafted. But if no arrangement occurring in that period can be proved, there can be no conviction of handling, because the goods were not "stolen" when they were received.[40]

15–14   In some cases, however, it is less clear whether the goods have been restored to lawful possession. In *Attorney-General's Reference (No. 1 of 1974)*[41] a police constable found in an unattended car packages of clothing that he suspected were stolen (as they proved to be). He removed the rotor arm from the car to immobilise it, and kept watch. When D appeared and tried to start the car, the constable questioned him. He gave an implausible explanation and was arrested. The trial judge directed D's acquittal on a charge of handling, ruling that the goods were no longer "stolen" when D came to the car. On a reference under the Criminal Justice Act 1972, s.36, however, the Court of Appeal's opinion was that whether the constable had taken possession of the goods "depended primarily on [his] intentions." Had he made up his mind to "reduce them into his possession or control, take charge of them so that they could not be removed and so that he would have the disposal of them"? Or did he act as he did simply to ensure that he would be able to question the driver about the goods when he appeared, having meanwhile an open mind as to whether the goods were to be seized? This was an issue that should have been left for the jury's determination.[42]

---

[37] See *Schmidt* (1866) L.R. 1 C.C.R. 15; *Villensky* [1892] 2 Q.B. 597. As to naming the victim in the indictment, see below, §15–59.
[38] *Attorney-General's Reference (No. 1 of 1974)* [1974] Q.B. 744 at 750; *Alexander and Keeley* [1981] V.R. 277. (It is doubtful whether the word "custody" adds much in the present context. In *Attorney-General's Reference* the words "possession", "custody" and "control" were used interchangeably by Lord Widgery C.J. (at 753).)
[39] See above, §15–02, at n. 4.
[40] But there may be a conviction of attempted handling or of conspiracy to handle: compare §15–02, above.
[41] [1974] Q.B. 744.
[42] *ibid.*, at 753–754. In the light of the Court of Appeal's opinion, some pre-Act cases on the present topic are now of little, if any, authority; especially *King* [1938] 2 All E.R. 662.

Cessation of right to restitution

Secondly, the goods will cease to be stolen when the person from whom   **15–15**
they were stolen "and any other person claiming through him have ... ceased
as regards those goods to have any right to restitution in respect of the theft."
For instance, the owner of goods which have been obtained from him by
deception may, on discovering the fraud, affirm the transaction in question
and so lose all title to the goods; a third party may have acquired a good title
to the goods by virtue of some exception to the rule *nemo dat quod non habet*;
or, exceptionally, the owner's title may have been extinguished by the expiration of six years following a conversion not "related to the theft."[43]

3. WHAT CONDUCT AMOUNTS TO HANDLING

Assuming that D has the necessary *mens rea*, he will be guilty of handling if   **15–16**
("otherwise than in the course of the stealing"[44]) he:

(a) receives stolen goods; or
(b) arranges to receive stolen goods; or
(c) undertakes or assists in the retention, removal, disposal or realisation
    of stolen goods by or for the benefit of another person; or
(d) arranges to act as in (c).

It is worth repeating that goods dealt with as in (a) or (c) must in fact be
stolen; and that an arrangement within (b) or (d) must relate to goods already
stolen.[45]

(a) Receiving

Before 1968 the corresponding offence under the old law was limited to   **15–17**
receiving and was called by that name. Receiving involved nothing less than
the acquisition of exclusive control of the property or of joint possession with
the thief or another receiver.[46] Handling is now a much wider offence, but
presumably the meaning of receiving itself remains as before.[47] If D examines
goods in the thief's presence while negotiating with him, he does not thereby
handle them in the technical sense. On the other hand, if, for example, the
thief leaves the goods with D by way of loan or on approval, D handles when
he knowingly accepts the possession so given to him; *a fortiori* if he acquires
possession of the goods by gift or purchase.

---

[43] Limitation Act 1980, ss.2, 3(2), 4. For elaborate consideration of the phrase "a right to restitution" in this context, see Smith (A. T. H.), paras. 30–74 *et seq*
[44] See below, §§15–45 *et seq*.
[45] See above, §15–02.
[46] *Hobson v. Impett* (1957) 41 Cr.App.R. 138; *Frost and Hale* (1964) 48 Cr.App.R. 284. D's control may, of course, be exercised through someone acting with his authority, or through a bailee
at will (from whom he may physically recover the property on demand): relevant authorities
were reviewed in *Cottrell* [1983] V.R. 143.
[47] See *Smythe* (1980) 72 Cr.App.R. 8.

15–18   The question whether a person who finds stolen goods and takes possession of them can be said to "receive" them has arisen in two unreported Court of Appeal cases. In one, the court apparently assumed that he could[48]; in the other it held that he could not.[49] The latter opinion is preferable. The word "receive" seems to imply an act of transfer by another to the receiver. One who finds goods whose owner might be discovered by taking reasonable steps steals those goods if he dishonestly decides to keep them. His realisation that they are already stolen goods, apart from tending to confirm his dishonesty in not reporting his finding to the police, is irrelevant to the occurrence of this further theft.[50]

15–19   It is not necessary in every case for the judge to direct the jury in detail about the meaning of "possession"; but an explanation of the word, suitable to the context of the case, will be called for where the question whether D acquired possession of the stolen goods (either alone or jointly with the thief) is crucial.[51] It may be crucial, for example, where D and the thief are found together with the goods[52] or where the goods are found on premises occupied by D. In the latter case, in order to prove a receiving by D it must be shown either that the goods came on his premises "at his invitation or by arrangement" (their acceptance by his employee, acting without authority or instructions to take them, will not suffice) or that after they came on the premises he "became aware of them and exercised some control over them."[53]

(b) Arranging to receive

15–20   If D negotiates with C, a thief, for the purchase of the stolen goods, D is not on this account guilty of handling. What is required is at least an arrangement by D to receive the goods. The conclusion of a bargain between C and D will normally involve at least such an arrangement. There must be an arrangement by D to acquire possession on his own account. Consequently, if D, when he buys from C, arranges for C to deliver the goods direct to E, a subpurchaser, D presumably does not "arrange to receive" the goods, though it appears that he assists in their realisation by C.[54]

Making an offer to buy from the thief, with a view to taking delivery if the offer is accepted, is an attempt to handle (an attempt to arrange to receive).

(c) Undertaking or assisting in retention, removal, disposal or realisation

15–21   Once he has accomplished his theft the thief faces major problems for which he may need all manner of facilities. The goods may need to be stored.

---

[48] *Kelly,* November 19, 1984, C.A. no. 5624/B1/83.
[49] *Haider,* March 22, 1985, C.A. (unreported).
[50] See below, §15–50: most handlers also commit new thefts by handling.
[51] *Apostoli and Apostoli,* November 15, 1984, C.A. (unreported); compare *Comerford* (1964) 49 Cr.App.R. 77.
[52] As, for example, in *Seiga* (1961) 45 Cr.App.R. 26.
[53] *Cavendish* (1961) 45 Cr.App.R. 374; compare *Lloyd* [1992] Crim.L.R. 361 (burglary).
[54] See below, §15–27.

They may have to be carried to a place of safety or to a purchaser. Gold and silver articles may require melting down. Stolen cars require new number plates and registration documents and the execution of skilled work to conceal their identity. Contact must be made with "fences" and negotiations conducted. Anyone who assists in or undertakes any of these or similar operations for the thief or for another handler is guilty of handling if he knows or believes the goods to be stolen and acts dishonestly. The net is flung very wide.

"Undertakes or assists ... by or for the benefit of another person"

The act undertaken or assisted must be "by or for the benefit of another **15–22** person."[55] This vital phrase qualifies each of the four nouns, "retention", "removal", "disposal" and "realisation".[56] The whole phrase is often recited, without attention to its meaning, even when part of it cannot apply. The House of Lords clarified the provision in the leading case of *Bloxham*.[57] What the handler "undertakes" must be an activity *for the benefit of* another person; what he "assists in" must be an activity undertaken *by* another person. Moreover, an activity is not "for the benefit of" another just because it happens to benefit him, but only if it is undertaken for his benefit. So, in particular, a seller does not sell goods "for the benefit of" his purchaser. It seems also that a person who makes a gift of stolen goods does not in doing so undertake their disposal "for the benefit of" the donee, even though only the donee will benefit from the transaction. The House of Lords effectively treats the notion of an act undertaken "for the benefit of another person" as that of an act done on behalf of another person; it is an act that the other might do himself. "[An] act of purchase" (or the receipt of a gift) "could not sensibly be described as a disposal or realisation of the stolen goods by [the purchaser]" (or the donee).[58] This reading satisfactorily fulfils, without going beyond, the legislator's purpose in providing the badly-drafted second limb of the offence.

Retention

It has been held that the meaning of "retain" is a matter of law. The word **15–23** means "keep possession of, not lose, continue to have".[59]

One who stores stolen goods as a bailee obviously undertakes their retention for the benefit of the bailor. Where D knows that stolen goods are on his premises, mere failure to reveal them to police officers who are searching for them may be evidence that he has permitted the goods to remain on his prem-

---

[55] Not being a person jointly charged with the same offence: *Roberts*, July 9, 1993, C.A. no. 93/0075/Z2.

[56] *Sloggett* [1972] 1 Q.B. 430.

[57] [1983] 1 A.C. 109. The House adopted the reading proposed by J. R. Spencer [1982] Crim.L.R. 682, in an article severely criticising the decision of the Court of Appeal in the same case ((1981) 72 Cr.App.R. 323) and anticipating all the arguments employed by the House.

[58] [1983] 1 A.C. at 114.

[59] *Pitchley* (1972) 57 Cr.App.R. 30.

ises and is thereby assisting in (or perhaps more accurately, undertaking) their retention. But it cannot itself amount to so assisting; to hold otherwise would be to encroach on the principle that one is not bound to answer police questions.[60]

The activity of "retention" of goods continues over time. It may begin innocent and continue guilty. One who discovers that property he is holding for another is stolen property must therefore be active to disburden himself of it. In *Pitchley*,[61] D received money from his son and paid it into his own post office savings account on his son's behalf. According to him he realised only afterwards that the money was stolen. It was held that even on that basis he was rightly convicted of handling, for after learning the truth he made no withdrawal from the account and had been (as the court doubtfully expressed it) "assisting in the retention of the money."[62]

15–24   A number of decisions have clarified the position of a person in the household or employment of a thief or handler who keeps stolen goods in the home or at the workplace. Merely "[being] willing for the goods to be kept and used in the house and thinking that it [is] nice to have them there, although they [are] stolen goods", does not constitute assisting in their retention[63]; nor does actively using them as a member of the family or an employee.[64] What is required is the doing of something, intentionally and dishonestly, for the purpose of enabling the goods to be retained, such as concealing them or telling lies (not necessarily successful lies) to the police to prevent their being found.[65]

Removal

15–25   This word obviously covers anyone carrying or transporting stolen goods for another's benefit or assisting therein. An illustration may conveniently be given here of the fact that D's act need not be done solely for the benefit of another. D may, for example, help C to carry C's stolen goods into D's shop, there to negotiate. In doing so D assists in the removal of the goods by C for

---

[60] *Brown* [1970] Q.B. 105.
[61] (1972) 57 Cr.App.R. 30. (The headnote is misleading as to the facts.)
[62] It should surely have been, if anything, "undertaking the retention of a thing in action", namely a debt owed to D by the bank. The argument would be that that debt was the proceeds of a realisation of the stolen money: see s.24(2). In fact it is highly doubtful whether the wording of s.24(2) was satisfied in *Pitchley*. At first sight the thing in action may appear to "represent ... the stolen goods in the hands of a *handler* ..." (s.24(2)(b)). But for this purpose the thing must be "the proceeds of [a] realisation of ... the stolen goods handled by him." At the time of the realisation, however, D did not know the money was stolen and therefore the goods realised were not "goods *handled* by him". It is thought that the conviction should have been quashed. There is a tendency even among lawyers to think of credit at the bank as being "money" for the purposes of the Act; in *Pitchley* itself there are many references to "money in the savings book" (*sic*). But "money at the bank" is a loose expression. See above, §2–17.
[63] *Kanwar* (1982) 75 Cr.App.R. 87.
[64] *Sanders* (1982) 75 Cr.App.R. 84; *Thornhill*, May 15, 1981 (unreported: referred to in *Sanders* and in *Kanwar*, above).
[65] *Kanwar*, above.

C's benefit; the fact that he also acts for his own purposes does not affect his liability for handling.

Disposal

This word seems apt to cover a wide range of acts, including destruction,   **15–26** dumping, transformation by heat or by chemical means and distribution by way of gift. This opinion is offered in the teeth of the weighty view of Professor Williams, who regards "disposal" as referring only to an "alienation" of the goods.[66] With respect, it is not clear that its meaning is so limited. One who melts down gold objects for the benefit of a thief or handler performs an act quite as significant as that of the person who then transports the metal to the point of sale. From the inclusion of retention and removal in the list of offending activities it seems that the offence was intended to cover virtually all those who lend assistance in dealing with stolen property.

A person does not "assist in" the thief's disposal of stolen goods just because the disposal benefits him; assisting requires an act of helping or encouraging.[67]

Realisation

Realisation of goods occurs when they are exchanged for money or any-   **15–27** thing else of value.[68] Realisation for the benefit of another occurs when an agent sells on behalf of a principal. A person selling on his own behalf does not "undertake" the sale "for" the benefit of the purchaser, even though the latter may derive a benefit from the transaction. So where D bought stolen goods without knowing they were stolen (and thus did not handle them by receiving) and later, having learnt that they were stolen, sold them to E, this realisation of the goods was not a handling under the second part of section 22(1).[69]

Where C (perhaps the thief) sells stolen goods, D who buys from him may perhaps be described as assisting in C's realisation of them (though it would normally be more appropriate to charge him with receiving them or, if delivery has not occurred, with arranging to receive them). In one case the Court of Appeal regarded the buyer's conduct as accurately described by an indictment alleging that he undertook the realisation of the goods[70]; but the House of Lords has since rejected the suggestion that a purchase of goods may be a realisation by the purchaser.[71]

---

[66] Williams, *Textbook*, p. 867; see also Smith (A. T. H.), para. 30–44.
[67] *Coleman* [1986] Crim.L.R. 56; compare above, §15–24.
[68] In *Tamm* [1973] Crim.L.R. 115, Judge David Q.C. ruled that D assisted in the realisation of goods by C if, having the power and duty to prevent payment to C for the goods, he permitted the payment to be made.
[69] *Bloxham* [1983] 1 A.C. 109. The result (as observed *ibid.*, at 114) is consistent with s.3(2)—a bona fide purchaser of property cannot steal it by anything done after learning that he has acquired no title by his purchase. But see below, §15–35.
[70] *Deakin* (1972) 56 Cr.App.R. 841.
[71] *Bloxham*, above, at 114.

(d) Arranging to act as in (c)

15–28   If D merely arranges to do or assist in doing any of the kinds of things referred to under the preceding head he will be guilty of the complete offence of handling. The Act is indeed remarkable, here as in theft, in the extent to which it treats as major substantive offences transactions of a preliminary or accessory character. It would be as well to bear this in mind in interpreting the word "arranges". Very little formality and precision need attend an arrangement—nothing in the nature of a contract or solemn promise; but there should be an element of finality.

To illustrate the problem and the kind of approach suggested, we may take the case of D who says that he is prepared to lend a hand in carrying some parcels from C's house to a lorry outside. It is suggested that—(i) if a time is fixed, there is an arrangement, however casually made; (ii) if all that occurs is D's expression of willingness in principle, there is no arrangement within the section; (iii) in any intermediate case the court should be most wary of finding an arrangement. Whether D has arranged to assist depends as a matter of degree on the details of the case. If, for instance, all is finally settled except the time of the operation, which C will communicate to D, it would not be improper to say that D has arranged to assist.

It may be noted that, the act of arranging being the complete offence, it will be mere mitigation that D in the end decided not to lend his assistance.

4. THE MENTAL ELEMENT

15–29   Handling is committed by one who knows or believes that the goods are stolen. Only knowledge or belief on the part of the person charged will satisfy the requirements of the section; it is not sufficient that any reasonable person would have realised that the goods were stolen.[72] What is required, of course, is knowledge of or belief in facts which result in the goods having as a matter of law, a stolen character. D may know or believe that the goods have been acquired in some way amounting to an offence of theft or obtaining by deception or by blackmail; but he may not know in just what kind of circumstances they were acquired, or he may positively believe in facts which, if true, would indeed result in the goods being stolen, but which are not the true facts. He will still be guilty: there is no need for him to identify the class of "theft" concerned.

Nor need D know the nature of the goods with which he is dealing. It is enough if he knows or believes, for instance, that the goods in the unopened suitcase he is looking after are stolen goods.[73]

Meaning of "knowing" and "believing"

15–30   D may know that goods are stolen from having witnessed the theft. Apart

---

[72] *Atwal v. Massey* (1971) 56 Cr.App.R. 6; *Stagg* [1978] Crim.L.R. 227; *Bellenie* [1980] Crim.L.R. 437.
[73] *McCullum* (1973) 57 Cr.App.R. 645.

from that obvious case, he "may be said to know", explained the Court of Appeal in the leading case of *Hall*,[74] "... when he is told by someone with first-hand knowledge", such as the thief himself. Belief, on the other hand,

"may be said to be the state of mind of a person who says to himself: 'I cannot say I know for certain that these goods are stolen, but there can be no other reasonable conclusion in the light of all the circumstances, in the light of all that I have heard and seen.'"

(This must have been *D's* state of mind if he is to be found to have believed the goods to be stolen. It is not enough that there was *in fact* no other reasonable conclusion but that they were stolen, although that will obviously help towards a finding that D himself reached that conclusion[75]). A person with such a state of mind "believes" although (misusing language) he also says to himself: "Despite all that I have seen and all that I have heard, I refuse to believe what my brain tells me is obvious."[76] Mere suspicion, however ("I suspect that these goods are stolen, but it may be on the other hand that they are not") is not within the words "knowing or believing".[77] This applies even to very strong suspicion.[78] Moreover, believing that the goods are probably stolen or that it is more likely than not that they are, is not "believing [them] to be stolen" within the meaning of the section.[79]

The Court of Appeal had at one time insisted that a trial judge should not **15–31** interpret the word "believing" for the jury.[80] In *Hall*, however, the court seemed quietly to abandon that position, expressing the opinion that a jury "should be directed along [the] lines" of its explanation of the word in that case. But other divisions of the court have since held that this direction is not necessary in every case.[81] The main concern appears to be that suspicion should not be treated as belief, so that "where much reference is made to suspicion, a judge [may well] think it prudent, if not necessary", to give a *Hall* direction.[82] The view that such a direction is not routinely required suggests that the court is not similarly concerned that the jury might without guidance treat belief that goods are probably stolen as belief that they are.

The Court of Appeal's interpretation of "believing" is not an inevitable **15–32** one. A person may also properly be said to "believe" something if he feels

---

[74] (1985) 81 Cr.App.R. 260 at 264.
[75] The need for this parenthesis is suggested by the misleading direction to the jury in *Brook* [1993] Crim.L.R. 455.
[76] *Hall* (1985) 81 Cr.App.R. 260 at 264.
[77] *Grainge* (1973) 59 Cr.App.R. 3; *Griffiths* (1974) 60 Cr.App.R. 14; *Smith (Albert)* (1976) 64 Cr.App.R. 217; *Grainge* [1984] Crim.L.R. 493.
[78] *Pethick* [1980] Crim.L.R. 242; *Moys* (1984) 79 Cr.App.R. 72. A different view is suggested by *Bellenie* [1980] Crim.L.R. 437, where it was said that suspicion is not enough unless it amounts to belief.
[79] *Reader* (1977) 66 Cr.App.R. 33.
[80] *Smith (Albert)*, above; *Ismail* [1977] Crim.L.R. 557; *Reader*, above.
[81] *Harris* (1986) 84 Cr.App.R. 75; *Toor* (1986) 85 Cr.App.R. 116.
[82] *Toor*, above, at 120.

that it is so likely to be true that he is prepared to act upon the assumption that it is, even if he is not confident enough to say that the evidence compels that conclusion. One who receives goods with such a strong impression that they are probably stolen is acting with a recklessness that might reasonably be brought within the offence of handling,[83] without, it is thought, improperly inhibiting dealings with goods of unknown provenance.[84] And if this view is unacceptable, consider the case where the receiver, strongly suspecting that the goods are stolen, but preferring not actually to "know" that they are,"[85] deliberately refrains from an inquiry that he might make to allay or confirm his suspicion. Such "wilful blindness" has been recognised as turning strong suspicion into "knowledge of the second degree"[86] for the purpose of some statutory requirements of knowledge. The case should be regarded as one of "knowing or believing" in the present context.

"Inferring" knowledge or belief

15–33   The cases before *Hall*[87] in fact contain many references to a person's "deliberately closing his eyes to the circumstances" or "shutting his eyes to the obvious". The leading theme is that a jury may infer D's knowledge or belief that the goods were stolen from the fact that, suspecting as much, he "deliberately closed his eyes to the circumstances"; but that it is a misdirection to advise them that, on such facts, they must as a matter of law find such knowledge or belief.[88] This, with respect, is obscure. It treats "wilful blindness" as something from which a state of mind can be inferred. But the jury have, *ex hypothesi*, already found a state of mind: "suspecting as much"— which is not enough. They are now to be invited to go on to find another: "knowledge or belief". It is not clear why the defendant is to be credited with two states of mind, one which does not suffice and one which does. There seems to be no reason why wilful blindness should be regarded only as evidence of knowing or believing. The principle, as suggested above, should rather be that "suspecting as much", coupled with a deliberate avoidance of knowledge, *is* "knowing or believing" within the meaning of section 22.

Time of knowledge or belief[89]

15–34   In a case of *receiving*, the offence is not committed unless D knows or

---

[83] See J. R. Spencer [1985] Crim.L.R. 92 and 440.

[84] See Glanville Williams [1985] Crim.L.R. 432, replying to Spencer, above.

[85] Apparently there are those who find dealing in stolen goods acceptable, and believe it to be less dangerous, if the origin of the goods, though well understood, is not made explicit ("stolen", "nicked"); and those who suppose that whatever is not spelt out in words is not known. See S. Henry, *The Hidden Economy*, pp. 56–57.

[86] See *per* Devlin J. in *Roper v. Taylor's Central Garage* [1951] 2 T.L.R. 284.

[87] Above, n. 74.

[88] See especially *Griffiths* (1974) 60 Cr.App.R. 14; *Moys* (1984) 79 Cr.App.R. 72.

[89] See V. Tunkel (1983) 133 New L.J. 844, for a diagram analysing the position of "the innocent receiver with subsequent *mens rea*."

believes at the time he receives the goods that they are stolen.[90] And the same must be true of an *arranging* to receive or to do any of the other acts listed in the section; the guilty knowledge or belief must exist at the time of the arranging. But there is no reason why it should exist when D begins *assisting in*, or *undertaking*, one of those acts; to continue the assistance or the operation involved in the undertaking[91] after learning or divining the truth must surely be an offence. This will be no less the case where the undertaking, itself originally innocent, follows upon an innocent receiving. D receives the goods and then begins to deal with them for the benefit of another; he handles them when he continues to deal with them after learning that they are stolen.[92]

If D is a bona fide purchaser of goods, no subsequent dealing with them **15–35** after he learns that they are stolen goods can be *theft*. But section 3(2), which so provides, does not explicitly protect against *handling* liability and cannot be read as impliedly doing so.[93] It seems that D, although innocent of handling by receiving when he buys the goods, may be guilty of handling by a later dealing with them for the benefit of E, a sub-purchaser (as by undertaking retention for E or assisting in E's sale to F). And if E knows that the goods are stolen when he buys from D, D may be guilty as a secondary party to the handling E commits by receiving them. It is doubtful whether these results were intended.

Proof of knowledge or belief

Where D has handled goods there may be little or no evidence tending to **15–36** prove directly that he knew or believed them to be stolen; but the prosecution may be assisted in this proof by (i) any inference to be drawn from his unexplained possession of the goods or (ii) evidence of previous conduct rendered admissible by section 27(3).

(i) *Inference from unexplained possession*

(a) *Failure to account for possession on arrest or at trial.* Suppose that **15–37** stolen goods are in D's posession, or in the place where he is, when he is arrested by a constable. The arresting or another constable may reasonably

---

[90] *Alt* (1972) 56 Cr.App.R. 457; *Grainge* (1973) 59 Cr.App.R. 3; *Smythe* (1980) 72 Cr.App.R. 8 (receiving is "a single finite act").

[91] "Undertakes" must mean "conducts" rather than "takes on" or "embarks upon".

[92] As in *Pitchley* (1972) 57 Cr.App.R. 30 (subject to the special doubt about that case expressed in n. 62, above). An inconsistent ruling in *Williams* [1994] Crim.L.R. 934 seems to have been *obiter*.

[93] Though it may influence the interpretation of the handling section: see above, §15–27 at n. 69.

believe that the presence of the goods may be attributable to D's "partici-pation ... in the commission of an offence specified by the constable"—say, handling the goods[94]; and D may be so informed and requested to account for the presence of the goods. The effect (in part) of the Criminal Justice and Public Order Act 1994, s.36, is that if D fails or refuses to do so (despite being told what the effect of the section would be if he should fail or refuse), then, on his trial for the offence, the court or jury may draw such inferences from the failure or refusal as appear proper. One such inference might be that D came by the goods (which are independently proved to have been stolen goods)[95] dishonestly and knowing or believing that they were stolen. The court or jury may think it proper to draw a similar inference (permitted by section 35 of the 1994 Act) from a failure by D to give evidence at his trial.

15–38   (b) *"Recent possession."*[96] If D is proved to have been in possession of goods which had recently been stolen, and gives no explanation, or no cred-ible explanation, of how he came by them, the jury are entitled, if they think fit, to infer from this "recent possession", as it is strangely called, that when he received the goods he knew that they were stolen. The principle that they *may* draw this inference[97] (they are not, of course, bound to do so) is too often dignified with the title "the doctrine of recent possession". It is in fact a mere piece of common sense[98] which has long been recognised. It has not been displaced by the provisions referred to in (a) above. It may operate, for exam-ple, if D does give evidence but fails to account plausibly for his possession of the goods; or the fact that the goods were recently stolen may tend to strengthen any suggestion that an inference of guilty knowledge should be drawn from his failure to account for their possession on arrest or to give evidence at his trial.

It has been said that the inference, if drawn, is drawn from the unexplained fact of recent possession—not (in a case where D offers no explanation at all) from silence viewed as tacit admission[99]; and, in particular, that no adverse inference is to be drawn from silence after caution, the principle not being an exception to "the right of silence".[1] These statements appear to remain true

---

[94] It must be permissible for the constable to say that he believes that D may have stolen the goods or may have handled them, with the consequence stated in the text in the event of pro-ceedings for either offence.

[95] s.38(3) prohibits conviction solely on an inference permitted by s.36; so it would not be per-missible for the court of jury to conclude from D's silence that the goods were stolen by another person *and* that D received them knowing or believing them to be stolen, and to convict on that basis. (S.38(3) likewise prohibits conviction solely on an inference drawn from an accused per-son's silence under caution before charge, or on being charged (s.34) or from his failure to give evidence or to answer any question at his trial (s.35).)

[96] A person's possession of recently stolen goods may alternatively be evidence that he was the thief or involved in the theft. See below, §15–52.

[97] With "the proper degree of assurance" (*Greaves, The Times*, July 11, 1987)—that is, beyond reasonable doubt.

[98] *D.P.P. v. Nieser* [1959] 1 Q.B. 254 at 266–267.

[99] *Bruce v. The Queen* (1987) 61 A.L.J.R. 602 (High Court of Australia).

[1] *Raviraj and Others* (1986) 85 Cr.App.R. 93; and see *Bruce v. The Queen*, above, at 603: "the absence of any reasonable explanation must not itself be explicable in a manner consistent with innocence."

(except, in the case of the second, where D has been asked on arrest to account for his possession). A suspect or accused person continues to be told that he does not have to say anything; and this is qualified only by advice reflecting the possibility that inferences may be drawn from his failure to mention a fact he may later rely on in his defence.[2]

The principle was originally stated as applying to a case of receiving, to which alone the corresponding offence under the old law was limited. But the Court of Appeal (rejecting an argument to the contrary in earlier editions of this book and disapproving an earlier dictum of its own[3]) asserted in *Ball*[4] that the principle now applies to all modes of handling. In that case D and E were found in a car at 2.45 a.m. with 30 citizen's-band radios. E was not a dealer in such goods; yet D (on his own eventual story) was going to help E sell them. At his first interview with the police D told some damaging lies. It is plain that his knowledge that the radios were stolen might properly be inferred from these facts, whether the theft had occurred two days before (as was the case) or much less recently. The more there is of other evidence tending to justify a conclusion that the defendant knew the goods were stolen, the less relevant (it is submitted) becomes the fact that the theft was a recent one. The fact acquires true significance where there is no, or very little, other evidence from which guilty knowledge can be inferred. For it is, undoubtedly, alone enough to establish a case to answer against one who has received exclusive control of the goods. But section 22(1) covers, at the other extreme, one who briefly lends a casual hand with carriage of the goods. It remains, with respect, unclear why such menial involvement should inevitably raise a case to answer just because the goods were stolen two days before. It is stubbornly submitted that whether it is proper to infer that the defendant knew the truth depends on the common sense of the individual case[5]; that "recent possession" has variable relevance to the commonsense judgment; and that the inference of knowledge was plainly justifiable in *Ball* irrespective of the time of the theft. "Recent possession" should not be a shibboleth uttered unthinkingly without regard to the total facts. **15–39**

(ii) *Evidence of previous conduct: s.27(3)*[6]

The statutory aid to the proof of *mens rea* is to be found in section 27(3). **15–40**

---

[2] Criminal Justice and Public Order Act 1994, s.34.
[3] See 4th edition of this book, §13–23; *Sloggett* [1972] 1 Q.B. 430 at 433.
[4] (1983) 77 Cr.App.R. 131.
[5] The nature of the goods is a relevant factor; see *Mason* [1981] Q.B. 881 (recent possession of antique silver wine coasters stolen five months previously); *Simmons* [1986] Crim.L.R. 397 (music centre; nearly a year: not "recent possession"); *Powers* [1990] Crim.L.R. 586 (car; 4 to 6 months: not "recent").
[6] See Roderick Munday [1988] Crim.L.R. 345 for a history and full consideration of this anomalous provision; J. C. Smith [1980] Crim.L.R. 174 (commentary on *Bradley*, below, n. 13).

This renders two classes of evidence admissible "for the purpose of proving that [D] knew or believed the goods to be stolen goods",—namely:

> "(a) evidence that he has had in his possession, or has undertaken or assisted in the retention, removal, disposal or realisation of, stolen goods[7] from any theft taking place not earlier than twelve months before the offence charged[8]; and
>
> (b) ... evidence that he has within the five years preceding the date of the offence charged been convicted of theft or of handling stolen goods."

Certain conditions must be satisfied before evidence becomes admissible under section 27(3): (i) D must be being proceeded against[9] only for handling stolen goods; (ii) evidence must first be given of D's having committed an act of handling in relation to the goods the subject of the charge; (iii) D's knowledge or belief that the goods were stolen must be a matter requiring proof[10]; and (iv) a conviction can be proved under paragraph (b) only if D[11] has had seven days' notice in writing of the intention to prove it. Subject to these conditions the evidence is admissible at any stage of the proceedings.

15–41   An important difference has emerged between paragraphs (a) and (b) in respect of the particularity of the evidence that they render admissible.

Paragraph (a) is very strictly construed. All that is admissible under it is the bare fact "that the defendant was on a previous occasion found to be in possession of stolen goods."[12] The jury is not to know any details of the earlier transaction; it will have no evidence as to whether the defendant's earlier possession was that of a guilty handler.[13] The Court of Appeal, in confirming this interpretation of the paragraph, appears to have been uncertain as to the paragraph's rationale; the jury, it was observed, might leap to the conclusion that the evidence had been introduced as evidence of a previous handling, and the task of conveying to them "that the only relevance of the fact is that the previous occasion would have served as a warning to be more careful in future (if indeed this is the rationale of paragraph (a))" will not be easy.[14]

---

[7] The words "stolen goods" have the same wide meaning here as they have in s.22: s.27(5).

[8] The evidence may relate to goods from a theft taking place after the offence charged: *Davis* [1972] Crim.L.R. 431. Possession of articles from two thefts may under this paragraph provide evidence of guilty knowledge in the receiving of each: *Simmons* [1986] Crim.L.R. 397. Evidence relating to possession of other stolen goods will also be admissible at common law, whether or not it is within s.27(1)(a), if there is a substantial nexus between the offences: *ibid.*

[9] This refers to the proceedings before the court at the time when the evidence is tendered; it is immaterial that some other offence was charged in the same indictment but has been severed and awaits trial: *Anderson* [1978] Crim.L.R. 223 (Judge Stroyan Q.C.).

[10] So the evidence was not admissible where dishonesty was the only live issue: *Duffus*, October 4, 1993, C.A. no. 93/2601/Z5 (*sub nom. Duffas, The Times*, October 9, 1993).

[11] Or, no doubt, his solicitor: compare *Bott* [1968] 1 All E.R. 1119. It is not essential for the notice to refer to the section: *Airlie* [1973] Crim.L.R. 310.

[12] *Wood* (1987) 85 Cr.App.R. 287 at 292.

[13] *Bradley* (1979) 70 Cr.App.R. 200; *Wood*, above.

[14] *Wood*, above, *per* Mustill L.J. at 292. This cannot be the rationale for the admission of evidence of a possession later than the present alleged offence.

Paragraph (b) was for a while similarly construed; it was thought permiss-   **15–42**
ible to adduce only the bare fact, and the time and place, of a previous conviction for theft or handling.[15] But the House of Lords has now held that
paragraph (b) has to be read with section 73(2) of the Police and Criminal
Evidence Act 1984.[16] Subsection (1) of that section provides that where evidence of a conviction in the United Kingdom (otherwise than by a Service
court) is admissible in any proceedings, proof of the conviction may be by
production of a certificate of conviction. Section 73(2) explains the phrase
"certificate of conviction". In the case of a conviction on indictment, it is "a
certificate ... giving the substance and effect (omitting the formal parts) of
the indictment and of the conviction ..."[17] It is such a certificate that should
be produced under section 27(3)(b); and the certificate will include whatever
the indictment reveals about the nature of the goods stolen or handled—
matter which is not a "formal part" but is "of the substance of the indictment
and the conviction". D was charged with handling the bodyshell of a Ford
Escort RS Turbo motor car; evidence of his previous handling conviction
properly revealed that it related to a Ford RS Turbo. But evidence under
paragraph (b) appears to remain limited to the contents of the certificate of
conviction, though the House of Lords did not confirm this.

Evidence rendered admissible by section 27(3) should not be admitted   **15–42a**
automatically. Section 27(3) merely gives the judge a discretion to admit it,
to be exercised only when the demands of justice warrant its admission.[18] It
will be the judge's duty to exclude the evidence if in the circumstances of the
case it can be of only "minimal assistance" to the jury; the assistance it can
afford must outweigh its prejudicial effect.[18a] In exercising his discretion in a
case involving a number of handling counts, the judge must bear in mind that
the evidence will be relevant only where there is an issue as to D's knowledge
or belief that the goods were stolen, and not relevant to any count in which,
for example, the only or primary issue concerns D's alleged possession of the
goods. If the evidence is admitted, the judge must take care to ensure that the
jury realise that it is relevant only to the issue of guilty knowledge.[18b]

Dishonesty

No one can be guilty of handling unless he acts dishonestly; and the   **15–43**

---

[15] *Fowler* (1988) 86 Cr.App.R. 219.
[16] *Hacker* [1994] 1 W.L.R. 1659; [1995] 1 All E.R. 45.
[17] A certificate of a summary conviction consists of "a copy of the conviction" signed by the clerk
of the convicting court. The certificate must record the nature of the goods stolen or handled
"and the whole certificate ... is admissible"; *Hacker*, above.
[18] *Rasini, The Times*, March 20, 1986.
[18a] *Knott* [1973] Crim.L.R. 36; *Perry* [1984] Crim.L.R. 680. See *Herron* [1967] 1 Q.B. 107 and *List*
(1965) 50 Cr.App.R. 81, for examples of a situation in which the discretion to exclude should be
exercised. In *Canton*, June 2, 1992, C.A. no. 90/5242/X3, the Court of Appeal emphasised the
importance of the judge's informing himself of the circumstances of a conviction rendered
admissible by paragraph (b), so that he may assess its relevance and probative value.
[18b] *Wilkins* (1975) 60 Cr.App.R. 300.

dishonesty—like knowledge or belief that the goods are stolen—must coincide with the relevant act of handling. The test for dishonesty is that laid down in *Ghosh* with respect to deception offences and theft.[19] The question "Did D act dishonestly?" is one for the determination of the tribunal of fact; a conviction depends upon the tribunal's finding (i) that D's act was dishonest according to the ordinary standards of reasonable and honest people, and (ii) that D realised that it was dishonest according to those standards (but finding (ii) will normally be required only if there is evidence capable of raising a doubt about it[20]).[21]

15–44   The rule referring the judgment of dishonesty to the tribunal of fact must be subject to an exception where D intends, when he receives stolen goods, to do with them what the law requires—to seek their owner or inform the police. And it ought not to apply when D believes that he has in law the right to receive and retain the goods because he believes they are his own. As his receiving will not, as a matter of law, be dishonest for the purpose of theft (section 2(1)(a)), it would be absurd if D had to depend upon a jury to declare it not dishonest for the purpose of handling. But section 2(1)(a) is not made to apply to the offence of handling; and a *Ghosh* direction has been held to be required where a "claim of right" is relied upon in a case of obtaining by deception.[22] Perhaps the fact that deception somewhat taints the obtaining it achieves may serve to distinguish the deception and receiving cases; and the pressure to ensure that D's act is treated in the same way whether it is viewed as appropriation or as receiving feels peculiarly strong.

5. THE RELATIONSHIP BETWEEN HANDLING AND THEFT[23]

Handling can occur only "otherwise than in the course of the stealing"

15–45   If D1 and D2 are both parties to a theft, either or both of them may do acts generally prohibited as handling. D1 may take goods from P's house and hand them to D2 who is waiting outside: D2 thus "receives the goods". D1 and D2 may each carry some of the stolen goods away from the scene: then each "assists in their . . . removal . . . for the benefit of" the other. To avoid the liability of a thief for handling in such situations, it is provided that the acts prohibited by section 22(1) shall be handling only if done "otherwise than in the course of the stealing."

---

[19] [1982] Q.B. 1053; see above, §2–132.
[20] *Roberts* (1985) 84 Cr.App.R. 117. See further, above, §2–133, n. 32.
[21] R. J. Harvey [1972] Crim.L.R. 213 reports an anonymous trial (before the modern cases on dishonesty) at which Shaw J. ruled that D does not dishonestly assist in the realisation by the thief of stolen goods where he acts as an intermediary between owner and thief for the payment of ransom money for the goods.
[22] See above, §8–75.
[23] A. T. H. Smith [1977] Crim.L.R. 517.

What is "the course of the stealing"?

The phrase will first be considered on principle. It is clear that "the course   **15–46**
of the stealing" must last for some time beyond the first moment of appropriation or obtaining: "the stealing" cannot simply mean "that which renders
the goods stolen", for the goods must already be stolen if an offence of handling is to be in question at all. Presumably what is referred to is the total
process of effective appropriation, including the "get-away". But it is not at
all clear how long "the course of the stealing" lasts. If D1 and D2 take silver
goods, drive them 50 miles, melt them down and contract over the telephone
to sell the metal to E (without, as it were, pausing for breath), at what point
does their "stealing" cease? It is suggested that its "course" must be over at
the latest when they are "clean away", if not before—though this is, inevitably, to use one vague phrase to set a limit to the scope of another for the
purposes of just one kind of factual situation. If the suggestion is correct, each
of the thieves will be guilty of handling at least during the later stages of their
journey and thereafter.

This view would be consistent with the robbery case of *Hale*,[24] according to
which an appropriation (and therefore "the time of" the stealing) is not a
mere momentary event but endures for some time, obviously varying with
the circumstances. There must be a strong case for supposing that "the course
of the stealing" within the meaning of section 22 and "the time of" the stealing within the meaning of section 8 are the same period. If they are, however,
it seems that one who receives or relevantly deals with goods during the continuance of the appropriation must be guilty only of the original theft (as a
secondary party) and not of handling. This conclusion would be embarrassing if such a person was charged only with handling, as he might easily be.

Pitham and Hehl[25] is the only reported case directly raising the issue. One   **15–47**
M offered to sell to D the furniture of a man who was in prison. This offer was
an appropriation of the furniture. The rest of the facts are not quite clear, but
on one reading of the judgment it appears that D inspected the furniture on
two occasions before buying it and taking it away. His act of handling was
held to have occurred "otherwise than in the course of the stealing"—that is
to say, after the course of M's stealing was over. The Court of Appeal
referred to arguments such as that conducted above but found it unnecessary
to pass upon them. That seemed to confirm that the theft and the handling
were on separate occasions (though it did not explain why the course of the
stealing was not regarded as continuing until the offer for sale was accepted;
the acceptance, an arranging to receive, was surely D's first act of handling).
In a subsequent case, however, *Pitham* was said to be "a case ... of what
might be called instantaneous appropriation."[26] This suggests that a theft of
goods by offering to sell them lasts only as long as it takes to speak the words
and makes irrelevant the interpretation of the rest of the facts in *Pitham*. It

---

[24] (1978) 68 Cr.App.R. 415 (above, §3–08).
[25] (1976) 65 Cr.App.R. 45.
[26] *Gregory* (1981) 77 Cr.App.R. 41 at 46.

also tends to confirm that the principle of *Hale* applies to the more common, physical taking, kind of appropriation.

Is this an ingredient for the prosecution to prove?

15–48   The Court of Appeal held in *Cash*[27] that the prosecution do not in the ordinary case have the burden of proving that the alleged handler acted "otherwise than in the course of the stealing." This was said to be true "at least so far as 'recent possession' cases are concerned." But, as the court observed, the inference in such cases that D "was a guilty handler, includes the inference that he was not the actual thief"[28]; and since the former inference must be drawn beyond reasonable doubt, that seems to amount to proof that D was not the thief. So perhaps what is meant is this: first, that the jury can draw the inference of handling without, for example, receiving direct evidence that D was not present at the theft or that he had an alibi for the occasion when it occurred (such evidence, as the court pointed out, cannot be expected)[29]; secondly, that the jury need not be directed that they must make a positive finding that D's receiving or other act of handling was done "otherwise than in the course of the stealing."—not, that is to say, if no issue as to this arises on the evidence, as it would if D testified that he was indeed a party to the theft.[30]

The thief as handler

15–49   A former rule that a person could not be guilty both of stealing and of receiving the same goods has not survived the combination of the Criminal Law Act 1967 (which abolished all rules peculiar to felony) and the Theft Act.[31] Once beyond "the course of the stealing", therefore, a person guilty of theft may commit an offence of handling the same goods or part of them. D, a thief, may, for example, the "course of the stealing" being over:

(i) "undertake" acts within section 22(1) for the benefit of E, an accomplice in the theft, or "assist" in the performance of such acts by E;

(ii) receive the goods or part of them from another party to the theft, or from a handler, or from an innocent party into whose hands they have come;

(iii) give or sell the goods to E, a handler, or to F, an innocent party, and then help E or F to dispose of the goods (or retain or remove them for E or F)[32];

(iv) be liable as a secondary party to a handling by E (whether that handling is a receiving from D himself[33] or from another person, or some other act within section 22(1)).

---

[27] [1985] Q.B. 801; compare *Koene* [1982] V.R. 916.
[28] [1985] Q.B. 801 at 804–805.
[29] *ibid.*, at 806.
[30] See *Griffiths* (1974) 60 Cr.App.R. 14.
[31] *Dolan* (1975) 62 Cr.App.R. 36.
[32] See *Eighth Report*, para. 131.
[33] Possibility admitted in *Bloxham* [1983] 1 A.C. 109 at 115; compare *Carter Patersons and Pickfords Carriers Ltd.* v. *Wessel* [1947] K.B. 849.

The handler as thief

Handling stolen goods requires an act done "otherwise than in the course **15–50** of the stealing." But the "stealing" referred to is that by which the goods first acquire their stolen character. A person who subsequently deals with them may be guilty of theft as well as handling.[34] Almost any act of handling is likely to be an appropriation of the stolen goods with the intention of permanently depriving their owner of them. The only illustrative case given by the C.L.R.C. was that of a handling by receiving.[35] But an act of "retention, removal, disposal or realisation" may equally be an appropriation.[36] For the purposes of theft, the appropriation need not be made "for the thief's own benefit" (s.1(2)). And it cannot be said that, because the victim is already deprived, the handler has no intention of depriving him; for on that argument even a receiver would not steal—which, save exceptionally,[37] he certainly does.[38] It seems, therefore, that all handlers who actually deal with the goods themselves may also steal.[39]

Suppose that goods are "stolen" goods because they were obtained by **15–51** deception or by blackmail.[40] Then the "thief" may have acquired a voidable title to them. If so, the victim's right "as regards those goods to ... restitution in respect of the theft"[41] depends on a timely disaffirmation of the transaction by which the "thief" obtained them. Only if this right of disaffirmation and "restitution" is a "proprietary interest" in the goods within the meaning of section 5(1) will the goods for the time being continue to "belong to" the victim so that a handler of them can also be guilty of theft. It would not be wise to predict that a criminal court would be prepared to find a "proprietary interest" in this situation.

Handler or original thief?

A person found in possession of stolen goods, and without a satisfactory **15–52** explanation of his possession, may have acquired them as the original thief or may have subsequently received them as a handler. The circumstances, and

---

[34] *Sainthouse* [1980] Crim.L.R. 506.
[35] *Eighth Report*, para. 132.
[36] *Sainthouse*, above.
[37] Where he does not intend to deprive the victim permanently.
[38] *Stapylton v. O'Callaghan* [1973] 2 All E.R. 782; *Shelton* (1986) 83 Cr.App.R. 379.
[39] This would exclude one who only "arranges" to receive or to deal with the goods, and perhaps some who only "assist in", rather than "undertaking", an act within the section; but any of these might be a secondary party to someone else's theft. If the purpose or one of the purposes of an act of handling (*e.g.* retention or removal of the goods) is to assist the thief or another handler to escape apprehension or prosecution, the handler will also be guilty of assisting an offender under the Criminal Law Act 1967, s.4(1).
[40] See s.24(4).
[41] The language of s.24(3). When this right is lost, the goods cease to be "stolen goods".

particularly that of "recent possession",[42] may justify either inference.[43] This can give rise to a difficulty to which the law has so far found no satisfactory solution: even though one offence or the other must have been committed, how is a conviction of either to be ensured? Two methods of proceeding require consideration.

15–53   *Alternative counts.* It is permissible to include in an indictment alternative counts for theft (or robbery, or burglary involving theft) and handling,[44] even though those counts are "factually mutually contradictory in the sense that proof of one charge destroys the other"[45]; and the judge may leave both counts to the jury if a prima facie case is made out in support of each.[46] The jury may have no doubt, in the light of all the evidence, that the defendant came by the stolen goods dishonestly—that he is indeed guilty of one of the offences charged. It was, however, clear to the Judicial Committee of the Privy Council in *Attorney-General of Hong Kong v. Yip Kai-foon*[47] that the jury may not be directed simply to convict of the offence that seems more probably to have been committed. Such a direction "detracts, or may be thought to detract, from the obligation of the jury to be satisfied beyond reasonable doubt that the accused is guilty of the particular offence" of which they convict him.[48] The course approved by the Judicial Committee is to direct the jury to consider first whether they are satisfied beyond reasonable doubt of the defendant's guilt on the theft count; and, if they are not, to consider secondly whether they are satisfied "in relation to each of the ingredients of the alternative [offence] of handling."[49] One consequence may, of course, be a disagreement on each count, in which case the jury must be discharged.[50]

15–54   If the jury is not to convict of either offence on the basis that it is the one more probably committed, it might be thought that a common enough occur-

---

[42] See above, §15–38.
[43] In *Cash* [1985] Q.B. 801 at 806–807, the Court of Appeal (referring to *Seymour* (1954) 38 Cr.App.R. 68) appeared to limit the possibility of an inference of D's being a party to the theft to cases where the theft occurred very shortly before D was found in possession. But it is clear that every case depends on its own facts (see, *e.g. Smythe* (1980) 72 Cr.App.R. 8 at 11–12; *Greaves, The Times,* July 11, 1987), including the nature of the goods. Possession of stolen money is said to suggest participation in the theft more strongly than possession of stolen chattels: see *per* Lord Denning M.R. in *Stupple v. Royal Insurance Co. Ltd.* [1971] 1 Q.B. 50 at 70, citing the direction of Phillimore J. in *Fallon* (1963) 47 Cr.App.R. 160 at 165. *Smith* (1984) 148 J.P. 216 discourages invocation of the "doctrine" of recent possession as relevant to theft where other evidence implicates D in the theft. It is not clear why; does not recent possession more strongly justify an inference of guilt when aggregated with other evidence? See the discussion at §15–39, above.
[44] *Shelton* (1986) 83 Cr.App.R. 379.
[45] *Bellman* [1989] A.C. 836 at 847.
[46] *Bellman*, above, for the general principle relating to "mutually destructive" counts.
[47] [1988] A.C. 642.
[48] *ibid.,* at 656.
[49] *ibid.*
[50] *ibid., Shelton* (1986) 83 Cr.App.R. 379 at 385.

rence would be an agreement that neither the defendant's involvement in the theft nor his subsequent receipt of goods stolen by another has been proved beyond reasonable doubt[51]: an outcome strictly leading to a totally unmeritorious acquittal.[52] But a crucial passage in the Judicial Committee's opinion in *Yip Kai-foon* contrives (doubtfully and illogically, it is submitted) to avoid this result. Suppose that (as in *Yip Kai-foon* itself) the jury first decide that they are not satisfied that D was guilty of theft; they therefore acquit him of that offence. The jury now come to consider the handling charge. The Committee rejected a submission that, because handling could only be committed "otherwise than in the course of the stealing", the trial judge should have specifically directed the jury that they must be satisfied beyond reasonable doubt that the defendant did not receive the goods in the course of theft. In the Committee's opinion, the parenthesis in section 22(1) "called for no specific direction", because the jury's decision to acquit of theft rendered the question of his involvement in the theft "no longer a live issue. The presumption that he was innocent of the theft . . . was . . . never rebutted."[53] D is therefore to be taken, apparently, not to have come by the goods as the original thief; *ergo* (since the jury are satisfied that he was either the thief or a handler) he was a handler. This interpretation of the Committee's opinion[54] appears to be accepted by the Court of Appeal.[55] But of course the jury may think it more probable that D was the original thief but not be sufficiently sure; and then (if they do not rebel against the reasoning they are being asked to apply) they are constrained to convict him of the offence they think it less likely that he committed. This is worse than the result outlawed by the Committee's principal ruling—conviction of the offence thought merely more probable.[56]

A widely-drawn theft charge. Suppose that goods are stolen on January 1   **15–55** and found in D's possession on January 8. He may have been the original thief; or he may have received the goods, knowing them to be stolen, between January 1 and 8. Whichever is the truth, he stole the goods, because a handling by receiving is itself theft. It is accurate to say that on a day between

---

[51] Compare *Bellman*, above, at 847, considering mutually contradictory charges of supplying heroin (for payment) and obtaining by deception payment for a harmless substance proffered as heroin.

[52] In practice, one suspects, the jury are likely to avoid this outcome "pragmatically"—by convicting of the more probable offence.

[53] [1988] A.C. 642 at 658; applying the reasoning in *Griffiths* (1974) 60 Cr.App.R. 14 and *Cash* [1985] Q.B. 801 (see above, §15–48).

[54] Propounded by Sir John Smith (see now Smith (J. C.), para. 13–43) but repeatedly deplored by him. see commentaries on cases in next note.

[55] *Foreman* [1991] Crim.L.R. 702; applied in *Ryan and French v. D.P.P.* [1994] Crim.L.R. 457.

[56] *Yip Kai-foon* was disapproved by a majority of the High Court of Australia in *Gilson v. The Queen* (1991) 172 C.L.R. 353 at 362. The Court held that the jury should be instructed, that if they are satisfied beyond reasonable doubt that D is guilty either of stealing or of receiving stolen goods but are unable to say which, they should convict of the less serious offence, the judge directing them which offence they should regard as the more serious in the circumstances of the case.

January 1 and 8 he appropriated the goods by assuming possession of them. Can the dilemma be solved by obtaining a conviction of theft on a charge in such terms? The case of *Stapylton v. O'Callaghan*[57] first suggested that it can. D was tried on informations charging, respectively, theft and handling (by receiving) of a driving licence. It was clear that the licence had been stolen and that D, in whose possession it was found not long afterwards, had come by it dishonestly and intended to keep it. But the magistrate, not being satisfied as to which of the informations was appropriate, dismissed both. The Divisional Court directed a conviction of theft, because, on any view, D "dishonestly possessed himself of the licence and meant to keep it."[58] And in *Shelton*,[59] where D was in possession of a cheque book on the day it was stolen, the Court of Appeal upheld a theft conviction because, on any view, "on the day specified in the indictment [D] had dishonestly appropriated" the cheque book.[60]

15–56   But the court spoke with two voices in *Shelton*. On the one hand it asked: how could the problem of the ambiguous possessor "be solved by an indictment in sufficiently wide terms to cover both ... appropriations ... without breaching the rules against duplicity?"[61] On the other hand, it rationalised the conviction by, in effect, understanding the charge of theft to mean, "D appropriated the property either by taking it from the owner at such-and-such a time (and place) or by receiving it from the thief at such-and-such a later time (and, no doubt, other place)". The court seems in the end to have conquered its anxiety about duplicity. It is submitted that it was right to do so. The charge of theft by an assumption of possession on a named date, or between named dates, alleges only one offence, committed in an identified manner. The prosecution cannot further particularise but rely upon D's possession as evidence of an assumption of possession that, whenever it occurred, constituted the offence. It is sufficient that the jury are satisfied that he took possession dishonestly and with the required intention; it is immaterial when and where he did so[62] and immaterial that different members of the jury may prefer different theories as to when he did so.[63]

15–57   There may be a case where it is desired to obtain a handling conviction as accurately reflecting D's apparent role, but in which it is feared that the whole of the evidence at the trial may make the case less clearly one of hand-

---

[57] [1973] 2 All E.R. 782.
[58] See also *Gregory* (1983) 77 Cr.App.R. 41; *Devall* [1984] Crim.L.R. 428; *More* (1986) 86 Cr.App.R. 234 (in the Court of Appeal). The suggestion in *Devall* of a separate theft count giving particulars of an alleged "second appropriation" merely reproduces the difficulty discussed in the text above.
[59] (1986) 83 Cr.App.R. 379.
[60] *ibid.*, at 384.
[61] *ibid.*, at 383.
[62] See *More* (1986) 86 Cr.App.R. 234 at 246; *Shelton* (1986) 83 Cr.App.R. 379 at 385; *Dowdall and Smith* (1991) 13 Cr.App.R. (S.) 441 (theft by taking from owner or by finding; alternative counts inappropriate).
[63] Compare J. C. Smith [1988] Crim.L.R. 335 at 343.

ling than it began. Such a case, it is suggested, is suitable for a widely-drawn theft charge (assuming that to be permissible) presented as an alternative to a handling charge. The judge could invite the jury to consider first whether they are satisfied that D was a handler and, if they are not, to consider secondly whether they are satisfied that he committed theft as alleged in the alternative count.[64]

6. INFORMATIONS AND INDICTMENTS

Section 22(1) creates a single offence[65] and an information simply alleging **15–58** handling contrary to the section is not bad for duplicity. But where D may be embarrassed by an absence of particulars as to the mode of handling alleged, the information should set out particulars or an application for particulars should be acceded to.[66]

Similarly, although a conviction may be had upon an indictment in which the particulars of offence allege simply that D dishonestly handled certain goods, knowing or believing them to be stolen,[67] the particulars ought to allege the mode of handling it is proposed to establish, with adequate detail.[68] Where a particular mode is alleged (*e.g.* receiving), there cannot be a conviction of a different species of handling (*e.g.* assisting in removal)[69]—or there cannot, at any rate, without amendment of the indictment. Where the mode is uncertain, there should be separate counts to cover different modes.[70] It is neither necessary nor helpful, however, to cover every possible alternative[71]; normally two counts are the most required, one alleging receiving, the other alleging an act within the second part of section 22(1).[72]

A count alleging an undertaking or assisting in the retention, removal, disposal or realisation of goods or an arranging to do so should include the words "by or for the benefit of another".[73]

---

[64] A passage in the judgment of Lord Widgery C.J. in *Stapylton v. O'Callaghan* [1973] 2 All E.R. 782, at 784, may appear to discourage this procedure by suggesting that whenever "the facts justify the conclusion that the offence of stealing was committed, the right . . . course is to convict of stealing" and not to consider handling "with the added penalty which might arise". Compare *Shelton* (1986) 83 Cr.App.R. 379 at 385: "handling is the more serious offence, carrying a heavier penalty because those who knowingly have dealings with thieves encourage stealing." But it is not thought that small-time handlers are in practice punished more severely than the thieves from whom they receive; and in any case a conviction clearly describing the offender's role seems desirable in principle.

[65] *Contra*, Lord Bridge in *Bloxham* [1983] 1 A.C. 109 at 113; but the dictum is inconsistent with the authorities cited below.

[66] *Griffiths v. Freeman* [1970] 1 W.L.R. 659; [1970] 1 All E.R. 1117.

[67] *Ikpong* [1972] Crim.L.R. 432; *Kirby* (1972) 56 Cr.App.R. 758; *Pitchley* (1972) 57 Cr.App.R. 30.

[68] *Alt* (1972) 56 Cr.App.R. 457.

[69] *Nicklin* (1976) 64 Cr.App.R. 205 (in which the principles stated in this paragraph were reaffirmed); applied in *Samms*, October 16, 1992, C.A. no. 91/3723/Y2: evidence of assisting in removal of stolen goods; conviction of handling by receiving quashed.

[70] *Sloggett* [1972] 1 Q.B. 430; *Marshall* (1971) 56 Cr.App.R. 263.

[71] *Ikpong*, above.

[72] *Willis and Syme* (1972) 57 Cr.App.R. 1; *Deakin* (1972) 56 Cr.App.R. 841 at 849, where a formula is offered of particulars of a count alleging handling within the second part of s.22(1).

[73] *Sloggett*, above. (In some cases the words "by or" or "or for the benefit of" will strictly be inappropriate.)

The particulars of a count for handling should include an averment of knowledge or belief that the goods were stolen.[74]

15–59   There are some cases in which it is necessary to name the owner of the stolen goods in the indictment—cases, that is to say, "where the property is of a common and indistinctive type" and "where, unless the ownership be assigned in the particulars of the charge, the accused may be at a loss to understand fully the nature of the charge which he has to meet."[75] But this certainly does not mean that whenever the goods are of a common type, the attribution of ownership will be a material averment so that the prosecution must fail if that ownership is not proved; on the facts it may be immaterial from whom the goods were stolen.[76]

15–60   There may sometimes need to be a compendious count covering a "hoard" of goods, possibly received over a period of time; this will be when particular goods are not identifiable as the proceeds of particular thefts. (Similarly, a single charge of receiving a sum of money between named dates, being the total of various unidentifiable sums received on unknown dates from the same person, is unobjectionable[77].) But where some at least of the goods in a compendious count are shown to have been received on different occasions from different thefts, a single conviction on that count of handling all the goods cannot be substituted for defective convictions of the thefts. In such a case the indictment should have been differently drawn.[78]

15–61   Section 27 contains provisions permitting the charging in one indictment, and the trial together, of any number of persons alleged to have handled, whether at different times or at the same time, goods deriving from the same theft (s.27(1)); and the conviction of any of two or more accused indicted for jointly handling any stolen goods if he handled all or any of the goods, whether or not he did so jointly with any of the other accused (s.27(2)).[79] The latter provision permits the conviction of two persons jointly charged who are proved to have been guilty of successive handlings of the same goods.[80]

7. ADVERTISING REWARDS FOR RETURN OF GOODS STOLEN OR LOST

15–62   It is convenient to mention here that section 23 (which reproduces a

---

[74] *Amos* [1971] Crim.L.R. 352.
[75] *Gregory* (1972) 56 Cr.App.R. 441, where a late amendment of the assertion as to ownership was improper as giving rise to a risk of injustice.
[76] *Deakin*, above, referring to r. 6(1) of the Indictment Rules scheduled to the Indictments Act 1915, which had, however, been revoked by the Indictment Rules 1971 and not replaced.
[77] *Cain* [1983] Crim.L.R. 802 (citing cases referred to at §2–159, above). But a charge wrapping up several specified handling offences, with the intention of proving one as a sample, was bad.
[78] *Smythe* (1980) 72 Cr.App.R. 8. Compare *Malhi* [1994] Crim.L.R.755: different kinds of handling of goods and cash from the same theft.
[79] See *Eighth Report*, pp. 132–133 (notes on draft Bill).
[80] *French* [1973] Crim.L.R. 632.

pre-existing offence) prohibits the use of certain words—*e.g.* words to the effect "no questions asked"—in public advertisements of rewards for the return of stolen or lost goods. The offence, which carries a maximum fine on summary conviction of £400,[81] may be committed by the advertiser, the printer or the publisher.[82] It is an offence of strict liability; the printer or publisher (*e.g.* of a newspaper) will commit it although he does not know of the offending advertisement.[83]

---

[81] Originally £100; thus, level 3 on the standard scale (Criminal Justice Act 1982, ss.37, 38), currently £1,000 (Criminal Justice Act 1991, s.17(1)).

[82] The advertising manager of a newspaper is one who publishes advertisements in it: *Denham and Scott* (1983) 77 Cr.App.R. 210.

[83] *ibid.* For the fascinating history behind this provision and its forebears, see Hall, *Theft, Law and Society* (2nd ed.), pp. 70–76.

Chapter 16

GOING EQUIPPED

1. DEFINITION. ENFORCEMENT

16–01   Section 25(1) (read with subs. (5)) makes it an offence for a person to have with him, when not at his place of abode, any article for use in the course of or in connection with any burglary, theft (which includes for this purpose an offence under section 12(1) of taking a conveyance other than a pedal cycle) or "cheat" (that is, an offence of obtaining property by deception under section 15).

The offence is punishable on conviction on indictment with imprisonment for three years (s.25(2)).[1] Where it is committed "with reference to the theft or taking of motor vehicles" the offender may be disqualified for holding or obtaining a driving licence.[2] An offence under section 25 may justify an order under section 43 of the Powers of Criminal Courts Act 1973, operating to deprive the offender of his rights, if any, in the article involved, on the ground that it was intended by him to be used for the purpose of committing, or facilitating the commission of, an offence.

Arrest and search

16–02   Although punishable with a maximum of only three years' imprisonment, the offence created by section 25 is an arrestable offence (as is conspiring or attempting to commit, or inciting, aiding, abetting, counselling or procuring the commission of, such an offence).[3] The powers of arrest without warrant provided by the Police and Criminal Evidence Act 1984, s.24(4)-(7), therefore apply; and one who does an act with intent to impede the apprehension or prosecution of an offender may be convicted under section 4(1) of the Criminal Law Act 1967, as amended by Schedule 6 to the 1984 Act.

Enforcement of the section is facilitated by the power given to constables by section 1 of the 1984 Act to search persons and vehicles for prohibited articles.[4]

---

[1] This remains so even where the intended offence is taking a conveyance, now a summary offence punishable with no more than six months' imprisonment.
[2] Road Traffic Offenders Act 1988, Sched. 2, Pt. II.
[3] Police and Criminal Evidence Act 1984, s.24(2)(d) and (3). Section 25(4) of the Theft Act has been left unrepealed. It partially duplicates the 1984 provisions, at least as to a citizen's arrest; as to constables, see the 1984 Act, s.26(1)(a).
[4] See the 1984 Act, s.1(7)(b) and (8), for relevant prohibited articles. See also the Criminal Justice and Public Order Act 1994, s.60.

2. THE DETAILS OF THE OFFENCE

The articles covered by the section

The C.L.R.C. offered a convenient list of typical articles covered by the **16–03** section:

> "The offence will apply, for example, to firearms and other offensive weapons, imitation firearms, housebreaking implements, any articles for the purpose of concealing identity (for example, masks, rubber gloves and false car number-plates) and ... car keys and confidence tricksters' outfits"[5];

and it will apply to a vehicle for use in getting to or from the place of a crime. Indeed it can be any article whatsoever so long as it is intended for a relevant criminal purpose.

"When not at his place of abode"

It is important to stress that the offence is limited to occasions when the **16–04** possessor of the article is not at his place of abode. The professional burglar is safe in his possession of the tools of his trade as long as he keeps them at home. No doubt the possession at home of a burglar's kit or of a confidence trickster's outfit is some indication of a general intention to use that equipment; but when the intending offender takes his equipment with him away from home it will usually be safe to regard him as having a particular crime in contemplation or at least as intending to use the equipment on that occasion if an opportunity to do so presents itself, and it is at this point that the section becomes an acceptable and very important weapon in the armoury of crime control. The section in fact goes a little further than this. For D may, for instance, make his mask or skeleton key at his place of work, intending to take it home to add to his stock-in-trade. Nevertheless, if caught at work in possession of an article capable of being shown to have an intended criminal use covered by the section, he is clearly within the section.

One is "at his place of abode" only if he is on a site where he intends to abide; so a person who has equipment for theft with him in a vehicle in which he lives commits an offence under the section except when the vehicle is on such a site.[6]

"Has with him"

D has an article "with him", of course, when it is about his person or in the **16–05** vehicle in which he is travelling. But can an article be "with him" if he is physically separated from it so that it is not immediately available to him? The Court of Appeal has adopted a purposive approach to the interpretation of the phrase "has with him" in the context of an offence of having with one a firearm with intent to commit an indictable offence. In that context the ques-

---

[5] *Eighth Report*, para. 148.
[6] *Bundy* (1977) 65 Cr.App.R. 259.

tion for the jury concerns the accessibility of the firearm for its intended purpose, judged as a matter of common sense.[7] This test can no doubt be adapted for use in connection with section 25. The judgment of accessibility may be affected by whether the article was intended for use in connection with an offence which D was in the act, or on the point, of committing at the relevant time, or whether the intended offence or some as yet undetermined offence lay in the future: a finding that he had the article "with him" in the latter case might be based on circumstances of less immediate accessibility than in the former.

D may also have an article "with him" if he and E are in company and E has with him an article within the section, but only if he knows that E has it[8] and he is jointly with E a party to a relevant enterprise in which the article will be available for use.[9]

16–06   In *In the Matter of McAngus*,[10] D was held to have counterfeit designer shirts "with him" when he showed them to E, a prospective purchaser (not the intended victim of a contemplated "cheat"), as they lay in a bonded warehouse that they had visited for the purpose. This seems to carry section 25 beyond the mischief for which it was designed. D was not abroad "with" the shirts in order to make use of them in an offence; he merely visited the shirts, which happened to be elsewhere than at his home. The language of the marginal note to the section, although not having the status of a definition,[11] is at least suggestive: D could not be described as "going equipped".

"For use in the course of or in connection with" an offence

16–07   D must have an article with him "for use in the course of or in connection with" one of the stated offences. He may intend it to be used (not necessarily by himself) for an offence already determined upon—even one embarked upon by the performance of preparatory acts[12]—or an offence for which opportunity may present itself.[13] But if he has not decided whether he will use it, given the opportunity, he does not have it "for use".[14]

16–08   The use of the phrase "in connection with" widens the scope of the section by providing for a case in which an article is intended for use in preparation for a crime or, for instance, in escaping after it has been committed.[15] But an intended use of documents to obtain a job that will afford opportunities for

---

[7] *Pawlicki and Swindell* (1992) 95 Cr.App.R. 246; see above §4–42.
[8] Compare *Lester and Byast* (1955) 39 Cr.App.R. 157; *Harris* [1961] Crim.L.R. 256; *Webley and Webley* [1967] Crim.L.R. 300.
[9] Compare *Thompson* (1869) 11 Cox C.C. 362; *Jones* [1979] C.L.Y. 411.
[10] [1994] Crim.L.R. 602.
[11] *D.P.P. v. Schildkamp* [1971] A.C. 1.
[12] *Minor v. D.P.P.* (1987) 86 Cr.App.R. 378 (possession of syphoning equipment after removing car petrol cap).
[13] *Ellames* (1974) 60 Cr.App.R. 7.
[14] *Hargreaves* [1985] Crim.L.R. 243.
[15] *Ellames*, above.

theft is too remote from the proposed thefts to be "in connection with" them.[16]

In *In the Matter of McAngus*[17] (already mentioned) D proposed to sell shirts falsely bearing a brand name to E, who knew of their counterfeit character. It was held that D had the shirts "for use in the course of or in connection with" the cheat that he anticipated E would commit by selling them on as genuine. (E was in fact an undercover agent.) This is a second respect in which the decision stretches the ambit of the offence. D did not have the shirts "for use in the course of" a cheat—for E was not to be deceived and E's further activities were a matter of indifference to D. And it is a liberal reading of the statutory language that describes D's proposed sale of the shirts to E as their use "in connection with" E's expected offence. Perhaps what justifies it is the fact that D's conduct would make him a party to the contemplated cheat.

The contemplated offences

The article may be intended for use in the course of or in connection with   **16–09**
any:

(i) *burglary*

The offence of "possessing housebreaking implements"[18] by night was a weapon of long standing in the armoury of preventive justice; and the main function of the broader generalisation achieved in section 25 no doubt remains the control of the intending burglar. Not that the section is used only when a criminal enterprise has proceeded no further than the stage of preparation. Sometimes it cannot be proved, although it is the case, that a person was involved in a burglary, and a conviction under section 25 is all that can be obtained. And a burglar (or a thief[19]) may sometimes be convicted of both the preparatory and the substantive offences; and in such a case, although it was all one criminal activity, it has been held, surprisingly, that consecutive sentences of imprisonment are not improper.[20]

(ii) *theft*

Taking a conveyance contrary to section 12(1) is treated as theft for this purpose (s.25(5)).

(iii) *cheat—that is, an offence under section 15*

All the authorities on this form of the offence concern a troublesome kind   **16–10**
of case in which D intends to sell the article in question in fraud of a third

---

[16] *Mansfield* [1975] Crim.L.R. 101.
[17] [1994] Crim.L.R. 602; above §16–06.
[18] See cross-heading above s.25. See latterly, Larceny Act 1916, s.28(2).
[19] *Minor v. D.P.P.* above.
[20] *Ferris* [1973] Crim.L.R. 642, cogently criticised by D. A. Thomas at 643.

person (T). According to these authorities, the offence requires reference to the hypothetical state of mind of a notional person—namely, any unsuspecting customer. This approach may be misconceived (a matter considered below); but, as will be explained, there ought at least to be reference to D's state of mind as to a customer's likely state of mind. The offence of going equipped for cheat plainly requires careful handling.

Going equipped for cheat: the elements of the offence

16–11   T, the ultimate intended victim of D's fraud, has in most of the cases been D's employer. D (a railway buffet car steward[21] or a waiter in a restaurant[22]) has food or drink of his own for sale to T's customers, with the intention of keeping the proceeds of sale for himself. He does not intend the customers to know that he is selling his own goods. It has authoritatively been said[23] that what has to be proved in a prosecution under section 25 is: first, "that there was an article for use in connection with the deception"—that is, the goods to be sold; secondly, "that there was a proposed deception"—"deception of [the customers] into believing that the proffered [goods were T's] and not [D's]"; thirdly, "an intention to obtain ... by means of the deception", and of course to keep, the money of the customers; fourthly, "dishonesty"—that is, "the lying to and misleading of [the customers] so that there is a deception of them"[24]; and fifthly, "that the obtaining would have been, wholly or partially,[25] by virtue of the deception." This way of summarising the offence, however, does not draw attention to a crucial aspect of the proposed deception: it must be "deliberate or reckless".[26] In one case a conviction was quashed because the jury were not told that, in order to convict, they must be satisifed that D believed that a prospective purchaser would decline to purchase if he knew the truth.[27]

The notional deceived customer

16–12   The cases treat as relevant the question whether a person to whom D might sell his own goods in fraud of his employer would be induced to buy the goods by an implied representation that they belong to the employer. Would a customer buy if he knew the truth?[28] The answer to this question has been said to depend in any particular case on "the detail of the evidence, particularly that

---

[21] *Rashid* (1976) 64 Cr.App.R. 201; *Corboz* [1984] Crim.L.R. 629; *Cooke* [1986] A.C. 909.
[22] *Doukas* (1977) 66 Cr.App.R. 228.
[23] *Doukas*, above, at 231; approved in *Cooke*, above, at 934; followed in *Corboz*, above; *Whiteside and Antoniou* [1989] Crim.L.R. 436 (selling pirated copies of cassette tapes on the street).
[24] Dishonesty *vis-à-vis* T is not a necessary element of the offence: *Cooke*, above, *per* Lord Mackay at p. 934.
[25] These words caused unnecessary difficulty in *Whiteside and Antoniou*, above. They appear to be redundant; it is axiomatic that the deception need never be the only factor inducing the victim to act as he does.
[26] s.15(4).
[27] *Rashid* (1976) 64 Cr.App.R. 201. Realisation that he might decline to purchase is surely enough for reckless deception.
[28] See above, §8–46.

relating to the attitude and understanding of [the purchasers]."[29] But it is not necessary that any deceived person should give evidence[30]; indeed, there may have been no purchasers, D having simply had the articles with him but not used them. The offence does not require an obtaining by deception but only an intention to do so. The question must therefore rather be as to the effect that the intended deception would have on a notional purchaser.[31] One matter relevant to that question is the nature of the commodity being sold.[32] Another is the fact that a customer who was aware that the goods belonged to D would realise that D was practising a fraud on his employer. In the leading case the court was confident that a diner in a restaurant would be unwilling to participate in such a fraud.[33] But others have declined to assume that railway passengers would refuse to buy refreshments because they knew that the buffet staff were practising a "fiddle".[34] Such scepticism, however, does not mean that the question ought not to be left to a jury.[35]

Criticism of the case law

The case law, then, looks for an intention to obtain property by what would **16–13** in fact be an operative deception. But a search for the state of mind of the notional person-to-be-deceived is misdirected.[36] The only relevant state of mind is that of D himself. What is necessary—but, equally, all that is necessary—is that D intends to obtain property by deception, that is, by behaving in a way that he believes will (or may) induce another to act otherwise than as he would if he knew the truth. Whether D's intended behaviour is capable of deceiving the other and thereby of inducing the desired transaction is not, substantively, to the point (although, of course, any view that the jury has on that matter may assist them in divining the view of it that D himself had).

Proof of the criminal purpose

The fact that D intended the article to be used in the course of, or in con- **16–14**

---

[29] *Cooke* [1986] A.C. 909, *per* Lord Mackay at 934; and compare the approach of the court in *Whiteside and Antoniou* [1989] Crim.L.R. 436.

[30] *Whiteside and Antoniou*, above.

[31] "[T]he question has to be asked of the hypothetical customer: . . . if you had been told the truth, would you or would you not have bought the commodity?": *Doukas* (1977) 66 Cr.App.R. 228 at 232.

[32] *Rashid*, above, at 203 (contrasting food bought on a train with a watch bought in a jeweller's shop); *Doukas*, above, at 232 (jury may be expected to find that a diner is induced to buy wine in a restaurant by the supposition that it is the restaurant's wine).

[33] *Doukas*, above, at 233. (Compare *Lambie* [1982] A.C. 449; above, §8–46.) This consideration justified the trial judge's leaving the matter to the jury.

[34] *Rashid*, above, at 203 (*obiter*; prosecution regarded as misconceived); *Cooke* [1986] A.C. 909, *per* Lord Bridge at 921.

[35] And a conviction was upheld in *Corboz* [1984] Crim.L.R. 629.

[36] Compare J.C. Smith, commentary on *Whiteside and Antoniou* [1989] Crim.L.R. 436 at 437–438; Parry, *Offences against Property*, para. 2.38. The case law is defended by Smith (A. T. H.), para. 31–12.

nection with, one of the stated offences must be proved by the prosecution. Commonly that intention will be suggested forcibly enough by the nature of the article and the circumstances in which D had it with him; and then an explanation from D seems called for. This commonsense proposition is rendered statutory in relation to a limited class of articles by section 25(3), which provides that:

> "proof that [D] had with him an article made or adapted for use in committing a burglary, theft or cheat shall be evidence that he had it with him for such use."

Some comments may be made upon this provision.

16–15   First, it seems to do little if anything more than state the obvious. The subsection surely means merely that possession of an article of the kind to which it refers is, in itself, evidence from which a jury may infer the necessary criminal purpose. Even in the absence of a credible explanation consistent with innocence, possession of an article within the subsection is only "evidence" of such a purpose and is not necessarily conclusive. Still less does such evidence place on D a burden of positively persuading the jury of his innocent purpose.[37] No doubt he must come forward with some explanation if he can; but that would be no less true without the subsection.

Secondly, the phrase "made ... for use ... " may be unfortunate. As noted earlier in the context of aggravated burglary, an article is to be regarded as "made" for a particular use if it was originally made for such use.[38] But there are many articles, which have long been known as "house-breaking implements" and are probably meant to be within the scope of subsection (3), which are not in the normal sense "made" for housebreaking. Assuming subsection (3) to have any substantial value at all, it may therefore be necessary to give the phrase "made ... for use ... " a special meaning here, and one different from that which we have assumed it to bear in section 10. This indeed seems to be implied by the C.L.R.C.'s reference in this context to skeleton keys, possession of which "in itself calls for explanation by the accused."[39] A locksmith may make a skeleton key for a perfectly legitimate purpose. If such a key is in D's possession when not at his place of abode, it is surely not the Committee's intention that the application of subsection (3) should depend upon whether D is a locksmith and, if he is, on proof of his purpose in making the key; or, if D is not a locksmith, on proof of the source of the key and of the original purpose of its making.

16–16   In summary, subsection (3) appears to distinguish needlessly and clumsily between different kinds of case. It is submitted that the question in all cases should be—and is—whether the circumstances taken together amount to evidence of a relevant criminal purpose. If three men are found late at night in a van with a torch and some carpenter's tools, and each man has a stocking

---

[37] See on subs. (3), *Eighth Report*, paras. 151–153.
[38] See above, §4–38, on s.10(1)(*b*).
[39] *Eighth Report*, para. 151.

in his pocket, there is clearly evidence of an intention to wear the stocking on the head. An explanation is called for—no less in this case than in a case within the terms of subsection (3), however interpreted. It is suggested that such a case will be dealt with in practice identically with a case within the subsection, except that it will not be proper to direct the jury in terms of subsection (3).[40]

---

[40] *Harrison* [1970] Crim.L.R. 415.

Chapter 17

JURISDICTION

1. INTRODUCTION

17–01   The jurisdiction of the criminal courts of England and Wales is in principle territorial. Subject to statutory exceptions, only an offence committed in England and Wales—that is, an offence the last constituent element of which occurs in England and Wales—is triable here.[1] To take a simple and obvious example; our courts have no jurisdiction in relation to conduct abroad which, if it had occurred here, would have constituted the offence of burglary.[2] Moreover, inchoate offences are, in general, limited to agreements, attempts and incitements to commit offences that would, if completed, be triable here.

This basic position has come to be recognised as too restrictive, and as productive of unacceptable technical difficulties, in relation particularly to offences of dishonesty. Much economic crime nowadays involves activity in more than one country or activity in one country having its damaging effects in another (often as a result of electronic communication). The demands of international law enforcement have therefore led to substantial reform of the jurisdiction rules, specifically in respect of fraud offences. Jurisdiction remains territorial in character save in so far as it is affected by Part I of the Criminal Justice Act 1993. That legislation, which implemented recommendations of the Law Commission in *Jurisdiction over Offences of Fraud and Dishonesty with a Foreign Element* (1989: Law Com. No. 180), fundamentally alters the law with respect both to the majority of Theft Act, and some other, offences and to related offences of conspiracy, attempt and incitement. In what follows statutory references are to provisions of the 1993 Act unless otherwise stated.

---

[1] An exception anticipating the Criminal Justice Act 1993, s.3(2)(a) (below, §17–09), was recognised by the Privy Council in *Liangsiriprasert v. U.S. Government* [1990] 2 All E.R. 866 and confirmed by the Court of Appeal in *Sansom* [1991] 2 Q.B. 130: agreement abroad to commit an offence in England and Wales. The Privy Council expressed itself (at p. 878) as applying a principle extending generally to "inchoate crimes committed abroad which are intended to result in the commission of criminal offences in England." The Theft Act 1968, s.14(1), renders amenable to justice in England and Wales, as guilty of an offence or an attempt to commit an offence under the Act, a person who, outside England and Wales, (a) steals or attempts to steal, or (b) commits robbery, attempted robbery or assault with intent to rob involving the theft of or an intent to steal, a mail bag or postal packet in the course of transmission between different jurisdictions in the British postal area (as defined in s.14(2)).

[2] G. R. Sullivan and C. Warbrick [1994] Crim.L.R. 650 maintain that the proposition is one of substantive law as well as of jurisdiction—that the conduct abroad constitutes no offence in terms of English law. On this ground they object to the decision in *Atakpu and Abrahams* [1994] Q.B. 69 (above, §2–94), which proceeds on the basis that a person may "commit" abroad, once for all, an offence defined in terms of English law, so as to be incapable of subsequently committing that offence within the jurisdiction with respect to the same property.

274

2. PART I OF THE CRIMINAL JUSTICE ACT 1993

[NOTE: The legislation was not yet in force on March 15, 1995]

Substantive offences

Most offences under the Theft Acts are designated "Group A offences"[3];   **17–02**
and it is provided that a person may be guilty of a Group A offence if any
"relevant event" occurred in England and Wales.[4] A "relevant event" is "any
act or omission or other event (including any result of one or more acts or
omissions) proof of which is required for conviction of the offence."[5]

It is further provided, by section 4, (a) that property is obtained in England
and Wales if it either despatched from or received at a place in England and
Wales; and (b) that there is a communication in England and Wales of any
information, instruction, request, demand or other matter if it is sent by any
means from a place in England and Wales to a place elsewhere, or vice versa.[6]

Application to particular offences

Theft. The only act or event which must be proved for conviction of theft is   **17–03**
an appropriation of property. As the law now stands, any act that an owner of
property alone is entitled to do in relation to the property is an appropriation
of it.[7] This includes an act of authorising another to deal with the property.
Thus, the act of issuing a cheque drawn on a bank account, or of typing a telex
message instructing a bank to deal with funds in an account, may be a complete appropriation of the account[8]—and therefore a "relevant event" within
the meaning of the 1993 Act. The offence is triable in England and Wales if
that is where the act took place, although the account is situated abroad.

What of the converse case, in which an act of appropriation is done abroad
in relation to property in England and Wales? If that act involves the sending
of (say) an instruction to a place in England and Wales, the communication
of that instruction occurs in England and Wales[9] and so it seems that the
appropriation also occurs there.[10] Where there is no such international communication, however, jurisdiction would seem to depend upon the notion,
for which there is no clear authority, of the appropriation's continuing[11] until
(without further activity on the part of the appropriator) the act has the

---

[3] s.1(2): offences under ss.1, 15, 16, 17, 19, 20(2), 21 and 22 of the 1968 Act, and under ss.1 and 2
of the 1978 Act. Other Group A offences are those under ss.1–5 of the Forgery and Counterfeiting Act 1981 and the common law offence of cheating in relation to the public revenue.
[4] s.2(3). It is immaterial whether the person was a British citizen, or was in England and Wales,
at any material time: s.3(1).
[5] s.2(1). "For the purpose of determining whether or not a particular event is a relevant event in
relation to a Group A offence, any question as to where it occurred is to be disregarded": s.2(2).
[6] Section 4 applies also in relation to "Group B" offences—as to which, see §17–08, below.
[7] See above, §2–69.
[8] See above, §§2–151, 2–152.
[9] s.4(b): above, §17–02.
[10] This was the Law Commission's intention; see Law Com. No. 180, para. 2.31, especially n. 57.
[11] For authority on theft as a more than momentary event, see above, §2–96.

intended effect upon property in England and Wales[12] and of its then occurring where that effect occurs.[13]

17–04   *Deception offences.* The new provisions have their most obvious application in relation to an offence of obtaining by deception any property or other thing that is the subject of one of the Theft Act deception offences. D will be guilty of such an offence if his deceptive communication is sent from, or is sent to, a place in England and Wales (wherever he may, as a result, obtain the property or other thing) or if he obtains the property or other thing in England and Wales (as a result of a deception practised anywhere in the world). So, for example, D may be convicted in England of obtaining property by deception (i) if he received property in France as a result of a lying letter that he posted in England to P in Belgium, or that was delivered to P in England by a courier to whom D had entrusted it in Germany; or (ii) if, as a result of a deception practised in Canada, he receives property in England or receives in Scotland property despatched from somewhere in England.

Another example is provided by section 16(2)(b) of the Theft Act 1968, which makes it an offence to obtain by deception the "pecuniary advantage" of being allowed to borrow by way of overdraft. The offence will be triable in England and Wales if the deception emanates from, or is received in, England and Wales; or if that is where the bank account in question is held and thus where the pecuniary advantage is obtained.[14]

17–05   *False accounting.* Section 17(1) of the Theft Act 1968 creates two offences.

(a) In *Governor of Pentonville Prison, ex parte Osman*,[15] the Divisional Court thought it impossible to lay down a general rule as to where the offence of falsifying a document required for an accounting purpose is committed, where the document is falsified in one place and required for an accounting purpose in another. In terms of the 1993 Act, however, the only "relevant event"—that is, the only "act or omission or other event" required to be proved—is that of destroying, defacing, concealing or falsifying referred to in section 17(1)(a). Jurisdiction only exists, therefore, if that act or omission occurred in England and Wales.

(b) A person may commit the offence under section 17(1)(b) if "in furnishing information for any purpose" he "produces or makes use of" a misleading, false or deceptive accounting document. As "furnishing information" involves "a communication ... of ... information", it seems clear that there is jurisdiction to try this offence if the document was either sent from or sent to a place in England and Wales.[16]

---

[12] This concept is suggested for another purpose at §2–153, above.

[13] "Prima facie a theft takes place where the property is appropriated; prima facie appropriation takes place where the property is situated": *Tomsett* [1985] Crim.L.R. 369, cited from the transcript by Lloyd L.J. in *Governor of Pentonville Prison, ex p. Osman* (1988) 90 Cr.App.R. 281 at 294. The idea is, in part, that the latter principle may operate although on the facts the appropriation also occurs elsewhere.

[14] *Bevan* (1986) 84 Cr.App.R. 143.

[15] (1990) 90 Cr.App.R. 281, at 289.

[16] See s.4(b), above, §17–02.

Blackmail involves the making of a demand with menaces.[17] The effect of **17–06** section 4 is that a relevant demand sent from a place in England and Wales to a victim abroad, or sent from a place abroad to a victim in England and Wales, is treated as made in England and Wales; so that in either case a "relevant event" occurs in England and Wales and the offence is triable here.

(a) *Demand sent from England and Wales.* So far as concerns a letter posted in England and Wales, the Act does not affect the pre-existing position under the House of Lords decision in *Treacy v. D.P.P.*,[18] according to which a demand contained in such a letter is "made" upon posting, whether or not the letter reaches its addressee.

(b) *Demand sent from abroad.* It is not clear whether a demand despatched abroad is within section 4 if it does not arrive in England and Wales. On the one hand, the section requires in terms only that the demand be "sent ... to" a place in England and Wales. It might indeed have seemed a statement of the obvious to say that there is a communication in England and Wales if a message is "received" here. On the other hand, that word occurs in the relevant paragraphs of the Law Commission's Report, suggesting that that is all that the Commission intended and understood their draft provision (using the same language as section 4) to achieve[19]; and it seems improbable that the despatch at a place abroad of an unarrived demand should be declared triable here as a complete blackmail. It may be safer to treat it as a mere attempt, triable by virtue of section 3(3).[20]

Handling stolen goods may be committed by receiving stolen goods; or by **17–07** undertaking or assisting in the retention, removal, disposal or realisation of such goods; or by arranging to do either. It must be proved that the goods were "stolen"—that is, had been the subject of theft (which includes being obtained by deception or blackmail[21]). The theft may have occurred "in England or Wales or elsewhere."[22] But the question arises whether the theft is a "relevant event", as an "act ... or other event ... proof of which is required for conviction of the offence", so that handling, wherever committed, may be tried in England and Wales on the sole basis that that is where the goods were stolen. Nothing in the 1993 Act clearly qualifies the definition of a "relevant event"; and the theft is, literally, an "event ... proof of which is required." On the other hand, there is reason to believe that the definition was intended to refer only to the conduct and the results of conduct making up the "elements" of the offence itself.[23] It is thought, on balance, that the mere fact that the goods were originally stolen in England and Wales, whatever their subsequent history, does not suffice to make handling triable here; but the point is not clear.

---

[17] Theft Act 1968, s.21.
[18] [1971] A.C. 537; above, §14–12.
[19] Law Com. No. 180, paras. 2.31, 2.32.
[20] See below, §17–10.
[21] Theft Act 1968, s.24(4).
[22] *ibid.*, s.24(1).
[23] Law Com. No. 180, para. 2.28.

Inchoate offences

17–08   Conspiracy, attempt and incitement to commit a Group A offence, and conspiracy to defraud, are designated "Group B offences."[24] The general effect of the 1993 Act in relation to a Group B offence is that it becomes triable in this country (i) if the substantive offence was intended to be committed in this country (wherever the agreement was made or the act of attempt or incitement occurred), or (ii) if an act in relation to or in pursuance of an agreement, or an act of attempt or incitement, was done in this country and the agreement was for, or the attempt or incitement was directed to, the commission of an offence abroad.[25] More particularly:

Conspiracy[26]

17–09   (a) *Conspiracy to commit a Group A offence in England and Wales.* A person may be guilty, under the Criminal Law Act 1977, s.1(1), of such a conspiracy even if he became a party to it outside England and Wales, and even though no act or omission or other event in relation to the conspiracy occurred in England and Wales.[27]

    (b) *Agreement for the commission of a Group A offence outside England and Wales.* Such an agreement is an offence of conspiracy under the Criminal Law Act 1977 if two conditions are satisfied: (i) there is a local connection with the agreement: either a party to it, or a party's agent, did something in England and Wales in relation to it before its formation; or a party to it became a party in England and Wales; or a party to it, or a party's agent, did or omitted something in England and Wales in pursuance of it[28]; and (ii) the agreed course of conduct would involve commission of an offence, however described, under the relevant foreign law.[29]

Attempt

17–10   (a) *Attempt to commit a Group A offence in England and Wales.* Section 3(3) provides that a person may be guilty, under the Criminal Attempts Act 1981, s.1(1), of an attempt to commit a Group A offence although the attempt was not made and/or had no effect in England and Wales. The case evidently contemplated is that where the act constituting the attempt is intended to bring about a "relevant event"[30] in England and Wales.

---

[24] s.1(3).
[25] A person may be guilty of a Group B offence whether or not he was a British citizen, or was in England and Wales, at any material time: s.3(1).
[26] Principles stated here in relation to conspiracy to commit a Group A offence apply also, *mutatis mutandis*, to conspiracy to defraud: see ss.3(2), 5(3).
[27] s.3(2).
[28] Criminal Law Act 1977, s.1A, added by the 1993 Act, s.5(1). If any of these facts is true of one party, the conspiracy is an English conspiracy for all purposes: "We consider that if, for example, A enrols B in London, B enrols C in Paris and C enrols D in Rome, all four of them, and not only A and B, should be triable here": Law Com. No. 180, para. 5.16.
[29] s.6(1)(3). As to proof of foreign law, see above, §15–03, n. 8.
[30] See above, §17–02.

(b) *Attempt in England and Wales to commit a Group A offence outside*   **17–11**
England and Wales. If an act is done in England and Wales that is more than
merely preparatory to the commission abroad of a Group A offence, the act
would seem to be almost inevitably a "relevant event"[31] in relation to that
offence, if completed. If so, the offence would be triable here as an indictable
offence by virtue of section 2(3). It is therefore an offence to which section
1(1) of the Criminal Attempts Act applies; and the act, done with the intent
to commit it, is an attempt to commit it, contrary to that subsection.

It does not appear that much more (if anything) is added by section 5(2),
which inserts a new section 1A into the Criminal Attempts Act. This provides
that if an act (a) is done in England and Wales and (b) would fall within
section 1(1) of the Criminal Attempts Act as more than merely preparatory
to the commission of a Group A offence but for the fact that that offence, if
completed, would not be an offence triable in England and Wales, "what the
person doing the act had in view shall be treated as an offence to which section 1(1) ... applies"; which is as much as to say that the person is guilty of an
attempt to commit that offence. This is qualified by the further requirement
that what the person "had in view" would involve commission also of an
offence, however described, under the relevant foreign law.[32] But, as said
above, the intended offence most probably *would* be an offence triable in
England and Wales by virtue of a "relevant event" occurring there.

Incitement

(a) *Incitement to commit a Group A offence in England and Wales.* The   **17–12**
Law Commission recommended that such an incitement need not occur in
England and Wales; and this is undoubtedly an intended effect of the provision in section 3(1)(b) that a person may be guilty of a Group B offence
whether or not he was in England and Wales at any material time.[33] It might
have been better to provide expressly that the incitement need neither ema-
nate from nor be received in a place in England and Wales.[34]
(b) *Incitement to commit a Group A offence outside England and Wales.* If
D incites E to commit a Group A offence abroad, the incitement is not "an
act ... or other event ... proof of which is required for conviction" *of E* of the
incited offence if it occurs. So the incitement is not a "relevant event" in
relation to the Group A offence (even though proof of the incitement would
be required for conviction *of D* as a party to the offence). It seems, therefore,
that the incitement, not being of an offence triable in England and Wales,
would probably not itself be an offence but for section 5(4), as qualified by

---

[31] *ibid.*
[32] s.6(2)(3). As to proof of foreign law, see above, §15–03, n. 8.
[33] Law Com. No. 180, para. 4.14, relating to the time of any "relevant event" (defined as in s.2(1)).
[34] This appears, however, to be the position at common law, according to the broad statement of
the Privy Council in *Liangsiriprasert v. U.S. Government* [1990] 2 All E.R. 866 at 878, cited
above, n. 1.

section 6(2). The effect of these provisions, however, is that a person may be guilty of incitement of a Group A offence to be committed outside the jurisdiction if (i) the incitement takes place in England and Wales[35] and (ii) the intended offence would involve commission also of an offence, however described, under the relevant foreign law.[36]

---

[35] An incitement to commit an offence takes place in England and Wales if the communication containing the incitement is despatched abroad and received here by the incitee, or despatched here and received abroad: s.4(b).
[36] As to proof of foreign law, see above, §15–03, n. 8.

Chapter 18

RESTITUTION AND COMPENSATION

1. TITLE TO PROPERTY

Section 31(2) provides that the title to property that has been stolen or **18–01** obtained by fraud or other wrongful means shall not be affected by reason only of the conviction of the offender. It was formerly the law that if goods were stolen and a title to the goods was acquired by a third party by purchase in market overt, the effect of a conviction of the thief after such purchase was to cause the property in the goods to revest in the original owner or his personal representative. There was no justification for the continuance of this rule in modern times. The relevant statutory provisions[1] were repealed by the Act. Section 31(2) ensures, if express provision for the purpose was required, that the title to property shall depend on the operation of civil law principles and not on the outcome of criminal proceedings.

2. RESTITUTION AND COMPENSATION[2]

Not only is the title to property which has been the subject of an offence **18–02** unaffected by criminal proceedings against the offender. It is also clear that disputes concerning the title to such property are not appropriate for litigation in those proceedings. Nevertheless it is desirable to make available to criminal courts procedures whereby, in cases where no dispute as to title appears to exist, they may make orders for the restoration of property or for the compensation of losers at the conclusion of their proceedings. Special provisions for this purpose are contained in section 28, as amended.[3]

The powers of the court under section 28 may be exercised where:

"goods have been stolen and either a person is convicted of any offence with reference to the theft (whether or not the stealing is the gist of his offence) or a person is convicted of any other offence but such an offence as aforesaid is taken into consideration in determining his sentence .... " (s.28(1)).

In this context, as in that of handling, the words "stealing", "theft" and so on refer to offences of obtaining property by deception and blackmail as well as to theft, and to such offences whether committed in England or Wales or abroad (s.28(6)). "Goods" means all kinds of property except land, but including things severed from the land by stealing (s.34(2)(b)). The exact scope of the phrase "any offence with reference to the theft" is not clear. It

---

[1] Sale of Goods Act 1893, s.24(1); and see Larceny Act 1916, s.45.
[2] Hodgson et al., *The Profits of Crime and Their Recovery* (1980).
[3] See Thomas, *Current Sentencing Practice*, J3.

281

obviously includes handling. It may include offences such as conspiracy to steal, or assisting the thief contrary to the Criminal Law Act 1967, s.4(1). The phrase "taken into consideration in determining sentence" has in a related context been held to be the "well-known term of legal art" referring to the conventional procedure for the admission on conviction of further offences to which the offender invites the court to have regard in sentencing.[4]

The convicting court[5] may on the conviction, even if the passing of sentence is in other respects deferred, make any of a number of orders. These will be set out and briefly discussed; after which we shall deal with some matters relevant to the section as a whole.

Restoration of the stolen goods: s.28(1)(a)

18–03   Section 28(1)(a) empowers the court to order anyone having possession or control of stolen goods to restore them to anyone entitled to recover them from him.

Such an order can be made by the court of its own motion. But it is unlikely to be made in practice without an application. Most commonly that application will be made by the police, who may wish for their own protection to have the formal authority of a court order for the return of the goods to the victim of the offence. A return of the goods to the owner at the conclusion of the criminal proceedings without any order for that purpose being made is a course that can have its hazards.[6] Where the proceedings end in an acquittal the police, seeking judicial sanction for parting with the property to a particular claimant, must take separate proceedings for the purpose in a magistrates' court under the Police (Property) Act 1897.[7] Where there has been a conviction, an application to the convicting court under section 28(1)(a) is clearly more convenient. The paragraph may be of similar service to anyone other than the police who may have stolen property in his hands at the end of a trial.

18–04   Of course an application for restoration may be made by the victim of the offence or anyone else claiming to be entitled to recover the property. It is not appropriate to consider at length the problems of title that could theoretically arise on such an application. For the jurisdiction of the court under this section, which is entirely discretionary, should not be exercised in any case raising difficult questions of civil law. To embark upon such questions would be beyond the proper province of a criminal court. The court will

---

[4] *D.P.P. v. Anderson* [1978] A.C. 964 at 977.
[5] But where a magistrates' court commits an offender to the Crown Court for sentence, the power to make an order under s.28 passes to the Crown Court and is not to be exercised by the committing court: Criminal Justice Act 1967, s.56(5); *Blackpool JJ., ex p. Charlson and Gregory* (1972) 56 Cr.App.R. 823.
[6] See, *e.g. Winter v. Bancks* (1901) 84 L.T. 504.
[7] See below §18–15. For an illustration of the value of such proceedings to the police, see *Bullock v. Dunlop* (1876) 2 Ex.D. 43.

make an order only in a clear case.[8] Normally such a case will be one in which it is apparent that neither the offence itself nor any subsequent dealing with the property by the offender has had any effect upon the title to the property.[9] It may be anticipated, therefore, that the vast majority of orders will be made in cases of theft in the narrow sense. But they may also be made in some cases of obtaining property by deception or blackmail in which the original offender is caught before disposing of the property obtained by the offence.[10] Where a person guilty of obtaining by deception or blackmail has transferred the property to a third person (other than a person convicted of handling) there is always liable to be an issue as to title between the transferee and the original owner; for the offender may have acquired a voidable title by his offence and, if he has, may have passed a good title to his transferee[11] before his own title was avoided by the act of the victim.

Goods representing the stolen goods: s.28(1)(b)

The convicted person (the thief or a handler) may be proved to have property into which the stolen property or some part of it has been directly or indirectly converted, as by the spending of stolen money or the sale of stolen goods. A person entitled to recover such identifiable proceeds of the stolen property from the convicted person may obtain an order under section 28(1) (b) that those proceeds be delivered or transferred to him.[12] Such an order, in contrast to orders under paragraphs (a) and (c), requires an application by the person in whose favour it is to be made. He must be able to show a right under the civil law to follow the stolen goods into the goods that represent them. It must be clear that he can do this, for it will not be appropriate for the

18–05

---

[8] *Ferguson* (1970) 54 Cr.App.R. 410 (applying to s.28 the principles laid down in *Stamp v. United Dominions Trust (Commercial) Ltd.* [1967] 1 Q.B. 418, for the exercise of the corresponding jurisdiction under the Larceny Act 1916, s.45, and the Magistrates' Courts Act 1952, s.33); *Church* (1970) 55 Cr.App.R. 65. A possible reason for the refusing of an order even when the question of title is clear would be the claim of the possessor that, believing in his good title to the goods, he has improved them since acquiring them. On the making of an order under para. (a) he would not be able to obtain an allowance for the improvement, as he would in proceedings against him for wrongful interference: Torts (Interference with Goods) Act 1977, s.6(1).

[9] Mann, *The Legal Aspect of Money* (5th ed.), p. 4, says that "it is an open question whether money passed and accepted bona fide from hand to hand as currency is 'money' for the purpose of an order for restitution" (referring to "money" in the definition of "goods" in s.34(2)(b), and citing *Moss v. Hancock* [1899] 2 Q.B. 111). It is submitted that this is the wrong question. The question should be whether anyone is "entitled to recover" the money from its possessor; and the answer might well turn on the negotiable character of money as currency (compare coins as curios: *Moss v. Hancock*, above).

[10] See *George* (1901) 65 J.P. 729; *Cohen* (1907) 71 J.P. 190, in each of which property found in the possession of the prisoner was identifiable as the proceeds of property obtained by false pretences (see now s.28(1)(b), below). The prisoner's title to the property had been avoided, not by the conviction (*cf.* s.31(2)), but by the victim's disaffirmation of the transaction between himself and the prisoner. In *Cohen* the order was made against the opposition of the prisoner's trustee in bankruptcy.

[11] By virtue of the Sale of Goods Act 1979, s.23, or of corresponding common law principles.

[12] Orders may be made under both paragraph (b) and paragraph (c) of s.28(1), but not so that the person in whose favour the orders are made recovers in total more than the value of the stolen goods: s.28(2).

court to decide difficult questions of the law of tracing for the purpose of enabling itself to make an order.

The court has no power under this paragraph to order a sale of goods and the distribution of the proceeds among different losers.[13]

Money taken out of convicted person's possession: s.28(1)(c)

18–06   The convicted person may not have been found in possession of the stolen goods, but it may be clear that had they been in his possession some person (usually the victim of the offence) would have been entitled to recover them from him. In such a case the court may,[14] under section 28(1)(c), order a sum not exceeding the value of the stolen goods to be paid, out of the convicted person's money[15] taken out of his possession on his apprehension, to any person who, if those goods were in the possession of the convicted person, would be entitled to recover them from him.[16]

The Criminal Justice Act 1972, s.6(2), provides that an order under paragraph (c) may be made "without any application being made in that behalf or on the application of any person appearing to the court to be interested in the property concerned."

D may be convicted of handling part only of a larger quantity of stolen goods. If all the goods the subject of the conviction have been recovered, it is an incorrect exercise of discretion to make an order under paragraph (c) for the payment to P of money found on D so as to compensate P for the loss of the other goods with which, so far as his conviction shows, D was not concerned.[17]

"Taken out of his possession on his apprehension"

18–07   For an order to be made against a person under paragraph (c) the money must have been "taken out of his possession on his apprehension." This does not mean that it must actually have been found on his person at the time of his arrest. First, it may be found elsewhere, though in his "possession". In *Ferguson*[18] it was in a safe deposit box at Harrods store, the box being in his name and he holding the key. Secondly, it may be found some time after the arrest. In *Ferguson* the Court of Appeal had no doubt that there was power to make an order under the paragraph in respect of money found and taken 11 days after the arrest. This reading—the result of "giving the words 'on his apprehension' a common-sense meaning"[19]—is quite strikingly expansive.

---

[13] *Thibeault* (1982) 76 Cr.App.R. 201; 4 Cr.App.R.(S.) 375.
[14] With no obligation to have regard to the convicted person's means: *Lewis* [1975] Crim.L.R. 353.
[15] The limitation of para. (c) to money taken out of D's possession may have escaped attention in *Hammond* [1983] Crim.L.R. 571; see commentator's note at 572.
[16] See n. 12, above.
[17] *Parker* (1970) 54 Cr.App.R. 339. In fact there may be no power to make an order in these circumstances; the point was reserved in *Parker*.
[18] (1970) 54 Cr.App.R. 410.
[19] *ibid.*, at 412.

Perhaps the decision stretches this far and no farther: that money will be "taken out of [D's] possession on his apprehension" if it is in his legal possession (on his person; in his house or his safe deposit box; in the keeping of his servant) both when he is arrested and when it is found and taken, he being still in custody when the latter event occurs.

Although the police may lawfully have taken money out of a person's possession on his apprehension, they do not have power to retain it pending trial solely in anticipation that the court may on his conviction make an order under paragraph (c).[20]

Offenders other than thieves or handlers

The operation of paragraph (c) depends upon the hypothesis that, if the convicted person had possessed the stolen goods, the person in whose favour the order is to be made would have been entitled to recover them from him. But the victim of theft will usually be entitled to recover the stolen goods from almost anyone in possession of them. It does not seem right to make any convicted person liable to pay their value simply by notionally attributing possession to him. To be so liable he should surely be guilty either of the substantive offence or of a handling that amounts to the tort of conversion. Most convicted persons within the section will be so guilty, but not all. It is submitted that the paragraph should be interpreted (or at least applied, by virtue of the court's discretion) in this limited way.   **18–08**

Compensation for a bona fide purchaser or lender: s.28(3)

The person against whom an order for restoration of the stolen goods is made under section 28(1)(a) may be one who has, in good faith, bought the goods from the convicted person or has, in good faith, lent money to the convicted person on the security of the goods. Section 28(3) provides that in such a case the court may order the payment of compensation to the purchaser or lender out of the convicted person's money taken out of his possession on his apprehension. The compensation is not to exceed the amount paid for the goods or the amount owed in respect of the loan. The Criminal Justice Act 1972, s.6(2),[21] applies to this subsection as to section 28(1)(c).   **18–09**

Summary procedure for use in clear cases

The point has been made several times above that the jurisdiction under section 28 is only to be exercised in very clear cases.[22] The procedure is an   **18–10**

---

[20] *Malone v. Metropolitan Police Commissioner* [1980] Q.B. 49; approved by a majority of the court in *Chief Constable of Kent v. V* [1983] Q.B. 34.
[21] See above, §18–06.
[22] See cases cited in n. 8 above.

essentially summary one, to be exercised as a matter of convenience at the tail-end of a criminal trial. No procedure is provided for giving notice to a person not already before the court that he may make a claim or that an order under section 28(1)(a) may be made against him. Such a person, even though not concerned in the criminal trial, may, of course, know of the proceedings and be present for the purpose of making or resisting an application; and there is no doubt that he may be heard in person or by counsel.[23] But a third party to whom, for instance, money found in the convicted person's possession might belong has no *locus standi* before the court and might be unjustly affected by an order for payment of that money to the victim of the theft. Nor does the criminal court have the necessary machinery (especially the process of discovery) for resolving issues as to title.[24]

Materials on which and time at which order to be made

18–11   The summary nature of the procedure is further emphasised by the provisions of section 28 as to the materials on which an order under the section is to be made and as to the time for making the order.

Section 28(4) provides that none of the powers conferred by the section is to be exercised

> "unless in the opinion of the court the relevant facts sufficiently appear from evidence given at the trial or the available documents,[25] together with admissions made by or on behalf of any person in connection with any proposed exercise of the powers ..."

For the purpose of section 28(4) the trial comes to an end when sentence is passed,[26] so that there is no power to make an order based on facts appearing from evidence given after that time. And an order under section 28(1) must be made "on the conviction", which has been said to mean "immediately after the conviction".[27] All in all, the intention seems to be that the court is not to resolve disputed questions of title upon the basis of the evidence, documents and admissions referred to in section 28(4), but rather that that material, to justify an order, should reveal that there is no dispute to be resolved.

Suspension of orders

18–12   There are provisions for the suspension of orders under section 28 to allow time for appeal.

---

[23] Compare *Macklin* (1850) 5 Cox 216.
[24] *Ferguson* (1970) 54 Cr.App.R. 410. And see *Church* (1970) 55 Cr.App.R. 65, suggesting questions as to the rights of an insurance company which has paid the victim of the theft under a policy covering the stolen goods.
[25] For the meaning of this phrase, see the full text of s.28(4) in Appendix 1.
[26] *Church* (1970) 55 Cr.App.R. 65.
[27] *ibid*. The language of Lord Esher M.R. in *Justices of the Central Criminal Court* (1886) 18 Q.B.D. 314 at 318 remains appropriate; " ... it seems that the order can, and what is more, ought to be, made practically at the time of the trial; I do not say that it must be made at the minute, but it must be made as one of the conclusions of the trial."

Where any order under the section is made *by a magistrates' court*, it is automatically suspended unless (in the case of an order made under subsection (1)(a) or (b)) the court directs otherwise because it is of the opinion that title to the property affected by the order is not in dispute. The suspension is for the period for the time being prescribed by law for the giving of notice of appeal against a decision of a magistrates' court, or until the determination of an appeal of which notice was given during that period.[28]

There is similar automatic suspension of the operation of "an order for the restitution of property to a person" made *by the Crown Court*.[29] Any order under section 28 is to be treated for this purpose as an order for the restitution of property (section 28(5)). The suspension occurs unless the Crown Court[30] directs to the contrary for the reason mentioned above. It lasts until there is no further possibility of an appeal on which the order could be varied or set aside.[31]

Appeals

Order made on conviction on indictment. The Court of Appeal may by order annul or vary any order made by the court of trial under section 28, although the conviction is not quashed.[32] A convicted person may also, with leave, appeal against an order under the section as a "sentence".[33] But a person who has been refused an order or a third party claiming to be prejudiced by an order has no right of appeal,[34] though in an appropriate case he may apply for judicial review.[35] **18–13**

Order made on summary conviction. A convicted person against whom an order under section 28 is made by a magistrates' court may appeal to the Crown Court against the order by way of an appeal against sentence.[36] And any person aggrieved by an order of a magistrates' court under section 28

---

[28] Criminal Justice Act 1972, s.6(5).
[29] Criminal Appeal Court 1968, s.30(1), as substituted by the Criminal Justice Act 1988, s.17(1), Sched. 15.
[30] s.30(1) of the Criminal Appeal Act says "the Court", which usually in that Act means the Court of Appeal but must here mean the Crown Court.
[31] Disregarding any possibility of leave to appeal out of time: *ibid.*
[32] Criminal Appeal Act 1968, s.30(2) (as substituted by the Criminal Justice Act 1988, s.170(1), Sched. 15), read with the Theft Act 1968, s.28(5).
[33] Criminal Appeal Act 1968, ss.9(1), 50(1); see also *Parker* (1970) 54 Cr.App.R. 339. For appeal against an order made in respect of an offence taken into consideration, see Criminal Justice Act 1972, s.6(4)(b).
[34] He cannot appeal either to the criminal division (*Elliot* [1908] 2 K.B. 452) or to the civil division (*Justices of the Central Criminal Court* (1886) 18 Q.B.D. 314) of the Court of Appeal. (But the Criminal Appeal Rules 1968 contemplate that the Court of Appeal may wish a person "immediately affected by an order of the judge of the court of trial" to be represented at the hearing of a convicted person's appeal: rr. 22(2)(a), 25(1). A clearer right to be heard was formerly provided: Criminal Appeal Rules 1908, r. 9, now revoked.) The absence of a right of appeal is another reason why an order should not be made under s.28 except in a clear case: see *Stamp v. United Dominions Trust (Commercial) Ltd.* [1967] 1 Q.B. 418 at 430.
[35] See, *e.g. London County JJ., ex p. Dettmer & Co.* (1908) 72 J.P. 513.
[36] Magistrates' Courts Act 1980, s.108(1)(3).

may appeal to the Divisional Court by way of case stated on the ground that the order is wrong in law or is in excess of jurisdiction.[37]

Enforcement of orders under section 28

18–14   An order made under section 28 by the Crown Court will be enforceable by committal for contempt.[38]

Disobedience to an order made by a magistrates' court, other than an order for the payment of money, may be punished under the Magistrates' Courts Act 1980, s.63(3). The person in default may be ordered to pay a sum not exceeding £50 for every day during which he is in default[39] or a sum not exceeding £5,000,[40] or may be committed to custody until he has remedied his default[41] or for a period not exceeding two months.

Other procedures

18–15   There are some other procedures available either for the restoration of stolen property to its rightful owner or for the compensation by order of the criminal courts of the victims of offences under the Act.

Procedures relating to stolen property

It has already been mentioned that the police may act quite informally by returning stolen property to the owner after the termination of criminal proceedings. Alternatively, either the police or any person claiming the property can invoke the Police (Property) Act 1897, under which a magistrates' court may make an order for the delivery of the property to the person appearing to the court to be the owner.[42] If the owner cannot be ascertained the court may make "such order ... as to the ... court may seem meet."[43]

An order under the Police (Property) Act does not prevent a person taking proceedings for the recovery of property against any person in possession of it as a result of the order, but such proceedings must be brought within six months of the order.[44] In the case of property that has not been the subject of an order under section 28 or under the 1897 Act, a person claiming to be entitled to it is of course left to his civil remedies, which are unaffected by the fact that an order under section 28 has been refused or not applied for.[45]

---

[37] *ibid.*, s.111.
[38] R.S.C., Ord. 52. Compare *Wollez* (1860) 8 Cox 337.
[39] But not more than £5,000.
[40] Sum substituted by the Criminal Justice Act 1991, s.17(3), Sched. 4, Part I.
[41] But not more than two months in all.
[42] "Owner" means owner in its ordinary popular meaning of the person entitled to the goods: *Raymond Lyons & Co. Ltd. v. Metropolitan Police Commissioner* [1975] Q.B. 321. The court should not make an order under the Act except in a straightforward case where there is no real issue of law or difficulty in determining whether a person is the owner: *ibid.*, at 326.
[43] Police (Property) Act 1897, s.1(1). The Police (Disposal of Property) Regulations 1975 (S.I. 1975, No. 1474), made under s.2(1), provide for the disposal of property whose owner has not been ascertained and in respect of which no order of a competent court has been made.
[44] Police (Property) Act 1897, s.1(2).
[45] Compare *Ex p. Davison* (1896) 60 J.P. 808; *Scattergood v. Sylvester* (1850) 15 Q.B. 506.

Compensation

Under section 35 of the Powers of Criminal Courts Act 1973 (as amended)　　**18–16**
a person convicted of an offence may be ordered by the convicting court[46]

> "to pay compensation for any personal injury, loss or damage resulting from that
> offence or any other offence which is taken into consideration[47] by the court in
> determining sentence" (subs. (1)).

The order may be made "instead of or in addition to dealing with [the
offender] in any other way." In the case of an offence under the Theft Act,

> "where the property . . . is recovered, any damage to the property[48] occurring while
> it was out of the owner's possession shall be treated . . . as having resulted from the
> offence, however and by whomsoever the damage was caused" (subs. (2)).

Compensation orders made by a magistrates' court are subject to a maximum of £5,000 in respect of any offence of which the court has convicted the
offender, and in effect, where compensation is ordered in respect of offences
taken into consideration by a magistrates' court, the total compensation in
respect of all offences may not exceed £5,000 multiplied by the number of
offences of which the offender has been convicted.[49]

In determining whether to make an order, or the amount of compensation　　**18–17**
to be paid, a court must have regard to the offender's means so far as they
appear or are known to the court (subs. (4)). The court will decide what
amount is "appropriate, having regard to any evidence and to any representations that are made on behalf of the accused or the prosecutor" (subs.
(1A)).
　　Where both a fine and a compensation order would be appropriate, but the
offender has insufficient means to pay both, the court is to give preference to
compensation (subs. (4A)). A sentencing court must give reasons for not
making a compensation order where it has power to do so (subs. (1)).
　　The principles governing the making of compensation orders are elaborated in a substantial case law, for which reference should be made to works
on sentencing.[50]

---

[46] But see n. 5, above, reading that note as applying to compensation orders as to orders under
s.28.
[47] That is, is the subject of formal "t.i.c." procedure: compare *D.P.P. v. Anderson* [1978] A.C. 964
(above, n. 4).
[48] But not, in the case of taking a car without consent contrary to s.12, other property damaged by
the offender when driving the car: *Quigley v. Stokes* (1976) 64 Cr.App.R. 198 (see subs. (3)).
[49] This is the effect of the Magistrates' Courts Act 1980, s.40(1) (formerly Powers of Criminal
Courts Act 1973, s.35(5)), as amended by the Criminal Justice Act 1991, s.17(3), Sched. 4, Part I.
[50] *e.g.* Thomas, *Current Sentencing Practice*, J2.

APPENDIX 1

Theft Act 1968

(1968 c. 60)

ARRANGEMENT OF SECTIONS

Definition of "theft"

Theft, robbery, burglary, etc.

Fraud and blackmail

Offences relating to goods stolen, etc.

Possession of house-breaking implements, etc.

Enforcement and procedure

General and consequential provisions

Supplementary

An Act to revise the law of England and Wales as to theft and similar or associated offences, and in connection therewith to make provision as to criminal proceedings by one party to a marriage against the other, and to make certain amendments extending beyond England and Wales in the Post Office Act 1953 and other enactments; and for other purposes connected therewith. [26th July 1968]

Definition of "theft"

Basic definition of theft

1.—(1) A person is guilty of theft if he dishonestly appropriates property **19–01** belonging to another with the intention of permanently depriving the other of it; and "thief" and "steal" shall be construed accordingly.

(2) It is immaterial whether the appropriation is made with a view to gain, or is made for the thief's own benefit.

(3) The five following sections of this Act shall have effect as regards the

interpretation and operation of this section (and, except as otherwise provided by this Act, shall apply only for purposes of this section).

"Dishonestly"

19–02   **2.**—(1) A person's appropriation of property belonging to another is not to be regarded as dishonest—

(a) if he appropriates the property in the belief that he has in law the right to deprive the other of it, on behalf of himself or of a third person; or

(b) if he appropriates the property in the belief that he would have the other's consent if the other knew of the appropriation and the circumstances of it; or

(c) (except where the property came to him as trustee or personal representative) if he appropriates the property in the belief that the person to whom the property belongs cannot be discovered by taking reasonable steps.

(2) A person's appropriation of property belonging to another may be dishonest notwithstanding that he is willing to pay for the property.

"Appropriates"

19–03   **3.**—(1) Any assumption by a person of the rights of an owner amounts to an appropriation, and this includes, where he has come by the property (innocently or not) without stealing it, any later assumption of a right to it by keeping or dealing with it as owner.

(2) Where property or a right or interest in property is or purports to be transferred for value to a person acting in good faith, no later assumption by him of rights which he believed himself to be acquiring shall, by reason of any defect in the transferor's title, amount to theft of the property.

"Property"

19–04   **4.**—(1) "Property" includes money and all other property, real or personal, including things in action and other intangible property.

(2) A person cannot steal land, or things forming part of land and severed from it by him or by his directions, except in the following cases, that is to say—

(a) when he is a trustee or personal representative, or is authorised by power of attorney, or as liquidator of a company, or otherwise, to sell or dispose of land belonging to another, and he appropriates the land or anything forming part of it by dealing with it in breach of the confidence reposed in him; or

(b) when he is not in possession of the land and appropriates anything forming part of the land by severing it or causing it to be severed or after it has been severed; or

(c) when, being in possession of the land under a tenancy, he appropriates the whole or part of any fixture or structure let to be used with the land.

For purposes of this subsection "land" does not include incorporeal hereditaments; "tenancy" means a tenancy for years or any less period and includes an agreement for such a tenancy, but a person who after the end of a tenancy remains in possession as statutory tenant or otherwise is to be treated as having possession under the tenancy, and "let" shall be construed accordingly.

(3) A person who picks mushrooms growing wild on any land, or who picks flowers, fruit or foliage from a plant growing wild on any land does not (although not in possession of the land) steal what he picks, unless he does it for reward or for sale or other commercial purpose.

For purposes of this subsection "mushroom" includes any fungus, and "plant" includes any shrub or tree.

(4) Wild creatures, tamed or untamed, shall be regarded as property; but a person cannot steal a wild creature not tamed nor ordinarily kept in captivity, or the carcase of any such creature, unless either it has been reduced into possession by or on behalf of another person and possession of it has not since been lost or abandoned, or another person is in course of reducing it into possession.

"Belonging to another"

5.—(1) Property shall be regarded as belonging to any person having possession or control of it, or having in it any proprietary right or interest (not being an equitable interest arising only from an agreement to transfer or grant an interest). **19–05**

(2) Where property is subject to a trust, the persons to whom it belongs shall be regarded as including any person having a right to enforce the trust, and an intention to defeat the trust shall be regarded accordingly as an intention to deprive of the property any person having that right.

(3) Where a person receives property from or on account of another, and is under an obligation to the other to retain and deal with that property or its proceeds in a particular way, the property or proceeds shall be regarded (as against him) as belonging to the other.

(4) Where a person gets property by another's mistake, and is under an obligation to make restoration (in whole or in part) of the property or its proceeds or of the value thereof, then to the extent of that obligation the property or proceeds shall be regarded (as against him) as belonging to the person entitled to restoration, and an intention not to make restoration shall be regarded accordingly as an intention to deprive that person of the property or proceeds.

(5) Property of a corporation sole shall be regarded as belonging to the corporation notwithstanding a vacancy in the corporation.

"With the intention of permanently depriving the other of it"

19–06   **6.**—(1) A person appropriating property belonging to another without meaning the other permanently to lose the thing itself is nevertheless to be regarded as having the intention of permanently depriving the other of it if his intention is to treat the thing as his own to dispose of regardless of the other's rights; and a borrowing or lending of it may amount to so treating it if, but only if, the borrowing or lending is for a period and in circumstances making it equivalent to an outright taking or disposal.

(2) Without prejudice to the generality of subsection (1) above, where a person, having possession or control (lawfully or not) of property belonging to another, parts with the property under a condition as to its return which he may not be able to perform, this (if done for purposes of his own and without the other's authority) amounts to treating the property as his own to dispose of regardless of the other's rights.

Theft, robbery, burglary, etc.

Theft

19–07   **7.** A person guilty of theft shall on conviction on indictment be liable to imprisonment for a term not exceeding ten years.

Robbery

19–08   **8.**—(1) A person is guilty of robbery if he steals, and immediately before or at the time of doing so, and in order to so, he uses force on any person or puts or seeks to put any person in fear of being then and there subjected to force.

(2) Any person guilty of robbery, or of an assault with intent to rob, shall on conviction on indictment be liable to imprisonment for life.

Burglary

19–09   **9.**—(1) A person is guilty of burglary if—

   (a)   he enters a building or part of a building as a trespasser and with intent to commit any such offence as is mentioned in subsection (2) below; or
   (b)   having entered any building or part of a building as a trespasser he steals or attempts to steal anything in the building or that part of it or inflicts or attempts to inflict on any person therein any grievous bodily harm.

(2) The offences referred to in subsection (1)(a) above are offences of stealing anything in the building or part of a building in question, of inflicting on any person therein any grievous bodily harm or [raping any person] therein, and doing unlawful damage to the building or anything therein.

[(3) A person guilty of burglary shall on conviction on indictment be liable to imprisonment for a term not exceeding—

(a) where the offence was committed in respect of a building or part of a building which is a dwelling, fourteen years;
(b) in any other case, ten years.

(4) References in subsections (1) and (2) above to a building, and the reference in subsection (3) above to a building which is a dwelling, shall apply also to an inhabited vehicle or vessel, and shall apply to any such vehicle or vessel at times when the person having a habitation in it is not there as well as at times when he is.]

[*The words in square brackets in subsection (2) were substituted by the Criminal Justice and Public Order Act 1994, s. 168(2) and Sched. 10, para. 26. Subsections (3) and (4) were substituted by the Criminal Justice Act 1991, s. 26(2).*]

Aggravated burglary

10.—(1) A person is guilty of aggravated burglary if he commits any bur-   **19–10** glary and at the time has with him any firearm or imitation firearm, any weapon of offence, or any explosive; and for this purpose—

(a) "firearm" includes an airgun or air pistol, and "imitation firearm" means anything which has the appearance of being a firearm, whether capable of being discharged or not; and
(b) "weapon of offence" means any article made or adapted for use for causing injury to or incapacitating a person, or intended by the person having it with him for such use; and
(c) "explosive" means any article manufactured for the purpose of producing a practical effect by explosion, or intended by the person having it with him for that purpose.

(2) A person guilty of aggravated burglary shall on conviction on indictment be liable to imprisonment for life.

Removal of articles from places open to the public

11.—(1) Subject to subsections (2) and (3) below, where the public have   **19–11** access to a building in order to view the building or part of it, or a collection or part of a collection housed in it, any person who without lawful authority removes from the building or its grounds the whole or part of any article displayed or kept for display to the public in the building or that part of it or in its grounds shall be guilty of an offence.

For this purpose "collection" includes a collection got together for a temporary purpose, but references in this section to a collection do not apply to a collection made or exhibited for the purpose of effecting sales or other commercial dealings.

(2) It is immaterial for purposes of subsection (1) above, that the public's

access to a building is limited to a particular period or particular occasion; but where anything removed from a building or its grounds is there otherwise than as forming part of, or being on loan for exhibition with, a collection intended for permanent exhibition to the public, the person removing it does not thereby commit an offence under this section unless he removes it on a day when the public have access to the building as mentioned in subsection (1) above.

(3) A person does not commit an offence under this section if he believes that he has lawful authority for the removal of the thing in question or that he would have it if the person entitled to give it knew of the removal and the circumstances of it.

(4) A person guilty of an offence under this section shall, on conviction on indictment, be liable to imprisonment for a term not exceeding five years.

Taking motor vehicle or other conveyance without authority

19–12   **12.**—(1) Subject to subsections (5) and (6) below, a person shall be guilty of an offence if, without having the consent of the owner or other lawful authority, he takes any conveyance for his own or another's use or, knowing that any conveyance has been taken without such authority, drives it or allows himself to be carried in or on it.

(2) A person guilty of an offence under subsection (1) above shall [be liable on summary conviction to a fine not exceeding level 5 on the standard scale, to imprisonment for a term not exceeding six months, or to both].

[(3) *Repealed by the Police and Criminal Evidence Act* 1984, *s.*18, *Sched.* 7.]

(4) If on the trial of an indictment for theft the jury are not satisfied that the accused committed theft, but it is proved that the accused committed an offence under subsection (1) above, the jury may find him guilty of the offence under subsection (1) [and if he is found guilty of it, he shall be liable as he would have been liable under subsection (2) above on summary conviction].

(5) Subsection (1) above shall not apply in relation to pedal cycles; but, subject to subsection (6) below, a person who, without having the consent of the owner or other lawful authority, takes a pedal cycle for his own or another's use, or rides a pedal cycle knowing it to have been taken without such authority, shall on summary conviction be liable to a fine not exceeding [level 2 on the standard scale].

(6) A person does not commit an offence under this section by anything done in the belief that he has lawful authority to do it or that he would have the owner's consent if the owner knew of his doing it and the circumstances of it.

(7) For purposes of this section—

(a) "conveyance" means any conveyance constructed or adapted for the carriage of a person or persons whether by land, water or air, except that it does not include a conveyance constructed or adapted for use only under the control of a person not carried in or on it, and "drive" shall be construed accordingly; and

(b) "owner," in relation to a conveyance which is the subject of a hiring agreement or hire-purchase agreement, means the person in possession of the conveyance under that agreement.

[*Subsections* (2) *and* (4) *were amended by the Criminal Justice Act* 1988, *s.*37(1). *Subsection* (5) *was amended by the Criminal Justice Act* 1982, *s.*46(1).]

Aggravated vehicle-taking

12A.—(1) Subject to subsection (3) below, a person is guilty of aggravated taking of a vehicle if— **19–12A**

(a) he commits an offence under section 12(1) above (in this section referred to as a "basic offence") in relation to a mechanically propelled vehicle; and
(b) it is proved that, at any time after the vehicle was unlawfully taken (whether by him or another) and before it was recovered, the vehicle was driven, or injury or damage was caused, in one or more of the circumstances set out in paragraphs (a) to (d) of subsection (2) below.

(2) The circumstances referred to in subsection (1)(b) above are—

(a) that the vehicle was driven dangerously on a road or other public place;
(b) that, owing to the driving of the vehicle, an accident occurred by which injury was caused to any person;
(c) that, owing to the driving of the vehicle, an accident occurred by which damage was caused to any property, other than the vehicle;
(d) that damage was caused to the vehicle.

(3) A person is not guilty of an offence under this section if he proves that, as regards any such proven driving, injury or damage as is referred to in subsection (1)(b) above, either—

(a) the driving, accident or damage referred to in subsection (2) above occurred before he committed the basic offence; or
(b) he was neither in nor on nor in the immediate vicinity of the vehicle when that driving, accident or damage occurred.

(4) A person guilty of an offence under this section shall be liable on conviction on indictment to imprisonment for a term not exceeding two years or, if it is proved that, in circumstances falling within subsection (2)(b) above, the accident caused the death of the person concerned, five years.

(5) If a person who is charged with an offence under this section is found not guilty of that offence but it is proved that he committed a basic offence, he may be convicted of the basic offence.

(6) If by virtue of subsection (5) above a person is convicted of a basic offence before the Crown Court, that court shall have the same power and duties as a magistrates' court would have had on convicting him of such an offence.

(7) For the purposes of this section a vehicle is driven dangerously if—

    (a) it is driven in a way which falls far below what would be expected of a competent and careful driver; and

    (b) it would be obvious to a competent and careful driver that driving the vehicle in that way would be dangerous.

(8) For the purposes of this section a vehicle is recovered when it is restored to its owner or to other lawful possession or custody; and in this subsection "owner" has the same meaning as in section 12 above.

[*This section was added by the Aggravated Vehicle-Taking Act* 1992, *s.*1(1).]

Abstracting of electricity

19–13   **13.** A person who dishonestly uses without due authority, or dishonestly causes to be wasted or diverted, any electricity shall on conviction on indictment be liable to imprisonment for a term not exceeding five years.

Extension to thefts from mails outside England and Wales, and robbery, etc. on such a theft

19–14   **14.**—(1) Where a person—

    (a) steals or attempts to steal any mail bag or postal packet in the course of transmission as such between places in different jurisdictions in the British postal area, or any of the contents of such a mail bag or postal packet; or

    (b) in stealing or with intent to steal any such mail bag or postal packet or any of its contents, commits any robbery, attempted robbery or assault with intent to rob;

then, notwithstanding that he does so outside England and Wales, he shall be guilty of committing or attempting to commit the offence against this Act as if he had done so in England or Wales, and he shall accordingly be liable to be prosecuted, tried and punished in England and Wales without proof that the offence was committed there.

(2) In subsection (1) above the reference to different jurisdictions in the British postal area is to be construed as referring to the several jurisdictions of England and Wales, of Scotland, of Northern Ireland, of the Isle of Man and of the Channel Islands.

(3) For purposes of this section "mail bag" includes any article serving the purpose of a mail bag.

Fraud and blackmail

Obtaining property by deception

15.—(1) A person who by any deception dishonestly obtains property **19–15** belonging to another, with the intention of permanently depriving the other of it, shall on conviction on indictment be liable to imprisonment for a term not exceeding ten years.

(2) For purposes of this section a person is to be treated as obtaining property if he obtains ownership, possession or control of it, and "obtain" includes obtaining for another or enabling another to obtain or to retain.

(3) Section 6 above shall apply for purposes of this section, with the necessary adaptations of the reference to appropriating, as it applies for purposes of section 1.

(4) For purposes of this section "deception" means any deception (whether deliberate or reckless) by words or conduct as to fact or as to law, including a deception as to the present intentions of the person using the deception or any other person.

Obtaining pecuniary advantage by deception

16.—(1) A person who by any deception dishonestly obtains for himself or **19–16** another any pecuniary advantage shall on conviction on indictment be liable to imprisonment for a term not exceeding five years.

(2) The cases in which a pecuniary advantage within the meaning of this section is to be regarded as obtained for a person are cases where—

[(a) *any debt or charge for which he makes himself liable or is or may become liable (including one not legally enforceable) is reduced or in whole or in part evaded or deferred; or*]

(b) he is allowed to borrow by way of overdraft, or to take out any policy of insurance or annuity contract, or obtains an improvement of the terms on which he is allowed to do so; or

(c) he is given the opportunity to earn remuneration or greater remuneration in an office or employment, or to win money by betting.

(3) For purposes of this section "deception" has the same meaning as in section 15 of this Act.

[*Subsection* (2)(a) *was repealed by the Theft Act* 1978, *s.5(5).*]

False accounting

19–17   **17.**—(1) Where a person dishonestly, with a view to gain for himself or another or with intent to cause loss to another,—

(a) destroys, defaces, conceals or falsifies any account or any record or document made or required for any accounting purpose; or
(b) in furnishing information for any purpose produces or makes use of any account, or any such record or document as aforesaid, which to his knowledge is or may be misleading, false or deceptive in a material particular;

he shall, on conviction on indictment, be liable to imprisonment for a term not exceeding seven years.

(2) For purposes of this section a person who makes or concurs in making in an account or other document an entry which is or may be misleading, false or deceptive in a material particular, or who omits or concurs in omitting a material particular from an account or other document, is to be treated as falsifying the account or document.

Liability of company officers for certain offences by company

19–18   **18.**—(1) Where an offence committed by a body corporate under section 15, 16 or 17 of this Act is proved to have been committed with the consent or connivance of any director, manager, secretary or other similar officer of the body corporate, or any person who was purporting to act in any such capacity, he as well as the body corporate shall be guilty of that offence, and shall be liable to be proceeded against and punished accordingly.

(2) Where the affairs of a body corporate are managed by its members, this section shall apply in relation to the acts and defaults of a member in connection with his functions of management as if he were a director of the body corporate.

False statements by company directors, etc.

19–19   **19.**—(1) Where an officer of a body corporate or unincorporated association (or person purporting to act as such), with intent to deceive members or creditors of the body corporate or association about its affairs, publishes or concurs in publishing a written statement or account which to his knowledge is or may be misleading, false or deceptive in a material particular, he shall on conviction on indictment be liable to imprisonment for a term not exceeding seven years.

(2) For purposes of this section a person who has entered into a security for the benefit of a body corporate or association is to be treated as a creditor of it.

(3) Where the affairs of a body corporate or association are managed by its members, this section shall apply to any statement which a member publishes or concurs in publishing in connection with his functions of management as if he were an officer of the body corporate or association.

Suppression, etc. of documents

20.—(1) A person who dishonestly, with a view to gain for himself or an-   **19–20**
other or with intent to cause loss to another, destroys, defaces or conceals any valuable security, any will or other testamentary document or any original document of or belonging to, or filed or deposited in, any court of justice or any government department shall on conviction on indictment be liable to imprisonment for a term not exceeding seven years.

(2) A person who dishonestly, with a view to gain for himself or another or with intent to cause loss to another, by any deception procures the execution of a valuable security shall on conviction on indictment be liable to imprisonment for a term not exceeding seven years; and this subsection shall apply in relation to the making, acceptance, indorsement, alteration, cancellation or destruction in whole or in part of a valuable security, and in relation to the signing or sealing of any paper or other material in order that it may be made or converted into, or used or dealt with as, a valuable security, as if that were the execution of a valuable security.

(3) For purposes of this section "deception" has the same meaning as in section 15 of this Act, and "valuable security" means any document creating, transferring, surrendering or releasing any right to, in or over property, or authorising the payment of money or delivery of any property or evidencing the creation, transfer, surrender or release of any such right, or the payment of money or delivery of any property, or the satisfaction of any obligation.

Blackmail

21.—(1) A person is guilty of blackmail if, with a view to gain for himself or   **19–21**
another or with intent to cause loss to another, he makes any unwarranted demand with menaces; and for this purpose a demand with menaces is unwarranted unless the person making it does so in the belief—

(a) that he has reasonable grounds for making the demand; and
(b) that the use of the menaces is a proper means of reinforcing the demand.

(2) The nature of the act or omission demanded is immaterial, and it is also immaterial whether the menaces relate to action to be taken by the person making the demand.

(3) A person guilty of blackmail shall on conviction on indictment be liable to imprisonment for a term not exceeding fourteen years.

Offences relating to goods stolen, etc.

Handling stolen goods

19–22   **22.**—(1) A person handles stolen goods if (otherwise than in the course of the stealing) knowing or believing them to be stolen goods he dishonestly receives the goods, or dishonestly undertakes or assists in their retention, removal, disposal or realisation by or for the benefit of another person, of if he arranges to do so.

(2) A person guilty of handling stolen goods shall on conviction on indictment be liable to imprisonment for a term not exceeding fourteen years.

Advertising rewards for return of goods stolen or lost

19–23   **23.** Where any public advertisement of a reward for the return of any goods which have been stolen or lost uses any words to the effect that no questions will be asked, or that the person producing the goods will be safe from apprehension or inquiry, or that any money paid for the purchase of the goods or advanced by way of loan on them will be repaid, the person advertising the reward and any person who prints or publishes the advertisement shall on summary conviction be liable to a fine not exceeding one hundred pounds.

Scope of offences relating to stolen goods

19–24   **24.**—(1) The provisions of this Act relating to goods which have been stolen shall apply whether the stealing occurred in England or Wales or elsewhere, and whether it occurred before or after the commencement of this Act, provided that the stealing (if not an offence under this Act) amounted to an offence where and at the time when the goods were stolen; and references to stolen goods shall be construed accordingly.

(2) For purposes of those provisions references to stolen goods shall include, in addition to the goods originally stolen and parts of them (whether in their original state or not),—

(a)   any other goods which directly or indirectly represent or have at any time represented the stolen goods in the hands of the thief as being the proceeds of any disposal or realisation of the whole or part of the goods stolen or of goods so representing the stolen goods; and

(b)   any other goods which directly or indirectly represent or have at any time represented the stolen goods in the hands of a handler of the stolen goods or any part of them as being the proceeds of any disposal or realisation of the whole or part of the stolen goods handled by him or of goods so representing them.

(3) But no goods shall be regarded as having continued to be stolen goods after they have been restored to the person from whom they were stolen or to other lawful possession or custody, or after that person and any other person claiming through him have otherwise ceased as regards those goods to have any right to restitution in respect of the theft.

(4) For purposes of the provisions of this Act relating to goods which have been stolen (including subsections (1) to (3) above) goods obtained in England or Wales or elsewhere either by blackmail or in the circumstances described in section 15(1) of this Act shall be regarded as stolen; and "steal," "theft" and "thief" shall be construed accordingly.

Possession of housebreaking implements, etc.

Going equipped for stealing, etc.

25.—(1) A person shall be guilty of an offence if, when not at his place of abode, he has with him any article for use in the course of or in connection with any burglary, theft or cheat.   **19–25**

(2) A person guilty of an offence under this section shall on conviction on indictment be liable to imprisonment for a term not exceeding three years.

(3) Where a person is charged with an offence under this section, proof that he had with him any article made or adapted for use in committing a burglary, theft or cheat shall be evidence that he had it with him for such use.

(4) Any person may arrest without warrant anyone who is, or whom he, with reasonable cause, suspects to be, committing an offence under this section.

(5) For purposes of this section an offence under section 12(1) of this Act of taking a conveyance shall be treated as theft, and "cheat" means an offence under section 15 of this Act.

Enforcement and procedure

Search for stolen goods

26.—(1) If it is made to appear by information on oath before a justice of the peace that there is reasonable cause to believe that any person has in his custody or possession or on his premises any stolen goods, the justice may grant a warrant to search for and seize the same; but no warrant to search for stolen goods shall be addressed to a person other than a constable except under the authority of an enactment expressly so providing.   **19–26**

[(2) *Repealed by the Police and Criminal Evidence Act* 1984, *s.*18, *Sched.* 7.]

(3) Where under this section a person is authorised to search premises for stolen goods, he may enter and search the premises accordingly, and may seize any goods he believes to be stolen goods.

[(4) *Repealed by the Criminal Justice Act* 1972, *s.*64(2), *Sched.* 6.]

(5) This section is to be construed in accordance with section 24 of this Act; and in subsection (2) above the references to handling stolen goods shall include any corresponding offence committed before the commencement of this Act.

Evidence and procedure on charge of theft or handling stolen goods

19–27   27.—(1) Any number of persons may be charged in one indictment, with reference to the same theft, with having at different times or at the same time handled all or any of the stolen goods, and the persons so charged may be tried together.

(2) On the trial of two or more persons indicted for jointly handling any stolen goods the jury may find any of the accused guilty if the jury are satisfied that he handled all or any of the stolen goods, whether or not he did so jointly with the other accused or any of them.

(3) Where a person is being proceeded against for handling stolen goods (but not for any offence other than handling stolen goods), then at any stage of the proceedings, if evidence has been given of his having or arranging to have in his possession the goods the subject of the charge, or of his undertaking or assisting in, or arranging to undertake or assist in, their retention, removal, disposal or realisation, the following evidence shall be admissible for the purpose of proving that he knew or believed the goods to be stolen goods:—

(a) evidence that he has had in his possession, or has undertaken or assisted in the retention, removal, disposal or realisation of, stolen goods from any theft taking place not earlier than twelve months before the offence charged; and

(b) (provided that seven days' notice in writing has been given to him of the intention to prove the conviction) evidence that he has within the five years preceding the date of the offence charged been convicted of theft or of handling stolen goods.

(4) In any proceedings for the theft of anything in the course of transmission (whether by post or otherwise), or for handling stolen goods from such a theft, a statutory declaration made by any person that he despatched or received or failed to receive any goods or postal packet, or that any goods or postal packet when despatched or received by him were in a particular state or condition, shall be admissible as evidence of the facts stated in the declaration, subject to the following conditions:—

(a) a statutory declaration shall only be admissible where and to the extent to which oral evidence to the like effect would have been admissible in the proceedings; and

(b) a statutory declaration shall only be admissible if at least seven days before the hearing or trial a copy of it has been given to the person charged, and he has not, at least three days before the hearing of trial or within such further time as the court may in special circumstances allow, given the prosecutor written notice requiring the attendance at the hearing or trial of the person making the declaration.

(5) This section is to be construed in accordance with section 24 of this Act;

and in subsection (3)(b) above the reference to handling stolen goods shall include any corresponding offence committed before the commencement of this Act.

Orders for restitution

28.—(1) Where goods have been stolen, and either a person is convicted of **19–28** any offence with reference to the theft (whether or not the stealing is the gist of his offence) or a person is convicted of any other offence but such an offence as aforesaid is taken into consideration in determining his sentence, the court by or before which the offender is convicted may on the conviction [(whether or not the passing of sentence is in other respects deferred)] exercise any of the following powers—

   (a) the court may order anyone having possession or control of the goods to restore them to any person entitled to recover them from him; or

   (b) on the application of a person entitled to recover from the person convicted any other goods directly or indirectly representing the first-mentioned goods (as being the proceeds of any disposal or realisation of the whole or part of them or of goods so representing them), the court may order those other goods to be delivered or transferred to the applicant; or

   (c) the court may order that a sum not exceeding the value of the first-mentioned goods shall be paid, out of any money of the person convicted which was taken out of his possession on his apprehension, to any person who, if those goods were in the possession of the person convicted, would be entitled to recover them from him.

(2) Where under subsection (1) above the court has power on a person's conviction to make an order against him both under paragraph (b) and under paragraph (c) with reference to the stealing of the same goods, the court may make orders under both paragraphs provided that the person in whose favour the orders are made does not thereby recover more than the value of those goods.

(3) Where under subsection (1) above the court on a person's conviction makes an order under paragraph (a) for the restoration of any goods, and it appears to the court that the person convicted has sold the goods to a person acting in good faith, or has borrowed money on the security of them from a person so acting, the court may order that there shall be paid to the purchaser or lender, out of any money of the person convicted which was taken out of his possession on his apprehension, a sum not exceeding the amount paid for the purchase by the purchaser or, as the case may be, the amount owed to the lender in respect of the loan.

(4) The court shall not exercise the powers conferred by this section unless in the opinion of the court the relevant facts sufficiently appear from evidence given at the trial or the available documents, together with admissions made by or on behalf of any person in connection with any proposed exercise

of the powers; and for this purpose "the available documents" means any written statements or admissions which were made for use, and would have been admissible, as evidence at the trial, the depositions taken at any committal proceedings and any written statements or admissions used as evidence in those proceedings.

(5) Any order under this section shall be treated as an order for the restitution of property within the meaning of [section 30 of the Criminal Appeal Act 1968 (which relates to the effect on such orders of appeals)].

(6) References in this section to stealing are to be construed in accordance with section 24(1) and (4) of this Act.

(7) An order may be made under this section in respect of money owed by the Crown.

[*Subsections* (1) (*other than the words in square brackets*), (2) *and* (3) *are printed as substituted by the Criminal Justice Act* 1972, *s.*64(1), *Sched.* 5. *The words in square brackets in subsection* (1) *were added by the Criminal Law Act* 1977, *s.*65(4), *Sched.* 12. *The words in square brackets in subsection* (5) *were substituted by the Criminal Justice Act* 1988, *s.*170(1), *Sched.* 15. *Subsection* (7) *was added by ibid. s.*163.]

Jurisdiction of quarter sessions, and summary trial

19–29   **29.**—[(1) *Repealed by the Courts Act* 1971, *s.*56, *Sched.* 11.]
[(2) *Repealed by the Criminal Law Act* 1977, *s.*65(5), *Sched.* 13.]

General and consequential provisions

Husband and wife

19–30   **30.**—(1) This Act shall apply in relation to the parties to a marriage, and to property belonging to the wife or husband whether or not by reason of an interest derived from the marriage, as it would apply if they were not married and any such interest subsisted independently of the marriage.

(2) Subject to subsection (4) below, a person shall have the same right to bring proceedings against that person's wife or husband for any offence (whether under this Act or otherwise), as if they were not married, and a person bringing any such proceedings shall be competent to give evidence for the prosecution at every stage of the proceedings.

[(3) *Repealed by the Police and Criminal Evidence Act* 1984, *s.*18, *Sched.* 7.]

(4) Proceedings shall not be instituted against a person for any offence of stealing or doing unlawful damage to property which at the time of the offence belongs to that person's wife or husband, or for any attempt, incitement or conspiracy to commit such an offence, unless the proceedings are instituted by or with the consent of the Director of Public Prosecutions:
Provided that—

   (a) this subsection shall not apply to proceedings against a person for an
       offence—

(i) if that person is charged with committing the offence jointly with the wife or husband; or

(ii) if by virtue of any judicial decree or order (wherever made) that person and the wife or husband are at the time of the offence under no obligation to cohabit [*and*

(b) *Repealed by the Criminal Jurisdiction Act* 1975, *s.*14(5), *Sched.* 6.]

(5) Notwithstanding [section 6 of the Prosecution of Offences Act 1979] subsection (4) of this section shall apply—

(a) to an arrest (if without warrant) made by the wife or husband, and
(b) to a warrant of arrest issued on an information laid by the wife or husband.

[*Subsection* (5) *was added by the Criminal Jurisdiction Act* 1975, *s.*14(4), *Sched.* 5. *The words in square brackets were substituted by the Prosecution of Offences Act* 1979, *s.*11(1), *Sched.* 1.]

Effect on civil proceedings and rights

31.—(1) A person shall not be excused, by reason that to do so may **19–31** incriminate that person or the wife or husband of that person of an offence under this Act—

(a) from answering any question put to that person in proceedings for the recovery or administration of any property, for the execution of any trust or for an account of any property or dealings with property; or
(b) from complying with any order made in any such proceedings;

but no statement or admission made by a person in answering a question put or complying with an order made as aforesaid shall, in proceedings for an offence under this Act, be admissible in evidence against that person or (unless they married after the making of the statement of admission) against the wife or husband of that person.

(2) Notwithstanding any enactment to the contrary, where property has been stolen or obtained by fraud or other wrongful means, the title to that or any other property shall not be affected by reason only of the conviction of the offender.

Effect on existing law and construction of references to offences

32.—(1) The following offences are hereby abolished for all purposes not **19–32** relating to offences committed before the commencement of this Act, that is to say—

(a) any offence at common law of larceny, robbery, burglary, receiving stolen property, obtaining property by threats, extortion by colour of office or franchise, false accounting by public officers, concealment of treasure trove and, except as regards offences relating to the public revenue, cheating; and

(b) any offence under an enactment mentioned in Part 1 of Schedule 3 to
this Act, to the extent to which the offence depends on any section or
part of a section included in column 3 of that Schedule;

but so that the provisions in Schedule 1 to this Act (which preserve with
modifications certain offences under the Larceny Act 1861 of taking or killing deer and taking or destroying fish) shall have effect as there set out.

(2) Except as regards offences committed before the commencement of
this Act, and except in so far as the context otherwise requires,—

(a) references in any enactment passed before this Act to an offence abolished by this Act shall, subject to any express amendment or repeal
made by this Act, have effect as references to the corresponding
offence under this Act, and in any such enactment the expression
"receive" (when it relates to an offence of receiving) shall mean
handle, and "receiver" shall be construed accordingly; and

(b) without prejudice to paragraph (a) above, references in any enactment, whenever passed, to theft or stealing (including references to
stolen goods), and references to robbery, blackmail, burglary, aggravated burglary or handling stolen goods, shall be construed in accordance with the provisions of this Act, including those of section 24.

Miscellaneous and consequential amendments, and repeal

33.—(1) The Post Office Act 1953 shall have effect subject to the amendments provided for by Part I of Schedule 2 to this Act and (except in so far as
the contrary intention appears) those amendments shall have effect throughout the British postal area.

(2) The enactments mentioned in Parts II and III of Schedule 2 to this Act
shall have effect subject to the amendments there provided for, and (subject
to subsection (4) below) the amendments made by Part II to enactments
extending beyond England and Wales shall have the like extent as the enactment amended.

(3) The enactments mentioned in Schedule 3 to this Act (which include in
Part II certain enactments related to the subject matter of this Act but already obsolete or redundant apart from this Act) are hereby repealed to the
extent specified in column 3 of that schedule; and, notwithstanding that the
foregoing sections of this Act do not extend to Scotland, where any enactment expressed to be repealed by Schedule 3 does so extend, the Schedule
shall have effect to repeal it in its application to Scotland except in so far as
the repeal is expressed not to extend to Scotland.

(4) No amendment or repeal made by this Act in Schedule 1 to the Extradition Act 1870 or in the Schedule to the Extradition Act 1873 shall affect the
operation of that Schedule by reference to the law of a British possession; but
the repeal made in Schedule 1 to the Extradition Act 1870 shall extend
throughout the United Kingdom.

Supplementary

Interpretation

34.—(1) Sections 4(1) and 5(1) of this Act shall apply generally for pur-   **19–34**
poses of this Act as they apply for purposes of section 1.
(2) For purposes of this Act—

(a) "gain" and "loss" are to be construed as extending only to gain or loss
    in money or other property, but as extending to any such gain or loss
    whether temporary or permanent; and—
        (i) "gain" includes a gain by keeping what one has, as well as a gain
    by getting what one has not; and
        (ii) "loss" includes a loss by not getting what one might get, as well
    as a loss by parting with what one has;
(b) "goods," except in so far as the context otherwise requires, includes
    money and every other description of property except land, and
    includes things severed from the land by stealing.

Commencement and transitional provisions

35.—(1) This Act shall come into force on the 1st January 1969 and, save as   **19–35**
otherwise provided by this Act, shall have affect only in relation to offences
wholly or partly committed on or after that date.
(2) Sections 27 and 28 of this Act shall apply in relation to proceedings for
an offence committed before the commencement of this Act as they would
apply in relation to proceedings for a corresponding offence under this Act,
and shall so apply in place of any corresponding enactment repealed by this
Act.
(3) Subject to subsection (2) above, no repeal or amendment by this Act of
any enactment relating to procedure or evidence, or to the jurisdiction or
powers of any court, or to the effect of a conviction, shall affect the operation
of the enactment in relation to offences committed before the commencement of this Act or to proceedings for any such offence.

Short title, and general provisions as to Scotland and Northern Ireland

36.—(1) This Act may be cited as the Theft Act 1968.   **19–36**
[(2) *Repealed by the Northern Ireland Constitution Act* 1973, *s.*41(1),
Sched. 6.]
(3) This Act does not extend to Scotland or ... to Northern Ireland, except
as regards any amendment or repeal which in accordance with section 33
above is to extend to Scotland or Northern Ireland.
[*The words omitted in subsection* (3) *were repealed by the Northern Ireland
Constitution Act* 1973, *s.*41(1), *Sched.* 6.]

SCHEDULES

Section 32   SCHEDULE 1

OFFENCES OF TAKING, ETC. DEER OR FISH

Taking or killing deer

19–37   [**1.** *Repealed by the Deer Act* 1980, *s.*9(2).]

Taking or destroying fish

19–38   **2.**—(1) Subject to subparagraph (2) below, a person who unlawfuly takes or destroys, or attempts to take or destroy, any fish in water which is private property on which there is any private right of fishery shall on summary conviction be liable to a fine not exceeding fifty pounds or, for an offence committed after a previous conviction of an offence under this subparagraph, to imprisonment for a term not exceeding three months or to a fine not exceeding one hundred pounds or to both.

(2) Subparagraph (1) above shall not apply to taking or destroying fish by angling in the day-time (that is to say, in the period beginning one hour before sunrise and ending one hour after sunset); but a person who by angling in the daytime unlawfully takes or destroys, or attempts to take or destroy, any fish in water which is private property or in which there is any private right of fishery shall on summary conviction be liable to a fine not exceeding twenty pounds.

(3) The court by which a person is convicted of an offence under this paragraph may order the forfeiture of anything which, at the time of the offence, he had with him for use for taking or destroying fish.

(4) Any person may arrest without warrant anyone who is, or whom he, with reasonable cause, suspects to be, committing an offence under subparagraph (1) above, and may seize from any person who is, or whom he, with reasonable cause, suspects to be, committing any offence under this paragraph anything which on that person's conviction of the offence would be liable to be forfeited under subparagraph (3) above.

Section 33(1)(2)   SCHEDULE 2

MISCELLANEOUS AND CONSEQUENTIAL AMENDMENTS

PART I

Amendments of Post Office Act 1953

19–39   1. The Post Office Act 1953 shall have effect subject to the amendments provided for by this Part of this Schedule (and, except in so far as the contrary intention appears, those amendments have effect throughout the British postal area).

2. Sections 22 and 23 shall be amended by substituting for the word "felony" in section 22(1) and section 23(2) the words "a misdemeanour," and by omitting the words "of this Act and" in section 23(1).

3. In section 52, as it applies outside England and Wales, for the words from "be guilty" onwards there shall be substituted the words "be guilty of a misdemeanour and be liable to imprisonment for a term not exceeding ten years."

4. In section 53 for the words from "be guilty" onwards there shall be substituted the words "be guilty of a misdemeanour and be liable to imprisonment for a term not exceeding five years."

5. In section 54, as it applies outside England and Wales,—

   (a)   there shall be omitted the words "taking, embezzling," and the words "taken, embezzled," where first occurring;

(b)   for the words "a felony" there shall be substituted the words "an offence" and the word "feloniously" shall be omitted;

(c)   for the words from "be guilty" to "secreted it" there shall be substituted the words "be guilty of a misdemeanour and be liable to imprisonment for a term not exceeding fourteen years."

6. In sections 55 and 58(1), after the word "imprisonment," there shall in each case be inserted the words "for a term not exceeding two years."

7. In section 57—

(a)   there shall be omitted the words "steals, or for any purpose whatever embezzles," and the words from "or if" onwards;

(b)   for the word "felony" there shall be substituted the words "a misdemeanour."

[8. *Repealed by the British Telecommunications Act* 1981, *s.*89, *Sched.* 6.]

9. Section 69(2) shall be omitted.

10. For section 70 there shall be substituted the following section—

"Prosecution of certain offences in any jurisdiction of British postal area.

70.—(1) Where a person—

(a)   steals or attempts to steal any mail bag or postal packet in the course of transmission as such between places in different jurisdictions in the British postal area, or any of the contents of such a mail bag or postal packet; or

(b)   in stealing or with intent to steal any such mail bag or postal packet or any of its contents, commits any robbery, attempted robbery or assault with intent to rob;

then, in whichever of those jurisdictions he does so, he shall by virtue of this section be guilty in each of the jurisdictions in which this subsection has effect of committing or attempting to commit the offence against section 52 of this Act, or the offence referred to in paragraph (b) of this subsection, as the case may be, as if he had done so in that jurisdiction, and he shall accordingly be liable to be prosecuted, tried and punished in that jurisdiction without proof that the offence was committed there.

(2) In subsection (1) above the reference to different jurisdictions in the British postal area is to be construed as referring to the several jurisdictions of England and Wales, of Scotland, of Northern Ireland, of the Isle of Man, of the Channel Islands; and that subsection shall have effect in each of those jurisdictions except England and Wales."

11. In section 72 there shall be added as a new subsection (3)—

"(3) In any proceedings in England or Wales for an offence under section 53, 55, 56, 57 or 58 of this Act, section 27(4) of the Theft Act 1968 shall apply as it is expressed to apply to proceedings for the theft of anything in the course of transmission by post; and in the case of proceedings under section 53 of this Act a statutory declaration made by any person that a vessel, vehicle or aircraft was at any time employed by or under the Post Office for the transmission of postal packets under contract shall be admissible as evidence of the facts stated in the declaration subject to the same conditions as under section 27(4)(a) and (b) of the Theft Act 1968 apply to declarations admissible under section 27(4)."

12. In section 87(1), the definition of "valuable security" shall be omitted but, except in relation to England and Wales, there shall be substituted:—

" 'valuable security' means any document creating, transferring, surrendering or releasing any right to, in or over property, or authorising the payment of money or delivery of any property, or evidencing the creation, transfer, surrender or release of any such right or the payment of money or delivery of any property, or the satisfaction of any obligation."

PART II

Other amendments extending beyond England and Wales

19–40

Act amended	*Amendment*
[*Entry relating to the Extradition Act* 1873, *Sched.: repealed by the Extradition Act* 1989, *s.*37, *Sched.* 2.]	
The Public Stores Act 1875 (38 & 39 Vict. c. 25)	For section 12 (incorporation of parts of Larceny Act 1861) there shall be substituted:— "(1) Any person may arrest without warrant anyone who is, or whom he, with reasonable cause, suspects to be, in the act of committing or attempting to commit an offence against section 5 or 8 of this Act. (2) If it is made to appear by information on oath before a justice of the peace that there is reasonable cause to believe that any person has in his custody or possession or on his premises any stores in respect of which an offence against section 5 of this Act has been committed, the justice may issue a warrant to a constable to search for and seize the stores as in the case of stolen goods, and the Police (Property) Act 1897 shall apply as if this subsection were among the enactments mentioned in section 1(1) of that Act."
The Army Act 1955 (3 & 4 Eliz. 2, c. 18)	For section 44(1)(b) there shall be substituted— "(b) handles any stolen goods, where the property stolen was public or service property, or". For section 45(b) there shall be substituted— "(b) handles any stolen goods, where the property stolen belonged to a person subject to military law, or". In section 138(1) for the words from "receiving" to "stolen" there shall be substituted the words "handling it". In section 225(1) after the definition of "Governor" there shall be inserted— " 'handles' has the same meaning as in the Theft Act 1968"; and for the definition of "steals" there shall be substituted— " 'steals' has the same meaning as in the Theft Act 1968, and references to 'stolen goods' shall be construed as if contained in that Act".
The Air Force Act 1955 (3 & 4 Eliz. 2, c. 19)	The same amendments shall be made in sections 44, 45, 138 and 223 as are above directed to be made in the corresponding sections of the Army Act 1955, except that in the amendment to section 45(b) "air-force law" shall be substituted for "military law".
The Naval Discipline Act 1957 (5 & 6 Eliz. 2, c. 53)	For section 29(b) there shall be substituted— "(b) handles any stolen goods, where the property stolen was public or service property, or". In section 76(1) for the words from "receiving" to

Act amended	Amendment
The Naval Discipline Act 1957 (*cont.*)	"embezzling" there shall be substituted the word "handling". In section 135(1) the same amendments shall be made as are above directed to be made in section 225(1) of the Army Act 1955.
The Army and Air Force Act 1961 (9 & 10 Eliz. 2, c. 52)	Section 21 shall be omitted.

[*Entry relating to the Road Traffic Act 1962, Sched. 1, Part II; repealed by the Road Traffic Act 1972, s.205(1) Sched. 9.*]

PART III

Amendments limited to England and Wales

19–41

Act amended	Amendment
The Gaming Act 1845 (8 & 9 Vict. c. 109)	In section 17 (punishment for cheating at play, etc.) for the words "be deemed guilty of obtaining such money or valuable thing from such other person by a false pretence" and the following words there shall be substituted the words— "(a) on conviction on indictment be liable to imprisonment for a term not exceeding two years; or (b) on summary conviction be liable to imprisonment for a term not exceeding six months or to a fine not exceeding two hundred pounds or to both".

[*Entry relating to the Pawnbrokers Act 1872, s.38: repealed by the Consumer Credit Act 1974, s.192(3)(b), Sched. 5.*]

[*Entry relating to the Bankruptcy Act 1914, s.116: repealed by the Insolvency Act 1985, s.235, Sched. 10.*]

[*Entry relating to the House to House Collections Act 1939, Sched.: repealed by the Charities Act 1992, s.78(2), Sched. 7.*]

[*Entry relating to the Magistrates' Courts Act 1952, Sched. 1, para. 8: repealed by the Criminal Law Act 1977. s.65(5), Sched. 13.*]

The Visiting Forces Act 1952 (15 & 16 Geo. 6 & 1 Eliz. 2, c. 67)	In the Schedule there shall be inserted in paragraph 1(a) after the word "buggery" the word "robbery", and in paragraph 3 there shall be added at the end— "(g) the Theft Act 1968, except section 8 (robbery)".
The Finance Act 1965 (1965 c. 25)	In Schedule 10, in the Table in paragraph 1, for the words "Sections 500 to 505" there shall be substituted the words "Sections 500 to 504".
The Finance Act 1966 (1966 c. 18)	In Schedule 6, in paragraph 13, for the words "Sections 500 to 505" there shall be substituted the words "Sections 500 to 504", and the words from "together with" to "the said section 505" shall be omitted.

[*Entry relating to the Criminal Law Act 1967, Sched. 1: repealed by the Courts Act 1971, s.56, Sched. 11.*]

The Firearms Act 1968 (1968 c. 27)	Schedule 1 (offences in connection with which possession of a firearm is an offence under section 17(2)) shall be amended, except in relation to a person's apprehension for an offence committed before the commencement of this Act, by substituting for paragraph 4— "4. Theft, burglary, blackmail and any offence under section 12(1) (taking of motor vehicle or other conveyance without owner's consent) of the Theft Act 1968":

Act amended	*Amendment*
The Firearms Act 1968 (*cont.*)	by omitting paragraph 7: and by substituting in paragraph 8 for the words "paragraphs 1 to 7" the words "paragraphs 1 to 6".

SCHEDULE 3

Repeals

19–42

[*This Schedule repealed penal enactments superseded by this Act and obsolete and redundant enactments and effected certain consequential repeals.*]

APPENDIX 2

Theft Act 1978

(1978 c. 31)

ARRANGEMENT OF SECTIONS

SECT.

An Act to replace section 16(2)(a) of the Theft Act 1968 with other provision against fraudulent conduct; and for connected purposes.

[20th July 1978]

Obtaining services by deception

1.—(1) A person who by any deception dishonestly obtains services from another shall be guilty of an offence.   **20–01**

(2) It is an obtaining of services where the other is induced to confer a benefit by doing some act, or causing or permitting some act to be done, on the understanding that the benefit has been or will be paid for.

Evasion of liability by deception

2.—(1) Subject to subsection (2) below, where a person by any deception—   **20–02**

(a) dishonestly secures the remission of the whole or part of any existing liability to make a payment, whether his own liability or another's; or

(b) with intent to make permanent default in whole or in part on any existing liability to make a payment, or with intent to let another do so, dishonestly induces the creditor or any person claiming payment on behalf of the creditor to wait for payment (whether or not the due date of payment is deferred) or to forgo payment; or

(c) dishonestly obtains any exemption from or abatement of liability to make a payment;

he shall be guilty of an offence.

(2) For purposes of this section "liability" means legally enforceable

315

liability; and subsection (1) shall not apply in relation to a liability that has not been accepted or established to pay compensation for a wrongful act or omission.

(3) For purposes of subsection (1)(b) a person induced to take in payment a cheque or other security for money by way of conditional satisfaction of a pre-existing liability is to be treated not as being paid but as being induced to wait for payment.

(4) For purposes of section (1)(c) "obtains" includes obtaining for another or enabling another to obtain.

Making off without payment

20–03   **3.**—(1) Subject to subsection (3) below, a person who, knowing that payment on the spot for any goods supplied or service done is required or expected from him, dishonestly makes off without having paid as required or expected and with intent to avoid payment of the amount due shall be guilty of an offence.

(2) For purposes of this section "payment on the spot" includes payment at the time of collecting goods on which work has been done or in respect of which service has been provided.

(3) Subsection (1) above shall not apply where the supply of the goods or the doing of the service is contrary to law, or where the service done is such that payment is not legally enforceable.

(4) Any person may arrest without warrant any one who is, or whom he, with reasonable cause, suspects to be, committing or attempting to commit an offence under this section.

Punishments

20–04   **4.**—(1) Offences under this Act shall be punishable either on conviction on indictment or on summary conviction.

(2) A person convicted on indictment shall be liable—

(a) for an offence under section 1 or section 2 of this Act, to imprisonment for a term not exceeding five years; and

(b) for an offence under section 3 of this Act, to imprisonment for a term not exceeding two years.

(3) A person convicted summarily of any offence under this Act shall be liable—

(a) to imprisonment for a term not exceeding six months; or

(b) to a fine not exceeding the prescribed sum for the purposes of [section 32 of the Magistrates' Courts Act 1980] (punishment on summary conviction of offences triable either way: £1,000 or other sum substituted by order under that Act), or to both.

[*The words in square brackets in subsection* (3) *were substituted by the Magistrates' Courts Act* 1980, *s.*154(1), *Sched.* 7.]

Supplementary

5.—(1) For purposes of sections 1 and 2 above "deception" has the same   **20–05**
meaning as in section 15 of the Theft Act 1968, that is to say, it means any
deception (whether deliberate or reckless) by words or conduct as to fact or
as to law, including a deception as to the present intentions of the person
using the deception or any other person; and section 18 of that Act (liability
of company officers for offences by the company) shall apply in relation to
sections 1 and 2 above as it applies in relation to section 15 of that Act.

(2) Sections 30(1) (husband and wife), 31(1) (effect on civil proceedings)
and 34 (interpretation) of the Theft Act 1968, so far as they are applicable in
relation to this Act, shall apply as they apply in relation to that Act.

[(3) *Repealed by the Extradition Act* 1989, *s.*37, *Sched.* 2.]

(4) In the Visiting Forces Act 1952, in paragraph 3 of the Schedule (which
defines for England and Wales "offences against property" for purposes of
the exclusion in certain cases of the jurisdiction of United Kingdom courts)
there shall be added at the end—

"(*j*) the Theft Act 1978."

(5) In the Theft Act 1968 section 16(2)(a) is hereby repealed.

Enactment of same provisions for Northern Ireland

6. An Order in Council under paragraph 1(1)(b) of Schedule 1 to the   **20–06**
Northern Ireland Act 1974 (legislation for Northern Ireland in the interim
period) which contains a statement that it operates only so as to make for
Northern Ireland provision corresponding to this Act—

(a) shall not be subject to paragraph 1(4) and (5) of that Schedule (affirm-
     ative resolution of both Houses of Parliament); but
(b) shall be subject to annulment by resolution of either House.

Short title, commencement and extent

7.—(1) This Act may be cited as the Theft Act 1978.   **20–07**

(2) This Act shall come into force at the expiration of three months beginning with the date on which it is passed.

(3) This Act except section 5(3), shall not extend to Scotland; and except
for that subsection, and subject also to section 6, it shall not extend to Northern Ireland.

INDEX